MATTHEW'S
CHRISTIAN-JEWISH
COMMUNITY

Chicago Studies in the History of Judaism

Edited by
William Scott Green and
Calvin Goldscheider

MATTHEW'S
CHRISTIAN-JEWISH
COMMUNITY

Anthony J. Saldarini

The University of Chicago Press
Chicago and London

Anthony J. Saldarini is professor of theology at Boston College.

The University of Chicago Press, Chicago 60637
The University of Chicago Press, Ltd., London
© 1994 by The University of Chicago
All rights reserved. Published 1994
Printed in the United States of America

03 02 01 00 99 98 97 96 95 94   5 4 3 2 1

ISBN (cloth): 0-226-73419-6
ISBN (paper): 0-226-73421-8

Library of Congress Cataloging-in-Publication Data

Saldarini, Anthony J.
    Matthew's Christian-Jewish community / Anthony J. Saldarini.
        p.   cm. — (Chicago studies in the history of Judaism)
    Includes bibliographical references and index.
        ISBN 0-226-73419-6 — ISBN 0-226-73421-8 (pbk.)
        1. Bible. N.T. Matthew—Criticism, interpretation, etc.   2. Jews
    in the New Testament.   3. Jewish Christians—Middle East.   4. Church
    history—Primitive and early church, ca. 30–600.   I. Title.
    II. Series.
    BS2575.6.J44S35   1994
    226.2'067—dc20   93-5607
                                                                           CIP

⊗ The paper used in this publication meets the minimum
requirements of the American National Standard for Information
Sciences—Permanence of Paper for Printed Library Materials,
ANSI Z39.48-1984.

For Daniel and Bryan

"A wise son makes his father glad."
(Proverbs 10:1)

"Your sons will be like olive plants around your table."
(Psalm 128:3)

Contents

Introduction

The Gospel of Matthew is a complex text. It has generally been recognized as the most Jewish of all the gospels because it refers in a sustained and serious way to the Bible, to specific Jewish customs and beliefs, and to the general Jewish cultural and religious thought world of the first century. When the author of the gospel argues for his position or grapples with the intricacies of biblical texts, he does so with sophistication and detailed attention to alternative Jewish positons. At the same time, the Gospel of Matthew virulently attacks Jewish leaders (esp. chap. 23) and disputes many viewpoints and practices within the Jewish community.[1] The authority and teachings of Jesus (chaps. 5–7) and of the Matthean group (chaps. 16, 18) replace the guidance of the Pharisees, scribes, chief priests, and elders.[2] Matthew emphasizes and exalts Jesus to a much greater extent than the messiahs and prophets who appear in other Jewish literature. Thus many commentators interpret Matthew as a former Jew reacting against Judaism in support of Christianity, and they theorize that Matthew's now-Christian group has broken completely or substantially with the Jewish community, whether in the immediate past or earlier.

This study will argue that the Matthean group and its spokesperson, the author of the Gospel of Matthew, are Jews who believe in Jesus as the Messiah and Son of God. The Matthean group is a fragile minority still thinking of themselves as Jews and still identified with the Jewish community by others. Despite its sharp conflicts with the leaders of the Jewish community and its experience of standard disciplinary measures, or better, because of these negative relationships, the Matthean group is still Jewish. It has been labeled deviant by the authorities and by many members of the Jewish community in its city or area. Matthew's response to this conflict can be seen in the gospel's polemics and apologetics.[3] Being treated as deviant, far from driving a group out of society, often keeps it in. Social theory has established that nonconformity, resistance to social structures, and deviance are, paradoxically,

1

always part of any functioning society.[4] Thus the hasty conclusion that evidence of conflict implies a complete break with the Jewish community is contrary to normal sociological processes. In addition, the use of the terms Judaism and Christianity in this context as the denominators for two separate religions is a major historical anachronism and category error.

Thus the usual question over whether Matthew's group is still Jewish, that is, whether it is still in contact with the Jewish community or has irrevocably broken away, is misstated.[5] Categories which place Matthew's group either in or out of Judaism are too absolute and sociologically rigid to be useful analytical tools. Mediating positions, such as Graham Stanton's hypothesis that Matthew is separated from Judaism but defines his group's stance against Judaism, are vague concerning the nature of the relationship and require clarification. A group which has "broken away" from a parent community retains multiple relationships and cannot be understood in isolation.[6] (Even after nineteen hundred years, Christianity must still be defined partly with reference to Judaism.) A traditional community is always a complex symbolic and social reality which includes many subcommunities, systems, and groups with shifting boundaries.[7] Most analyses of Judaism and Christianity give too much credence to the majority groups and leaders, who define boundaries, orthodoxy, orthopraxy, morality, and belief with artificial clarity. What groups say about themselves and each other often reflects what they wish were true rather than what is actually the case. Accepting the consensus of scholars that Matthew's Jewish community of believers-in-Jesus had been engaged in a lengthy conflict with Jewish authorities and had recently withdrawn from or been expelled from the Jewish assembly, I will argue that it still had close relations with the Jewish community, both negative and positive, and many common symbolic elements. In fact, Matthew still hoped that he would prevail and make his program normative for the whole Jewish community.

Matthew and Judaism

The numerous problems that have plagued and divided the commentators on Matthew stem from differing understandings of Matthew's social relationships, audience, and goals. Most studies of Matthew and Judaism concentrate on four problems: whether Matthew's group is made up of Jewish-Christians or gentiles, whether Matthew thinks Israel can still be saved, whether Matthew's group is still Jewish or has broken away entirely from Judaism, and whether his polemics against

Judaism can be separated somehow from anti-Semitism. These studies, mostly by Christians, are Matthew-centric and Christian-centric; that is, they focus on the viewpoint and thought of a "Christian" Matthew who is independent of and equal in stature to his Jewish opponents the way church and synagogue relate today. But we shall argue that Matthew's group is a small and relatively uninfluential part of the first-century Jewish community in the eastern Mediterranean.

The sharp distinction of first-century Christianity from Judaism in New Testament study and also in some modern Jewish theology derives most recently from late nineteenth-century liberal Protestant theology. In order to make a place for Christianity in a modern and increasingly antireligious and antitheological world, theologians stressed the this-worldly, cultural, ethical, and universal values of Christianity and deemphasized both the other-worldly and the so-called particularistic aspects of the tradition, especially connections with Judaism. Christianity was treated as a new, universal religion and was then distinguished from Judaism (in reality, Judaisms), understood as a particularistic, ethnic religion.[8] The false distinction between Judaism as a religion of law and Christianity as a religion of love is also part of this schematization. Hegel was a decisive influence on the universalistic interpretation of Christianity, and Adolf Harnack its most famous and influential exponent.[9] Alfred Loisy, a Semitist, ably refuted Harnack's attempt to separate Christianity from Judaism, but Harnack's view has remained so influential that Christian books still casually refer to Judaism as legalistic and particularistic.[10] In addition, it has become a commonplace in Christian treatment of the first century to place the separation of Christianity from Judaism in the 80s and 90s, after the destruction of the Temple. Both the Jewish and Christian communities are viewed as tightening their boundaries and focusing more sharply their identities so as to weather the crisis caused by the loss of the Temple. Specifically, the alleged promulgation of the Birkat Ha-Minim (the "blessing"/curse against heretics) is cited as a widely employed disciplinary measure aimed at the Jewish-Christians, which drove them away from the synagogue in an irrevocable split.[11] This institutionally crisp account of the late first century is unlikely. Conflicts between Jewish and Christian groups varied greatly according to time and place.

Harnack's influence has extended into Jewish scholarship as well. In order to protect Judaism from the threat of absorption into Christianity and in order to validate first-century Judaism, Jewish views of Christianity have normally accepted Jesus as a Jewish reformer and

Paul as the villain who transformed Jesus' teaching into a new, non-Jewish Hellenistic religion called Christianity. Harnack's thesis that after the Bar Kosiba War Jews turned inward and ceased to take part in the larger society of the empire has been effectively attacked, though it is still repeated.[12] Christian literature shows that the rivalry, conflict, and contact between Jews and Christians continued in various places for centuries and provided the context both for Jewish and Christian exclusive claims and the rejection or ignoring of the other.[13] Gentile interest in both Judaism and Christianity fueled the rivalry between Jews and Christians, especially since many people could not distinguish clearly between them within the larger Greco-Roman context. For many in the first century, believers-in-Jesus did not form a different functioning religion but were seen as part of the Jewish community. Matthew's group was part of the Jewish community; hence the designation "Christian-Jewish."

Method and Theology

In this study, Matthew is read as concretely as possible in the light of our increased knowledge of the first-century social history of Jews and Jewish believers-in-Jesus in greater Syria. The final composition of the text and its setting within first-century Judaism are the key to understanding Matthew's view of Judaism and his group's place within it. The historical-critical method and contemporary literary studies of the narrative are used, and special attention is given to the nature of the social relationships and of the groups implied by Matthew's narrative. The numerous claims for Jesus, the exhortations to faith in Jesus, the apologetic refutations of charges made against believers-in-Jesus, and the polemics against the opponents of the Matthean group are all interpreted as part of the Matthean group's relationship to Judaism within the larger context of the Roman Empire and the Hellenistic Near East. In explaining the Matthean narrative, hermeneutical priority is given to indigenous Jewish thought, practices, conflicts, and history in the eastern Mediterranean rather than to later second-century Christian theological concerns.

Looked at in this way, the Gospel of Matthew (dating from the last two decades of the first century) fits not only into the development of Christian theological thought but also into the Jewish debate after 70 C.E. over how Judaism was to be lived and how that way of life was to be articulated in order to ensure the survival of the Jewish community without the Temple and its related political institutions. Thus, the Gospel of Matthew should be read along with other Jewish postdestruction literature, such as the apocalyptic works 2 Baruch, 4 Ezra, and Apocalypse of Abraham, early strata of the Mishnah, and Josephus. All this Jewish literature tried to envision Judaism in new circumstances, reorganize its central symbols, determine concretely the will of God in a new changed world, and propose a course of action for the faithful community. The Jews of Matthew's group believed that Jesus was the crucial person sent by God to save them, and thus they made him the center of their understanding of Judaism.

This study of the Gospel of Matthew presupposes the widely held position that the final author exercised strong compositional and creative control over the documents and traditions at his disposal. He ordered and edited them to fit the needs of his group, to convey his understanding of the Jesus movement, and to promote his solutions to group problems.[14] Thus the story of Jesus in Matthew reflects the experience of Matthew's group and its social situation.[15] We will concentrate mostly on the narrative itself, with its significant action and teaching, and refer less to the history of traditions and Matthean redactional contributions to them. The final literary product, the gospel, with the claims it makes for Jesus, the story it tells about him, and the way its presents Jesus' world will be at the center of our textual analysis. At the same time, sustained attention will be given to both the narrative world and its referential relationship to first-century-Judaism, insofar as this is possible. Many interpreters have utilized anachronistic or erroneous assumptions about the first-century Jewish and Christian world. Social and institutional structures and distinctions from later centuries and fully articulated theological systems have a tendency to creep into reconstructions of early Christianity and Judaism. Thus we will address in detail the author's understanding of his group's relationship to the Jewish community, as communicated indirectly in the story of Jesus, and of his understanding of Jesus' teaching and relationship with God and humans.

The relationship of the Gospel of Matthew and its author and audience to the larger Jewish community is crucial to the gospel's interpretation because many descriptions of the Matthean group have assumed its "Christian," as opposed to Jewish, identity and in an a priori or subjective fashion relegated the strongly Jewish exhortations and tone of the gospel to the earlier history of its tradition. Thus instructions to keep the whole law (5:17–19) and legal arguments that are so detailed as to presume observance (12:1–14) are supposed to have come from an earlier stage in the community's history in which the membership was Jewish and observant. This earlier stage is contrasted with the "present" membership and situation of the Matthean group, in which large numbers of members are gentiles and Jewish law is no longer observed. According to this theory, Matthew sought to preserve the older Jewish traditions as much as possible and to integrate them into the newer Christian understandings of Scripture. A small but significant group of scholars even hold that both Matthew and his group were gentiles.[16]

Many understand Matthew to claim that Christianity has replaced Judaism (21:43) as the true or new Israel and that all hope of preaching Jesus to his fellow Jews has been relinquished (28:19). This understanding is based on the salvation-history approach, which dominated Matthean studies during the sixties and seventies and resulted in elaborate schemes in which the Matthean group was portrayed as having been heavily Jewish, before being expelled from the synagogue and finally absorbing a large number of gentiles. According to this view, the mission to the Jews was completed by Jesus and the early Matthean group, and the mission to the gentiles bespoke a later stage, not only in the group's history, but also in God's plan. Integral to this theory of Matthean composition is the separation of earlier and later layers of the narrative and the denial that Matthew's teachings about Jewish law were addressed to his immediate community and its behavior. A few key passages or terms, themselves subject to multiple interpretations, became the lever by which the mass of Jewish material in Matthew was moved to the periphery of the narrative and author's world. This sorting of materials by how Jewish they are tends to be arbitrary, circular, and based on a priori Christian theological schemes which purport to account for an evolutionary Christian development away from Judaism. More improbably, many assign the anti-Jewish polemics (e.g., 6:1–18; 10:17–23; 21:28–22:14; 23:1–36; 27:63) to earlier stages in the community history and hold that the break with Judaism was so final that there was no conflict for the later Matthean group.[17]

The salvation-history approach to Matthew reflects a mid second-century reading of the gospel. It assumes that the Jewish and Christian communities are for the most part separate and should be separate. Christianity is understood as an independent established religion which replaces or supersedes Judaism.[18] The mission to convince the whole Jewish community that Jesus was sent by God to teach, heal, and save is viewed as a stage which is over. Such an approach also denies that much of the Gospel of Matthew reflects real history, that is, real people in a struggle for the future of Judaism. The later imposition of eras of salvation on Matthew's text has obscured the Jewishness of Matthew's group and his engagement in late first-century Jewish community struggles in the name of Jesus.[19] Matthew does not simply preserve Jewish-Christian traditions which were operative earlier in the century, nor does he effect a synthesis of earlier Jewish with current Christian traditions and customs.[20] The outlook and practice which Matthew promotes in his gospel is thoroughly Jewish and based on the Bible as understood through the teachings and actions of Jesus. Matthew seeks to carry on Jesus' reform of Judaism and convince his fellow Jews that his understanding of Judaism is God-given (11:25–27) and necessary for Israel and for the gentiles, too.

The Purpose of the Gospel

We will argue that the final document, the Gospel of Matthew, is an integral and coherent whole reflecting a Christian-Jewish group which keeps the whole law, interpreted through the Jesus tradition. The author considers himself to be a Jew who has the true interpretation of Torah and is faithful to God's will as revealed by Jesus, whom he declares to be the Messiah and Son of God. Matthew promotes "a perfected or fulfilled Judaism brought to its goal by the long-awaited Christ."[21] He seeks to promote his interpretation of Judaism over that of other Jewish leaders, especially those of emerging rabbinic Judaism.[22] Despite his conflicts with various community leaders and his relatively small following, the author of Matthew considers himself to be Jewish. He seeks to legitimate his particular form of Judaism by utilizing the sources of authority in the Jewish community (see chaps. 5–6 and his use of Scripture generally) and by delegitimating the Jewish leaders (see esp. chap. 23).[23] His motivational accounting system is still Jewish. Significantly, he has no name for his group. He does not call it Israel or the people *(ho laos)*; he uses these terms either in their biblical setting or to designate the Jewish people whom Jesus and the Matthean group have tried to instruct and influence. These terms designate all Jews and provide no identifying distinctions among groups within Israel. Matthew does not even use the terms "new" or "true" Israel. Rather, members of the Jewish community who reject Jesus, especially the leaders, are excoriated in the prophetic mode as unfaithful members of Israel, but members nonetheless. Israel is the concrete community of Jews from which Matthew has been banned, but to which he still thinks he belongs.[24]

   The conflicts Matthew has with the Jewish community leaders and even his alienation from their assembly do not affect his Jewishness sociologically or psychologically. He considers himself a Jew and fights for his interpretation of Jewish life. He is seen as a Jew by the surrounding communities, by the Jewish authorities who discipline him, and by other believers-in-Jesus. He affirms the validity of Jewish law understood in the correct way (5:17–20) and the authority of the Jewish community leaders, though not their practice or their legal interpretations (23:1–36, esp. 2–3). He mitigates Christian rejection of purity and dietary laws (15:1–20; cf. Mark 7:1–23, esp. 19) and gives reasons for letting his disciples pick grain on the Sabbath (12:1–8; cf. Mark 2:23–28). Thus he seems to be one of a diminishing number of Christian Jews who accept the whole Jewish law and way of life (understood according to the teaching of Jesus) as normative.

Though Christians usually understand Matthew's program as distinct from Judaism, what Matthew teaches and promotes is thoroughly consistent with the variety of belief in first-century Judaism, both before and after the destruction of the Temple.[25] The later sharply defined categories of Christian and Jew are inaccurate for the late first century among Jewish groups in Syria and Israel and do not fit Matthew's situation. In fact, Jewish influence remained so strong in the East that during the second century, Marcion felt compelled to revise Christian symbols and boundaries radically in order to separate Christianity from Judaism. Also during the second century, various churches fought over changing the commemoration of Jesus' death and resurrection from 14 Nisan (Passover) to a Sunday, In the late fourth century, John Chrysostom excoriated his gentile Christians for worshiping with Jews during the synagogue festivals as well as in church services.[26]

If, as we shall argue, Matthew wished to attract the bulk of his fellow Jews to acceptance of Jesus, he lost his battle. Within Christianity his way of following Jesus, as a Jew loyal to the law as interpreted by Jesus, died out for the most part during the following generation. His gospel was used by later Christians in order to make sense out of Christianity's relationship to Judaism, but fidelity to Torah in Matthew's sense was nonoperative, and so "fulfillment" of Torah was understood in a different way.[27] From the viewpoint of deviance theory, Matthew's group or its successors were engulfed by their deviant role and adopted their deviance as a "master status," that is, as the set of values and characteristics that defined and controlled all other aspects of their lives.[28] Within a short time, because of both rejection by the majority of the Jewish community and the dominance of non-Jewish Christians, most communities like Matthew's became sociologically Christian. That is, they lost their identification with Judaism and became part of a separate, competing religion. Second-century sources begin to testify to the separate identity of many Christians, but also to the difficulties inherent in separating Christianity from its religious and cultural place of origin.

The later lines of demarcation were not drawn sharply in the first century. As we shall see in later chapters, Matthew is very vague in his naming of groups and positions. This bespeaks a fluid social situation with imprecise boundaries, ongoing conflict, and unresolved tensions. Matthew's symbolic world and symbol system is being modified, but it has not emerged as a consistent whole that can clearly be differentiated from Judaism. Thus the so-called early Jewish-Christian views found in Matthew cannot be eliminated as inconsistent with later Christian views. The second century interpreters made this move, but not Matthew.

Plan of the Book

In order to substantiate this position, chapter 1 shows the diversity characteristic of Judaism in late antiquity, especially before the development and ascendancy of the Mishnah and Talmuds. Subsequent chapters show that Matthew's world view and specific teachings, even those about the most central Christian figure, Jesus, fit within the Jewish intellectual, religious, and symbolic world.

To elaborate on the contents and argument of the book more fully: chapter 1 reviews the varied and complex development of both Judaism and Christianity in the first two centuries. The variety of Judaisms characteristic of the second Temple period continued after the destruction of the Temple in 70 C.E. Only gradually did the rabbinic movement create and impose its views on all of Israel. Similarly, the believers-in-Jesus began as a Jewish sect before growing into a varied religious movement of its own. A significant branch of believers-in-Jesus continued to live Jewish life, and the majority of Christians remained heavily influenced by and attracted to Judaism and the Jewish community. Chapter 2 argues that Matthew's use of various terms such as "Israel," "people," and "crowds" indicates that he understood the people in both the narrative and his own community as constituting Israel. Needless to say, the thesis of some commentators that Matthew announces the end of the Jewish mission, describing the complete failure of Israel to respond to God and the replacement of Israel with the gentiles, will be rejected. The third chapter demonstrates that Matthew's vitriolic polemics, far from showing that he is anti-Jewish and outside the Jewish community, testify to his engagement in inner-Jewish sectarian politics. His attacks are directed against the leaders of the Jewish community who oppose him and occasionally against people who follow those leaders and to definitively reject Matthew's teaching. Chapter 4 argues that Matthew's use of the word "nations" matches normal Greek usage and does not communicate a theology of the gentiles which removes Israel as God's people. Rather, Matthew takes for granted the presence of many gentiles outside of Israel, as do all Jews, and also opens the boundaries of Israel to interested, believing gentiles. Though peripheral, gentiles are nevertheless firmly present and given an integral relationship to Israel.

The fifth chapter uses modern sociological categories, especially those drawn from the study of deviance, sects, and kinship, to describe Matthew's understanding of his group's place in Judaism. His view of the disciples, of God as Father, and of the household assembly will be analyzed in detail in order to overcome the simplistic dichotomies between Judaism and Christianity, synagogue and church, outside and inside, and so on, which are often used in scholarly literature. Chapter 6 argues that Matthew's extended discussions of Jewish law, custom, and practice fit within the acceptable range of legal debate in first-century Judaism, that Matthew defends his positions with sophisticated arguments comprehensible to the Jewish community, and that Matthew sees himself as an authoritative teacher within the Jewish community, not as the spokesperson for a new religion. In the seventh chapter, the figure of and claims made for Jesus in the narrative are shown to be closely connected to the thought world of first-century Judaism. Even the most exalted claims for Jesus find analogies in the literature of Second Temple or early postdestruction Judaism. Thus even in speaking of Jesus, Matthew remains within the orbit of Judaism, though at its far edges.

I

Matthew within First-Century Judaism

Since the Gospel of Matthew was read and preserved by the second-century Christian community and later became part of the New Testament collection, it is assumed to be a Christian writing and thus not a Jewish work. But the use of the word "Christian" for this gospel, its first-century author, and his audience of believers-in-Jesus is troubling and imprecise. In the first century, many groups of believers-in-Jesus were either integral parts of the Jewish community or not yet completely separated from Judaism. Especially in greater Syria, the boundaries between Jewish communities and the Christian groups emerging from them remained porous and indistinct a long time. To say that Matthew is Christian, meaning a member of a clearly separate religion which is not Jewish, contradicts the complex and overlapping relationships among varieties of Jews, including some groups who believed in Jesus.

Modern views of Matthew are usually guided by a second-century interpretation of Matthew rather than by what the gospel narrative means in a first-century Jewish context. From the second century on, the Gospel of Matthew was read as a non-Jewish, Christian work and valued because it was seen as explaining the relationship of Christianity to its Jewish origins. The frequent references to Scripture and to Jewish tradition, law, and custom were seen as attempts to synthesize the Jewish past with the Christian present or to show how Christianity fulfilled Judaism by reinterpreting it or to prove that Christianity had replaced Israel.[1] These conclusions reached by later interpreters have often been attributed to the author of the gospel. However, if the affirmations of Jewish law and custom, the Jewish assumptions and modes of argument, and the heavily Jewish milieu and agenda in the gospel are taken seriously as teachings of the author (rather than being attributed to hypothetically earlier Jewish-Christian traditions which the author no longer affirms), then a more Jewish author, gospel, and audience begin to emerge.

In order to judge where Matthew stands in relation to Judaism, an accurate description of the diversity within the first-century Jewish community in the Roman Empire must be developed. Many assumptions about first-century "Judaism" have been wrong, especially those which attribute to it a normative unity and essentialist identity that would exclude many early believers-in-Jesus. Thus a review of early Judaism and of its varied and complex relationships with "Christianity" is necessary before Matthew's relationship to Judaism can be worked out. Only then will the further explorations of the text show in detail that the teaching of the Gospel of Matthew fits within the compass of first-century Judaism. Though the author affirms the centrality of Jesus Christ as Son of God and Savior, this affirmation does not in his eyes contradict an authentic Jewish interpretation of the Bible or the Jewish way of life. Rather, the author understands Jesus and those who believe in him as the faithful and reliable interpreters of God's will and of the biblical tradition. The author is well aware of the tensions and conflicts which have plagued his group's relationship with the larger Jewish community, but he does not yet consider his to be a different religion from Judaism, nor does he see in his group the new or true Israel that will replace the old. For us to comprehend Matthew's view, the usual understandings of Judaism and Christianity found in textbooks and often repeated in popular and scholarly works must be modified to fit the first century.

Research in the past twenty-five years has established and emphasized three characteristics of Judaism and Christianity in late antiquity: the variety of groups within each community, the gradual (rather than sudden and complete) development and ascendancy of rabbinic Judaism and orthodox Christianity, and the constant interaction of Jewish and Christian groups with one another and their larger cultural world.[2] While earlier treatments of Jewish and Christian history have acknowledged many of these phenomena, they have often been treated as heretical or as epiphenomenal. The fixed, classical forms of each religion were viewed anachronistically as normative. Consequently, many forms of Christianity were ignored and the rich variety of second- and third-century Christianity was lost to the orthodox consensus.[3] Similarly, the vitality and variety of local Jewish communities and traditions, especially in the diaspora, have been ignored or treated as insignificant deviations from the normative and dominant tradition.[4] Talmudic Judaism and the "Great Church" tradition were often retrojected into the pre-Mishnaic and New Testament periods so that the very limited power and influence of early rabbinic and orthodox church leaders were heightened and the strength of other important movements and groups was diminished. Some of the blame for this situation must be laid to the surviving sources, which were edited and preserved by the dominant groups. Competing movements and views were refuted, maligned, or ignored. Yet the perdurance of numerous groups of Jewish believers-in-Jesus and the continued attraction of gentile Christians to Jewish worship and community activities during the first five centuries is notable. Many discussions in the Talmud suggest that rabbinic leaders struggled to establish and maintain clear boundaries and a distinct identity for the Jewish community in the face of the attractions of the Greco-Roman world and Christianity.[5] A review of certain data will allow the development and relationships of Judaism and Christianity to be understood according to a paradigm which takes account of the variety of Jewish and Christian communities in late antiquity, of the close relationships, positive and negative, among many of them, and of the long, complex process which resulted in the classical forms of each religion.

Diversity within Judaism

Recent studies of the development of rabbinic Judaism after the destruction of the Temple demonstrate that the rabbis gained influence and then power in Palestinian society only gradually, over several centuries. The loss of much of the national leadership in Jerusalem (the chief priests, wealthy families, Hasmoneans, and Herodians) in 70 C.E. led to confusion and competition for Roman favor and authority. Various groups maneuvered for power, including the surviving priests, Herodians, and a variety of other, less influential groups.[6] Local authority, as always, remained in the hands of village elders, wealthy families, and landlords as well as local priests, scribes, and popular leaders. Similarly, synagogues continued to be governed by local community leaders.[7] Archaeological evidence shows that dedicated synagogue buildings only became common in the third and fourth centuries in Palestine.[8] In the first two centuries, local synagogues were probably regular assemblies for prayer and discussions of community business under the guidance of local leaders. No evidence points to rabbinic control over synagogues. If rabbis lived in a town or village, they may have had influence or a leadership position in a synagogue, but they certainly did not control the community or synagogue, nor was their presence necessary.[9] Rabbinic literature often retrojects the dominant social and political position of third- and fourth-century

rabbis into the first two centuries. In fact, the group which gathered at
Jamnia in 70 c.e. did not set up a council to rule all Israel, nor did its
leaders, first Johanan ben Zakkai and then Gamaliel II, actually govern
Israel as a prince or patriarch. It is unlikely that Rabban Gamaliel II was
recognized as an official representative of the Jewish community with
Rome; if he did have some recognition, his control over the community
was still very limited.[10] The so-called Council of Jamnia, which allegedly decided numerous cases regarding observance of biblical law in
the new circumstances of the postdestruction period, is really a scholarly creation made from fragments of texts. The meetings of rabbis in
Jamnia were probably informal and sporadic, and any decisions they
made applied only to their voluntary association. The myth of Johanan
ben Zakkai establishing a full-blown institution to govern Israel on the
model of the council in Jerusalem is an idealization based on predestruction and later talmudic governing bodies.[11] The promulgation of
the Birkat Ha-Minim and the fixing of the canon of Scripture are often
attributed to the Council of Jamnia, but the canon was essentially fixed
in the second century b.c.e. and the Birkat Ha-Minim developed and
spread only gradually in the early centuries of the common era.[12]

Many social, religious, and political movements competed for influence and power among Palestinian Jews in the late first century. Re-
sentment and resistance to Rome did not cease with the defeat in 70.
The dominant, long-term response to Rome was political resistance,
which led to another war sixty years later under the leadership of Bar
Kosiba. Apocalyptic groups fostered the aspirations of the community
for reform and the fulfillment of the promises of God's rule in the land.
Mystical trends appeared in apocalyptic movements, at Qumran and in
Hellenistic Jewish communities.[13] Later collections testify to the complexity and variety of response to that task and the richness of the mystical tradition.[14] Though the midrashic and talmudic texts manifest
great reserve toward apocalypticism and mysticism, they flourished.[15]
In other circles, Jews who accepted Jesus promoted their own versions
of messianic teaching and Jewish practices. Alongside all these groups,
the early rabbinic movement created a tightly bonded group of re-
formers who sought to understand and live fully the way of life divinely given to Israel. They reconstructed a Judaism which included in
its vision the Temple and sacrifices that no longer existed and a pro-
found grasp of all of the details of life governed by divine command.[16]
In this way, they began the process that would lead to a self-sufficient
community able to exist under alien rule anywhere.

After the Bar Kosiba War with Rome (132–35) and the concomitant
devastation of Judea, many Jews, including rabbis, migrated to Gal-

ilee. This resulted in a loss of coherence and influence for the rabbinic movement, since it had to reestablish its economic and social base and seek to regain influence in the Galilean villages and cities.[17] Galilee had its own Jewish culture and traditions, a fact perhaps reflected in the rabbinic view that the Galileans had not consulted Johanan ben Zakkai to decide cases.[18] In fact, Galilee was as complex and thoroughly Jewish as Judea.[19] In the coastal cities and in territories surrounding Galilee, Jewish communities were probably Greek speaking and had to deal with a variety of tensions and problems which required innovative solutions.[20] The rabbis who migrated from Judea to Galilee originally settled in outlying areas and only gradually penetrated the cities and became influential on the community as a whole.[21] Rabbi Judah the Prince was the first rabbinic leader to exercise the aristocratic power common to social leaders in the Roman Empire. He was wealthy, supported a circle of retainers and clients, controlled a small but dedicated group of social and religious leaders, and claimed Davidic descent to bolster his legitimacy. Origen calls his successors ethnarchs and compares them, with midrashic exaggeration, to the kings of Judah.[22] Like other intellectuals during the Second Sophistic, Rabbi used his learning and influence for social leadership. His formulation of the Mishnaic code took place in the context of the intellectual efforts of the Second Sophistic, when Greco-Roman authors created digests, compendia, and codes and Christian authorities began the canonization of the New Testament.[23] However, the patriarch's power and influence varied with the social and political fortunes of both Galilee and his own group, declining during parts of the third century and increasing, paradoxically, under Christian imperial control in the fourth.[24] Thus, late first- and second-century Judaism was less a finished product or a coherent community and tradition and more a group of communities within a varied and changing tradition that was developing toward the comprehensive, unified, and relatively stable talmudic system of later centuries. The early rabbinic group was struggling to gain influence and power in the Jewish community and only began to gain widespread power at the end of the second century under Rabbi Judah the Prince. The process whereby rabbis became judges, officials, and village leaders continued with varied results in Galilean villages and cities throughout the third, fourth, and early fifth centuries.

Similarly, the many Jewish communities scattered around the Roman Empire varied greatly from one another and had adapted significantly to local conditions. Jews were a major ethnic group in the empire, comprising perhaps 5 to 7 percent of the empire's population.

Their social and political importance can be seen in the grave danger they presented to the empire in a series of popular uprisings usually called Trajan's War (115–17). Jewish communities were found in small villages and towns and in large cities. Many were well established and influential with the authorities. The Acts of the Apostles probably reflects diaspora conditions in the late first century when it shows influential Jewish leaders appealing successfully to the authorities to keep order by disciplining a disruptive new teacher named Paul (Acts 13:50; 14:4–6; 17:5–9). The prosperity, power, and accomplishments of the Alexandrian Jewish community aroused political opposition and controversy, as Philo and others testify.[25] Excavations in Sardis have shown that the Jewish community had a synagogue in a public building on the town square that was expanded and renovated several times during the first four centuries of the common era. Many other communities had meeting halls which went through various stages of development and served multiple purposes.[26] Some Jewish communities were poor and uneducated. The Jewish inscriptions from Rome show that, though the Roman community had a number of synagogues, the members of many of these synagogues were neither prosperous nor well educated.[27] A welter of archaeological and historical evidence suggests that numerous Jewish communities flourished in the eastern empire for several centuries until Christianity dominated society and suppressed Judaism in the fifth century.[28] Around Antioch in Syria, in the fourth century, Jewish tenant farmers successfully sued their landlord, Libanus, without any legal hindrance or disability.[29] At the same time, Libanus, a famous orator and social leader, corresponded on equal terms with the patriarch (Gamaliel VI?) concerning his son's Greek studies in Antioch and other subjects proper to aristocrats of high station.[30] The educated ruling classes in fourth-century Syria-Palestine included Jews, and close ties were maintained between Jewish communities in Antioch and Palestine.[31] John Chrysostom himself testifies to the high regard in which Jews were held.[32] Each Jewish community had its own structure and relationship with the local population. Their leaders bore various titles, such as head of the synagogue, leader, elder, scribe; they were women as well as men.[33] Justin Martyr refers to the Jewish leaders with whom he is in conflict as "teachers" *(didaskaloi)*.[34] Nowhere are rabbis mentioned. The extension of rabbinic influence from Palestine and Babylonia to the whole Mediterranean world would take several centuries. Meanwhile in the Roman diaspora, Jewish communities flourished in many unique ways.

On the whole, Greek-speaking Jews had more open boundaries

than some Jews in Palestine, especially under emerging rabbinic Judaism. Many of them shared with their fellow Hellenistic citizens a common ethic, apprehension of divine power, and appreciation of philosophical wisdom.[35] They also engaged in religious practices such as magic and the cult of the dead and struggled with demonic powers.[36] Yet Jewish life had some constant features that were well recognized in the Greco-Roman world, including exclusive monotheism; circumcision; Sabbath, new moon, and festival celebrations; purification after sexual relations and touching impure things, wearing tassels and phylacteries.[37] Jews were admired for their monotheism, ancient Scriptures, worship, and ethics. But they had incorporated a variety of world views and practices. Texts, inscriptions, and testimonies speak of Jewish mysticism, magic, healing, miracle working, and so on.[38] Though the Talmud attempts to control miracles and magic, their presence and reality is taken for granted.

Jewish movements, sects, and heretics *(minim)* also testify to the variety and vitality of Judaism. Charges of heresy and sectarianism were used by both rabbinic and Christian leaders to establish their own groups and delegitimate their opponents.[39] In turn, those other groups met the rejection of the main body of believers with counterclaims of having exclusive possession of the truth. Justin Martyr dismissed as godless and impious heretics certain Christians who rejected his belief in the millenium.[40] He claimed that they were no more Christians than various sects of Jews—Sadducees, Genista, Meristae, Galileans, Hellenians, Pharisees, Baptists—were really Jewish.[41] But sects, dissidents, and deviants are sociologically always members of their society, even when they are rejected. Paradoxically, the health of society demands dissidents; they are part of the larger social processes associated with stability and change, continuity and adaptation. Interaction between deviants and their host society exposes a society's identity, boundaries, key structures and values, and its symbolic system.[42] To study what a society rejects is to study what it is.[43] Conflict within and at the boundaries of a society helps the processes of change and adaptation.[44] Furthermore, it is not clear to what extent these groups were constructed by the authors who criticized them or how much they fit reality.[45] Even making allowances for the homogenization of the talmudic tradition, some passages hint at disagreements among Jewish groups. The Sadducees seem to have endured in an uneasy relationship with the rabbinic groups (m. Nid. 4:2), and Pharisees were often treated as a sect.[46] Even though talmudic Judaism did not accept Samaritans as really Jewish, sociologically and historically they came from the Jewish tradition.[47] Heretics and people who said that there are two powers in heaven appear sporadically in the midrashim and Talmuds.[48] The identity of the groups alluded to under the categories *minim, nokhrim,* worshipers of stars and constellations, worshipers of two powers in heaven, and so on, most probably varied greatly over the centuries and may have included Jews who opposed rabbinic control or views, various types of Jewish-Christians, Jewish gnostics, and those who assimilated to Greco-Roman philosophy or practices too thoroughly.[49] However, the fact that *minim,* whoever they were, occur in rabbinic and also in patristic literature, argues for their importance within or near Jewish society. The relations between Jews and gentiles, as reflected in the laws of the Mishnah and Tosefta, testify to the constant effort required to maintain community identity and adjust boundaries. Jews had many habitual interactions with gentiles; problems associated with these relationships were solved in such a way as to preserve the boundaries and ethnic integrity of the community.[50] The opposition between the Jewish community and various of its neighbors and the intensity of Jewish devotion to Torah do not mean that there were no contacts, but the opposite. Jews remained a vital part of the empire and of its various provinces and cities all through antiquity.[51] Thus the Greco-Roman, Christian, and Jewish communities had many concrete contacts and engaged in many disputes for which we have only hints or allusions.

Jewish-Christian Relationships

Granted the great variety of Jewish communities, how should the relationship between Christianity and Judaism be understood? Most agree that Christianity began as a Jewish sect in the land of Israel, but that close relationship is treated as a brief chapter in its history. As was noted in the Introduction, Christian treatments of the first century often place the separation of Christianity from Judaism soon after the destruction of the Temple and attribute it to the alleged promulgation of the Birkat Ha-Minim. A hardening of attitudes and of self-definitions among Jews and Christians is said to have resulted from the years of crisis following the loss of the Temple. Indeed, Harnack's argument that Jews isolated themselves from the concerns of the larger society after the Bar Kosiba War is still influential.[52] But this broad thesis is improbable. Conflicts between Jewish and Christian groups varied greatly according to time and place. Even if the rabbinic group created a "blessing" against the heretics, they did not control the synagogues either in Palestine or in the rest of the Roman Empire. Thus any decisions made by them would have been limited to their own assemblies and to a minority under their influence. The textual development of the blessing and patristic allusions to anti-Christian Jewish prayers and attitudes are too ambiguous to prove the widespread circulation of the Birkat Ha-Minim.[53] It is by no means certain that the benediction was promulgated in the first century, nor that it was aimed at Christians, nor that it was accepted by a large number of Jewish communities. Rather, the process of separation of Christians from the synagogue was long and subject to local variation. Arguments from the Geniza text of the the Amidah and from various later interpretations only confirm the complexity of the development of the curse against the heretics and the many and continuing conflicts between Judaism and Christianity.

Christian historians and theologians admit to the continuing influence of biblical ideas and customs, but ignore any positive influence of Judaism after Jesus' death. They treat Judaism and Christianity as conceptually and historically distinct religions with clear boundaries, separate identities, and little in common. Jewish practices and ideas which survived in Christianity are understood to have been fundamentally transformed. The Jewish community and tradition is judged to be mistaken and valueless for Christian theology or life.[54] The reality is not so uniform or tidy.

That Christians and Jews continued to interact with one another, to compete for members, and most important, to create and defend boundaries, which were constantly crossed, can be see in many scattered texts both in rabbinic literature and patristic literature. Various texts dealing with Ben Stada or Ben Pantera (often identified as Jesus) and other *minim* dot talmudic literature.[55] However, the texts are allusive and their dates often late; thus their relevance for Jewish reactions to Christianity remains disputed. A number of recent articles have linked rabbinic interpretations of Scripture with anti-Christian apologetics or polemics.[56] For example, Sifre Deuteronomy defends the election of Israel, probably against the Christian claim that Israel has been rejected.[57] One section of the Mekhilta stresses faith (*'ămānāh*) as faithful observance of the commandments against a Christian, Pauline emphasis on faith versus law.[58] Pesikta de Rab Kahana offers a later Jewish alternative to Christian claims for Jesus' atoning death.[59] Since Christians often cited Jewish sin, especially the worship of the golden calf, as proof that Jews had rejected the covenant with Yahweh and that Christians were the true heirs of the covenant, the rabbis suppressed and explained away the golden calf.[60]

Origen, who lived in Caesarea during the third century, engaged in lively debate and scholarly exchanges with Jews.[61] Interpretations of

the Song of Songs indicate that Origen and Rabbi Johanan disagreed
systematically on five issues: the covenant, the value of the New Testament versus the Oral Torah, the roles of Christ versus Adam, the heavenly versus the earthly Jerusalem, and the status of Israel (repudiated
or disciplined).[62] Jacob Neusner has suggested that the shape and thematic structure of the Talmuds and some midrashic collections are
partly determined by a response to Christian dominance of imperial
politics.[63] Themes of sanctification and salvation, of hope and history,
knit these texts together and may be an implicit response to social pressures and Christian culture.

    Many other areas of evidence could be adduced to fill out the pic-
ture of Judaism as a varied community in vital contact with the world
around it. Patristic and rabbinic literature contain many unsystematic
but pervasive signs of contact.[64] As will be seen below, the synagogues
continued to attract both Christians and other Greco-Romans for worship and teaching.[65] Proselytism was only gradually legislated out of
existence in the late fourth and fifth centuries.[66] In fact, rabbinic efforts
at conversion may have increased during the third century in imitation
of Christian successes.[67] In fourth century Antioch, John Chrysostom
still perceived conversion to Judaism as a threat, though he does not
accuse the Jewish community of actively proselytizing.[68] Topics which
occur in both rabbinic and patristic literature suggest that Jews and
Christians in many places engaged in active debate and conflict, with
neither side holding a cultural or legal advantage.[69]

    The evidence which has been gathered here does not allow a com-
plete picture of Judaism in late antiquity nor of Jewish-Christian relations, but it does suggest that Jewish communities were growing and
changing with the Roman Empire and in response to local conditions.
The grand talmudic synthesis which was to guide Israel for centuries
was only gradually emerging and was accepted only by certain groups.
Jews in the first few centuries of the common era lived in varied communities, were enriched by the biblical and Hellenistic traditions and
were challenged and threatened by the many religions of the Roman
Empire.

Christian Identity in Relation to Judaism

False notions of a unitary and cohesive Christian development in the
first two centuries and a strong concern to establish Christian identity
have often lead to the assumption that a decisive break was made with
Judaism in the 80s, or at least by the early second century. Judaism and
Christianity are understood as conceptually distinct religions with

clear boundaries, separate identities, and cohesive communities. Actually, the Christian communities and writers of the first two centuries lived in varied relationships with Jewish communities. Some separated themselves from Judaism and others constantly drew upon their Jewish roots. All wrestled with the fundamental problem of Christianity's relationship with God's people Israel.

The Gospels of Mark and Matthew exemplify the disagreements and tensions among the late first-century communities of followers of Jesus. The Gospel of Mark was written about the time of the war with Rome, and the Gospel of Matthew, written in the 80s or 90s, made use of Mark.[70] Yet the authors differ dramatically in their attitudes toward Judaism. Mark declares Jesus "Lord of the Sabbath" (2:28), with the implication that Jesus' abrogates Sabbath observance. Mark interprets a dispute over handwashing and purity rules to mean that Jesus "declared all foods clean" (7:19). The author provides his (most probably) gentile Christian community with a (not completely accurate) account of purity regulations (7:3–4). He criticizes the Temple and its authorities by bracketing the scene in which Jesus overturns the tables of the moneychangers and those who sold pigeons with the cursing and subsequent withering of a fruitless fig tree (11:12–25). Mark has moved in the same direction as the Pauline communities, to a very selective observance of Jewish law based on its compatibility with the life and teachings of Jesus. The author of Matthew, as we shall see, is most probably a Jew who, though expelled from the assembly in his city, still identifies himself as a member of the Jewish community and who supports obedience to Jewish law according to the interpretation of Jesus.[71] The fact that Matthew is later than Mark shows that separation from Judaism was not a function of time and that it varied by geographical location. The relationship of the Jewish communities to the groups of believers-in-Jesus was a complex cultural phenomenon.[72]

Most New Testament and second-century Christian writings reflect concrete struggles between Jewish and Christian communities for members, social legitimacy, communal identity, and political influence.[73] Theological arguments served immediate, limited concerns but did not develop into a universally consistent theology of Israel. For example, the Gospel of John excoriates "the Jews," which in most cases means those Jews, especially the leaders, who have opposed and pressured the Johannine community. The sectarian atmosphere of John serves to differentiate the Johannine community from the world, those weak in faith, and "the Jews."[74] The deuteropauline Letter to Titus, written about 100 C.E., hints at conflict with Jewish communities in its strictures against law, speculations, and genealogies (1:10–16; 3:9).[75]

In the early second century, Ignatius of Antioch insisted on the clear distinction between Christians and Jews, reprimanded Christians who observed Jewish customs, and claimed that the biblical prophets explicitly spoke about Jesus Christ.[76]

Explicit, elaborate, and detailed rejection of the practice of Jewish customs and of the historical place of the Jewish people arises in the Epistle of Barnabas, in which the story of the broken tablets at Sinai (Exod. 32) anticipates Israel's rejection of the covenant of the beloved Jesus (4:8, 14). Just as the younger son, Jacob, was chosen over Esau, the elder, so "this people" (the believers-in-Jesus) are now first (13:1) and are a " new people" (chap. 5). Consequently, Barnabas allegorizes circumcision and dietary laws so that they speak of the moral life (chaps. 9–10), and he transforms the Jerusalem Temple into the temple of the saved human (chap. 16).[77] Matthew's nuanced interpretations of Jewish law and custom according to the teaching of Jesus have been replaced by a wholesale rejection of major portions of the law, and the historical Israel has given way to a new community, which is in fact struggling to establish a strong and distinct identity using the traditions of Israel.

Not all Christian writers attacked Judaism as inflexibly as the Epistle of Barnabas. Justin Martyr enclosed his exegetical defense of Christianity in a fictional dialogue with a Jew named Trypho, set sometime after the defeat of Bar Kosiba.[78] (The *Dialogue* itself was written after the *First Apology* in 155 and before Justin's death in the late 160s.) Justin is notable as the first writer to claim that Christians are the "true, spiritual Israel" and thus to substitute a new (third) group for the historical Israel.[79] He quotes long passages from the Septuagint to prove that only Christian teaching and interpretation of Scripture is true, that Jesus is the Messiah sent by God, and that the Christians are the new people of God. Many of the themes which persist in virulently anti-Jewish attacks in later centuries are laid down here. However, the mild tone of the *Dialogue with Trypho* is notable. Though the *Dialogue* is a Christian instruction that is fundamentally unfair to historical Judaism, the relationship between Justin and Trypho is generally respectful. The atmosphere of the work argues for a diaspora context in which ongoing conversation and debate between Jews and Christians was common.[80] Trypho, who does not know Hebrew and admits that he is not a religious expert, fits the type of the Hellenistic Jew who has a variety of contacts with gentiles and lives with permeable community boundaries.[81]

The author of 5 Esdras (the first two, Christian chapters of 4 Ezra) announces the replacement of Israel by the "coming people" (1:35,

38). Israel is rejected for her sins in a total and final way not found in the Bible or in Matthew. However, the coming people (the Christians) are not called new or a new Israel. Rather, they inherit God's name, the Bible, and the patriarchs, and they become the people of God. The author of 5 Esdras seeks a clear identity for his group by taking over the foundations and roles of Israel, not by denying their validity. This odd insistence on both discontinuity and continuity bespeaks ongoing conflict with the Jewish community in the middle of the second century as the author works out his community's identity in relationship to Judaism.[82]

Justin, the author of 5 Esdras, and the author of the Epistle of Barnabas sought to establish the identity of Christianity by rooting it in a particular interpretation of the Bible and Israel's tradition. All three understood Israel's story as reaching its conclusion in Jesus and read Israel's law and literature as a coded version of how to live as a Christian in the second century. Contemporaneously, the early rabbinic sages at Jamnia and at Usha in Galilee (after the Bar Kosiba War) were connecting their own stories to those of Israel and reinterpreting Israel's law. Much of their Mishnah concerned a Temple no longer physically available, but from which the sages derived a vision of a holy and integral society under God. Both groups adapted to changed circumstances that threatened their existence within a large and diverse empire, and both drew on and dramatically reinterpreted biblical traditions.

Though rabbis and Christian teachers opposed one another and sought to establish unique and stable identities, they had many common elements of tradition and practice. The elements that Jews and Christians shared in the eyes of the peoples of the empire can be seen in Theophilus of Antioch's apology for Christianity, the *Ad Autolycum*.[83] Theophilus is noted for his reticence on the subject of Christology—he never mentions the name of Jesus or speaks of his work explicitly.[84] His appeal to monotheism and morality is virtually identical to that of Hellenistic diaspora Judaism.[85] Theophilus offers vivid testimony to the persistence of close connections between Judaism and Christianity and of Jewish themes and interests in Syrian Christianity through the second century. The close relationship with Judaism and the struggle to create and maintain separate identities continued in the East during the following centuries. As late as the fourth century, the influence and vitality of Jewish communities was an embarrassment to Christian leaders. Though the emperor was Christian, the culture of the empire was not.[86] Close contact between Jews and Christians was common in Syria, and many Christians continued or adopted Jewish liturgical practices and other customs. This fourth-century tendency was most likely a tradition carried on from earlier times.[87] The Christian liturgical prayers passed on through the third-century collection the *Didascalia* to the late fourth-century collection the *Constitutiones Apostolorum* probably were originally second- or third-century Jewish prayers from Syria.[88]

Many groups of believers-in-Jesus in the east were Jewish-Christians, that is, people who accepted Jesus as Messiah but identified themselves primarily as Jews.[89] Ireneus, Epiphanius, and other heresiologists and historians named several groups of Jewish-Christians, but their reports are often based on inaccurate or misinterpreted information and biased by prior schematizations.[90] The Ebionites were probably several distinct groups, and the Elchesaites, whom Epiphanius names as founded by Elchasai, were actually a Jewish-Christian group that adopted the Book of Elchasai. The Book of Elchasai itself, however, was a second-century, Mesopotamian Jewish apocalypse with no original connection with Christianity.[91] Other documents reflect a diversity of community conflicts. The Christian community addressed in the *Didascalia* (third century) sought to establish and protect its orthodoxy, but it was probably a minority group reacting against a majority Jewish-Christian community.[92] Similarly, the community behind the hypothetical source of the Pseudo-Clementine literature, the *Kerygmata Petrou* (c. 200), was an independent Jewish-Christian group, as was the Jewish-Christian community behind the Ascents of James.[93] The so-called Judaizers within various Christian communities, against whom Christian writers complain, were often representatives of a different kind of Christianity.[94] This situation was normal throughout the East. Christians in Adiabene during the fourth century engaged in vigorous contact and debate with the Jewish community, as the writings of Aphrahat show. In fact, the Christians there may have been merely an offshoot of the Jewish community.[95] As late as the eighth century in Syria, the works of Sergius the Stylite suggest that ordinary Syrian Christians "could still not distinguish clearly between Judaism and Christianity. We can trace this uncertainty about the exact boundary between the two religions virtually from the emergence of the Syriac-speaking Church right down to its effective demise as a major cultural force in the Middle East. . . . [The ordinary laypeople] appear to have taken a more tolerant attitude to the differences between the two religions despite all the attempts of the Christian elite to create an image of the Jews which would frighten laypeople from having any contact with them."[96]

The very existence of many Jewish-Christian groups in the early centuries of this era warn against overly rigid definitions of Judaism and Christianity. Most accounts of Jewish-Christians assign to them a low Christology, in which Jesus is seen as human in the role of Messiah or prophet, and attribute to them rejection of Pauline Christianity and the practice of Jewish law. However, the data are more complex. The so-called Ascents of James (recovered from the Pseudo-Clementine literature) stem from a Greek-speaking Jewish-Christian community in the late second century that was law-observant, but accepted Jesus as a preexistent Christ.[97] Similarly, the Nazarenes, rightly defined and understood, were an early, independent group of Jewish believers-in-Jesus who survived until the fourth century. They affirmed the virgin birth and a high Christology, did not reject Paul, and continued the practice of Jewish law.[98]

Conclusions

The existence and persistence of Jewish Christianity for centuries, the continuing attraction of Judaism for gentile Christians, and the sustained engagement between the Christian and Jewish communities were not an accident nor an epiphenomenon of the dominant orthodox tradition. The Jesus movement and rabbinic Judaism began as two Jewish reform programs. The rabbinic program succeeded gradually in reforming all Jewish communities in Mesopotamia and the Roman Empire so that the talmudic halakah became the dominant and then the singular way of understanding and living Judaism. The Jesus movement succeeded among gentiles and became an independent but related religion. Yet especially in the East, many believers-in-Jesus retained a close association with Jewish communities and shared with them many cultural characteristics. At the level of lived religion, many Judaisms and Christianities found themselves in a variety of relationships, often much to the consternation of their more orthodox leaders.

All these communities existed within the larger Greco-Roman culture (and farther east, Parthian and Sassanian culture) and faced many of the same problems. They struggled to create a clear identity and maintain sharp boundaries. In doing so, they often overlapped one another, though their leaders sought to differentiate the groups through polemics. Despite Christian anti-Semitism, positive relationships between Jews and Christians continued. Origen in the third century and Jerome in the fourth knew and learned from Jewish scholars in Palestine and had contact with various Jewish-Christian groups. The paradigm of two great orthodox traditions and two independent religions from the first century on ignores a mass of archaeological, his-

torical, and literary data. The talmudic tradition and the orthodox
Christian theology and polity of the fifth and sixth centuries had yet to
be formed and dominate their respective communities.

Thus a sharp division between the postdestruction Jewish community and Matthew's Christian-Jewish group is both unnecessary and
unlikely. The Jewish and Christian communities in the eastern Roman
Empire were varied in their practice and thought as they responded to
a variety of local situations. This fluid situation provides the context
for Matthew's Christian-Jewish group somewhere in Syria or Coele
Syria in the late first century. Consequently, in order to understand
Matthew's views of God, Jesus, the Bible, righteousness, law, the kingdom of God, Israel, and the gentiles, a setting and a set of social and
intellectual relationships will have to be sought within the Judaisms of
the Roman Empire in the late first century.

II

Matthew's People: Israel

The Gospel of Matthew, like its source, Mark, has no name for the group of disciples Jesus gathered around him. Similarly, though the author often hints at circumstances and problems which affect his own group in the late first century in his description of the relationships of Jesus, his disciples, and the authorities, he neither names his group nor explicitly defines its identity in relation to other groups.[1] He does not claim that his group is Israel, or the true or new Israel, or the people of God, or true Jews. He attributes righteousness to his group, but unlike the authors of many apocalyptic writings, he does not use the substantive "the righteous" or "the just" as a technical designation to set his group apart from his opponents.[2] However, Matthew's terms and descriptions of the groups with which Jesus and his disciples had contact and his characterizations of the crowds and the community leaders in Galilee and Jerusalem provide some evidence for his view of his own group by way of apologetic and polemical contrast. In some cases Matthew draws sharp boundaries, for example, between Jesus' disciples and the scribes and Pharisees; in others, the boundaries are more porous, for example, between the disciples and the crowds, whom Jesus is trying to recruit. As we will see, the analysis of terms used for Galilean and Judaean Jews and of the characters, including group characters, who appear in the Matthean narrative provide a basis for accurate contrast of these groups with non-Jews and for a more exact characterization of Matthean group identity. The terms "Israel," "people," "crowds," "Jews," "this generation," "sons of the kingdom," and "children of Abraham" will be examined in this chapter, and the leaders of Israel (the chief priests, elders, scribes, Pharisees, and Sadducees) in the next. It is important to emphasize Matthew's sharp distinction between the people and their leaders. He continually appeals to his fellow Jews to accept Jesus and attacks the community leadership for rejecting him and keeping the people from following Jesus (and by implication, the Matthean group in the late first century).

Israel

Jews through the centuries have called themselves "Israel," and this is
the name used in first-century Jewish literature and, presumably, by
Jesus and his early followers. Though various Christian authors
claimed that they were the new or true Israel in subsequent centuries,
no New Testament writer claims this for the believers-in-Jesus.[3] In the
Gospel of Matthew, "Israel" refers to the land and to the historical, ethnic, religious group of people who lived in the land, believed in the
God of Israel, and accepted the writings and way of life associated with
their particular God. That is, Israel in Matthew refers to the Jewish
community as a whole, and thus Matthew's usage matches the normal
meaning of the word in Hebrew and Aramaic. For example, Israel
means land when Joseph, Mary, and Jesus return from Egypt to "the
land of Israel" (2:20−21) and when Jesus says that his disciples will
not have visited all the cities of Israel before the Son of Man comes
(10:23). More often Israel refers to the people or to both people and
land. Jesus declares that he has never seen faith in Israel like that of the
centurion (8:10); the crowds respond to an exorcism by saying that
nothing like this has been seen in Israel (9:33), and elsewhere the
crowd glorifies the God of Israel (15:31). Jesus promises that his disciples will judge the twelve tribes of Israel (19:28). The chief priest, elders, and scribes mock Jesus for allegedly claiming to be king of Israel
(27:42). Finally, a biblical paraphrase (27:9, supposedly Jeremiah)
uses the normal idiom, "the sons of Israel," for the inhabitants of the
land.

Matthew has one special usage of the term "Israel," which parallels
his use of "people" and "crowds" (both treated below). In three places,
he uses Israel to refer to a specific part of the people of Israel, namely,
those who are in need of leadership and care. Twice Jesus refers to the
lost sheep of the house of Israel (10:6; 15:24) and, in an adaptation of
Mic. 5:1−3 and 2 Sam. 5:2, the author says that Jesus will be a ruler
who will "rule [*poimanei*, pasture, feed] my people Israel" (2:6). In
these places, Jesus and his disciples are identified as leaders who have
been sent by God to care for their people.

People

The author of Matthew usually uses the word "people" (*laos*) in its ordinary sense to refer to the social and political entity of the land of Israel, that is, the Jewish people. He also uses it to specify subgroups
within Israel. "People" has a special Matthean theological weight only

in the first four chapters of the gospel, when the author is speaking of the peoples' need for leadership and salvation.[4] "People" as a designation for the political, religious community occurs five times in compounds characterizing various leadership groups. The "scribes of the people," along with the chief priests, are consulted by Herod (2:4). At the time of Jesus' arrest, the "elders of the people" are mentioned several times, sometimes along with the high priests and as members of the council (21:23; 26:3, 47; 27:1). In these cases, the qualifying clause "of the people" refers to their official status as community leaders. Thus, "the people" are the people of Israel in the land of Israel in the widest sense.

The ordinary relationship of leaders to people also is implied in two passages in the passion narrative. The chief priests and elders of the people fear to arrest Jesus by stealth and kill him during the feast "lest there be a tumult among the people" (26:3–5).[5] After Jesus' death the chief priests and Pharisees ask Pilate for a tomb guard so that the disciples of Jesus may not steal his body and "tell the people, 'He has risen from the dead'" (27:64).[6] In these two passages, the "people," like the "crowds" elsewhere, are well disposed toward Jesus and open to being won over to him. The Jerusalem leadership therefore seeks to control public opinion and separate the people from Jesus by careful maneuvering.

In four places in the first four chapters, the author of Matthew uses the word "people" in reference to the need of the people actually living in Israel for competent leadership and care. This usage overlaps that of the terms "Israel" and "crowds." In each case, Jesus is presented as the answer to the people's needs. The angel tells Joseph that Jesus "will save his *people* from their sins" (1:21). In the narrative "his people" refers to the people of Israel.[7] Soon after, the chief priests and scribes "of the people" (2:4) testify to Herod and the Magi that the Messiah will "govern my *people* Israel" (2:6). This clause, set within a Matthean adaptation of Mic. 5:1, is an almost exact reproduction of LXX 2 Sam. 5:2 (= 1 Chron. 11:2). The scriptural citation seeks to establish Jesus' authority over Israel, based on the role David played in the Bible, and also conveys the concrete first-century apocalyptic expectation of Israel's imminent restoration.[8] The passage is sharply ironic and critical of Israel's governance, since some of the leaders of the people (chief priests and scribes) tell another leader of the people (Herod) that Scripture promises that God will send a leader for the people.[9]

Jesus' preaching and healing in Galilee is introduced with Isa. 9:1, which claims that "the *people* sitting [= dwelling] in darkness have seen a great light." Specific reference is made to "the land" *(gē)* of the tribes of Zebulon and Naphtali, that is, the areas in Galilee where Jesus worked, and to the needs of the people there. Finally, a few verses later Matthew summarizes Jesus' activities: teaching in "their synagogues," preaching the gospel of the kingdom, and "healing every disease and every infirmity among the *people*" (4:23).[10] In all four passages in chapters 1–4, the author communicates something significant about Jesus, either through an edited scriptural citation or a concise summary statement. In each case the narrative refers to the people themselves as the object of Jesus' concern and activity. Matthew's insistent repetiton of the needs of the people, Israel, and the crowds testifies to his continued interest in and identification with his people.

In chapter 15, the author cites from Isaiah an attack on the people of Israel for being far from God. However, Matthew uses the passage to indict the leaders—the Pharisees and scribes who are arguing with Jesus concerning handwashing—not the people. This polemic against the leaders is typical of Matthew. In it Jesus first argues that the Pharisees and scribes void the word of God with their own traditions (15:6) and then launches an *ad hominem* argument against them as hypocrites (7–9).[11] Following Mark, the author of Matthew attacks the leaders using a close approximation of LXX Isa. 29:13, which charges that "this people" honors God only with their lips, not with their heart (Matt. 15:9). Matthew, however, changes the order of words and thus the meaning of the last line. The Septuagint has "teaching the precepts of man and teachings [of men]" *(didaskontes entalmata anthrōpōn kai didaskalias).* Matthew has "teaching [as] teachings the precepts of men" *(didaskontes didaskalias entalmata anthrōpōn).* The quotation in this form supports Matthew's main point in this section, that the Pharisees and scribes put their traditions in place of God's commands. The biblical term "people" here is made to refer to a subgroup of leaders, an interpretation which may be suggested by the whole oracle in Isaiah (29:13–21) in which God threatens those who hide their counsel from him (29:15), promises to destroy the wisdom of the wise and understanding of the prudent (29:14), and condemns those who dispense justice unjustly (29:21). Those being condemned in Isaiah are only certain members of the people, and they are contrasted with the deaf who shall hear and the blind who shall see and the poor who shall rejoice. This Isaianic contrast parallels closely Matthew's frequent juxtaposition of the unfaithful leaders of Israel with the crowds and people who need leadership.

Two other passages use the word "people" to refer to the subgroup within Israel that is hostile or not responsive to Jesus. The people listening to the parables sermon (chap. 13) do not understand or accept

Jesus' message (13:15), and the people in Jerusalem at Jesus' trial before Pilate call for Jesus' crucifixion (25:27). These two passages have sometimes been interpreted as a reflection of Matthew's judgment that the Jewish people as a whole have rejected Jesus and that consequently the mission to bring them to belief in Jesus is closed.[12] However, Matthew's condemnations of the people are very specific and limited in each case and do not apply to the whole of the people of Israel. After the parable of the sower and before its interpretation, Matthew follows Mark in commenting on the people's lack of understanding. He also decisively distinguishes the crowds who listen to Jesus teach (13:2, 3) from the disciples who have committed themselves to Jesus. The controlling metaphor of the first part of chap. 13 is hearing. After the parable of the sower, the author has Jesus call for those who have "ears to hear" (13:9). Then Jesus tells his disciples that "it has been given" (= divine providence) to them to know the mysteries of the kingdom, but to "them" (the crowds in 13:2, 3) it has not been given because they do not really see, hear, or understand (13:13). Therefore, the crowds are instructed in parables, which veil the truth. Finally, the explanation of the parable of the sower (13:18–23) distinguishes different responses to the hearing of the word of the kingdom and shows that many fail to understand or respond. Matthew supports his interpretation of the crowd's misunderstanding by citing Isa. 6:10 in full (Matt. 13:14–15).[13] The crucial phrase is "This people's heart has grown dull, and their ears are heavy of hearing and their eyes they have closed." The whole quotation follows the Septuagint closely and is meaningful both in its biblical and Matthean contexts. Isaiah is told that his message will be rejected by many until most of Israel has been destroyed (Isa. 6:11–12), yet "the holy seed" is like the stump of a tree which endures (Isa. 6:13). Similarly, the author of Matthew in his explanation of the parable of the sower shows that many will reject the word of the kingdom and yet the kingdom will flourish. Though some have interpreted "people" in Isaiah to mean the whole people of Israel, clearly both in Isaiah and in Matthew, many in Israel, not all, are designated by the word "people."[14] Both in Isaiah and in Matthew some do listen, and all the hearers, those who fail to respond and those who do respond (the disciples in Matthew), are still part of the people of Israel.[15] For Matthew (as for Isaiah in a different context), Israel is a constant, not something to be replaced by the church, a new people, or a new Israel.

Since chap. 13 is Matthew's attempt to explain why many in Israel did not hear and accept Jesus and his teaching, the sharp contrast between the disciples and the crowds, between the disciples' private instruction and the use of parables to instruct (and leave confused) the crowds, makes sense. The disciples are identified with the many prophets and with righteous people who want to see and hear what the disciples see and hear, and they are contrasted with the crowds who hear but are not moved. Similarly, the crowds in whom the word of the kingdom does not bear fruit are paralleled to those in Isa. 6:10 who reject Isaiah's and God's message. In Isaiah and in Matthew's narrative, the people or crowds—some of whom accept and others of whom reject God's and Jesus' word—are both "Israel." They are not rejected in principle, nor are they declared to be "non-Israel."

His Blood Be upon Us and upon Our Children

The final use of the term "people" occurs during the passion narrative when "all the people" in Jerusalem take responsibility for the death of Jesus (27:25).[16] The crowds at the Passover festival are at first sympathetic to Jesus (21:8–10, 15, 46; 22:33), as they had been in Galilee (see below). But they are manipulated by the Jerusalem leadership (the chief priests, elders, and scribes) to oppose Jesus (26:47, 55; 27:15–26). When the crowd gathers for the Passover release of a prisoner (27:15–26), Pilate asks whether they want Barabbas or Jesus. "The chief priests and the elders persuaded the crowds [*tous ochlous*] to ask for Barabbas and destroy Jesus" (27:20). When Pilate declares that he is innocent of Jesus' blood, "all the people [*pas ho laos*] said, 'His blood [be] on us and on our children [*tekna*]'" (27:25).[17] This last verse has often been interpreted as Matthew's judgment against Israel and as the end of the Jewish mission.[18] However, the narrative of the trial before Pilate suggests a much less cosmic interpretation. In this scene, the terms "crowd" (27:15, 24), "crowds" (27:20), and "people" (27:25) are used synonymously for the same group. It is by no means to be *assumed* that Matthew has substituted "people" for crowds with theological intent.[19] As we have seen above, "people" is not a technical term with one meaning. In many passages, "people" is a political term for Jews ruled by Jewish leaders (2:4; 21:23; 26:3, 47; 27:1). Only at the beginning of the gospel (1:21; 2:6; 4:16, 23) does "people" refer to the whole people of Israel in a possibly theological sense. In these passages, the people are in need of divine assistance and are the object of the work of Jesus, who is God's emmisary and presence among his people. Here in Jerusalem "all the people," who are persuaded by their *leaders* to ask for Barabbas' release and Jesus' death, are not the people of Israel in a theological sense, but a subgroup who are led away from Jesus by the institutional leaders of Israel. They are neither all Jews throughout the Roman and Parthian Empires nor even all Jews in Israel, but the bulk of Jews in Jerusalem, both the inhabitants and those there for the festival, who support Jesus' execution. The author of Matthew uses the word "people" because the ironic prophecy of judgment which he has them pronounce upon themselves foreshadows the destruction of Jerusalem, its leaders, and the bulk of its population in the war against Rome in 70.[20] Thus in Matthew's view, the destruction of Jerusalem is explained as the punishment of God for the death of Jesus. This punishment is concretely directed, not against all Jews, but against the inhabitants of Jerusalem and their children ("us and our children"), that is, those who were in Jerusalem when Jesus died and those of the next generation, who were alive about forty years after Jesus' death when Jerusalem was destroyed.[21] This threat of judgment against Jerusalem had been specifically prepared for by Jesus' lament over Jerusalem and prediction of its destruction (23:37–24:2) just before his arrest. Thus Matthew excoriates an actual political and social segment of Jerusalem, not the people of Israel as a symbolic whole. Only by ignoring the narrative context of 27:25 and by removing Matthew from the historical events of the late first century can commentators discern a rejection of Israel as a whole in Matthew's attack on the Jerusalem leadership and those who followed them.

"All the people" in 27:25 is not a term burdened with salvation-historical weight, but a social and political description of the main body of Israel associated with the center: Jerusalem and its leadership. It is part of Matthew's ongoing attack on the leaders of Israel (see chap. 3 below) and is a symbolic condemnation of the leaders of the Jewish community of his own day, as well as of the people who follow them and persecute the Matthean group. In order to carry out his polemic, Matthew has thoroughly reworked the hearing before Pilate.[22] He has added the dream of Pilate's wife and Pilate's self-exculpation as a stark contrast to the determination of the Jewish leaders and people to have Jesus crucified. He has made the trial process more formal than Mark and has made Pilate twice ask the people what to do with Jesus (27:17, 22).[23] Their response (27:25) is formal and striking.[24] Matthew's continuous attack on the leaders of Israel and those people in Israel who follow them explains to his own Jewish subcommunity why many in Israel have not believed in Jesus and demonstrates the destructive consequences of rejecting Jesus and his teaching.[25] Matthew is not referring to the decision and fate of all Jews in his own time or for all time, but to the fate of Jerusalem and the cause of its destruction. He is also symbolically explaining the opposition he is experiencing from the Jewish community leadership in his own day.

This interpretation of Matthew 27:25 fits the whole gospel's view of

Israel, especially in those passages where the Jewish people are characterized or commented on. The analysis of Matthew's presentation of the crowds below will show that the gospel as a whole does not reject Judaism, or condemn it as a whole or declare that the Jewish mission is closed. The crowds and people are ambiguous all the way through Matthew, as are the disciples. Both groups are imperfectly responsive to Jesus. At the end of the gospel (28:16–20), the disciples still doubt, though they follow Jesus, and the people of Israel (who are included among the nations) are yet to be won over to Jesus' teaching.[26]

That Matthew severely judged and criticized his fellow Jews during the late first century is not improbable. His portrayal of the crowd (crowds, people) and Jerusalem leaders as responsible agents who will come under judgment fits the historical reality of the destruction of Jerusalem and was probably composed in response to it. Another post-destruction, first-century Jewish author, Josephus, had a similar view. He recounts that it was "the multitude" *(to plethos)* in Jerusalem who objected to the insulting action of the procurator Florus and finally instigated the revolt against Roman domination and compelled their leaders to go along with them.[27] Later in the conflict, numerous groups from around the countryside came to Jerusalem and joined the population there in the war, just as Passover pilgrims from the countryside were among the crowds at the time of Jesus' death.[28] In both Josephus and Matthew, the people and leaders in Jerusalem made disastrous decisions that had, in the eyes of these authors, far-reaching consequences. Both authors also put the major portion of blame on the people and leaders of Jerusalem and not on the Romans.

In summary, Matthew's use of the common Greek word *laos* (and its Hebrew equivalent *'am*) is conventional in most cases. It has a theological weight characteristic of Matthew only when he speaks of the needs of the people for leadership and salvation in the first four chapters. It is mostly used in its ordinary sense to refer to a social and political entity, the Jewish people in Israel, and to specific groups of people within Israel. Its usage often parallels Matthew's more frequent term for the people of Israel, "the crowd" or "crowds."

Jews

The polemical use of the term "people" (27:25) is similar to the single, equally polemical use of the term "Jew" in Matthew. "Jew" is used five times in Matthew, four times by non-Jews and once by the author in an editorial comment. "Jew" *(Ioudaios)* was a term used by Greeks and Romans, not a term Jews used to designate themselves within their own community.[29] Matthew follows normal Greek usage in the four cases in which non-Jews speak about Jesus' kingship. The Magi inquire concerning the king of the Jews (2:2), and Pilate asks Jesus if he is king of the Jews (27:11). The Roman soldiers mock Jesus as the king of the Jews (27:29), and the Roman charge against Jesus is that he was king of the Jews (27:37). (However, when the chief priests, scribes, and elders mock Jesus, they call him king of *Israel* [27:42].) Note that the understanding these gentiles have of Jesus fits the public, political categories widely used in Greco-Roman society.

Only once does the author of Matthew use the expression "Jews" for his own people. He does so in an explicitly polemical passage and in his own voice (28:15).[30] The chief priests and elders are said to have obtained a guard for Jesus' tomb to prevent Jesus' disciples from stealing his body and claiming that he has risen (27:62–66). Then, after the empty tomb story and the first appearance of Jesus (28:1–10), the chief priests, elders, and council are said to have bribed the guards to report that the body was stolen from the tomb while they slept (28:11–15). Clearly the author of Matthew is replying to a common charge of fraud made by Jews who did not accept Jesus and his resurrection. The author explains the origin of this charge by the story of the bribed guards and then comments, "and this story has been spread among the *Jews* to this day." The use of the term "Jews" this once in Matthew is peculiar. Some have concluded that the author is a gentile outsider referring to hostile "others" even though the overwhelming evidence of the gospel is against this thesis.[31] Others more commonly have concluded that Matthew's group in the late first century was sharply separated from its fellow Jews and no longer identified with them.[32] It is clear that the author of Matthew is referring to the Jews in his own day because the comment is editorial and outside the narrative action; it is not a comment on the people or leaders in Jerusalem during Jesus' lifetime. The author of Matthew attacks a particular group within Israel with the gentile designation for Israel. He judges that the part of Israel which has accepted the story of the theft of Jesus' body is unreachable because they are under the influence of the Jewish community leaders who oppose and slander Matthew and are thus shut off from any possibility of hearing and believing the teachings and deeds of Jesus. Their distance from Matthew is conveyed by the gentile usage "Jews." However, not all those in Israel, but only some, those who have rejected Jesus' resurrection, are included in this designation. In contrast with them, the (Jewish) crowds all through the narrative are neutral or well-disposed to Jesus, as we shall see; they represent those in the late first-century Jewish community who are open to Matthew's message about Jesus and the kingdom. Finally, the Jews who say that Jesus' body was stolen are sharply contrasted with the disciples who, like the crowds, see Jesus with a mixture of faith and doubt in the next and final episode of the gospel (28:16–20).

Matthew's use of the term "Jews" does not indicate that he is no longer a Jew or that he is totally separate from his ethnic group and religion. Josephus, too, uses "Jew" in an ambiguous way to mean a part of the Jewish people. When recounting the early stages of the war against Rome, he often uses the term for those Jewish inhabitants of Israel who oppose and fight against the Romans, distinguishing them from the leaders loyal to Rome or at least unwilling to sanction armed revolt. When Cestius Gallus began his campaign against "the Jews," he was accompanied by Agrippa, who was of course Jewish; but Agrippa is not identified as such in Josephus' narrative.[33] After Cestius Gallus departed from Galilee, the "Jews" who had taken refuge in the hills counterattacked against the Syrians still pillaging the area. But the Roman army was welcomed into Sepphoris, and all the other cities remained peaceful. All the "rebels and brigands" in the area fled.[34] The inhabitants of these nonrebellious cities are not called Jews, even though the inhabitants of Galilee were overwhelmingly Jewish, because they were not in revolt. Cestius Gallus later entered Antipatris (northeast of Joppa) and attacked, not the whole city, but a large force of "Jews" assembled at a fortified tower. When he advanced on Jerusalem, the "Jews" rushed to arms and defeated him.[35] Interestingly, Silas the Babylonian deserted to "the Jews" from the army of (the Jewish) King Agrippa. It is likely that Silas was from the colony of Babylonian Jews settled in Batanaea, but Josephus calls him a Jew only when he opposes Rome.[36] With the Roman army in danger, Agrippa opened negotiations with the Jews, that is, with the rebels. Later in the battle, many of the leading citizens (gnorimoi) of Jerusalem (who were certainly Jewish) offered to surrender to Cestius, in contrast to the "Jews," who continued resisting the Roman attack on Jerusalem.[37] In a situation of conflict and division among the members of Israel, that is, the Jewish people, Josephus uses the gentile designation "Jews" for that part of the people he opposes. This usage recurs strikingly in his *Life*. When Josephus was commanding the Jewish forces in Galilee, two noble subjects of Agrippa II came as refugees from Trachonitis, smuggling horses, arms, and money for the revolt. "The Jews" would have forced them to be circumcised as a condition of residence, but Josephus opposed them and convinced the people to agree with him. Thus Josephus and the people, presumably all members of Israel, oppose another group in Israel whom Josephus labels "the

Jews." The author of the Gospel of Matthew uses "Jews" similarly in 28:15.[38]

Crowds

"Crowd" or "crowds" *(ochlos, ochloi)* are the terms most frequently used by Matthew to refer to the groups of people who gathered around, heard, and followed Jesus.[39] The crowds are anonymous, shifting, unstructured, and are thus contrasted with Jesus' disciples, who are a constant group, committed to Jesus, and given special instruction. The crowds are portrayed as fundamentally friendly, but also unreliable. Most often they are Jesus' audience; they follow him, listen, marvel at his teaching or miraculous deeds, are astonished, or are simply there (4:25; 5:1; 7:28—8:1; 9:8; 9:33; 12:23, 46; 14:13; 15:10, 30—31; 17:14; 19:2; 20:29; 22:33; 23:1). They are seen as sheep without a shepherd (10:6) who are searching and need Jesus' compassion, healing (9:36; 11:25—27; 14:13—15; 15:32—33), leadership, and instruction (11:1). For the most part, the crowds are presented as neutral or good-willed.[40] The crowds in Galilee and Jerusalem support John the Baptist and consider him a prophet (14:5; 21:26); similarly, the crowds in Jerusalem treat Jesus as a prophet (21:8—9, 46).

Unlike the disciples, who stay with Jesus and understand his teaching, the crowds are dismissed by Jesus after various events (8:18; 13:22—23, 36; 15:39). They are not instructed the way the disciples are and do not understand (13:2, 10—17, 34, 36). In a few cases, crowds are negative toward Jesus: The crowd of mourners at Jairus' house laughs at him (9:23—25). When the disciples cannot heal the epileptic boy, Jesus laments this "faithless generation" (17:17), an expression which refers to the crowds, though perhaps also to the disciples.[41] When the blind men call out to Jesus for help at Jericho, the crowds rebuke them for disturbing him (20:31). In this they are like the disciples who rebuke both those bringing children to Jesus to be blessed (19:13—15) and the Canaanite woman (15:23). However, Jesus does not rebuke the crowd for their incomprehension because less is expected of them than of the disciples.[42] In the latter half of the gospel, chapters 14—26, Jesus is presented as apart from the crowds and with his disciples often (15:40—17:14; 17:19—18:36; 19:16—20:28; 24:1—26:46). Though the crowds are clearly distinct from the disciples and not committed to Jesus, they generally are not hostile to him nor are they condemned by Matthew. Rather, the crowds of Israel are the audience whom Jesus addresses and hopes to attract as followers. They are not directly attacked as the leaders are, but rather are seen as misled

(9:36; 10:6); they are excoriated and rejected only when linked to their leaders in such a way that Jesus' and Matthew's appeal to them is rejected by a whole city (Chorazin, Bethsaida, Capernaum in 11:20–24; Jerusalem in 23:27–29 and 27:20–25). It is likely that the author of Matthew meant the crowds to symbolize the Jewish community of his day, which he hoped to attract to his brand of Judaism.[43]

Only in Jerusalem near the end of the narrative are the crowds characterized as hostile: A large crowd armed with swords and clubs sent by the chief priests and elders of the people accompany Judas to arrest Jesus (26:47). Jesus rebukes them for earlier letting him teach in the Temple and only now arresting him (26:55). But this crowd is associated with the Temple and is under the influence or control of the Temple authorities, so Jesus seems to be referring, not to the populace in general, but to a specific group of people.[44] Only when guided by the Jerusalem leaders, who are false guides in Matthew's eyes, do the crowds take hostile action against Jesus. This is also true when the crowd that is gathered in Jerusalem for the feast appears before Pilate to ask for Jesus' execution (27:15–26). The Jerusalem leadership, the chief priest and elders—have influenced the crowds to ask for Jesus' death and Barabbas' release (27:20). As was noted above in the treatment of the term "people" in 27:25, the group referred to seem to be the inhabitants of Jerusalem, and the scene is thus a foreshadowing of the destruction of Jerusalem and its population in the war against Rome.[45]

To understand Jesus' relationship to the crowds in Matthew's narrative, a few remarks concerning social groups and the relationships of people to their leaders in antiquity are necessary. The crowds are never the whole Jewish people, nor are they the institutionally constituted society of Israel. They are subgroups of Israel, thrown together for a time, mostly in need and potentially available to Jesus as followers. Only occasionally do they oppose Jesus under the influence of the traditional community leadership. The crowds which gather around Jesus are open to multiple influences. They are sociologically typical of the lower classes in antiquity. Ninety percent of the population were peasants and artisans. They were mostly illiterate, lived at a subsistence level, lacked social mobility, and had no direct access to power, unlike the middle classes today, which have a stable economic base, marketable skills, and access to political power and influence. Most of the time, the lower classes were led (and often oppressed) by the 10 percent of the population that made up the ruling classes, including the wealthy, the military, the bureaucracy, the priesthood, and the merchants. For the most part, the peasants worked their fields, which surrounded villages and towns in the countryside; other workers lived in large towns and cities, engaged in various necessary tasks.[46] However, shifting political and economic forces could cause unrest. Frequently in the first century, the people were attracted by popular leaders who claimed to be prophets or to be anointed by God and who promised victory over the Romans. Other dissidents lived outside the system as social bandits.[47] People could also be moved by holy men, a common type of popular leader in the eastern empire. Holy men were usually noted for their persuasive and wise teaching and divinely given powers to heal and do other wonders.

Jesus fits well into this social situation as a popular leader who has gained noninstitutional influence among the people through his teaching and wonder-working. The crowds attracted to him were looking for something more than what they found within established social relationships. Jesus' central symbol of the kingdom of God gave the promise of a renewed covenantal relationship with God and a clearly articulated identity as God's people. It also promoted just social, political, and economic relationships within Israel and thus was an implied critique of the local elders and landowners, the Jerusalem leadership, and the Roman Empire. In modern sociological terms, Jesus' following can be best understood as an incipient social movement which had not reached the level of differentiation required for a social movement organization. When social activity is diffuse and lacking in organization, it is often referred to as a "movement." The term covers a variety of phenomena. It is defined very abstractly and psychologically as "an effort by a large number of people to solve collectively a problem that they feel they have in common."[48] More concretely, a social movement is aimed at promoting or resisting change in a society at large. Such social movements can range from popular sentiment that might result in social activity to complex reformist or revolutionary groups. They often begin as diffuse aggregates of people with minimal organization and gradually change into voluntary, noncorporate groups with some shape and form. They may then become corporate "social movement organizations," for example, coalitions, political interest groups, and reform groups.[49]

Matthew presents the crowds as a shifting, unorganized, but interested group, present with Jesus from the beginning of his public life to the end. They are not committed to Jesus the way the disciples are, nor do they have any structure or leadership. In contrast to the crowds, the disciples have the Twelve, especially Peter, as leaders (10:1–4; 16:17–19), receive special instruction from Jesus (13:11, 36, 51), and are expected to be faithful in times of distress (10:26–33; 26:31–35, by contrast). Despite the distinctions set up between them, Jesus continually addresses both groups, with varied success.[50] Both groups are called to accept Jesus and his teachings and to enter the kingdom. Both abandon Jesus when he is arrested. The disciples, however, rejoin Jesus after the resurrection and believe, if sometimes imperfectly (28:17). Presumably, after the disciples began fulfilling their commission to spread Jesus' teachings, some in the crowds addressed by these early Palestinian followers of Jesus also believed.

For the author of Matthew and his second-generation group, the crowds seem to represent the people of Israel who must still be won away from their false leaders.[51] The obstacle to winning them over is the traditional community leadership, which keeps its people in line and away from the followers of Jesus (23:13). For this reason, Matthew is unsparing in his attacks on the scribes and Pharisees all through the gospel and especially in the climactic polemic in chapter 23, which is addressed to the crowds as well as the disciples (23:1).[52] Matthew seeks, without much success it seems, to disengage the Jewish community of his day from its leaders, whom Matthew judges to be false, hypocritical misleaders. As for the crowd, when it listens to Jesus and is open to his message, it is good; when it listens to its community leaders, it is bad.

Other Characterizations of Israel

Several times Jesus refers in a polemical way to "this generation." Matthew has thematized and elaborated these sayings, several of which are taken from Q and Mark, in order to attack those in the Jewish community of his day who reject Jesus.[53] Three of the passages which speak of "this [evil] generation" refer to the Pharisees and other Jewish leaders.[54] After the Pharisees have accused Jesus of receiving his power from the devil, the scribes and Pharisees ask Jesus for a sign. Jesus calls them an "evil and adulterous generation" and offers only the sign of Jonah (12:38–42). The scribes and Pharisees are compared unfavorably with gentiles, specifically the people of Ninevah and the Queen of the South (Sheba), and are threatened with judgment by them. The evil fate of "this generation" is reinforced by the story of the unclean spirit that returns to the man from whom it was exorcized with seven more evil spirits (12:43–45). The parable concludes with a threat found only in Matthew: "So shall it also be with this evil generation." The parable's close association with the condemnation of the scribes and Pharisees in the sign of Jonah pericope suggests that for Matthew this parable refers to the scribes and Pharisees. In chapter 16, Jesus' attack on the teaching of the Pharisees and Sadducees begins with their asking for a sign and his referring to them as an "evil and adulterous generation" and again offering the sign of Jonah (16:1–4). Here the saying about the evil and adulterous generation is added to the Q saying by Matthew as an explicit cross-reference back to the dispute over Jesus' source of power in chapter 12.

The first and last passages in which Matthew speaks of "this generation" do not explicitly refer to the leaders, though they may be an object of the polemic. In the first, Jesus has identified himself to the disciples sent by John the Baptist and has praised John for his strength and for his role as God's messenger (11:2–15). He then attacks "this generation" for trifling with both John and himself (11:16–20) and condemns the unrepentant cities where he has worked (11:21–24). He follows this with an appeal to those who are burdened to come to him (11:25–30). Jesus does not directly condemn "this generation," as he does when they are identified explicitly as the Pharisees,[55] but he criticizes them for inconsistently accusing John the Baptist of being possessed because of his austerity and Jesus with being a libertine for not being austere enough. He uses children teasing one another as a simile for the lack of seriousness among the adults he addresses. Only some Galilean Jews are included in this criticism, namely, those who reject or ignore Jesus or take him lightly. The focus of Jesus' polemic is made clear by the following pericope in which Jesus attacks the Galilean towns where he has preached, threatens them with judgment, and compares them unfavorably with Tyre, Sidon, and Sodom.

A final condemnation of this "generation" comes during Jesus' climactic attack on the scribes and Pharisees in chapter 23 (see chap. 3 below). The seventh woe accuses them of murdering the biblical prophets (23:29) and the prophets, wise men, and scribes of the Matthean group (23:34). Finally, Matthew lays upon them all the righteous blood shed since Abel and prophesies that "all this will come upon this generation" (23:36). The prophetic threat is followed by the lament over Jerusalem for being unresponsive to Jesus (23:37–39) and the prediction of Jerusalem's destruction (24:1–2). The sequence of threats and prophecies just before the final discourse and arrest of Jesus suggests that Matthew has taken a traditional polemic from Q (cf. Luke 11:49–51) and applied it to the fate of Jerusalem.[56] Its context, at the end of the attack on the scribes and Pharisees in chapter 23, suggests that these leaders are especially culpable.

In sum, Matthew uses the sayings about "this [evil, adulterous] generation" to attack those who reject Jesus, especially the leaders of the Jewish community both in Jesus' day and his own. He does not condemn all of Israel, nor does he simply identify "this generation" with the crowds, who are sheep without a shepherd and who approach Jesus for healing and teaching. "This generation" is an expression which gains its precise meaning from its polemical contexts. Matthew's thematic use of this term, with cross-references among passages in chapters 11–12 and 16, show that the problem of nonresponsiveness to and rejection of Jesus by many of his fellow Jews was a major problem for Matthew and his group.

Two other titles are used for Israel in Matthew: "sons of the kingdom" (8:12) and "children of Abraham" (3:9). Since these passages are sometimes used to support the thesis that Matthew envisions a rejection of Israel, they require brief comment. The story of the cure of the centurion's servant addresses several issues, including Jesus' authority, faith, and the relationship of gentiles to Jesus and Israel (see chapter 4 for a full treatment). Matthew has appended to the story a Q saying about the eschatological banquet in order to rebuke Israel's lack of acceptance of Jesus. Jesus says that the "sons of the kingdom" will be cast out of the heavenly banquet, and that many from the east and west will come to sit with the patriarchs (8:11–12). In the Matthean version of this story faith is the entrance criterion, and this saying plus the story of the centurion's faith is used to explain the relationship of Jewish and gentile believers.[57] The title "sons of the kingdom" presumes Israel's privileged relationship with God. It is not, as some commentators suggest, a key link in a Matthean argument that all Israel has been alienated from Jesus.[58] The heavenly banquet is presided over by the patriarchs, and no explicit or implicit claim is made that Israel is excluded. Rather, the saying explains why some Jews have not believed in Jesus and why gentiles have joined Israel in the kingdom, that is, have recognized and accepted God's rule. It is also a typical prophetic condemnation of Israel's infidelity, used to provoke repentance (see 12:41–42 for the same tactic). Matthew continues to appeal to his fellow Jews to accept Jesus.

Similarly, John the Baptist's warning to the Pharisees and Sadducees not to rely on their descent from Abraham (3:9) is not a rejection of Judaism or Jewish descent.[59] It is a call to Israel, specifically, to its leaders, for repentance and a prophetic threat of judgment. The threat is supported by the saying "God is able from these stones to raise up children to Abraham."[60] There is no covert reference to the gentiles replacing Israel or of Israel being separated from Jesus. The leaders, the Pharisees and Sadducees, are rebuked for not producing fruit and threatened with judgment. This attack on the Pharisees and other leaders rises to a crescendo as the narrative unfolds, but the polemic against the leaders does not include all Israel. Rather, an adequate definition of a faithful Israelite is developed, one that from Matthew's point of view can explain the faith of the gentiles.[61]

Conclusion

Contrary to the claims of the usual salvation-history schemes, Israel is not rejected and the Jewish mission is still open in Matthew.[62] This can be seen especially in his portrayal of the Jewish crowds. His treatment of the Galilean crowds is fundamentally friendly, if sometime ambivalent. Usually they are Jesus' audience and marvel at his teaching or miraculous deeds (e.g., 7:28; 22:33; 12:23). Matthew does not usually attack those in the crowds directly. When they are deaf to Jesus' message, they are said to have been misled (9:36). They are condemned only when their leaders persuade a whole city to reject Jesus' and Matthew's appeal (11:20–24; 23:37–39; 27:25). Matthew still hopes to win part of Israel away from the false leaders. For this reason the crowds, who represent the people of the Jewish community with whom Matthew was in contact, are often portrayed as searching, as needing leadership and instruction, and as neutral or goodwilled.[63] At other times, they are criticized for rejecting Jesus or for ill will, that is, for following the traditional Jewish leaders instead of Matthew (26:47, 55; 27:15, 20–25).[64] But the Jewish people are still recruitable, still not judged as beyond salvation or irrevocably condemned (as they are in later Christian literature). Thus, even as Matthew urges his group to undertake a gentile mission, he continues to appeal to fellow Jews.

In summary, the author of Matthew uses the usual terms for the Jewish community in a flexible and concrete way. This indicates that he has a living relationship with and a differentiated view of the Jewish community. No neat lines demarcate his group from other Jewish groups. The boundaries of these groups are consequently in dispute, and their legitimacy in relation to Jewish tradition is at stake in the aftermath of the war with Rome. The identities of the groups are being reshaped in the face of new circumstances and the development of new central symbols. The leaders of the communities are competing with one another to win adherents to their way of living Jewish life and interpreting Jewish tradition. The author of Matthew is one of these leaders, and his gospel is an attempt to both solidify his group and win new followers from the Jewish community and also from the gentiles.

III

Matthew's Opponents:
Israel's Leaders

The various leaders of Israel are the only groups unequivocally rejected by Matthew.[1] The Pharisees, scribes, chief priests, elders of the people (all appearing frequently), Sadducees (16:1; 22:23), and Herodians (22:16) are known from historical documents and the other gospels, but they function in special ways within Matthew's narrative.[2] The Pharisees and scribes are found in both Galilee and Jerusalem, and they dog Jesus' footsteps everywhere. They argue with Jesus over Sabbath observance, food laws, ritual purity, blasphemy, the signs of his ministry, and his authority.[3] In Jerusalem the national leadership, the chief priests, elders, and high-ranking scribes seek to blunt his influence on the crowds. All are members of the ruling classes, who opposed Jesus' teaching and popular authority with the people. They are viewed by Matthew as evil and hypocritical guides who have misled the crowds, the "sheep without a shepherd" (10:6). In Matthew's view, Jesus died because of these leaders, with whom he was in competition. Matthew and his group, like Jesus, are in competition with later Jewish community leaders for the hearts of the Jewish community. Matthew seeks to tear down the effective authority of the community leaders and to exercise his own leadership instead in order to bring about the reforms Jesus taught.

Building upon the conclusion of the last chapter, we must emphasize again that Matthew nowhere rejects "Judaism" or the "Jewish people." Nor, contrary to the view of many commentators, has he turned away from the Jewish community in favor of a new Christian community. None of Matthew's polemics are aimed at Judaism or the Jewish people as a whole, but rather at certain interpretations of Judaism, and at opposing leaders and occasionally the people who follow them in rejecting Matthew's group and its understanding of God's will. We shall see that even the verse asserting that the kingdom will be taken away from "you" and given to an *ethnos* producing its fruit (21:43) is an inner Jewish polemic, not an affirmation of Christianity against Judaism.

However, we must emphasize that despite Matthew's highly negative view of the Jewish leaders, their behavior, analyzed according to conventional social norms, was neither unusual nor evil. Though the scribes and Pharisees are presented as asking Jesus hostile questions and bringing negative charges against him, they never engage in extended vilification of Jesus (in contrast to Jesus' polemics against them). This may, of course, be part of Matthew's narrative technique to underscore the charges against the Jewish leaders and minimize their objections to Jesus. Even if this is so, Matthew has not disguised the fact that many of the questions asked by the Pharisees and scribes are legitimate matters for discussion in first-century Judaism. They raise questions about proper Sabbath observance (12:2, 10), divorce (19:3), association with sinners (9:11), blasphemy (9:3), handwashing (15:1), the signs of Jesus' authority (12:38; 16:1), and taxes (22:15–22). The one explicitly hostile charge against Jesus is that of witchcraft (9:34; 12:24), to which Jesus provides a lengthy defense in chapter 12.[4] All of these disputes over Jewish law and the disputants' status and authority in the community are normal conflicts found in any society. The laws and customs debated by Jesus and the leaders are standard fare in Jewish literature in late antiquity. Similarly, the disputes over Jesus' authority in Jerusalem (chapters 21–22), involving the chief priests and elders, are to be expected when a popular teacher with no official standing gains a following in the capital city.

Even though tensions are to be expected between the new popular teacher and the Jewish authorities, Matthew's Jesus is engaged in rancorous attacks on the Pharisees, scribes, Sadducees, chief priests, elders, certain Galilean cities, Jerusalem, and "this generation."[5] Within the narrative, the virulence of Jesus' polemic against his opponents is out of all proportion to their attacks on him. Thus, Matthew's portrayal of Jesus must be motivated by other considerations, one of which is surely an apologetic for the execution of Jesus. The embarrassing fact of Jesus' crucifixion must be explained by the ill will of those who unjustly had an innocent man condemned. Matthew is also attacking the Jewish community leaders of his own day in the figures of the Second Temple leaders. Matthew's purpose can be seen most clearly in his climactic attack on the scribes and Pharisees in chapter 23, so we shall begin there. Then the polemics and controversies in Jerusalem (chaps. 21–22) will provide a context for this attack. Finally, the attacks on Jesus during the passion narrative and during his Galilean ministry will be related to the attacks on the Jewish leaders in chapters 21–23.

The Cursing of the Scribes and Pharisees

Recent interpretations of Matthew 23 have stressed the composite nature of the chapter and Matthew's fidelity to early tradition in composing it. Some have concluded that Matthew is merely preserving past polemics and not himself attacking Israel.[6] Such exegeses treat this passage as part of a Jewish-Christian apology for Jesus' rejection by Israel and for the destruction of the Temple. Our thesis is that the author of Matthew specifically seeks to undermine the traditional, established leadership of the Jewish community in order to legitimate his own group and its leadership.[7] The origin, structure, and tone of the attack on the Pharisees and scribes strongly indicate that Matthew is engaged in serious controversies with the Jewish community of his day and that he is attacking its leaders through Jesus' polemic.[8] Clearly the author of Matthew is dissatisfied with the Jewish community in his city or area. In chapter 23, as in other parts of the gospel, he does not deny the fundamental legitimacy of Israel, its law, and its community structures. To do so would be to destroy the basis for his own group, which is so closely tied to Israel. Rather, he attacks the leaders' rule over the Jewish community by attacking their personal integrity and the accuracy of their interpretation of Jewish law and the divine will.

That Matthew's attack on the Jewish leaders is not a mere preservation of older Jesus traditions or a way of solving an inner Christian problem can be seen in the way he structures early traditions, adds his own material, and gives them all an original and striking context. The final product, with its seven woes, its mocking of Jewish practices, and its exaggerated accusations against the Jewish authorities, is an attempt to delegitimate the traditional leaders and the way of living Judaism that they promote.

Before we analyze Matthew 23, a brief word on the process of legitimation and the inelegant neologism, delegitimation, is appropriate.[9] In the sociology of knowledge, as synthesized and developed by Berger and Luckmann, society is created and experienced as an objective reality through processes of institutionalization.[10] The objective and necessary nature of these institutions is justified, explained, and passed on to new generations by the processes of legitimation.[11] The meanings attached to disparate social institutions are integrated into a symbolic universe, which is a coherent and comprehensive explanation for all of life in a given society. "Legitimation 'explains' the institutional order by ascribing cognitive validity to its objectivated meanings. Legitimation justifies the institutional order by giving normative dignity to its practical imperatives."[12] Note that knowledge and values are inextricably linked. First we become convinced of the way things are, and then we affirm certain values appropriate to reality as we perceive it.

When two groups are at odds with one another, usually their symbolic universes and institutional structures come into conflict. When a large group is faced with a dissident small group (a sect or heresy in the religious sphere), it responds by rearranging its legitimations in order to reaffirm its symbolic universe and institutions.[13] It also attacks the other group by a process called nihilation and rejects it by assigning it a lower ontological status. The established group may also try to explain away the dissident group through apologetics, accounting for its deviance through the cognitive terms of its own symbolic universe and ascribing the disagreement to the misunderstandings and bad faith of the smaller group.

Matthew seeks to break up the symbolic universe of his opponents and the theories which legitimate their various institutions.[14] He is not denying the whole Jewish symbolic universe and system, as many hold, but proposing from within an alternative understanding of it and its actualization in life. Consequently, he reduces the plausibility of his opponents' symbolic universe by creating contradictions in it as well as conflicts in values, a different symbolic center (Jesus) and a modified understanding of God's will (the kingdom of heaven). In addition, he deemphasizes certain sectarian practices and values (purity, tithes) and stresses alternative practices and values. Finally, just as the larger body accounts for the deviance of the smaller body by attributing to it error and bad faith, Matthew delegitimates the Jewish leaders and their interpretation of the Jewish symbolic universe and institutions by accusing them of bad faith, misunderstanding of Scripture and God's will and malfeasance.

The author of Matthew begins chapter 23 by acknowledging the authority of the scribes and Pharisees, but he then undercuts it with attacks on their titles, laws, and intentions and proposes an alternative model of community leadership.[15] His introductory acknowledgment of their authority is strikingly contradictory to the argument of the chapter and has long troubled New Testament commentators: "The scribes and Pharisees sit on Moses' seat; so practice and observe whatever they tell you, but not what they do; for they preach but do not practice" (vv. 2–3).[16] Even if this saying is a pre-Matthean, Jewish-Christian tradition, its use by Matthew must be explained.[17] In citing this affirmation of the authority of the scribes and Pharisees, Matthew admits either the official positions of his opponents in the Jewish community or their influence on those in power. The emerging coalitions seeking power after 70 contained elements of the Second Temple Pharisaic and scribal groups. It seems that these groups had attained some influence in Matthew's area. Matthew, faced with this kind of competition and especially with a wholesale rejection of Jesus and his interpretation of Scripture and law, attacks the rival leaders and those who follow them. In the same sentence in which he acknowledges their de facto power, he attacks their conduct of their office. He levels against them the usual charge of hypocrisy (vv. 4–7) and introduces the discussion of a new model of leadership (vv. 8–12), which he supports with an attack on the traditional, institutional forms of Jewish leadership and their interpretation of community norms. He attacks the scribes and Pharisees for failing to practice Judaism sincerely, to guide others to live Judaism correctly, to interpret the Bible adequately, and to attend to the major principles of the law and Jewish way of life. They are used as negative examples for how a community leader should act (vv. 4–7) and are contrasted with proper leaders, who by implication would not use titles such as "rabbi" and "master" and would be characterized by lowliness (vv. 8–12).[18]

The powers and status of the established authorities are graphically portrayed (vv. 4–7): they impose burdens, wear special insignia, claim privileged positions, and seek public honor. Against this common Near Eastern social hierarchy, Matthew forbids the use of titles and the exercise of highly authoritative roles (vv. 8–12). Honorific titles are to be avoided because Jesus is the one leader and all his followers are brethren. The members of the group are to be "servants" to one another. This resistance to hierarchically structured roles, plus the emphasis on equality, is typical of sects and reform movements.[19] All the members have begun a new life together and are to participate fully and equally in the emerging community. The Matthean group, which is being rejected by a broad constituency in the Jewish community, is being forced into the role of a sect that defines itself by differing from the traditional mode of community organization. Usually, the elders of established families and officials appointed by the government oversaw the application of community laws and customs, adjudicated disputes, and maintained public order. The members of Matthew's group have been cut off from their network of family and friends and have begun a new, nontraditional association. Matthew's attack on the established authorities intends to weaken their legitimacy and to establish the authority of his own group and its claim to be the genuine leader of Judaism.

Matthew's attack on his opponents in chapter 23 is part of an ongoing confrontation throughout the gospel. Here and in many other polemical passages, Matthew exhibits the characteristics of a sectarian leader protecting his group from the dominant social institution and from rival sects. Matthew attacks the community norms proposed by rival leaders, including several cited in chapter 23, and modifies many points of law and practice to conform to the teachings of Jesus and the way of life which derives from his teaching. Like any good sectarian leader, the author of Matthew claims to have the only legitimate interpretation of the practice of many Jewish customs, all of which he interprets in relationship to Jesus.

Matthew's attack on the Jewish community leadership is contained in seven woe oracles, in which Jesus condemns the scribes and Pharisees seven times (vv. 23:13, 15, 16, 23, 25, 27, 29).[20] His opening formula, "Woe to you, Pharisees, scribes, hypocrites" (used six times), drives home the contrast between inner attitudes and outward behavior, a contrast found also in the Sermon on the Mount.[21] The central charge that the Jewish leaders are insincere and of ill will and the image of blindness, repeated five times, undercut their authority (see also 15:14).[22] The woe oracles are not a random selection of complaints, but a structured series of charges aimed at key aspects of the leadership roles exercised in the Jewish community. The first two woes concern rival interpretations of community identity. According to Matthew, the Jewish leaders both prevent their members from following Jesus' teachings and attract gentiles to their way of life in the Jewish community, thus frustrating the major goal of Matthew's community, teaching all nations to observe Jesus' commands. In other words, Matthew charges that his rivals' teachings frustrate God's purpose embodied in Jesus' message of the kingdom of heaven. The next three woes, concerned with oaths, tithes, and purity, attack prevailing interpretations of the law, economy, and customs that hold the Jewish community together and set its boundaries. Matthew suggests an alternative understanding and practice of Jewish law. Finally, the last two woe oracles bring to a climax the attack against the personal ethics and intentions of the leaders with the charges of lawlessness and murder. Let us look at the import and intent of these seven woe oracles in detail.

The *first woe* accuses the leaders of gross malfeasance: "You shut the kingdom of heaven against men; for you neither enter yourselves, nor allow those who would enter to go in" (23:13). The image of shutting recalls that Matthew claims for his assembly the ability to open the kingdom of heaven (16:19).[23] The leaders of the Jewish community try to prevent their members from accepting Matthean teaching about

Jesus and thus stand in diametrical opposition to Matthew, who through Jesus has the keys to the kingdom. This first woe oracle contains a blanket charge which sets the theme for the rest of the attack on the legitimacy and competence of his rivals for leadership of the Jewish community.

The *second woe* testifies to Jewish success in attracting gentile members and attacks the conversion of gentiles to the form of Judaism opposed by Matthew.[24] In Matthew's view, the missionary activities of his rivals threaten to cut off the bulk of gentiles from Jesus' teaching. Since the gospel of Matthew ends with a command to preach to all nations, this frustrates the commands of Jesus. The author's desperation can be seen in the hyperbole of his charge: "When [a gentile] becomes a proselyte, you make him twice as much a child of Gehenna as yourselves" (23:15).[25] In the view of the author of Matthew, by moving to mainstream Judaism gentiles removed themselves even farther from salvation through Jesus than they had been.

In attacking oaths, tithes and purity rules in the third through fifth woes, the author of Matthew attacks his opponents' views on the law, economy, and customs that give the Jewish community its identity. He has already rejected the popular ancient custom of taking oaths as inconsistent with Jesus' teaching (5:33–37); though he does not deny the validity of tithes and purity rules, he deemphasizes these important boundary-setting mechanisms and thus changes the nature of the community. In each case, a biblical law has been actualized through custom and interpretation and forms part of the recognizable texture of the Jewish community. The author of Matthew rejects these established customs and accuses his community leaders of perverting the true meaning of Scripture.

In the *third woe,* Matthew mocks rules concerning oaths and vows.[26] His tone stresses what he judges to be hypocrisy and inconsistency in deciding which vows are valid or not. In the *fourth and fifth woes,* he does not reject or omit Jewish laws concerning tithing herbs and preserving ritual purity in the consumption of food, but he relativizes their importance and changes their meaning.[27] The contribution of tithes to the Temple, even of herbs, is affirmed but subordinated to "the weightier matters of the law, justice, and mercy and faith." The ritual cleanliness of cups and plates remains a valid concern, but it is subordinated to the contrast of the inner and outer human being and the cleansing of the inner self from extortion and intemperance. Matthew's distinction of inner and outer and adjudication of more and less important laws viciously caricatures the self-understanding of one type of Judaism. He proposes "justice, mercy, and faith" (v. 23) as central criteria for community membership, ignoring the fact that all first-century Jewish sects and movements supported these virtues in their own ways. The Pharisees and early rabbis stressed the purity laws as a way of articulating Israel's sanctifying relationship with God and supporting the community's commitment to "justice, mercy, and faith." Matthew is not only arguing fine points of Jewish law, but rejecting the fabric of his opponents' interpretation of their common tradition. He also accuses the established leaders of bad faith and lack of integrity.

The *sixth woe* uses the contrast between the inside and outside of tombs to charge the scribes and Pharisees with hypocrisy and lawlessness.[28] The charge of lawlessness against those who interpret, create, and promote a distinctive set of Jewish laws is noteworthy and ironic. Though they promote accurate interpretation and adherence to the law, they are accused of lawlessness because in the eyes of the Matthean community they do not discern and do the true will of God.[29]

The hypocrisy and lawlessness, symbolized in the sixth woe oracle by the grave full of bones and uncleanness, come to full flower in the *seventh woe*. The scribes and Pharisees build tombs to prophets and martyrs whom they themselves (through their ancestors) killed.[30] This charge leads to a prophetic and apocalyptic judgment oracle (vv. 32–36), which foreshadows Jesus' death and predicts the persecution of his followers. The references to the blood of Abel and Zechariah condemn all the unjust killings in the whole of biblical history and compare the deaths and persecution of these just and faithful prophets, priests, and leaders to the fate of Jesus and his followers.[31] The charge of killing the prophets functions like the historical reviews in apocalypses, as a preparation for divine intervention and judgment to bring evil to an end. The final verse (36) warns of imminent judgment, as do the apocalypses. As in many apocalypses, the leaders of the community come in for special condemnation since they have failed to lead the people in the correct direction. The ironic curse "Fill up the measure of your fathers" may also point in the same direction. "Fulfill" (*plēroō*), is used often by Matthew to describe Jesus' relation to the Bible and Jewish history and to legitimate his views and standing. Here he uses the same word to reject the legitimacy of the Jewish leaders.

The climactic seventh woe oracle with its accusation of murder against the scribes and Pharisees reflects Matthew's view that the Jewish leaders persuaded the people to reject Jesus (27:20) and have continued to influence them to reject his followers. The disciplinary measures taken against the Jewish leaders who have accepted Jesus (the prophets, wise men, and scribes), namely, scourging and expulsion (23:34), fit synagogue practice and were mentioned previously by

Matthew (10:17).[32] Local communities were normally given broad responsibility for their own internal affairs, including keeping order, adjudicating disputes, punishing crimes, and maintaining community customs and laws. Paul received thirty-nine lashes at the hands of synagogue authorities (2 Cor. 11:24).[33] Matthew links these common disciplinary measures to the death of Jesus by accusing the scribes and Pharisees of also killing and crucifying the messengers of Jesus, a charge which is historically improbable but symbolically powerful.

Matthew's vitriolic tone and numerous, detailed accusations suggest strongly that he was attacking the Jewish leaders in his city. These leaders had disciplined and finally expelled from their assembly (synagogue) Matthew and other followers of Jesus. Matthew attacked them in order to legitimate his teaching and status and delegitimate theirs in the eyes of his followers and, he hoped, of the whole Jewish community. The position of some scholars that Matthew's group had no dealings with the Jewish community and merely used earlier polemic materials is unlikely. The construction of this long and sophisticated attack bespeaks strong and immediate provocation. The expulsion of Matthew's community from the synagogue would not have ended the conflict. The dispute was not about private religious preference, but public control of society. Community leaders had wide powers to regulate society, and the members of Matthew's community were dissident Jewish troublemakers who had to be disciplined. Matthew's new assembly *(ekklesia)* responded by seeking recognition as legitimate teachers of Judaism and as faithful leaders of the community.

The frequency of pejorative epithets like "hypocrite" and "blind" besmirches the morality of the scribes and Pharisees, undermines their authority, and leads to the ironic charge that they are "lawless" (v. 28), the very opposite of what they claim to be. The charge that they are murderers of the prophets and righteous (vv. 30–31, 35) seeks to explain and condemn their persecution of Matthew's group (v. 34) and to subvert their legitimacy. The sarcastic command to "fill up [fulfill] the measure of your fathers" contrasts their way of life with the Christian-Jewish way of life, which according to Matthew fulfills Scripture. This command, followed as it is by the threat in verse 36, the lament in verses 37–39, and the eschatological discourse (chaps. 24–25), invokes heavenly judgment as the final resolution of the conflict.

Jesus' Attack on the Jerusalem Leadership

The attempt to undermine the scribes and Pharisees' authority, the vision of Jewish society, and the interpretation of Israel's tradition in chapter 23 is part of a larger attack in chapters 21–25, which cover the period between the entry of Jesus into Jerusalem and his last meal with his followers.[34] This section is filled with disputes and conflicts between Jesus and the Jewish leaders in Jerusalem, which prepare the reader for the arrest and execution of Jesus. Judgment against those who reject Jesus and the God who sent him (on the model of prophetic condemnations) is common in these chapters and in Matthew in general. Chapter 24, speaking of the end of the world, deals with the destruction of the Temple and also the conflicts which will break out in Matthew's own group. Antichrists and false prophets are excoriated with the same vigor as Pharisees and scribes (24:5, 10–11). Both the deviant Christian-Jewish leaders in chapter 24 and the scribes and Pharisees in chapter 23 are presented as negative examples for Matthew's group. Chapter 23 summarizes the previous conflict between Jesus and his opponents and prepares for the arrest and death of Jesus, which follow in the narrative. This final public teaching of Jesus is wholly devoted to a rejection of the leadership of the Jewish community. The intent of Matthew is clear. The teachers in his group have been authorized by God and instructed by Jesus and thus have the true interpretation of Scripture and the Jewish tradition. They, not the Jewish leaders, should be listened to, for only their Christian-Jewish group is faithful to God. A few particulars will make this clear.

Chapters 21–22 contain a series of symbolic acts in and near Jerusalem, including Jesus' entry into Jerusalem and then the Temple, followed by five controversy stories and three parables that attack the Jerusalem leadership. Jesus is presented as a leader who will rule Jerusalem and restore its worship to its proper form. He fulfills Scripture by entering Jerusalem on a donkey (Isa. 62:11; Zech. 9:9). He is hailed by the crowd outside Jerusalem as the son of David who comes in the name of God and is escorted into Jerusalem (21:1–9). After he has entered Jerusalem, all the city is stirred up. The crowds who have welcomed him identify him as a prophet from Nazareth in Galilee (21:10–11). The description of a popular leader as a son of David or prophet was common in first-century Jewish society and would have made sense to Matthew's late first-century Jewish community as well.[35] The reactions of the crowds and the scriptural warrants invoked by Matthew focus the narrative precisely on his main concern, the struggle to wrest the leadership of Judaism from the traditional, institutional leaders.

The next day, Jesus exercises the office of reforming prophet and kingly leader by driving all commercial activities out of the Temple, implicitly criticizing the Temple authorities (21:12–13), by healing and by receiving the acclaim of children (21:14–15), and by refuting the objections of the chief priests and scribes (21:15–16).[36] Jesus conducts himself as a religious leader at the center of Judaism by caring for the people, correcting abuses, and disputing with the established leaders who reject his claim to authority.[37] Scriptural warrants are provided at every step. His Galilean leadership and ministry have been carried to Jerusalem and the Temple. The disputes over his role have also come to Jerusalem and will be developed in chapters 21–23, finally leading to his arrest and execution.

In the cleansing of the Temple, Jesus' program for renewal is compactly expressed through a biblical quotation—"My house shall be called a house of prayer" (Isa. 56:7)—but not explained. The contrasting charge, that the Temple priests and officials have made it a den of robbers, suggests injustice and social disorder.[38] Jesus promotes order and social health by healing in the Temple and by calling for a renewed, perfected worship according to the will of God.[39] Matthew here presents Jesus' program for Jerusalem and the Temple, supporting it with frequent biblical quotations and simultaneously highlighting his conflicts with the Jerusalem leaders.

The enigmatic cursing of the fig tree serves as an introduction to Jesus' concentrated attack on the Jerusalem leadership associated with the Temple.[40] The story fits into Matthew's theme of bearing fruit as a sign of fidelity to God, and it is similar to Jeremiah's oracle that threatens punishment for infidelity: "When I would gather them, says the Lord, there are no grapes on the vine, nor figs on the fig tree; even the leaves are withered" (Jer. 8:13).[41] Like the Matthean story of the fig tree, this oracle in Jeremiah is preceded by a critique of the leaders who are unfaithful to God, the scribes and wise men, prophets and priests who mislead the people (Jer. 8:8–12). Though the fig tree story has no explicit referent, Jesus' critique of the Temple authorities that precedes it and his conflicts with them that follow make them the implied objects of the symbolic story.[42] However, Matthew suppresses the symbolic thrust of the withered fig tree by turning the incident into a didactic narrative.[43] He emphasizes the miraculous nature of the event (as he often does) by having the tree wither immediately and turns it into a didactic rather than symbolic event by having the disciples question Jesus and Jesus teach them. He disconnects it from the cleansing of the Temple by uniting the story into one narrative (rather than the two-part narrative surrounding the cleansing in Mark 11:12–14; 20–26). Matthew probably sees and rejects the natural thrust of the fig tree symbol, that Israel is cursed and rejected, and his awkward use of the event to teach a lesson on faith and prayer is a testimony to his discomfort with any rejection of Israel as a whole.[44] Yet the attack on the Jerusalem leaders is not forgotten. The lesson on prayer which Matthew draws from the fig tree story supports the critique of the way the Temple is run implied by the cleansing story.[45] In addition, the image of fruitlessness is picked up and again applied to the leaders in the parable of the wicked tenants.

Five Controversies

Jesus' time in Jerusalem (21:23–22:46) is filled by Matthew with five controversies interrupted by three parables (21:28–22:14). Coherent themes unite the materials and link them to what has preceded and what follows, especially the attack on the Jerusalem leaders that begins with Jesus' entry and reaches its climax in chapter 23 and the prediction that Jerusalem will be destroyed (23:37–24:2). The five controversies concern crucial aspects of Jewish society and life: governance, taxes, life after death, Torah, and the messianic rule. The parables grapple with the lack of response and hostility to Jesus from the Jewish leaders.[46]

The first dispute (21:23–27) engages the central topic of this section of Matthew—authority in Israel—and it also introduces the three parables which further elaborate this topic and the response to Jesus. When Jesus returned to the Temple the day after he cleansed it and symbolically acted as ruler, the chief priests and elders of the people challenged his authority to teach and act as he had. The question concerning the source of Jesus' authority can admit of only one legitimate answer within the Jewish tradition: God. The underlying question concerns the governance of Israel. The priests and community elders are the institutional leaders of Israel, and given their place in Israel's tradition, they would claim divine approbation. Both Jesus and John the Baptist, whose case Jesus brings up, are popular leaders, supported by public recognition. They claim prophetic authority from God, an authority affirmed by the author of Matthew. Jesus does not directly answer the Temple leaders, but hangs them up between their rejection of the legitimacy of John the Baptist and their desire to influence the people who have supported John (and are now interested in Jesus). Thus, the Temple authorities undercut their own position by not rejecting John the Baptist and Jesus publically, and they reveal their ill will by their manipulation of the crowd.[47] This unwillingness to respond authentically to John and Jesus will be further condemned by the three parables which follow. Note that the crowd is clearly distinguished from the leaders; the crowd supports John the Baptist (21:26), as it supported Jesus earlier in the chapter.

Before exploring the meaning of the three parables, a quick review
of the other four controversies which follow them (22:15–46) will
show Matthew's main purposes and give the parables a context. As a
result of Jesus' attacks, the Pharisees plot against him (22:15) by sending their disciples and the Herodians to ask about Roman taxes
(22:16–22). The question proposed, like the one Jesus' asked them
about the authority of John the Baptist (21:25), is framed so that either
answer, to pay taxes or not, is dangerous.[48] They try to force him to
reject Roman taxes in order to preserve his integrity—"We know that
you are truthful, and teach the way of God truthfully, and care for no
man" (22:16)—and they hope that his acceptance of Roman taxes will
subvert his teaching authority. In response to their duplicity, Jesus accuses them of hypocrisy (22:18) and gives them a clever answer, just as
he did with the devil in the temptations (4:4, 7, 10). The Jerusalem
leaders are the indigenous political leaders of Israel within the context
of the Roman Empire. They attempt to use their position either to entrap a new, nonestablished, popular leader or to force him to submit to
Caesar. Jesus replies by distinguishing enigmatically the rule of God
and that of Caesar. Though Jesus seems to say "to each his own," the
premise of the question asked by the Pharisees and Herodians is that
Jesus must and will teach that Jews owe submission to God alone. Perhaps he does so in an indirect way.[49] The leaders understand that Jesus'
critique of the Temple and his reform program seriously challenge the
status quo, including relations with the Roman authorities. And
through Jesus' response Matthew attacks the status quo and cooperation with the empire, in his own day in good sectarian fashion.

The Sadducees follow the Pharisees in challenging Jesus by raising
the question of resurrection of the dead. The Sadducees, unlike Jesus
and the Pharisees, did not accept life after death.[50] It is probable that
the Sadducees, who came from the governing class, supported a traditional understanding of Judaism, with emphasis on this world where
they participated at the highest levels of institutional leadership. Reformist groups like the Pharisees and the Jesus movement stressed
God's rule and the imperfection of human rule in Israel. Thus the question about resurrection had social and political implications within Israel. If Jesus cannot defend his position on the afterlife, his standing as
teacher and his reform program will be discredited. Jesus survives the
test by an appeal to apocalyptic traditions which teach that the just will
be like angels in heaven.[51] The superiority of the heavenly and future
life with God relativizes and challenges the earthly social and political
arrangements with which the Sadducees are primarily concerned.
Note that the crowds are still favorable toward Jesus—"[The crowd]

was astonished at his teaching" (22:33)—and are not the object of Jesus' attacks.

In the third controversy, the Pharisees return to the attack a final time behind a lawyer asking a question about law (the Torah), a topic of great importance to them. Jesus responds by challenging them with a question about the Messiah, a topic of primary importance to the author of Matthew. Torah ("instruction") refers to a complex of symbols and commitments: the Bible, the will of God revealed in the Bible, the interpretation of the Bible, and in fact, the whole Jewish way of life. A question about the greatest commandment in Torah forces the respondent to reveal his interpretation of Jewish life and his symbolic center. For Matthew, the double love commandment (22:37–39) gives meaning and direction to the whole Torah. It is the coherent perspective for understanding and observing the biblical law. Implied is a rejection of the Pharisees' view of the law and Jewish life (as presented by Matthew). Note that, in contrast to Mark who makes the scribe friendly and has Jesus praise him (12:28–34), the questioner in Matthew does not affirm Jesus' teaching and in turn does not receive praise from Jesus. Matthew's attack on the Jewish leaders is not lightened by any hope of openness to Jesus among the leaders.

The final controversy between Jesus and the Pharisees in the gospel is initiated by Jesus and decisively settles the question of his authority in the author's eyes. This final challenge, which the Pharisees cannot answer—"And no one was able to answer him a word, nor from that day did any one dare to ask him any more questions" (22:46)—is immediately followed by an address to the crowds, the extended attack on the scribes and Pharisees in chapter 23. Jesus poses a question which refers back to his entry into Jerusalem when he was acclaimed son of David. He asks whose son the Messiah is and receives the conventional response, David's son. He then brings up a scriptural "contradiction" by quoting Ps. 110:1 in which (according to New Testament interpretation) David, the inspired author of the Psalms, refers to the Lord (God) enthroning David's Lord at his right hand. Clearly David's Lord, enthroned at God's right hand, is not David and cannot be David's son (i.e., subordinate).[52] Here Matthew uses this verse, which was very important in early Christianity, to suggest that if David is not the Messiah's father then God must be.[53] Thus the Messiah, traditionally called David's son, is really of higher status than David; he receives his ruling authority from God. Since the crowds have proclaimed Jesus as son of David and since the reader already knows that Jesus is the Messiah, the Son of God (16:16), Jesus' status is clear. The unclear affirmations of the crowds when Jesus entered Jerusalem have been clarified, the objections of the rulers in Jerusalem have been answered and the ruling authority of Jesus has been established. Finally, the establishment of Jesus' authority lays the foundation for the final attack on the authority of the Jewish community leadership in chapter 23 and also for the rejection of all titles for Matthean leaders (23:8–12).

Three Parables

The three parables (21:28–22:14) which follow the first controversy concerning Jesus' authority are often interpreted as a Matthean rejection of Judaism.[54] However, the context in which the parables are found suggests that those being rejected by Matthew are the Jewish leaders who opposed Jesus and now oppose Matthew.

THE PARABLE OF THE TWO SONS

The parable of the two sons (21:28–32) is a direct response to the chief priests and elders' duplicity and rejection of both Jesus' and John the Baptist's God-given roles and authority in the first controversy.[55] John the Baptist was a critic of Jewish society and the Temple leadership and preached in the prophetic mode that repentance was necessary. According to Jesus' interpretation of the parable (21:32), the two sons symbolize the two responses to John the Baptist. Israel's leaders, who should guide Israel in its response to God, represent those who say that they do God's will but really do not.[56] They did not believe John, who was a prophetic messenger sent by God, nor did they repent. The tax collectors and prostitutes (21:32), universally recognized as sinners and marginalized members of the Jewish community, are the opposite of the leaders in social standing, and ironically in the eyes of God as well, since they have responded to John's message, and by implication to Jesus' also. The author of Matthew, who has been rejected by the Jewish leaders of his day, identifies with the outcasts of the Jesus' tradition and opposes the leaders who exclude them and him.

THE PARABLE OF THE VINEYARD

The second parable concerns the wicked tenants of the vineyard who refuse to pay their rents and kill the owner's son. According to the standard interpretation, the tenants represent Israel rejecting and killing Jesus. As a result, the kingdom is taken from Israel (the vineyard) and given to a "nation" *(ethnos)* producing fruit, that is, to Matthew's Christian community or to Christianity in general.[57] According to this view, the "nation" is conceived of as Jews and gentiles (or sometimes just gentiles) who believe in Jesus and exludes Jews who have not believed

in Jesus. The vineyard, which is Israel, is replace by the fruitful "nation," which is Christianity.[58] This reading, which fits later Christian
supercessionist interpretations of Jewish-Christian relations, is beset
by several problems, the most obvious of which is that Matthew makes
the chief priests and Pharisees apply the parable to themselves (21:45),
not to Israel as a whole.[59] It is Matthew's understanding of the parable
that will be stressed here, whatever its original meaning may have
been.[60]

The first problem is the meaning of the common Greek word *ethnē*
("band, people, class, nation, etc.") in the crucial phrase which
threatens to transfer the kingdom to an *ethnos* producing fruit (21:43).
Most often the phrase is translated as "a nation producing fruit." The
nation is understood as the Christian community, which replaces the
Jewish nation. This interpretation is far from certain. The suitability of
ethnos as a description of the Christian community and the appropriateness of the translation "nation" is very debatable. The English
word "nation" is usually used with the modern meaning of a homoge-
neous people in a geographically defined area. In modern usage, "nation" refers to a nation-state, which may encompass many peoples,
languages, and cultures.[61] The English adjective "ethnic" and the
expression "ethnic group" are derived from this word, but they usually
refer to a group of people with a common language or customs or culture, and thus a more restricted group than a modern nation.

Ethnē and its derivatives are used by Matthew with a variety of
meanings that are consonant with the wide range of meanings and usages prevalent in Greek.[62] In Homer, *ethnos* has several meanings: a
number of people living together, a company or body of men (often
military), and a band of comrades. It is also used of a large number of
people (an *ethnos* of peoples, *ethnos laōn*) and of an ethnic group or tribe
with its own proper name. After Homer *ethnos* acquired the meanings
"people" and "nation," referring to a group of people with cultural,
linguistic, geographical, or political unity.[63] In the Roman period, the
Latin word *provincia* (province) was translated into Greek as *ethnos;* it
referred to a somewhat coherent body of people, at least in terms of the
governing bureaucracy.

Ethnos is also used in the Hellenistic-Roman period with various
specialized meanings other than "nation" and "people." *Ethnos* can refer to guilds and trade associations.[64] A social class of people can be
called an *ethnos,* as can a caste or other political subdivision. (Plato uses
ethnē for the various groups who have different functions and stations
in his ideal city [*Republic* 421c]). Orders of priests can be referred to as
the holy *ethnē. Ethnē* and *ethnikos* can also be used to designate

"others," as opposed to one's own group. In idiomatic Hellenistic Greek, *ethnē* can mean the rural folk, in contrast to city people. In the Septuagint, *ethnē* is often used to designate gentiles, that is, non-Jewish nations or peoples. The Greeks had a similar ethnocentric usage for the plural *ethnē* as a designation for non-Greek nations or peoples. In later patristic literature, *ethnos* and *ethnikos* were used in a parallel fashion by gentile Christians to refer to those who were neither Jews nor Christians.[65] This variety of usage makes it far from certain that the statement, "The kingdom of God will be taken away from you and given to a nation *(ethnei)* producing its fruits" (21:43), refers to a new nation to replace the old, rejected nation, Israel.[66] *Ethnos* should not be translated in Matt. 21:43 as "nation" because, first, Christians were not a nation. Second, there is an implied contrast with an *ethnos* that does not produce fruit, but the whole nation of Israel cannot be that *ethnos*. Finally, the narrator explicitly says that the parable applies to the chief priests and Pharisees; thus the *ethnos* being rejected is the Jerusalem leadership. Even if the Judean or Galilean nation is understood to be included in the warning to its leaders, Jews in the rest of the empire are not included. By the *ethnos* that produces fruit the author of Matthew certainly refers to a group that believes in Jesus. But what group? He does not say that believers-in-Jesus are a new or true Israel, nor that they are a replacement for Israel. Commentators who claim that Matthew implies this are reading in second-century Christian theology. Rather, the author of Matthew almost certainly refers to his own group as the *ethnos* which produces the fruit of the kingdom.[67] Even if he did mean all the Christian communities in the Roman Empire, and even if we imagine them as much more institutionalized than they seem to have been in the late first century, this *ethnos* would not match the definition of a nation or even that of a coherent ethnic group. Matthew, then, uses the term *ethnos* of his own group in a restricted sense. The ordinary meaning of *ethnos* that fits Matthew's usage is that of a voluntary organization or small social group. The Matthean *ethnos* is a small subgroup, whose exact make-up is not specified. The narrative criticizes the Jewish leadership for rejecting God's message, brought by his accredited messenger, Jesus. The parable assumes that the vineyard (Israel), though it has been badly managed, can be given to other tenants (leaders) who will make it bear fruit (21:41). Thus the *ethnos* bearing (literally "making") fruit (21:43) is a new group of tenants (that is, leaders of Israel) who will give the owner his share of the fruits at the appropriate time (21:41). Those who are rejected, the previous leaders, are a group who do not act appropriately by producing fruit for the owner.[68] The vineyard, Israel, remains the same; subgroups within Israel are blamed or praised.[69] The *ethnos* thus is a group of leaders, with their devoted followers, that can lead Israel well.

That the parable of the vineyard is a critique of Israel's leaders and not of Israel can be further substantiated by reference to the biblical background of the imagery. It is generally recognized that Matthew's description of the vineyard has been influenced by God's song of the vineyard (Isa. 5:1–7).[70] In Isaiah, Judah and Jerusalem are compared to a vineyard planted and cared for by God; the vineyard is the house of Israel and the vines are the men of Judah (Isa. 5:7). But the vineyard produces only foul grapes (identified as bloodshed and a cry by the oppressed), rather than good fruit, that is, true judgment and justice.[71] Consequently, God will knock down the hedge and wall and let nature destroy the vineyard. Note the contrast between Isaiah and Matthew: in Isaiah it is the vines, the people of Judah, who are unfruitful; in Matthew the vineyard itself and the vines are fruitful. The tenant farmers are at fault for not paying their dues to the owner, God. Matthew focuses on the leadership, not the people, who remain fruitful.[72]

Even in Isaiah, the prophetic condemnation of Judah and Jerusalem is focused and limited. It does not mean that all Israel is rejected. Some in Israel are suffering a lack of judgment and justice and are crying out to God. Others, presumably the powerful and wealthy, are acting contrary to judgment and justice and shedding blood. Thus there is an implication that the leaders of the house of Israel are at fault. This reading is supported by Isaiah's use of the vineyard elsewhere to bring legal charges against the leaders of Israel (3:13–15):

> The Lord has taken his place to contend,[73]
> he stands to judge his people.
> The Lord enters into judgment
> with the elders and princes of his people:
> "It is you who have devoured the vineyard,
> the spoil of the poor is in your houses.
> What do you mean by crushing my people,
> by grinding the face of the poor?"
> says the Lord God of hosts.

Though the people are mentioned, the attack is pointed at the leaders, the official representatives of the people, and the charge is that they are doing the people harm. Similarly, Matthew again and again accuses the leaders of the Jewish community of misleading the people, threatens them with judgment, and urges the people to follow a true leader, Jesus (and Matthew's group).[74] Matthew and Isaiah are alike also in focusing their attack on Jerusalem and the territory surrounding it, Judah (Isa. 5:3). When they complain about Israel and the people, they refer to the injustice of certain of the people, specifically the leaders.

Matthew's complaint against the tenants is that they have not paid their rent in the form of produce to the owner, and his threat is that the kingdom will be given to an *ethnos* producing its fruit, that is, to new tenants. Besides identifying the *ethnos,* we also need to identify the fruit expected by God. Usually the fruit is generalized as faith in Jesus and good deeds (righteousness). Thus the Jewish people as a whole is seen as lacking fruit, that is, as failing to accept Jesus. However, the presupposition of the parable is that the vineyard is fruitful but that the fruits are being misappropriated by the tenants. Thus Matthew attacks, not Israel (the fruitful vines in the vineyard) but the leaders of Israel (the tenants).[75] This image of fruitfulness and unfruitfulness is used to evaluate community leaders elsewhere in Matthew. John the Baptist tells the Pharisees and Sadducees to bear fruit (3:8–10). Prophets are known by their fruits (7:16–20), and Jesus applies this idea to the Pharisees (12:33–34). The parable of the fig tree (21:19) probably refers to the fruitlessness of the Jerusalem leaders.[76]

Three other internal elements of the parable suggest that it is directed at opposing community leaders. First, Jesus' interpretation of the parable is introduced by the citing of Ps. 118:22–23: "The very stone which the builders rejected has become the head of the corner; this was the Lord's doing, and it is marvelous in our eyes."[77] The narrative within this verse concerns leadership, that is, the activities of the builders and crucial role of the cornerstone (the "head" of the corner). Thus this verse is used in an attack on the Jerusalem leaders and it points to the replacement of them by Jesus.[78] Second, the punishment for the evil tenants is that the kingdom of God will be taken away from them and given to an *ethnos* which produces the fruits of the kingdom. What is the kingdom? The kingdom is the reign of God, present to believers and hoped for in the eschatological future. If the kingdom is taken from the vineyard (Israel), then Israel is no longer chosen nor ruled by God and has no hope for the future. But in the Matthean narrative, the kingdom is in fact taken from the Pharisees (21:45), and presumably from the other Jewish leaders. They are the ones who no longer are responsive to God, and their authority over the community has been delegitimated because they have not listened to God's messengers. Nor have they produced proper fruit for their God. Kingdom should here be understood in its most central sense as reign and ruling power. Thus, the leaders of the Jewish community are losing their ruling power because of malfeasance, and they are being replaced by a group *(ethnos)* of leaders who do listen to God and can guide the "lost sheep of the house of Israel" (10:6) correctly. The new leadership is, of course, the Matthean group, which is sent to teach all nations, including Israel, to observe all that Jesus taught (28:20). Third, here Jesus for the first time reveals in public his sonship, even though he does so in a veiled way through this allegorical parable.[79] The invitation for the community leaders to recognize Jesus as Son of God symbolizes a struggle over authority and control. Matthew attacks the established leaders of the Jewish community for not recognizing an authority greater than theirs.[80]

THE PARABLE OF THE WEDDING GUESTS

The *last of the three parables* is the story of the wedding guests' refusal of invitations to the wedding banquet (22:1–14); in this parable, too, the polemic against the leaders of Israel is continued. The rejection of the invitation by the invited guests and the subsequent invitation of people in the street is often understood as the rejection of Jesus by Israel and the acceptance of him by the gentiles. However, Matthew's version of the story has several features which argue against that interpretation. First, only the Matthean version has a banquet given by a *king*. Both Luke (14:15–24) and the Gospel of Thomas (no. 64) speak of a banquet given by a (presumably rich) man, not a king. Since the previous saying in the Gospel of Thomas (no. 63) is a warning about wealth, this parable is also a warning against wealth in the Gospel of Thomas. Luke, too, used the parable to address the issue of wealth by including the poor, maimed, blind, and lame (14:21) in the supper. In contrast, Matthew's focus on ruling power and authority, rather than wealth, stands out. Second, Matthew has molded the story to parallel the preceding parable of the wicked tenants. Some of the invitees "seized his servants, treating them shamefully, and killed them" (22:6), an occurrence clearly lacking verisimilitude, but recalling the tenants' killing of the owner's son in the previous parable. In response to this, the "king was angry, and he sent his troops and destroyed those murderers and burned their city" (22:7). This behavior is not consistent with the story of an invitation to a wedding feast, but it does match nicely Matthew's view of the fate of the Jerusalem leadership and the people who follow them (27:25).[81] Finally, though the parable contrasts those of high station and wealth, who are the proper invitees, with undistinguished people in the street, all are subjects of the one king. If the king is understood as God, then the people invited are Israelites. By contrast, Luke symbolizes the call of both Jews and gentiles by having the householder's servants go out twice to gather people for the supper, once within the city and once outside the city. This second gathering is the call to gentiles, a narrative feature Matthew lacks.[82] Rather, in Matthew's parabolic narrative, the guests invited to the king's son's wedding feast would be wealthy, powerful, high-ranking citizens of the kingdom, the leaders. The original invitees thus represent, not all Israel, but the leaders of Israel, and the subsequent invitees are the people of Israel, specifically, the "lost sheep of the house of Israel" (10:6), who need God's care. The author of Matthew is trying to explain the uneven reception Jesus had received in Israel and especially the rejection of him by Israel's leaders and their followers. He wishes to attract Israel to the banquet (that is, the kingdom which is both present and future) and to free Israel from its resistant leaders who do not accept Jesus. The mixed nature of Matthew's group is recognized in that both good and bad are invited (22:10), but a person without a wedding garment (22:11–14), that is, one who does not conform to the requirements of the kingdom, will be expelled. The presence of good and bad does not imply that those called are gentiles.

In summary, chapters 21–22, along with 23, are the climax of Matthew's attack on the leadership of the Jewish community. He attacks them because they are the established leaders of the community that has opposed him, his group, and their interpretation of Judaism. The attacks also serve his attempts to delegitimize the leaders and thus to wean the people of Israel away from those "blind guides" to Jesus and the Matthean group. In order to accomplish his goals, Matthew presents Jesus as a popular messianic leader who is opposed by the Temple authorities. Jesus bests them in a series of five controversies, thus demonstrating his teaching authority. The first controversy concerns Jesus' and John the Baptist's authority. The divine origin of his authority as Son of God and the culpable rejection of that authority are further communicated through the three parables in chapters 21–22. The chief priests and Pharisees understand that these parables are directed against them (21:45–46), and the Pharisees plot against Jesus (22:15) by asking him difficult and dangerous questions. Finally, Matthew attacks both the person and teaching of the scribes and Pharisees in the seven woes (chap. 23) and predicts the destruction of Jerusalem and its Temple along with the leadership (23:37–24:2).[83]

Israel's Leaders Elsewhere in Matthew

The intense attack on the highest leaders in Israel in chapters 21–23 is part of Matthew's constant polemic throughout the narrative against the Jewish community leaders in both Jerusalem and Galilee. Jesus is in Jerusalem and Judea only at the beginning and end of the narrative. In the infancy narrative at the beginning of the gospel, both Herod (2:1ff.) and his son Archelaus (2:22) are hostile to Jesus. In the passion narrative, the chief priest, scribes, and elders oversee Jesus' arrest and execution (26:14–15, 47–68; 27:1–10), turn the people against him (27:20–25), mock him themselves (27:41–43), secure a guard for the tomb (27:62–66), and begin the rumor that the resurrection was a hoax (28:11–15). John the Baptist attacks the Pharisees and Sadducees, who are presumably from Jerusalem (3:5), and tells them to repent (3:7–10).

Herod Antipas, the son of Herod the Great, who was the Roman client king ruling Galilee, is presented only once as hostile to John the Baptist and potentially to Jesus (14:1–13). Otherwise, the Pharisees are the chief opposition to Jesus, constantly disputing with him over what the law is and how it should be kept.[84] Some topics they differ on are purity (9:6–13; 15:1–20; 23:25–26), the Sabbath (12:1–14), fasting (9:14–17), oaths (23:16–22; 5:33–37), vows (15:4–6) tithes, (23:23) and divorce (5:31–32). The Pharisees, sometimes with the scribes or Sadducees, accuse Jesus of being possessed (9:32–34; 12:22–30) and demand a sign from him of his authority (16:1–4; 12:38). Jesus, in turn, warns his disciples against the teaching of the Pharisees and Sadducees (16:5–12), says that greater righteousness is needed than that of the scribes and Pharisees (5:20), and contrasts his teaching with theirs (5:21–48). The hypocrites attacked for their practice of fasting, prayer, and almsgiving (6:1–18) are probably to be identified as the scribes and Pharisees attacked in chapter 23. Finally, "the wise and understanding" from whom God has hidden Jesus' teaching and activities and whose own teaching is contrasted with Jesus' easy yoke and light burden (11:25–30) are probably also the Pharisees, who appear in the very next story as Jesus' opponents on Sabbath regulations (12:2). For Matthew the Pharisees are rival teachers, with an understanding and practice of Judaism distinct from and hostile to Jesus'. They symbolize the leaders of the postdestruction Jewish community of which Matthew is a dissident member.

The scribes are less prominent and less differentiated in Matthew than they are in Mark and Luke. Most often they are grouped with the Pharisees (5:20; 12:38; 15:1; 23:2, 15, 23, 25, 27, 29) or the chief priests in Jerusalem (2:10; 16:21; 20:18; 21:15). They occur once alone as opponents of Jesus (9:3) when they accuse him of blasphemy. Their teaching is taken as a socially recognized given (17:10), from which Jesus may differ (7:29). A scribe laudably wishes to follow Jesus

(8:19); Matthew's group seems to have had scribes in an established office (13:52; 23:34). This latter fact may explain Matthew's shift of focus from scribes to Pharisees as the opponents of Jesus; the category "scribe" has a positive meaning for Matthew's group.[85]

"Their Synagogues"

Another center of opposition to Jesus in the Gospel of Matthew is the synagogue. Matthew refers to synagogues nine times (4:23; 6:2, 5; 9:35; 10:17; 12:9; 13:54; 23:6, 34) as a common institution in Jewish villages and as a place where Jesus teaches and sometimes heals.[86]

In three cases, the synagogue is simply mentioned in a matter of fact way (6:2, 5; 23:6). In the other six, the synagogues are called *"their"* (or *"your"*) synagogues, which suggests those assemblies are hostile either to Jesus or to the Matthean group.[87]

Two passages claim that Jesus' followers and the Matthean group (symbolized by Jesus' disciples in 10:17 and as prophets, wise men, and scribes in 23:34) will be flogged in their/your synagogues. These passages probably refer to official discipline inflicted by the Jewish elders and authorities in various cities and villages on members of the Matthean group. The use of the pronouns "their" and "your" implies an estrangement from the Jewish assemblies, but not a lack of relationship or absolute separation. Indeed, the threatened floggings imply that members of Matthew's group be members of the Jewish community and subject to its discipline. The argument that the infliction of punishment was in the past and now the Matthean group is completely separate from the Jewish community is unnecessary and unlikely. There are rifts between the Matthean group and those presently administering the Jewish community, but that does not mean that the Matthean group is non-Jewish or considers itself to be non-Jewish.[88]

In two stories, Jesus gets into a controversy in "their synagogue" and is rejected. In both cases, Matthew has inserted the modifier "their" into a Markan story. In "their synagogue" (12:9), the Pharisees challenge Jesus when he cures the man with the withered hand and then make plans to destroy him (12:14). In his own country (*patrida,* presumably Nazareth) Jesus teaches in "their synagogue" (13:54), but the people take offense at him and he does not do many mighty works there (13:58). Both of these usages imply hostility and division. The cure of the man with the withered hand follows a controversy in the field with the Pharisees concerning harvesting on the Sabbath. The introduction to the story, "And he went from there, and entered their synagogue," implies that the assembly was controlled by Jesus' opponents, the Pharisees.[89]

Two Matthean summary statements that frame the early stage of Jesus' Galilean ministry use the expression "their synagogues" (4:23; 9:35), but these may not be polemical in intent. In the first, Jesus is said to travel around Galilee, teaching in their synagogues. In context, the expression "their" refers to the people's synagogues, that is, to the assemblies found in towns and villages. In the second, he goes to all the cities and villages, teaching in their synagogues. This usage, too, seems to refer to the assemblies belonging to each village and city, not to assemblies hostile to him or to the Matthean group, nor to assemblies controlled by Jesus' competitors.

It is clear that Matthew's group is part of the Jewish community. Even though he uses the expression "your/ their synagogue," this does not mean that he and his group are cut off from the Jewish community. Those passages which suggest hostility prove that Matthew's group is in conflict with the Jewish community, not totally separate from it. Simple dichotomies will not describe the relationship of the Matthean assembly (ekklesia) to the rival assembies (synagogue). The similarity, competition, and conflict among and within these groups must be explained as part of a long-lasting and complex relationship which began in the lifetime of Jesus or soon after and was still being worked out when Matthew wrote.[90]

Conclusion

Though Matthew has sometimes been portrayed as anti-Jewish, in fact he reserves his venom for hostile Jewish leaders and occasionally for people who have followed those leaders into a firm rejection of Jesus. Not only the leaders, but the institutions they control and the interpretations of Jewish law and custom they propose for Jewish society, are subject to constant and systematic attack. Matthew is not opposed to the Temple in itself, much less to Jewish (that is, biblical) law. Rather, he is against business as usual at the Temple, in Galilee, and among the leaders. Matthew's polemics are directed against rival leaders and their competing programs for understanding and living Judaism. Matthew and his group are in a struggle for the hearts and minds of their fellow Jews. They propose their teacher and leader, Jesus, and their understanding of God's will as the appropriate response to God, the law, and the prophets and as a viable response to the loss of the Temple and the execution of Jesus by hostile Jerusalem authorities.

IV

Matthew's Horizon:
The Nations

Some scholars have argued that Matthew's group is a mixed gentile and Jewish community, cut off from the main Jewish community. According to this hypothesis, the Matthean group has given up on the Jewish mission and is now oriented toward the gentiles. Others interpret Matthew's conflicts with Judaism as symptomatic of a mostly gentile group (and for some, a gentile author), long separated from the Jewish community. For all these positions, Matthew's group is no longer within Judaism according to commonsense, sociological, or religious-theological criteria. In the previous two chapters, we have criticized the assumptions underlying these positions and the principles used to interpret Matthew's narrative this way. An exposition of Matthew's view of non-Jews will clarify further his evaluation of Israel and of his group's place within Israel and the world. It will also show what the author expected of gentiles who believed in Jesus and how he envisioned their relationship to his group and Israel. Non-Jews appear frequently in the narrative world of the gospel. Their roles and relationships to other characters, especially Jesus, will be examined first. Then an analysis of Matthew's varied use of the Greek word *ethnē*, usually translated "nations" or "gentiles") will fill out the picture.

Characterization of Non-Jews

Most of the characters who appear in the Gospel of Matthew are Galilean or Judean Jews. Gentiles exist on the fringes of the story and appear in the lives and activities of Jesus and his fellow Galileans only occasionally. They are not permanent characters in the narrative, but rather emerge briefly and then disappear without a continuing relationship with Jesus or his followers. In some stories, they symbolize the relationship of the later Matthean group with the non-Jewish world and offer hope that gentiles will also become members of Matthew's Christian-Jewish group.[1] But they are so peripheral to the narrative and main characters that the thesis that the gospel is predominantly oriented toward a gentile mission or a gentile group is very unlikely.[2]

Several references to and stories about gentiles suggest their proper relationship to Matthew's group and the way for them to enter into relationship with God through Jesus. The genealogy which opens the gospel connects Jesus to Abraham and the Jewish people, associates him with David, the anointed king, and places him within Jewish history.[3] Yet even the genealogy, which purports to define strictly the Jewish ancestry of Jesus and the Davidic house, suggests the inclusion of non-Jews in Israel. Tamar (1:3), the widow of Jacob's eldest son, Er, bore Perez and Zerah by Jacob (Gen. 28). It is likely that Tamar, like Jacob's wife Shua (38:2), was a Canaanite. Rahab (1:5), the Canaanite prostitute who helped Joshua's spies at Jericho (Josh. 2: 6), is said to have been the wife of Salmon and mother of Boaz, even though she and Boaz are separated by more than two centuries.[4] Ruth (1:5), who marries Boaz, is a Moabite (Ruth 1:4). Bathsheba, the mother of Solomon, was the daughter of Eliam, son of Ahithophel from Gilo, who was one of David's chosen thirty warriors (2 Sam. 23:34). It is likely that she was an Israelite. However, in the genealogy she is refered to as the wife of Uriah (1:6). Uriah was a Hittite (2 Sam. 11:3), and so the way Matthew refers to Bathsheba stresses the gentile associations of David's illegitimately acquired wife. All these cases are suggestive rather than explicit. Each of these four women, along with Mary, who conceives Jesus in a marvelous manner (1:18−25), causes a disruption in the ideal genealogy one would wish for the Davidic king, the Messiah. Their presence in the genealogy suggests that more than pure Jewish descent is required to be a leader in Israel. Though ethnic groups often imagine that their communities are separate and boundaries impermeable, all peoples and groups absorb diverse outsiders over the course of time.[5] This process is clearly reflected and accepted at the beginning of the gospel. Jesus' ancestry includes non-Jews who were commited to Israel. Tamar saw to the carrying on of the name of Er, according to Jewish law; Rahab saved Joshua's spies; Ruth bound herself willingly to Israel; and Bathsheba intervened to assure Solomon's succession to the throne (1 Kings 1). Since first-century interpreters probably considered these women to be proselytes, they symbolize gentile converts to Matthew's own group of Christian-Jewish followers.[6]

The stories of the Magi who worship Jesus after his birth (2:1−12) and the guards at the crucifixion ("the centurion and those with him, who were keeping watch over Jesus") who recognize Jesus after his death (27:54) bracket the narrative of Jesus' life.[7] Both the Magi and the guards are gentiles and foreigners in Judea. Both stand in contrast to the Jewish authorities (Herod, the chief priests, and elders) who wish Jesus harm. The Magi know Jesus as king of the Jews, and the guards call him by the more generic title "Son of God."[8] They are moved, not by Jesus' teaching or deeds, but by divine portents that attest to Jesus' special status, namely, the star (2:1) and the apocalyptic events that attend Jesus' death (27:51–53). Both groups play an explicit, thematic role in Matthew's narrative, but their importance should not be overstated. Though these gentiles' recognition of Jesus is contrasted with the Jewish leaders' rejection of him, their understanding is limited. Neither the Magi nor the guards at the crucifixion become followers of Jesus, in contrast to the disciples who, though often "men of little faith" (8:26; 14:31; 16:8), persevere to the end with Jesus and dedicate themselves to him. The Magi and the guards may be symbolic of gentile acceptance of Jesus, but the acceptance is rudimentary and inchoate. No organized program or permanent relationship is established. The gentiles show promise and hint of things to come. In addition, the gentile recognition of Jesus takes place within the social and religious boundaries of Israel. The Magi and guards symbolize the attraction of Jesus for gentiles and the possibility of their being welcomed into Israel through their recognition of Jesus as Messiah and Son of God. In addition, the Magi, guards, and the Egyptians as well, to whom Joseph takes his family for safety (2:13–23), are ironically contrasted with the Jewish leaders, who fail to recognize and accept Jesus.[9] These themes are repeated by Matthew in a number of stories and comments about the gentiles.

The gentiles' ambiguous, marginal position in relation to Jesus (and in relation to the Matthean group as well) is confirmed in the stories of the healing of the centurion's servant (8:5–13) and the daughter of the Canaanite woman (15:21–28). These two stories have a number of similarities in structure and setting and convey a similar understanding of the gentiles. In addition, the centurion with an ill servant is in some ways parallel to the centurion at the cross. Near the beginning of the collection of miracle stories in chapters 8–9, the author of Matthew presents an account of a centurion who pleads for the cure of his ill boy and trusts that Jesus can effect this cure at a distance (8:5–13).[10] In response, Jesus marvels at this kind of faith, which he has not found in Israel, and uses the occasion to rebuke Israel and predict that many gentiles will sit at the banquet in the kingdom of heaven while the sons of the kingdom will be thrown into the outer darkness (8:11–12). The author of Matthew has set up a deliberate contrast between the confidence the gentile centurion has in Jesus and the lack of faith of the rightful heirs, the "sons of the kingdom." This passage has often been interpreted as a Matthean rejection of Judaism and an affirmation that the gentiles have taken over from the Jews as members of the kingdom, but such a reading can be supported neither by the immediate context nor by the gospel as a whole.[11] The comment about the gentiles participating in the heavenly banquet affirms that they will, like the centurion, believe and be rewarded, but their reward will be at a heavenly banquet presided over by the Jewish patriarchs. The imagery used here is that of the restoration of Israel, a restoration which includes both diaspora Jews and the gentiles.[12] The quoting of Isa. 8:23–9:1 in Matt. 4:15–16 and of LXX Isa. 42:1–4 and 11:10 in Matt. 12:18–21 as thematic guides to the narrative also suggest a context of the restoration of Israel. The granting of the believing centurion's request in the miracle story symbolizes the acceptance into the kingdom of gentiles who believe.[13] This acceptance of faithful gentiles is consistent with their acceptance in the parable of the sheep and goats (25:31–46). Similarly, in the parable of the wheat and weeds (13:24–30, 36–43) the "sons of the kingdom" (Jew and gentile) are included and the "sons of the evil one" are excluded. Ultimately, the same criterion of membership in the kingdom of God is applied to both Jew and gentile. Likewise, some of each will accept Jesus and fulfill the criterion and some will not. There is, however, no rejection of Israel as a whole.

The negative contrast of gentile faith with Israel's lack of faith is a commonplace in the tradition and similar to the prophetic rebukes and threats against Israel in the Bible.[14] The lack of response to Jesus in Chorazin, Bethsaida, and Capernaum is contrasted with the potential for repentance in Tyre, Sidon, and Sodom (11:20–24), all prototypical gentile cities. Similarly, the city of Nineveh repented more than "this generation" (the scribes and Pharisees, 12:38), and the Queen of Sheba was more responsive to the wisdom of Solomon than those who have failed to respond to Jesus (12:38–42). Note that not all in Israel are condemned, but only towns or leaders that reject Jesus totally. Jesus and his disciples continue to work in Israel, and the disciples are linked with the prophets and the righteous (13:16–17). In addition, the contrast of faithful gentiles with unfaithful Israel presumes the cultural stereotype of the sinful gentile as the foil for Jesus' surprise at their unusual faith. Matthew clearly sees Israel as central to the teaching and work of Jesus, but Israel does not exist in isolation from the nations. Rather, Jesus is God's servant with God's spirit (12:18–21), appealing to Israel, his primary focus, but through Israel to the nations as well. The quotation from Isaiah in chapter 12, that Jesus is God's chosen servant with God's spirit, applies most concretely to Jesus' work among the people of Galilee (12:1–14), but the text of Isaiah speaks of the nations: "He will proclaim justice to the nations" and will act gently "till he brings justice to victory; and in his name will the nations hope." Thus Jesus' activity as God's servant, with God's spirit, is not in principle limited to Israel, though it is to Israel he is primarily sent (10:5–6).

The story of the cure of the centurion's servant does not presage a wholesale turn from Israel to the gentiles by the Matthean group, as some commentators have suggested.[15] The story of this cure is bracketed by cures of Jews, namely, the leper who is told to fulfill the law concerning leprosy (8:2–4) and Peter's mother-in-law and many others who are ill or possessed (8:14–17). The leper is told to act within the framework of Jewish law, and the people who come to Jesus after the centurion story are the objects of his proper ministry, Galilean Jews. Within this Jewish context and in Jewish territory, the centurion seeks Jesus, the Jewish healer; Jesus does not seek him. Jesus does not go the centurion's house, which would be unclean, but he does enter the house of a good Jew, Simon's mother-in-law.[16] The centurion believes in Jesus' power and authority but does not become his follower. Thus, even though Jesus marvels at his faith and contrasts him with many Jews who do not accept him, the centurion is not a fully rounded symbol for the gentile church. He remains ancillary to the Jewish crowds to whom Jesus comes to teach and heal. Jesus remarks on the centurion's faith because he had expected little from gentiles and much from his own people, Israel.

The story of the Canaanite woman who requests that Jesus cure her daughter (15:21–28) has long been recognized as similar to the story of the centurion whose servant is cured. Only in these two incidents is the issue of gentile faith in Jesus raised. The leper fulfills the laws concerning purity, and the story of the Canaanite woman is preceded by a discussion of Jewish purity laws. Both stories are followed by the healing of many. Like the centurion, the Canaanite woman seeks out Jesus, perhaps in Jewish territory.[17] She asks for an exorcism with a clear awareness of Jesus' power and status, as does the centurion. Jesus praises her for her faith and exorcizes her daughter at a distance, as he cured the centurion's servant at a distance and praised his faith.[18] Thus at the beginning and in the middle of Jesus' Galilean activities, he responds to the faith of gentiles without changing his orientation from Israel. As already mentioned, at the end of the gospel, the centurion and guards at the crucifixion complete the set of faithful gentiles by recognizing Jesus as Son of God (27:51–54).

The story of the Canaanite woman manifests the tensions felt over the admission of gentiles into the Matthean group. Two details in Matthew's retelling of Mark's story are suggestive. First, Matthew's woman is a Canaanite, not "a Greek, a Syrophoenician by birth," as in Mark (7:26). Canaanite is a Semitic expression common in the Bible and designates a group Israel was to avoid.[19] Thus it suggests that the boundaries which separated Israel from the Canaanites are still at issue here, even though they are being breached. Second, though Mark has Jesus enter a house in order to escape notice (7:24), Matthew omits mention of Jesus' entering a house, probably because the house would have belonged to a gentile, and in socializing closely and eating with gentiles, Jesus would be violating dietary and purity laws. Since this story comes immediately after an argument concerning the washing of hands and impurity in both Mark and Matthew, its telling is influenced by each evangelist's views. Mark interpreted the argument over hand-washing and purity as an implied rejection of the biblical purity laws (7:19). Consistent with this understanding, he has Jesus enter the house of a gentile. Matthew omits the sweeping generalization that Jesus voided purity laws, keeping Jesus out of a gentile house and possibly out of gentile territory entirely. In this gospel, Jesus always obeys Jewish law because Matthew's group still keeps Jewish law (see chap. 6 below) and is only beginning to face the problems of assimilating gentiles into its fellowship.

The striking characteristic of the Canaanite woman, like that of the centurion before, is her unusual faith. Both turn to Jesus and ask for the healing of a household member who is not present. Matthew interprets this story of faith in the context of the needs of the "lost sheep of the house of Israel" in contrast to those of the gentiles (15:24; cf. 10:5–6). The author still sees Israel as the primary group needing instruction and persuasion.[20] This orientation of the Matthean group toward Israel is suggested further by a strange omission. In Mark, Jesus explains his reluctance to attend to the woman's needs with the excuse that the children (Israel) must be fed *first* and that their food cannot be thrown to the dogs (7:27). Matthew retains the excuse and metaphor but drops the temporal distinction (15:26). The objection is absolute and is only overcome by the woman's striking faith, which Matthew, but not Mark, remarks upon: "O woman, great is your faith!" (15:28). Three complementary inferences are possible. First, Jesus' power is in fact available to both Jews and gentiles at the same time, not first to the

Jews and then to the gentiles. However, access is easier for Jews because they are the primary focus of attention. Second, the reluctance to
include gentiles in the group is overcome by the gentiles' "great faith,"
which gets them what they desire, specifically, a cure for the woman's
daughter, and in Matthew's time, membership in his assembly *(ekklesia)*. Third, the Matthean group is still wrestling with the problem of
gentile membership; it justifies it by their great faith but maintains the
boundaries and practices of Judaism, interpreted in a different way
(15:1–20; 5:17–19).[21] Both here and in the mission discourse,
Matthew affirms the primacy of Jesus' mission to the lost sheep of the
house of Israel (10:5–6; 15:24) and in so doing upholds "the central
place of Israel in God's dealings with humanity."[22]

The cure of the Gadarene demoniacs (8:28–34) involves gentiles,
though Matthew does not use the story, for explicit reflection on the
missions to Israel and the gentiles. The ambiguity of relations with
non-Jews pervades the story but the main thrust seems to be Jesus'
power and the difficulty of following him. A scribe and a disciple are
instructed concerning the hardships involved in following Jesus
(8:18–22), and then Jesus and his disciples are caught in a storm crossing the Sea of Galilee, from which Jesus saves them (8:23–37). In the
danger of the storm, the disciples manifest a lack of faith: "you of little
faith" (8:25–26). When they arrive on the other side of the Sea of Galilee, they are in Gadarene territory.[23] Here, outside Israel, they are immediately met by two fierce demoniacs, whose evil spirits recognize
Jesus' power. Jesus frees the men from the demons, who enter a herd
of pigs that plunge into the sea. When the townspeople come out to
meet Jesus, they ask him to leave (8:28–34). Jesus does not teach
them, nor do they seek his aid. Their unease with Jesus is caused by his
extraordinary power and the loss of their herd. The presence of a herd
of pigs, the multiplicity and power of the demons, and the reluctance of
the people indicate that the people are gentiles (though the area had
both Jewish and non-Jewish residents). These particular residents of
the Decapolis are not the ones who are said earlier to have followed
Jesus (4:25). The gentile townspeople differ from the Jewish crowds
because they do not welcome and listen to Jesus, nor do they react
with awe at the exorcism he has performed. Rather, their reluctance to
have contact with Jesus is emphasized. In addition, Matthew eliminates elements of the Markan story (5:1–20) which suggest that gentiles spread the teachings of Jesus among their fellows. In Mark the
single demoniac requests to accompany Jesus, but Jesus commands
him to tell his friends what the Lord has done for him. As a result, the
man spreads the news throughout the Decapolis (Mark 5:18–20). The

Matthean author does not envision a mission to gentiles by gentile believers. In fact, the cured demoniac is not even allowed to manifest
faith in Jesus in Matthew's narrative. The healing is done without any
further effects, and Jesus returns to Jewish territory to continue his
mission (9:1). There is no faith in Gadara, in contrast to the faith of
those in Galilee who bring to Jesus a paralytic (9:2), a woman with a
hemorrhage (9:22), and two blind men (9:28–29). In Matthew's view,
gentiles can only have faith and meaningful contact with Jesus
through the mediation of Israel.

The non-Jews who appear in Matthew's narrative are peripheral
and occasional. They may have faith in or worship Jesus, and there are
hints that Jesus' message is for them, too. But they do not have independent standing in the narrative or in relationship with Jesus. They
must come to Israel to find Jesus, whose attention and efforts remain
firmly focused on Israel. Israel remains the context and concern of
Matthew, even as he cautiously seeks to include gentiles in the reformed Christian-Jewish community of believers-in-Jesus.

The Place of the Non-Jewish World

The beginning of Jesus's ministry in Galilee (4:12–17) is justified by a
scriptural passage containing an enigmatic reference to "Galilee of the
nations." The primary purpose of this formula is clearly to show that
the area in which Jesus taught and cured was willed by God and veri-
fied by Scripture, just as his name, birth, and early experiences were.[24]
Capernaum, where Jesus made his home, was in the territory of the
tribe of Naphtali on the northwest coast of the Sea of Galilee; the tribe
of Zebulon had territory south and west of Naphtali. Since this is the
area in which Jesus did most of his teaching and curing, Isa. 8:23–9:1
(LXX 9:1–2), which mentions these two tribes, is used as the prooftext.
These two tribes were among the first to go into exile (2 Kings 15:29),
and so according to Isaiah, they will be the first to be restored (Isa.
9:2ff.). "Galilee of the nations" in Isaiah probably refers to the conquest of Galilee by the Assyrians; in Matthew, the phrase may be an
oblique reference to the inclusion of gentiles in the Matthean group,
but it is none too clear.[25] If that is its import, at the beginning of Jesus'
ministry to Israel, then it and the final commission to teach all nations
(28:19) bracket Jesus' active life.[26] Contrary to a common older view,
Galilee was not heavily gentile in the first century, nor were the Jews
there nonobservant (of some kind of "normative" Judaism).[27] Galilee
was, however, a cosmopolitan crossroads on the trade routes and adjacent to territories inhabited by mixed Jewish and gentile or all-gentile

populations. Capernaum, near the shore of the sea, was also a boundary city, at the edge of the cultivated land and near the northern border
of Herod Antipas' territory. Thus Jesus' location in Galilee is potentially
open to both Jewish and non-Jewish people.

Jesus' wider appeal and openness to the non-Jewish world is hinted
at by several geographical notations in Matthew's introduction to
Jesus' Galilean ministry (4:23–25).[28] First, Jesus is said to go about
"the whole of Galilee," an exaggeration since his travels are for the
most part limited to lower Galilee and the northeastern region at that.
Then his fame is said to have spread to "the whole of Syria," by which
the author probably means the area north of Galilee, perhaps as far as
Antioch.[29] Finally, crowds not only from Galilee, but from the Decapolis, south and east of Galilee, from Jerusalem and Judea, and from
beyond the Jordan (Perea) followed Jesus.[30] The crowds who come
from Galilee, Judea, Perea, and the Decapolis are probably understood
to be Jews. Syria, where Jesus' fame spread, had a diverse population,
including a substantial Jewish minority. Galilee, Judea, Perea, and the
Decapolis, which were parts of biblical Israel settled by the twelve
tribes, had a heavily Jewish population, but with a mixture of gentiles.[31] Thus Matthew seems to envision the crowds from these areas,
who are the same crowds who hear the Sermon on the Mount in the
next verse (5:1), as Jewish, though gentiles would not be excluded.[32]

Several other stories and teachings support the thesis that the non-
Jewish world is present in Matthew's vision, but at the edge of the Jewish world. The three temptations of Jesus in their Matthean order
(4:1–11; cf. Luke 4:1–13) move from Jesus' own need for food in the
Judean desert to the Temple and Jesus' status among Jews, then to a
high mountain and his potential rule over all the kingdoms of the
world. The very high mountain where Jesus views all the kingdoms of
the world and is tempted to gain control over them by demonic power
is probably parallel to the mountain from which he sends his disciples
forth to teach all nations at the end of the gospel (28:16–20).[33] The
Temple, which is the center of the Jewish world, is linked to the non-
Jewish world, and both are in the purview of the Matthean group.
However, the nations are beyond the Jewish community and are
brought into relationship with God in due time. Similarly, in the Sermon on the Mount, Jesus' followers are to be the "light of the world"
(5:14) and let their light "shine before men" (5:16). The people to be
influenced are not limited to Jews, though presumably the majority of
the crowds listening to Jesus' very Jewish sermon are Jews.

Non-Jews are treated as simple outsiders in a number of cases. The
Sermon on the Mount and other sections of Jesus' teaching contain the

standard stereotypes of gentiles common to Jews. These stereotypes remain as part of Matthew's world view despite his openness to non-Jews who respond to Jesus. There is no blanket affirmation of nations, no affirmation of their chosenness and Israel's rejection. Rather, Matthew refers pejoratively to the verbosity of the prayers of the *ethnikoi* in contrast to his group's central prayer, the Our Father (6:7).[34] The *ethnikoi* are paired with tax collectors twice as groups who are on the borders of society and not respectable to associate with. If a group member does wrong and refuses correction, he is to be treated like the *ethnikos* and tax collector (18:15–17). Matthew does grant to the *ethnikoi* and tax collectors normal standards of social behavior, but he demands more of his own group (5:46–47). Matthew's negative attitude toward other nations can be found elsewhere: the rulers of the nations lord it over their subjects (20:25), their kings burn cities (22:7), and nations war with one another (24:6–7).[35]

Many commentators have interpreted John the Baptist's prophetic warning to the Pharisees and Sadducees (3:7–10) as a rejection of Israel and an affirmation of the ascendancy of the gentiles. Against their excessive trust in their Jewishness, John warns that the judgment will be based on deeds. He makes his point through a hyperbole that God can raise up children of Abraham from "these stones," presumably the stones of the Jordan River. He does not say that God is *actually* raising up sons of Abraham from stone, that is, replacing Israel with gentiles. The raising of children of Abraham from stones is thus not a rejection of all the present children of Abraham in favor of the gentiles, but a prophetic attack on leaders who are failing in their duty. Israel is defined as those Jews who are faithful to God; in the narrative, these Jews are coming to John in repentance. This definition of Israel allows Matthew to account adequately for the genesis and authenticity of his Christian-Jewish group. The images used leave an opening for a subsequent loosening of boundaries to permit repentant gentiles who believe in Jesus to join the Matthean group.

Non-Jewish Authorities

With the exception of the centurion at the cross and the centurion whose servant is cured, the gentile authorities who appear in Matthew are treated neutrally or negatively because they are not involved with Jesus on the substantial level of faith. The gentile authorities are simply there as the background to first-century Jewish society in the Roman Empire. When instructing his disciples concerning coming persecutions by their fellow Jews, Jesus speaks of being disciplined by councils and synagogues and then brought before governors and kings (10:17–18). What is envisioned is conflict within the Jewish community (10:23), which is then referred to the imperial authorities, on the model of what happend to Jesus. The disciples teach among the people of Israel, but when the opportunity presents itself, they will witness to them (the non-Jewish authorities) and to the nations (10:18). Instruction of the nations occurs as an accidental accompaniment to the primary mission of announcing the kingdom to Israel (10:7).

In the account of Jesus' arrest and execution, the gentiles are relatively unrelated to Jesus. In the passion narrative, Pilate and the Roman soldiers are taken for granted as the agents of the empire, impersonal and uninformed in their dealings with Jesus. They are indifferent to Jesus and in no way open to his influence. Although they do not seek to harm him, they are not well disposed to him. Though Matthew supports Jesus' innocence with the story of Pilate's wife's warning Pilate not to condemn him (27:19), Pilate still operates as a detached Roman governor trying to maintain social control (27:24). Though he knows that Jesus is innocent (27:18), he is not influenced by his wife's dream. He neither wishes Jesus well nor ill, but acts in the interests of the state, finally condemning Jesus to keep civil order. Finally, the sermon concerning the end of the world (chaps. 24–25) generally treats all people equally in the face of final judgment. The destruction of the world (24:29–30) affects all. The "days of Noah" (24:36–44) symbolize the fate of the whole world, and the four judgment parables (24:45–25:46) seem to treat Jew and non-Jew equally.

The Meanings of *Ethnē* (Nations)

As we saw in chapter 3, the Greek word *ethnos/ethnē* has a variety of meanings. It can designate an ethnic group or tribe with its own proper name or a larger group, that is, a people or nation with its own cultural, linguistic, geographical, or political unity. It can also refer to guilds and trade associations, social classes of people, political subdivisions, and rural in contrast to urban residents. In the Septuagint and other Jewish literature *ethnē*, the "nations" (Hebrew *goyim*), often means non-Jews in contrast to Israel.[36] In this meaning, "nations" is often translated by the specialized English term "gentiles." Matthew uses the word *ethnē* in several of its meanings, and commentators have disagreed about when he means gentiles in contrast to Israel. The discussion of *ethnē* in Matthew should be guided by the following four considerations. First, *ethnē* is not always a technical term for non-Jews. Second, its use is not always theologically weighted. Third, the definition of who was within and who outside the Jewish community was far less clear in the first century than it became in later centuries after the development of more precise and elaborate talmudic categories. Numerous gentiles had a variety of relationships with the Jewish community, and what was required to be a member of the community varied in time and place.[37] Not only were the actual practices and relationships diverse, but more important for understanding Matthew, members of the Jewish community disagreed in their understandings and evaluations of community life and practice.[38] Consequently, the primary cultural divisions are not always between Israel and the "nations." Sometimes Israel and certain nations or gentiles have relationships that are more positive than those between groups within Israel.[39] Fourth, the Pauline distinction between Jewish believer-in-Jesus and gentile believer-in-Jesus, which determined for Paul whether or not one was bound to observe the whole biblical law, should not be read into the Matthean situation. Paul labored to define and defend the gentile exemption from much of biblical law. Though his views ultimately prevailed, they met with much opposition in the first century within his own communities, as his letters show, and from non-Pauline, Jewish-Christian groups. Even among Paul's followers, the boundaries between the long-established Jewish and the new gentile communities of believers-in-Jesus were often not sharp, as Paul may have intended.[40] As we argued in chapter 1 above, the relationships between Jews and believers-in-Jesus remained flexible in various places for a long period. Within this varied situation, Matthew seeks to incorporate non-Jewish believers-in-Jesus into his renewed Jesus-centered, but still Torah-observant Jewish community. Thus the nations, insofar as they are responsive to Jesus, are candidates for membership in Matthew's group.

The Greek word *ethnos/ethnē* should not be understood as a nation in the modern sense, that is, a pluralistic political unit in a geographically defined area.[41] Matthew uses this flexible Greek word in several different senses that match normal Greek usage. In several places, he uses *ethnos* and its adjectival form, *ethnikos*, in the common, pejorative sense to refer to outsiders, that is, non-Jews whose conduct is expected to be less ethical than that of a Jew, whether a believer-in-Jesus or not. The nations (gentiles) worry about material goods rather than trusting in God (6:32). They do not love their enemies (5:47), and they babble at length when they pray (6:7). They are associated with tax collectors, another rejected group (6:46–47; 18:17). This usage is similar to the Greeks' pejorative use of *ethnē* for non-Greeks and also for common, ill-mannered rural folk. In other places *ethnē* is used as a simple descriptive word for non-Jews. Jesus sends his disciples to Israel, not to the gentiles

(nations) who are round about (10:5). The Roman or non-Jewish judicial authorities who condemn Jesus (20:19) and his followers (10:18)
belong to the nations. The references to these nations are not hostile,
especially compared with some apocalyptic literature; the nations are
simply inhabitants of the social and political landscape. They are not
totally rejected, for in another passage, these same nations can hope for
justice from Jesus (12:18, 21, quoting Isa. 42:1–4).

Sometimes Matthew's usage of *ethnē* is ambiguous or includes both
Jews and non-Jews. His introductory summary of Jesus' work (4:12–
17) contains a quotation from Isaiah (8:23–9:1; LXX 9:1–2) which
mentions as one the lands of Zebulun and Naphtali, Galilee of the nations, and a needy people who have seen a light. In the first century
Galilee was heavily Jewish, so the tribes, people, and nations mentioned in the quotation refer to groups who were predominantly
Jewish.[42] Matthew, who seeks to include all nations, Jewish and non-
Jewish, in his group, may be hinting at the salvation of gentiles. However, the primary referents of Isaiah's tribes and nations in Matthew's
narrative were Galilean Jews in need of Jesus' teaching and healing.[43]

The term "nation" can refer to any established people, including the
Jews. All the nations, including Israel, are lumped together in the common, proverbial observation that "the rulers of the nations lord it over
them and their great men excercise authority over them" (20:25).
Against this common model of leadership, Matthew promotes service
(20:26–27) and avoidance of honors (23:4–12) among the members
of his group.[44] Similarly, at the end of the world, nations and kingdoms
will rise against one another (24:7) and will hate the Matthean group
(24:9). The nations referred to include the leaders of the Jewish nation,
who even now persecute the Matthean group (10:17).[45] Matthew uses
nations here to refer to all groups hostile to his own. Thus the use of the
word "nations" does not automatically refer to the Jew-gentile distinction, but to insiders and outsiders vis-à-vis Matthew's group. An even
wider usage may be operative in the parable of the judgment of the
sheep and the goats (25:31–46). When the Son of Man comes in glory,
"all the nations" will be gathered before him for judgment. The identity of the nations and of the little ones who must be cared for has been
a subject of strong disagreement.[46] Some have suggested that the judgment of the gentiles only is meant, but most schemes for distinguishing
a Jewish judgment from a gentile one depend on elaborate periodiza-
tions of salvation history and forced distinctions of various groups.
That all people and groups are finally subjected to an ultimate, comprehensive justice is much more likely. The saved are symbolized by
sheep; this suggests that they join the sheep of the house of Israel

(10:6; 15:24) in the end. The parable comes at the end of Jesus' last sermon concerning the end of the world, and it immediately precedes the story of Jesus' arrest and execution. The role of the Son of Man as judge is intimately connected with his execution and resurrection. The criterion by which people are judged is whether they have cared for Jesus, who is identified with the least of his brethren. This presupposes both Jesus' resurrection and the existence of the Matthean group, whose helpers and opponents are both Jews and gentiles.[47] Thus ordinary national and ethnic boundaries are transcended in order to focus on the relationship to Jesus and his group of believers as the ultimate criterion for the judgment of all.

In the final scene, the climax of the gospel, Jesus commands his followers to go and make disciples of all the nations (28:19). This command is anticipated in the sermon about the end of the world, when Jesus predicts that "this gospel of the kingdom will be preached throughout the whole world, as a testimony to all the nations; and then the end will come" (24:14).[48] Within the narrative, Jesus' prediction and command refer to the teaching of his message in lands beyond Israel, the sphere to which he had restricted himself (10:5–6). Thus the nations would include Jews not living in Israel as well as non-Jews everywhere. For the author and his group, the nations throughout the whole world are all the peoples of the Roman Empire. If the Matthean group is still predominantly Jewish, as is argued here, then these statements encourage the widening of the group's teaching mission, membership, and sense of self to include non-Jews.[49] The nations to be won over to the teachings of Jesus certainly include non-Jews predominantly, but Jewish communities within the empire and within Israel and southern Syria may also be meant.

In conclusion, Matthew's uses of the Greek words *ethnos/ethnē* and *ethnikos* follow normal Greek usage closely.[50] Sometimes "nations" has its technical Jewish meaning, "gentiles." Often it refers to recognizable national groups, including the Jews. It also refers to a voluntary subgroup: the Matthean group or its leadership. Matthew's understanding of these words does not include a theology of gentile acceptance and Jewish rejection of Jesus, as some commentators have claimed. Matthew distinguishes, rather, those who respond faithfully to God and those who do not.

Conclusion

Gentiles are part of Matthew's Jewish world in several ways. Imperial officials are taken for granted and play their assigned political roles in a

relatively neutral way, especially in connection with the trial and execution of Jesus. Gentiles as a stereotypical social category are referred
to pejoratively from time to time. They are outsiders who neither behave or believe in an acceptable way. They do not know God or Jesus.
When confronted with Jesus, they are incapable of recognizing him or
his importance. In this view of gentiles, Matthew is at one with his fellow Jews. For the most part, apocalyptic literature views the nations as
evil enemies who will be defeated and punished by God at the end
of the world.[51] Some diaspora literature, for example, Joseph and
Aseneth and the Third Sibylline Oracle, takes a more positive view of
gentiles. Later rabbinic literature is also instructive. It does not give
gentiles an independent treatment, but catalogs and interprets them
through existing biblical and rabbinic categories as relevant for rabbinic interests. "The rabbinic comments on the gentiles paint a varied
and complex picture of the non-Israelites," which seems to reflect the
diversity of the situation which confronted, or was imagined by the authors of Mishnah-Tosefta. Yet "it is the complexity and inconsistency of
the image of the non-Israelite which is one of the most striking facts.
. . . The gentiles are not merely projections from the Bible, imagined or
theoretical 'others,' or 'normal' human beings. They are all three."[52]
Matthew's view of gentiles is equally complex.

Some gentiles have a special role in the foreground of Matthew's
narrative. They are praised for their recognition of Jesus (the Magi and
centurion at the cross) and for their faith and confidence in Jesus'
power to heal (the centurion and Canaanite woman). They are contrasted with unfaithful Jews who reject Jesus (the Magi versus Herod;
the centurion verses the "sons of the kingdom"; the centurion at the
cross verses the Jewish leaders who have condemned Jesus). The gentiles do not, however, become disciples, with all that that commitment
implies. They are praised for their faith or partial recognition of Jesus.
Matthew may be implying that they have the potential to be members
of his group of believers-in-Jesus, but they are not yet members, nor
does the narrative indicate that they will become so. Matthew may
have in mind the phenomenon of the gentiles sympathetic to the synagogue who were not Jews, but who were nevertheless not totally
other.[53] Within the narrative, the gentile characters are secondary to
members of Israel, and their story is partial and unfinished.

Matthew's portrayal of Jesus' occasional positive relations with
gentiles, of their faith, which provokes a response from him, and of his
interest in marginalized Jews as well as gentiles has the effect of loosening, redefining, and opening the borders of the Jewish community.
Various scriptural passages which mention the nations (Matt. 4:15–

16; 12:18–21) support Matthew's view that the nations have an integral relationship to Israel. In Matthew's version of a reformed Judaism, gentiles are peripheral, but firmly present. Israel, its destiny and Jesus' mission to reform Israel and instruct it in God's will is central to the Matthean narrative and to Matthew's world view. However, gentiles are to be brought into Israel through faith in Jesus and obedience to his teaching. Moreover, the core of Jewish practice and identity is not compromised. Matthew declines to void the purity laws (chap. 15), in contrast to Mark (7:19). Gentiles attain positive status by coming closer to Israel and Jesus and by affirming the law.

V

Matthew's Group of Jewish Believers-in-Jesus

Nothing is certainly and directly known about the group within which and for which the Gospel of Matthew was written—not its size, nor the background of its members, not its organization and internal relations, nor its social relations with other groups, not even its place or date of origin. Most commentaries and studies have a brief section in which hypotheses about some aspects of Matthew's community are generated and briefly defended on the basis of the literary and doctrinal characteristics of the text. A limited number of topics are addressed, usually including the relationships and conflicts of the Matthean group with Judaism, the background of the members (Jewish, gentile, or both), the social location of the community (urban or wealthy?), and its geographical location (various cities or areas in greater Syria). Little attempt is made to describe the Matthean group as a complex social entity or to determine accurately its boundaries and relations with other groups or segments of society.

This chapter attempts a more comprehensive analysis of the group behind Matthew's narrative, using three bodies of evidence: modern sociological and anthropological theories concerned with group formation, Matthew's metaphors and narrative, and ancient Jewish and gentile modes of association. Commonly used terms such as "group" and "community" are scrutinized. Then processes leading to group conflict and identity formation are investigated in order to understand Matthew's polemics against other groups and his claims for his own. The modern sociological understanding of deviance helps to explain both the ties that bind Matthew to the Jewish community and the tensions that so mark that relationship that his group can be characterized as an active deviant association and sect within Judaism. The fictive kinship relationships and master-disciple bond in Matthew lead to the hypothesis that Matthew's group is a household assembly of Jews who believe in Jesus. This assembly has its own understanding of the Bible and God's will as interpreted by Jesus; though not highly institutionalized, it has its own leadership. The Matthean household assembly is similar to several types of voluntary association common in Greco-Roman society. Serious attention to ancient and modern groups and social processes leads to a more precise and conceptually useful description of the Matthean group than is usual in commentaries and studies. On the basis of this group definition, the teachings on law and Jesus covered in the next two chapters will become more comprehensible and coherent.

Reading a text in order to understand the group and social situation underlying it is a difficult and treacherous procedure. The story of Jesus and his disciples is not an allegory of the experience of the author and his group in the late first century.[1] Yet the majority of commentators argue convincingly that the story of Jesus and his disciples reflects the experience of Matthew's group and its social situation.[2] Most important, the disciples serve as a transparency for the later Matthean group and symbolize their attitudes and behavior.[3] The correspondence is not, of course, one-to-one, and so the dynamics of the narrative and the clues provided by Matthew's style, composition, and general outlook must be used to reconstruct his view of his society.[4] Though many aspects of Matthew's group remain obscure, some stand out. For example, the virulent attack on Israel's leaders, analyzed in chapter 3, almost certainly mirrors Matthew's battles with local authorities in the late first century. The social relations of the disciples inform us about Matthew's group and its social relationships. These materials from Matthew allow a provisional characterization of Matthew's group and its place within the Jewish community.

Group and Community

Various modern and ancient categories used to describe and characterize the Matthean group will be treated at appropriate points in this chapter. Two deserve immediate attention: "group" because it is the most general of all terms, and "community" because it is used for Matthew's group so frequently in the literature. A group is a number of individuals gathered in some way or perceived as having common characteristics. Sociology usually understands groups to be aggregates of people who interact with one another. "Group" has been used especially for small gatherings whose members know one another personally and interact closely (primary groups).[5] Social psychologists define a group as "a social unit that consists of a number of individuals who,

at a given time, have role and status relations with one another, stabilized in some degree, and who possess a set of values or norms regulating the attitude and behavior of individual members, at least in matters
of consequence to them."[6] The author of Matthew is addressing a cohesive group which meets this definition. Adherence to the Bible and
teachings of Jesus, confidence in God, the actualization of God's rule in
Jesus, and hope for vindication in a final judgment characterize the
world view of Matthew's associates. Since the author uses kinship
terms for the group's internal relationships and envisions personal
conflict-resolution (18:15–17), his group must be small and somehow
distinct from the larger set of social relations that hold together his city
or region, and even from the structures that hold together the Jewish
community. Since he eschews many, but not all, official roles and titles
(23:1–12 versus 23:34), his group must have some formal organization but is not highly institutional. His usage of terms like "Israel" and
"people" suggests that his group is a new subgroup of the Jewish community which is in conflict with the majority leadership (see chaps. 2–
3 above). The task before us is to discern in greater detail the "roles and
relations," the "set of values or norms," the "attitudes and behaviors,"
and the "matters of consequence to them" from the data in the text.
And on the basis of that analysis, we must more precisely characterize
the type of group out of which the gospel of Matthew came and its relationship to the Jewish community at large.

Most treatments of the Gospel of Matthew refer to the Matthean
community. The term "community" is popular in theological, sociological, and daily usage because it is vaguely and yet richly connotative of
the close, warm social relationships which have been lost in the ano-
nymity of modern industrial society. It also suggests the deep, loving
relationships which should unite Christians to one another. But "community" is a complex term, and it must be analyzed and then related to
a number of other sociological terms for groups. "Community" was
traditionally used for a group of people inhabiting a geographical area
who constituted a self-governing and self-sufficient social and economic unit. During the last century, the sociologies of Tonnies and We-
ber understood community as a group characterized by natural
relationships and by common values and feelings of belonging to one
another (communion). Community was contrasted with bureaucratic
society, which was rational, utilitarian, and impersonal. In addition,
modern society was identified with the economic inequalities of class,
in contrast to the more just and equitable relationships of interpersonal
community. "Community" thus has acquired a romantic aura, recalling a simpler, more personal type of association lost in complex, mod-

ern society. The term is also used in a more restricted sense for groups which are set off from society at large by unique ways of thinking and doing things, for example, the Jewish community in the Roman Empire or in Israel.[7] Theological and religious authors usually imply that community members are related to one another by vital and close relationships that transcend geographical and social separation. Community implies the presence of a strong sense of identity and a common set of deeply held values and perceptions, which result in close, supportive, loving contact. The Jewish community fits this description because of its history, literature, strong social organization, and rich cultural life. Though the Matthean group is in some senses a community, we will argue that it is first part of the larger Jewish community. Thus, in the preceding chapters, Matthew and his associates have been called a "group," the most general name available, because the designation "community" implies to many people separation and independence from Judaism. How Matthew's group is a part of the larger Jewish community will become clear as we review and analyze the evidence. It is also part of an emerging network of groups that form the Christian community, a topic we will reserve for the concluding chapter.

Processes of Social Conflict and Identity

The early Jesus movement and Matthew's group have often been characterized as sects or movements within Judaism or the Greco-Roman world. When such categories are rigidly or narrowly defined, they distort the evidence in the text and produce misreadings based on anachronistic comparisons with modern religious associations. Even when sects and movements are supposedly used as ideal types, those reified forms are imposed upon the real life of the first century. In order to critique and use a more nuanced and flexible understanding of sects and movements, attention must first be given to the processes of cohesion and conflict which characterize any society and which underlie the creation of such categories. A brief consideration of social conflict, identity, and deviance in the light of Matthew will lay the foundation for understanding the nature of Matthew's group.

The fragmentary and occasional nature of much of the Matthean evidence can be given some shape by social psychology, which stresses social interaction as determinative of groups. Group membership is known through action, when members of one group interact with members of another group in terms of their group identification.[8] This approach does justice to groups as active participants in society, especially in conflict situations. Social psychologists and interactionists see

conflict among groups and individuals as fundamental to society because the formation of groups brings order out of the chaos of life even
as it makes group conflict inevitable. Matthew's group, according to
this theory, would view itself as bringing order to a disordered universe
and to a needy Israel. In contrast, the leaders of Israel presumably
viewed Matthew's group of believers-in-Jesus as a threat to divinely
mandated holiness, righteousness, and order.[9]

How can we understand the human and social dynamics affecting
the formation of Matthew's group? Realistic conflict theory, social
identity theory, and deviance theory, including sect analysis, each con-
tribute to understanding the social relations implied by Matthew's text.
Realistic conflict theory throws light on some aspects of Matthew.[10] It
takes as a presupposition that people affiliate for reasons of self-interest,
such as competing for scarce resources, providing self-defense, and
maximizing rewards, including the sharing of mutual positive attitudes (i.e., affection).[11] The social structure of a group is a "network of
relationships linking individuals together through regularized exchanges" that have as their purpose maximizing rewards.[12] Group
identity is stronger when the group is perceived as conferring benefits
while avoiding costs, for example, when the group defends its members against hostile outsiders.[13] Many sociologists theorize in terms of
real, meaning material, needs, thus foreclosing any religious or transcendent motivation. This very functional understanding of groups reflects modern theories of human nature in which human desire and
emotion are primary. According to these theories, conflict among
groups arises over empirically verifiable human needs. It can be overcome by focusing the groups on a common goal, desirable to all, which
demands the involvement of all for its achievement and thus transcends narrow self-interest. Clearly the Gospel of Matthew, though it
includes such concerns, is built upon a different understanding of human needs, motivation, and activity. The rewards and benefits sought
by groups can be expanded to include the transcendent rewards that
are the objects of attention in Matthew. In addition to people's material
needs, their real inner needs can be ascertained and met, often with a
change in attitude or a new understanding of a situation.[14] For those
seeking a deep sense of belonging and relationship with the divine,
with history and with the transcendent goals of human life, a new understanding or experience of life beyond the material is a crucial goal
and the answer to a deep need. In the religious sphere, people can find
rewards for their social efforts in so-called universal compensators,
which are otherworldly rewards promised for the future.[15] The re-
liability of such compensators depends on faith-based explanations of

the situation in which rewards cannot be immediately achieved. Universal compensators offer rewards of great scope and therefore substitute for more immediate, attractive rewards and goals. The kingdom of God, the future coming of Jesus, and the promise of a judgment of good and evil are all active and vital parts of Matthew's world. They are goals toward which Matthew's group strives, and they compensate for the losses suffered in ordinary relations, especially in social conflict with the Jewish community and the rest of the world. Thus even a theory of religion based on exchange theory, which postulates as a prime motivator and rational guide the selfish human desire for rewards and avoidance of personal and material costs, can make room for widely experienced and recognized transcendent concerns. The members of Matthew's group combine a sharp critique of some community attitudes and practices with a deeply renewed sense of fundamental Jewish values, that is, divine rule (kingdom of God) and care (justice/righteousness), which has been communicated by God's emissary and son, Jesus. Their desire for a renewed relationship with God through Jesus and their conflict with the rest of the Jewish community combine to produce a strong sense of group identity, a complex web of social relationships, and a powerful set of transcendent goals and concerns.

Further insight into the nature of Matthew's group can be gained from close attention to his world view. *Social identity theory* stresses the role of cognition in group formation in contrast to the realistic conflict approach, which stresses needs and desires (emotions).[16] It explains the strength and permanence of the long-lasting and deeply ingrained group identification which was characteristic of ancient society, and it will be useful in analyzing the understandings of God, Jesus, Israel, and the world put forward by Matthew.[17] Social identity theory argues that group membership has primarily a perceptual or cognitive basis and that self-identity is important in itself.[18] Groups ask who they are before they ask whether they need or like other people or things. Thus, if one sees oneself as a follower of Jesus, as a member of Israel, and as a member of the kingdom of God, this generative self-understanding will lead to certain types of communal relationships, norms, goals, beliefs, and behaviors. It will cause creative initiatives and conflicts as well. People are not simply seeking an absolute identity, but are continually comparing, distinguishing, and evaluating their group with others, seeking to strengthen their group identity and make it more valued. What gives a group its identity is not known a priori, nor is it inevitable. The normal, objective criteria we think of as establishing group membership (sex, color, nationality, profession, political affiliation, etc.) are only decisive if another group is present with contrasting

characteristics.[19] The social categories used to distinguish individuals
and groups should not be thought of as inert characteristics inhering in
groups. They are valued ways of being in relation to others and imply
certain ways of acting and thinking. In Matthew, the special relationship the disciples have with Jesus and God, the importance of faithfulness to God and just (righteous) behavior, the correct interpretation of
the law as a communication of God's will, the presence of God's rule,
the promise of the final triumph of good, and the appeals made to Israel
and gentiles to accept and observe Jesus' teachings are all valued indicators of the identity, goals, needs, and rewards sought by the Matthean group.

Matthew's exhortations of the disciples, polemics against those who
oppose Jesus, appeals to the crowds, promises of the kingdom, and ex-
altation of Jesus as Son of God make perfectly good sense in the context of group formation and conflict within Judaism. In the previous
chapters, we have seen that Matthew's group still is part of Israel but is
in great conflict with the community authorities. Its members are
struggling with the rejection of Jesus by the majority of their fellow
Jews and trying to adapt to their explusion from the Jewish assembly
(synagogue). The group has also begun to look toward the gentiles as
potential members. Thus it is in great tension with its social and inner
theological world. The powerful story of Jesus—his teachings and his
close relationship with God, even in death—and the comprehensive
hope offered by Matthew for a renewed world under God's rule and for
ultimate satisfaction in life through the promise of resurrection and
vindication create a deep and stable identity for his audience, which
believes in Jesus.

The Matthean Group's Social Relations
Kinship Terminology and the Household

These sociological observations must be complemented by an examination of the internal convictions, attitudes, and goals of the group.
Their inner life may be discerned from the set of metaphors and symbols which the author of Matthew uses in describing his associates and
their relationships. Kinship is the dominant metaphor in Matthew for
internal group relationships. Father-son and brother-to-brother relationships are most common. Closely related to these kinship metaphors is the master-disciple relationship, since in antiquity teachers
and disciples forged close personal bonds. Both kinship and master-
disciple relationships were fostered within the household, and we shall
see that Matthew's group most probably assembled in a household.

This is not surprising, for Jewish assemblies (synagogues) and Greco-Roman disciples and teachers often met in houses.

The Matthean group had not yet developed formal institutions, such as a publically recognized leadership. Its struggles with the established teachers and officials of the Jewish community even made it reluctant to use the terms "master" and "teacher" of anyone but Jesus (23:8–12). The Matthean group was held together by fictive kinship relations and probably met in members' houses for worship and instruction. One of the functions of the large ancient household was education through tutors, client scholars, and traveling preachers and philosophers. The author of Matthew, like other early bearers of Jesus' teaching, probably worked in such a setting.[20] In the Greco-Roman world, philosophers who had high status could influence public institutions. The Cynics influenced the public by forcing themselves upon people in the marketplace. However, conversion of others to a philosophical way of life most often took place in private settings such as households, which were more appropriate places for developing strong bonds and personal commitments.[21] In order to find the setting of Matthew's group and expose its inner fabric, we turn first to kinship terminology and the master-disciple relationships, then to the household, which was the seat of education and governance of life, and finally to the assemblies which met in the household.

The use of kinship language for a variety of social relationships is normal in most languages. For example, in Greek the term "brother" refers most narrowly to the son of the same mother, then to half-brothers, cousins, family members, and other kinsmen, and finally to fellow members of a group or those who are colleagues and associates in a variety of social situations. Similarly, Matthew uses the terms father, mother, brothers, and sisters in the normal way for family members a number of times (4:18, 21; 12:46–47; 19:29). He affirms the traditional ties and duties that bind families together, that is, the command to honor father and mother (15:4–5; 19:19). But Matthew relativizes these family relationships in favor of a new commitment to Jesus. To follow Jesus' teaching, one must often leave brothers and sisters, mothers and fathers and children (19:29; 8:21–22; 4:21–22). Jesus graphically demonstrates this teaching by affirming that his true family is not his "mother and brothers" but his disciples and those who do the Father's will (12:46–50) and by referring to group members as brothers (18:15–20). That this substitution of new relationships for kin is highlighted probably reflects the divisions in families and the Jewish community in the late first century. As conflict sharpened between the believers-in-Jesus and some Jewish community leaders, the followers of Jesus were alienated from their families and excluded from the assembly of the majority group of Jews. These divisions are reflected in the story of Jesus' visit to his home country *(patridi),* where the people know his family and reject him as the teacher of a new family of disciples. (13:53–58). The division between Matthew's group and the larger community are also reflected in the references to "your/their" synagogues (4:23; 9:35; 10:17; 12:9; 13:54; 23:34), that is, the assemblies of those Jews who reject Matthew (see chap. 3 above).

Of most interest to this study is the use of "brother" for members of the Matthean group. A brother who has sinned against a brother must be corrected, by the group as a whole if necessary (18:15–17). Brotherhood connotes a relationship prescribed by Torah and safeguarded by group discipline.[22] Discipline is personally administered and unitive in purpose; it is not mediated through specialized judicial roles or highly institutionalized procedures. Those who have a brotherly relationship participate in a heavenly family which includes God, the Father in heaven, who ratifies anything that his adherents on earth do as a group (18:19) and punishes those in the group who do not forgive their brothers (18:35). Brotherhood also implies nonhierarchical relationships; because group members are brothers, they are not to have leadership titles such as "rabbi" (23:8). Only Jesus is their teacher and master, and God is their Father (23:8–10), and group members have a direct relationship with both of them.[23] The closeness of the members within the group and with Jesus is reflected in Jesus' reference to the disciples as his brothers after his resurrection (28:10). Matthew's new group, like all fledgling movements, sects, and interest groups, values unity and closeness among members. Group identity and cohesion depend on common perceptions of social reality, on internalizing valued social categories, and on sharing positive contact.[24]

The criteria by which brotherly relationships are to be judged are found especially in the Sermon on the Mount (chaps. 5–7) and the sermon on forgiveness (chap. 18). Brothers should not sin against one another (18:15–17), but if they do, they should forgive one another without limit (18:15, 21–22, 35). In the Sermon on the Mount, the descriptions of proper behavior and attitude are particularly Jewish and are addressed to those who believe in Jesus (the disciples and the later Matthean group) or who might become believers (the crowds and the late first-century Jewish community). All these teachings suggest that Matthew is instructing a group of deviant Jews who believe in Jesus. The attack on those Jews who oppose the author and his group is clear in the charges of hypocrisy (6:2, 5, 16) and the rejection of the

"Pharisees'" righteousness (5:20–48). These sectarian charges and distinctions mirror the real disputes that faced the Matthean group daily in relationship with fellow Jews. The boundaries of the group also excluded normal gentile practices (5:47). Thus, if you are angry with a brother (a fellow member of the group), you should not offer a gift at the altar until reconciled. If you see a speck in a brother's eye, you should make sure you have no log in your own eye (7:3–5). This proverbial advice presupposes a close group relationship in which a person knows the faults of another and has the standing to bring them to the other's attention. It is clear that Matthew conceives of his group as a family that is separate from the nations and in conflict with Jews who do not accept Jesus.[25]

Brotherhood both characterizes internal relations and differentiates the group from hostile outsiders. This brotherhood language, which is common in Paul as well as Matthew, is not used in inscriptions and texts on Greco-Roman associations; it probably developed among the early Jewish believers-in-Jesus.[26] The in-group and out-group contrast is especially strong in apocalyptic literature, which had a strong influence on the early Jesus movement. The rejection of those who spurn the in-group's view of the world and its norms for behavior and commitment is typical of intergroup conflict.

Only a few preliminary remarks concerning Jesus' relationship with the Father will be offered here, since this relationship will be explored in chapter 7. According to Matthew, Jesus is God's presence in Israel (1:23), especially within Matthew's group (28:20). The stories concerning Jesus' birth (chaps. 1–2) unmistakably mark him as God's Son, as does the voice of God at his baptism (3:17) and transfiguration (17:5). Jesus' special closeness to his Father is proclaimed by Jesus himself (11:25–27), and his disciples acknowledge his power and sonship after they are saved from the storm (14:33) and in response to Jesus' formal inquiry (16:16). Jesus enters Jerusalem as king (21:1–17), is anticipated as judge at the final judgment (25:31), and promises his protection to his followers after his resurrection (28:20). All these roles spring from Jesus' relationship with the Father. Jesus is pictured by the author as bringing all who believe in him into a similar relationship with God.

The Matthean group's relationship with the Father further illuminates its self-perception. Jesus will acknowledge before the Father those who acknowledge him, that is, those who belong to the Matthean group (10:32–33). This new family is characterized by the behavior and attitudes described in the Sermon on the Mount, which make one give glory to the Father in heaven (5:16), be a son of the

Father (5:45), and be perfect like the Father (5:48). Acts of piety (6:1–18) are done for the Father and known by the Father. In turn, the Father cares for the group that does his will (7:21; see also 21:28–46), just as he cares for nature (6:26, 32; 7:11; see also 10:29). In the Sermon on the Mount, the relationship of reverence and obedience to God the Father replaces the normal familial relationships as the central focus (see also the contrast in 10:21–22). The group has only one Father (23:9), and its relationship with the Father mirrors Jesus' special relationship with him. At the judgment, the Son of Man calls the just the "blessed of my Father" (25:34), and at the end of the gospel, Jesus tells the disciples to initiate others into the group through baptism in the name of the Father, Son, and Holy Spirit (28:19). Membership in the Matthean group, with its attendant faith in God, acceptance of Jesus' teaching, and obedience to God's will, is understood as a familial relationship with God. However, though Matthew emphasizes that Jesus is the Son of God, he does not call the disciples "sons of God," even though God is their Father.[27] As noted above, he once exhorts them to act in such a way that they may be sons of their Father in heaven (5:45), but otherwise he reserves this terminology for Jesus' relationship to the Father. Nevertheless, the tightly knit relationships of God, Jesus, and Jesus' followers are linked to an understanding of kinship.

The strength and peace of the believer's relationship with God through Jesus contrasts sharply with the conflict and suffering revealed in the polemics and controversies dotting the gospel. Against the indifference or hostility of the larger political world, the author of Matthew has constructed a smaller unit of society, the household, under the control of a benevolent Father. And through his apocalyptic hopes and the metaphor of the kingdom, he has enlarged its prospects to eventually include the whole world.

Jesus' Disciples and Ancient Schools

After kinship, the master-disciple relationship is the most common metaphor for group relationships in the gospel. The disciples of Jesus are the most ubiquitous group in the gospel. Matthew's interest in the disciples is manifested in his use of that word (73 times) far more frequently than Mark or Luke.[28] The disciples are committed to Jesus, believe in him, receive special revelation and teaching from him (13:10–12, 36; 15:15; 16:5–20), and are finally appointed by him to carry on his work of teaching and gathering followers after his death (28:18–20).[29] They are promised the kingdom of heaven, encouraged to persevere in times of oppression, and given continual instruction throughout the gospel. Thus they constitute a permanent, committed group of followers, rather than the informal, rotating body of students often found in an institutional school or a faction dependent upon the personality and immediate presence of the leader.[30] Though the disciples often fail to understand Jesus or to behave properly, Matthew presents them as responsive to Jesus and as models, albeit imperfect models, of what a follower of Jesus should be.[31] The problems of the disciples in understanding and following Jesus, the opposition they meet (and are warned they will meet, chap. 10), and the roles and responsibilities they are given all pertain directly to the members of the late first-century Matthean group in their own struggle to understand and live life according to the teachings of Jesus. The author has chosen and arranged extensive teachings and numerous stories (Matt. 5–7, 13, etc.) to instruct his group how to live as followers of Jesus after Jesus' death. Matthew's group thought and acted according to a coherent set of norms based on an integral world view. Its many conflicts with its host society bespeak a clear group identity.

The use of the term "disciples" for Jesus' followers in Matthew implies some kind of teaching or schooling, but what exactly? The narratives of all the gospels fail to provide evidence that Jesus and his disciples engaged in any kind of institutional schooling. Thus Jesus' disciples were not left with a formal educational framework or process for continuing Jesus' work. The master-disciple model does not come from Second Temple Judaism, the cultural context in which Jesus worked. Though Jewish literature and schools for the elite were present in Second Temple Judaism, explicit reference to teachers, students, and schools are infrequent in Hebrew and Aramaic.[32] The Hebrew word for student, *talmîd,* appears infrequently in the Hebrew Bible and pre-Mishnaic Hebrew, in marked contrast to later rabbinic literature in which the master-disciple relationship is central.[33] In calling Jesus' followers "disciples," Matthew is following the Greek usage of Mark and, most likely, earlier Jesus traditions. He is using a Greek rather than Hebrew model for the relationship between Jesus and his associates. Similarly, Philo, another Greek-speaking Jew writing in a Greek milieu, refers frequently to the master-disciple relationship. At the same time, Matthew is resisting the early rabbinic movement in the late first century, which also stressed master-disciple relations. He seeks to differentiate himself from it by insisting that only Jesus is master and teacher and that the terms and roles may *not* be replicated in the life of his group (23:8–10). In treating the master-disciple relationship suspiciously, Matthew is true to Second Temple Jewish tradition, which did not emphasize this theme, even as he follows the early Jesus traditions and Greek usage.

What does the master-disciple relationship imply? The Greek word for disciple, *mathētēs,* is the generic term for a learner of any kind. It could also refer to a boy attending school or a member of a formal philosophical or sophistic school.[34] During the Hellenistic period, its most common referent was an adherent of a great master or teacher, one committed to a movement or way of life. Consistent with this usage, Matthew most often employs the word disciple in reference to life commitment to Jesus, his teachings, his way of life, and any suffering or opprobrium which comes with it.[35] Thus Matthew probably conceives of Jesus' relationship to his followers as that of master to student according to the general understanding prevalent in the Greek-speaking East.[36] However, he does not exploit this imagery, nor does he explicitly stress Jesus as a sage, teacher, rabbi, and master of disciples. Titles and roles associated with teacher (rabbi and master) are restricted to Jesus only and are not held up for replication in the group (23:8–10). In fact, the disciples do not call Jesus teacher, master, or rabbi. He is never referred to as "master" *(kathēgētēs)* in the narrative, except indirectly in 23:8–10, and he is called "rabbi" only by Judas in connection with his betrayal (26:25, 49). The title "teacher" is found in the narrative, but ironically: even though Jesus in fact teaches extensively, only nondisciples, "outsiders," call Jesus teacher (8:19; 9:11; 12:38; 17:24; 19:16; 22:16, 24, 36). Jesus refers to himself as teacher three times (10:24, 25; 26:18), but only in relation to how outsiders understand him. In Matthew's view, real disciples understand that Jesus is much more than a teacher and do not use that term. In fact, faithful disciples seldom call Jesus by any title.[37] In portraying them thus, Matthew takes his own advice to avoid titles (23:8–10). Although the master-disciple relationship was well known and accepted in both Greek and Near Eastern society, and though Matthew stresses Jesus' teaching and the role of the disciples as teachers, he does not use the title nor conceive of his group relating to Jesus primarily as teacher.

The question remains whether Matthew's group might have anything in common with the philosophical schools common in the Greek milieu in which Matthew lived. The question is complex and requires attention to several types of evidence. Teaching and learning are important to Matthew. As we have seen, Matthew uses the term "disciples" even more frequently than Mark. He also gathers Jesus' teachings into sermons and has Jesus command the disciples to "teach all nations" (28:20). Because Matthew frequently uses complex interpretations of biblical texts, especially the fulfillment quotations, some have held that the gospel may be the product of a formal school consisting of trained interpreters of the Hebrew and Greek Scriptures. However, detailed attempts to defend such a hypothesis, led by Krister Stendahl, have not met with success.[38] Matthew has a more developed wisdom Christology than the other gospels.[39] However, though Jesus is presented as analogous to the biblical figure of wisdom, the metaphor of wisdom is subordinate to those of son of God, Lord, and Son of Man.[40] If Matthew sees Jesus as wisdom incarnate, he does not emphasize this theme or connect it with a wisdom school. Thus the case for a formal Matthean school and scholastic outlook is very weak. That the author was learned and a subtle interpreter of his traditions is certain, but the context in which he worked cannot be shown from the text to be a formal school of the Greek or Jewish type.

Further reflection on schooling may prove helpful, even if Matthew's group is not formally or substantially like a Greco-Roman school, because it will lead us to a Matthean social context, the household, in which schooling and many other activities took place in the Greco-Roman world. Moral instruction was given in a wide range of places, including the home, private meetings, public assemblies, and on the street.[41] Schooling was most common among the wealthy and those whom the wealthy patronized, that is, talented young people destined to fulfill roles which demanded literacy.[42] Secondary and higher education in grammar and rhetoric was mostly limited to the upper classes. Education and intellectual activity in the homes of wealthy patrons were also common, including philosophical instruction and discussion. Early Christians, especially Pauline communities, were influenced by this milieu.[43] Christian communities were based in households and carried on vigorous programs of conversion and education. Similarly, Jewish education in Israel was influenced by Greek models, though it is difficult to say how much, since evidence for Jewish education in the Roman period mainly comes from later rabbinic sources.[44] Josephus' *Contra Apionem* emphasizes, and probably exaggerates, the extent and scope of Jewish education in order to defend Jews as learned in and faithful to their law and thus as respectable members of imperial society. Consistent with the metaphor of teaching and school, Matthew emphasizes Jesus' teaching as the will of God and a true interpretation of the Bible. He supports knowledge of and obedience to Jewish law as interpreted by Jesus.[45]

The role of the teacher was crucial in the Greco-Roman world. The teacher was expected to be a model for his students, and classical authors complained that many teachers and moral instructors were frauds, sought monetary gain, or lacked the courage to confront their audiences with the truth.[46] Thus Paul often points to himself and his associates as examples of Christian life and ministry, stressing especially his concern for his communities and his sufferings. This view of the teacher-student relationship has influenced Matthew. The disciples are characterized primarily by fidelity to Jesus and through him to God, not by simple intellectual learning. Even Jesus' confrontation with the authorities in Jerusalem and his execution are part of his role as a teacher. The true philosopher was expected not only to teach his students but to instruct and confront rulers, even if it meant danger of death from tyrants.[47] Thus Matthew's presentation of Jesus as a courageous and dedicated teacher and his rhetoric and exhortations directed at the disciples move in the direction of a total commitment, climaxing in the command to both baptize and teach all nations at the end of the gospel.[48] Complete loyalty to Jesus is demanded of Matthew's audience. Matthew includes the teacher-student relationship and knowledge of Jesus' teachings within the larger commitment of the disciples to Jesus. As we shall see in detail in chapter 7, Jesus is understood not simply as a teacher but as God's Son, risen Lord, and thus as a uniquely authoritative teacher and leader. But even in making these strong theological claims, Matthew draws upon the Greco-Roman assumptions concerning authentic teachers and the demands they make on their students and society.

One other aspect of the teacher-student relationship should be pointed out. In stressing that relationship, the author of Matthew moves his audience toward a strong social identity based both on Jesus and on his teachings. Social identity is defined as "that part of individuals' self-concept which derives from knowledge of their membership in a social group (or groups) together with the value and emotional significance attached to that membership."[49] People belong to many identifiable social groups and are constantly adjusting their priorities and the intensity of their commitments. This complex process of understanding and embracing the many groups, obligations, and goals within one unified and yet complex and differentiated self goes on constantly.[50] The author of Matthew is attempting to establish Jesus' teaching about the kingdom as central to his group's understanding of its own life, its relations with others, and of the world itself. The disciples, who are struggling to actualize this commitment, are contrasted with the crowds, who are interested in Jesus, listen to him, but who do not dedicate their lives to him and his teaching.[51] The disciples serve the crowds (14:19; 15:36) and are sent first to teach Israel (10:5–6) and later all nations (28:16–20). They have superior knowledge because they receive special instruction from Jesus, especially in chapters 13–22. Thus the disciples (the Matthean group) stand in a special relationship with Jesus and are a special subgroup within the Jewish people. The author conveys their distinguishing characteristics in the narrative in order to define and defend the social categories by which his group understands itself and differentiates itself from others. Social categories are classifications of the social environment based on understanding and evaluation. They are not just arbitrary concepts used to divide things from one another, but deeply held judgments of what is valuable. The group attitudes and norms which Matthew proposes for his audience define their social place, their core sense of self, and thus provide a basis for sustained action even against strong social disapproval and opposition.[52] At the core of Matthew's identity is the relationship of Jesus to God as Son and the analogous relationship of his disciples to God as sons and servants. These intense fictive kinship bonds are proper to the household.

The group's identity and boundaries can be seen in the recruitment of Jesus' disciples and the instructions they receive to recruit others. The first four disciples (Peter and Andrew; James and John) are called to follow Jesus (4:18–22), but they are not formally designated disciples. Rather, they are offhandedly referred to by that term when Jesus teaches at length for the first time in the Sermon on the Mount (5:1). This sequence implies that the disciples are those who follow Jesus when they are called. The verb "follow" is not used in all cases with a technical meaning, but it does indicate dislocation from normal social circumstances and a determined and persistent commitment.[53] The following of Jesus is preeminently connected with bringing of additional members to the group. In Jesus' initial call to the two pairs of brothers, he tells them that they will become "fishers of men." At the end of the gospel, the eleven remaining disciples are told to make disciples of "all the nations," which means baptizing and teaching them to observe all Jesus' teachings (28:19–20). In Jesus' most explicit instruction concerning missionary work, the disciples are compared to the laborers in a bountiful harvest and also to shepherds (9:36–37). These workers are to heal, exorcise, teach, suffer, and witness (10:1, 7–8, 26–28; 32–33). The metaphors of harvesting, shepherding, and fishing center on the recruitment of new group members and their subsequent care. The emphasis on recruitment of new members is consistent with the whole of Matthew's treatment of Jesus' disciples. The disciples accompany Jesus as he teaches, heals, and appeals to the crowds to follow him. They are taught by Jesus and aid him in his work of teaching and feeding the crowds. (10:1–15; 14:13–21; 15:32–39). They experience a number of difficulties: they frequently misunderstand Jesus, are attacked by Jesus' opponents (12:2; 15:2), and face both peril at sea (8:23–27; 14:22–27) and the threats to Jesus in Jerusalem. The experience of the disciples in the gospel narrative echoes the experience of the Matthean group, trying to survive and expand in an unfriendly environment. The instructions they receive prepare them to lead a life as "outsiders," to insist that they have the true understanding of what is right and willed by God, and to recruit a loyal group to live out Jesus' teachings. Matthew urges his group to take a sectarian stance within Judaism and to labor for its reform.

God's Household: Synagogue and Church

Granting that the author of the Gospel of Matthew uses kinship and school language, strives to create a social identity for his subgroup of believers-in-Jesus, and labors to refute rival Jewish teachers, what is the most likely social setting for Matthew's group in first-century society? To what type of groups might it have been similar? The two principle social orders in antiquity were political society and the family. Religion, economics, and private associations were all embedded in one or the other of these. The extensive use of kinship terminology in Matthew and the absence of sustained attention to political society, except during the story of Jesus' death, suggest that the author was writing for a group of people who associated within a private context. This hypothesis is consistent with the sparse surviving evidence from first- and second-century Judaism that indicates that Jewish synagogues in the diaspora, and probably in Israel as well, met in houses.[54] The Greek word *synagōgē* (συναγωγη) denotes a gathering of persons in the widest sense of the term. It includes both informal gatherings and formal public assemblies. In the Septuagint, synagogue is used of the whole congregation of Israel numerous times (e.g., Exod. 12:3). Only in the Hellenistic period does synagogue come to refer to Jewish diaspora assemblies and to their buildings. Even here, usage varies. In Egypt, the Jewish religious locations are for the most part called by the name "place of prayer" (*proseuchē*, προσευχη).[55] Josephus, quoting a decree of Augustus, uses the variant term *sabbateion* ("Sabbath place") for the location where sacred books and money were kept (*Ant.* 16.6.2 §164). Thus the use of the term "synagogue" for the Jewish assembly was not universal in the Greco-Roman period. Usage was probably influenced by the Septuagint practice of using "synagogue" for Israel assembled. There is little evidence for the use of this word or its Hebrew equivalent, *bēt kĕneset* (בת כנסת), in Israel in the first century or for a highly formal institution. Assemblies in villages and towns probably took place in a public square, a large house with a courtyard, or perhaps a multiuse public building. Rooms claimed as first-century synagogues at Herodium, Masada, and Gamla are assembly halls that may have been used for many purposes, including prayer and reading of Scripture.[56] They lack explicit religious architecture, iconography, and internal arrangements fashioned for worship. They have stone benches around the walls and an open space in the middle, without the raised platform *(bema)*, Torah ark *(aron)*, or mosaics found in some third- and fourth-century Galilean and Transjordanian synagogues.[57] What went on in the synagogues is not known.[58] Presumably prayer and Scripture reading were common (if the group was wealthy enough to own a scroll), as well as some form of teaching or exhortation. Who the leaders of the assembly were in Israel, how it functioned,[59] and how central this institution was is unknown. Synagogues became more thoroughly institutionalized and erected dedicated buildings regularly only in the third and fourth centuries in Israel.

Early Jewish and gentile believers-in-Jesus probably met for worship and instruction in house-based groups. Jewish groups of believers-in-Jesus would probably have replicated the Jewish model of assembly. In Asia Minor and Greece the evidence from Paul's letters for household gatherings is ample.[60] Other New Testament literature testifies to the importance of households as well.[61] The household codes in Col. 3:18–4:1, Eph. 5:22–6:9, and 1 Pet. 3:1–7 are notable, as is the language concerning house and home in 1 Peter.[62] Multigenerational families often lived in the same house, courtyard, or neighborhood and formed an economic and legal unit, especially among the wealthy. Such households could include a wide range of relatives, servants, and slaves, who interacted with one another in a multitude of spheres of life. Since religious observances, cultic activities, and behavioral norms were determined by the family, if some members differed from the others in significant ways, a great strain arose and relationships could be ruptured (Matt. 10:35–37).[63] Thus whole households often undertook new religious orientation or cultic practices as a unit. Poorer urban families usually consisted of the nuclear family living in a small apartment in an *insula*. Such families would have assembled in the home of a rich community member or in some available public space.

In view of the ancient household pattern, it is likely that Matthew's group of Jewish believers-in-Jesus met in houses both when they were members of the Jewish synagogue and after they were expelled and had to form their own assembly *(ekklesia)*. Households were the site for the meetings of disciples of philosophers and teachers, for the meetings

and meals of various Greek burial, occupational, and cultic associations (see below), for Jewish worship, and also for early Christian
worship.

The significance of the place of assembly for the nature of the group
is more difficult to ascertain. Many teachings, rules, and events in
Matthew's narrative can be connected loosely with the household, but
any unified view thus created is not Matthew's main point.[64] Granted
that Matthew mentions houses a number of times and even granted
that much of what he says may apply to household relations, the
household is not one of Matthew's central and generative metaphors
or symbols. It is less prominent than that of discipleship, and it lies in
the background of the central symbol of the narrative, Jesus' relationship with his God as son to father. However, the rule of the Father over
his people is carried not only by the metaphor of household, but also
by a political metaphor, kingdom. Thus the case of Matthew is more
complex than it at first appears.

Structure and Leadership in the Assembly

How may we understand the inner relations of Matthew's household
group, its goals, level of institutionalization, and leadership roles, its
view of itself, and its claims to legitimacy within Judaism? The inner
relationships and boundaries of the group begin to become clear in
Matthew's second reference to *ekklesia* (18:15–20). The members of
the group are "brothers," that is, bound by a fictive kinship relationship, and they are not to sin against one another.[65] The use of the term
"brothers" for members is typical of a new, face-to-face group that
stresses communal commitment and inner unity against hostile outside forces. Such reform movements and sects take some time to insti-
tutionalize and develop fixed roles and lines of authority.[66] Personal
relationships bind the members of the group together.[67] Thus the author instructs a person who has been sinned against to approach the
offending party privately in order to seek a reconciliation and preserve
a brother from sin.[68] This failing, two or three witnesses are to be
brought into the process, according to the biblical procedure (Deut.
19:15). Though the bringing of witnesses is the beginning of a legal
process, it also sets in motion the mediating influence of group members on one another. If none of these measures end the offense, the
assembly *(ekklesia)* of the members is the final arbiter of relationships
and norms, with the power to invoke (with divine sanction) the ultimate punishment for sin, exclusion from the assembly itself (18:17).[69]
Several things should be noted. The group does not turn to a strong

leader to enforce group regulations, or to an established judiciary system or list of rules to establish guilt. The group members are presumed to know what constitutes sin and are given the responsibility to work out conflicts and wrongs through personal confrontation or mediation. Only in an extreme case does the assembly as a whole become involved.[70] Thus the relationships binding the group together are more personal than structured, allowing flexible response to conflict. The presence of these rules, so similar to those at Qumran, and the following teachings about forgiveness (18:21–35) reflect the importance of maintaining unity and resolving disputes and anger within a small group. Groups are formed and endure to provide benefits to the members, as was noted above. Serious disputes or unjust behavior among members of a small group reduce the benefits of group membership and weaken the motivation to belong. In a small voluntary association, active membership depends on feelings of solidarity with other members of the group, satisfaction of one's needs, including spiritual and transcendent needs, and the perception of common characteristics among the members of the group. Disputes among group members accentuate differences, reduce satisfaction, and break down the relationships which hold the group together. Thus, Matthew's exhortations and procedures for resolving group discord in chapter 18 are central and crucial to the survival of his group.

The leadership roles of the group are not clearly reflected in the narrative, but some negative strictures and positive allusions yield information which can be coherently analyzed. The role of *scribe* is mentioned most often and positively. In itself "scribe" is a neutral term for Matthew, unlike "Pharisee," which is negative.[71] Scribes who are associated with Pharisees (23:13–36) are excoriated, and the ordinary scribes are contrasted with Jesus (7:28). But in a number of places, Matthew has removed the scribes as opponents of Jesus, probably because scribes were operative in Matthew's group.[72] The Matthean scribe, "trained for the kingdom of heaven," (13:52) has at his disposal both old and new, that is, received tradition and the new teachings and interpretations of Jesus. These scribes, along with prophets and wise men, have been sent to Israel, but they have been rejected by the leaders and persecuted, as were innocent just men and prophets of old (23:34–35). The gospel's careful attention to scriptural and legal interpretation and the final commission to teach (28:20) suggest strongly that learned teachers were important figures in the Matthean group.[73] The wise men who are mentioned along with the scribes (23:34) are not further defined in the text, but the designation "wise man," or "sage," which is ancient and widespread in the Near East, overlaps that of scribe.[74] The wise man was the traditional teacher, court official, interpreter of the tradition, and especially in the biblical tradition, a good person.

Prophets were common in early Christianity and were present in the Matthean group (10:41; 7:15; 23:34). The roles of prophets seemed to have included missionary work (10:41; 23:34) and leadership in the group (7:15). However, Matthew's attitude toward them is ambivalent, perhaps because there was some controversy over their role and over discerning false prophecy. True and false prophets are subjected to the usual Matthean criterion of justice: false prophets can be distinguished by their unjust deeds and words (7:15–20). Matthew's attacks on false prophets, on those who prophesy and do miracles and exorcisms in Jesus' name (7:15–23; 24:11, 23–24), and on false messiahs (24:5, 23–24) have generated the thesis that Matthew was opposed to charismatic, miracle working, and perhaps itinerant prophets. Miracle workers, prophets, and messiahs were all common in first-century Judaism and in the early Jesus movement, so it is not unreasonable to expect prophets in the Matthean group and miracle workers as well.[75] Though Matthew is clearly opposed to some kinds of prophets, the nature of their objectionable activities is not given in the text.[76] Matthew generally supports prophecy and prophets. He quotes the biblical prophets constantly and implies that prophets within his group have been sent to Israel (10:41; 23:34). But the nature of prophecy among the early followers of Jesus is complex.[77] The Didache, slightly later than Matthew, tries to regulate charismatic, itinerant prophets.[78] The Pauline communities struggled to regulate prophecy and itinerant teachers. It is thus likely that Matthew's group, like many others, had within it or as visitors charismatic prophets who taught in the name of Jesus. The difficult question concerns Matthew's precise problem with some prophets and their identity.

Overman argues that Matthew stresses the teaching role of the disciples and deemphasizes charismatic activity.[79] The traditional role of charismatic disciples curing and exorcizing as well as teaching (10:7–8) is not denied or rejected, but it receives less attention than in Mark and is replaced by a broad focus on teaching in the sermons and in the final commission (28:20). It is likely, then, that some conflict arose between the teachers like Matthew, who emphasized the more "scholarly" interpretation of Scripture and of Jesus' teachings, and the charismatic prophets and healers who stressed the palpable power of God experienced by emissary and recipient.[80] As noted above, Matthew plays down the thaumaturgical aspects of Jesus' activity, and he may have similarly treated charismatic and prophetic activities.

Granted Matthew's orientation toward teaching, what do the prophets and charismatics represent that arouses Matthew's condemnation? Both Matthew's text and context make it certain that he is not rejecting prophets and miracle workers in general. He must be objecting to certain practitioners or particular understandings of those roles. The diversity of contexts and statements concerning prophets and miracle workers make it likely that Matthew is not referring to one, clearly defined group that is in opposition to him, but to several groups and issues.[81] The warning against false prophets in the Sermon on the Mount, with its explanatory imagery of good and bad fruit, is almost certainly directed against people in leadership positions. The image of fruitfulness and unfruitfulness is used to evaluate group leaders elsewhere in Matthew, as we have seen. John the Baptist tells the Pharisees and Sadducees to bear fruit (3:8–10), and Jesus accuses the Pharisees of bringing forth bad fruit, by which he seems to mean their teaching (12:33–36). The parable of the fig tree (21:19) probably rebukes the fruitlessness of the Jerusalem leaders.[82] Since this warning against false prophets comes near the end of the Sermon on the Mount and immediately follows the proverb about entering by the narrow gate, it is likely that the warning refers to those teaching differently from Matthew. Though other teachers within the Jesus movement are usually suggested as the referents for the warning, Matthew may have been warning his followers against rival Jewish teachers, as he does in ch. 12.[83] That a warning against false prophets is a warning against false teachers is not improbable. Prophets in Matthew's circle are probably thought of as teachers and preachers (10:41).[84] In addition, the characteristics of prophets were assimilated to those of sages and teachers as early as Ben Sira (24:28–31; 39:1–11). Learned groups such as the Essenes and Pharisees were associated with prophecy, and the later rabbis saw themselves as heirs of the prophets who had passed the Torah on to them (m. Abot 1:1).[85] Thus the roles of sage, prophet, and teacher overlapped. Matthew's warning about false prophets to his Jewish group of believers-in-Jesus probably included a wide range of teachers, including his rivals in the emerging rabbinic movement.

The problem addressed in Matt. 7:21–23 is different from that in verses 15–20, though related. Hill suggests that the charismatic prophets, healers, and exorcists in verses 21–23 are different from those in verses 15–20.[86] In the former passage, they are accused of failing to do God's will according to the "behavioral tests" which Matthew applies as a criterion of the authenticity of prophets.[87] Charismatic activity must be subordinate to obedience to the law and good works, both of which articulate the will of God and are constitutive of righteousness and the kingdom of God. The charismatics who invoke Jesus as Lord are specifically within the Jesus movement, but they may be leaders who differ from Matthew on how Jesus' teaching is to be understood and lived.[88] They are not outsiders who come into Matthew's groups, as the wolves in sheep's clothing may be (7:15), but their status is the same: they do not represent God's will accurately. The deviant leaders being addressed in 7:15–23 are not precisely identified but seem to include a wide range of behavior and outlook.

In the discourse concerning the end of the world (chaps. 24–25), the author warns against false messiahs and false prophets (24:4–5, 11, 23–37). The understanding of a popular leader as an anointed son of David or prophet was common in first-century Jewish society and would have made sense to Matthew's late first-century Jewish community as well.[89] The issue here, as in Matthew 7, is true and false leadership and teaching, and the warning is against being led astray. Granted that such warnings against being misled are common in apocalyptic literature, Matthew is probably connecting his understanding of the end with the present situation of his group and the struggle for leadership of Judaism between the Jesus movement and the traditional, institutional leaders.[90]

All the titles used for group leaders (scribe, wise man, and prophet) are drawn from the biblical tradition and were in use in first-century Jewish society. Matthew is not creating a new society or differentiating his leadership and authority from the Jewish tradition. Rather, he is adopting a selection of roles and titles which are recognized and acceptable and which are not exclusively identified with his opponents. His selection is limited; he does not claim to have priests, elders, Pharisees, or rabbis as members of his group because the priests were hereditary and declining in influence, the elders of the community were opposed to him, as were the remnants of the Pharisees and the emerging group of rabbis. Matthew sorts out authoritative titles in his polemic against the scribes and Pharisees when he instructs his group not to call each other rabbi (interpreted as teacher) or master because they have only one teacher and master and they are all brothers (23:8, 10).[91] The author subverts the influence, authority and access to power of his opponents by denying the legitimacy of the titles and roles they have assumed. Matthew is also remaining true to his guiding metaphor of fictive kinship. The followers of Jesus are brothers, not rabbis, teachers, or masters to one another (23:8–10). Only Jesus is rabbi, teacher, and master, and only God is Father. This egalitarianism is common to new religious and reform movements, but it is quickly followed by the development of differentiated and hierarchized roles. The author of Matthew resists this natural development.

Finally, Matthew's group most probably contained missionaries of some type and was engaged in the attempt to persuade fellow Jews and also gentiles to accept the teachings of Jesus. The latter half of Matthew 10, contains an extended exhortation to persevere in a Jewish mission. Though many commentators have tried to place these sayings at an earlier stage of the Matthean group, the emphasis and shape given them by the author argue to their relevance in his own situation. The emphasis on teaching in the gospel and the encouragement given to converting non-Jews (28:18–20) indicate that the role of missionary had changed from that of charismatic healer to teacher and that its object had been widened.[92] The sending of someone in the name of a disciple (10:42; contrast Mark 9:41, in the name of Christ) may indicate that a group of specialists were engaged in missionary work.[93] Certainly there were specialized teachers (scribes, wise men), and part of their role may have been persuading others to join the Matthean assembly.

Matthew's Group as Deviant Jews

Where is Matthew's group to be located in society, and what is its relationship to Judaism and the Jewish community? As was noted in chapters 1 and 3, the conflict the author of Matthew has with some Jews and aspects of Judaism has led many commentators to claim that Matthew has left Judaism and adopted a completely separate Christian identity. However, conflict and the struggle for identity are processes which go on continually *within* larger communities, often producing subgroups within them. The presence of conflict does not in itself indicate that a group is separate, much less cut off from those with whom it is in conflict. The choice is not a black and white either/or. The nuances of the relationship of Matthew's group and the larger Jewish community can be understood through the concept of deviance, which depends on an analysis of changing tensions in the social environment. This concept allows a more sophisticated use of categories, such as deviance association, sect, movement, and cult, as characterizations of Matthew's group, enabling us to understand what he means when he calls his group an *ekklesia* ("assembly," usually translated with anachronistic overtones as "church").

Within society, competing groups often label one another deviant as they struggle for influence and power over people and seek to articu-

late their view of reality and of what is significant in life. Calling the
Matthean group deviant is, in traditional categories, a pejorative labeling. Most ancient and many modern societies treat deviant behavior as
objectively evil because it is seen as contrary to divine or natural order
or as inspired by evil powers (demonic possession, witchcraft, etc.).[94]
Within the taken-for-granted, everyday world, moral and cultural
norms are right and good and that which is different is at best strange
and at worst wrong and evil. This commonsense judgment of deviance
has been severely qualified by cross-cultural comparisons and modern
theories of deviance, which show that social consensus and explicit
norms for what is considered deviant change with time. Customs,
mores, social relationships, and laws develop and adapt to new circumstances and outlooks. Even "hard" deviance, such as murder and
theft, are defined differently according to culture and era.

In modern sociology, deviance is treated as a relationship between
two individuals or groups, not as an objective state. A powerful or majority group makes or enforces the rules which define what is normal
in society, and those individuals or groups who do not conform with
the rules are labeled and stigmatized as deviant.[95] Criminals, minor-
ities, and people of other cultures, for example, are customarily labeled
as not normal, or deviant; they may be accepted with reservations or
rejected. When the deviance which provokes rejection is minor, for example, how one dresses or socializes with others, sanctions are also
likely to be minor, for example, disapproval or social pressure. Deviance may also be serious, for example, murder or participation in a
culturally unacceptable religion, and will be sanctioned by severe pen-
alties or total avoidance. Within a given culture, conflict, tension, and
serious differences can be understood as subcultural deviance.[96]

Deviance relationships may vary greatly in their intensity. The degree of deviance of a group from society at large depends on the degree
of tension with society. Religiously deviant groups are usually labeled
sects. However, the term "sect" is often narrowly defined in opposition
to "church" and then misapplied to antiquity when churches were
much less institutionalized and were themselves sects. A review of the
larger theoretical concept of deviance, of which sect is a subordinate
category, provides surer guidance for understanding ancient society
and groups. In an attempt to understand and organize coherently the
many types of religious groups and their overlapping social, symbolic,
and relational traits, Benton Johnson originally proposed that the
church-sect distinction, that is, the distinction between dominant and
deviant groups, be defined at a high level of generality according to one
criterion, the relationship of the group to the social environment: "*A*

church is a religious group that accepts the social environment in which it exists. A sect is a religious group that rejects the social environment in which it exists. "[97] This criterion has been adopted by Stark and Bainbridge, who place religious groups along a spectrum based on the state of tension or lack of tension between the group and its sociocultural environment.[98] Sects are in greater tension with the environment than churches, though churches are usually in some tension with society as well. Within the religious sphere, churches and sects are in tension and often in conflict with one another.

The church-sect distinction, which has arisen in a Christian context, can be generalized if the distinction is transformed into one between religious institutions and religious movements. Religious institutions are stable social structures with roles, norms, values, and activities closely integrated into society.[99] Religious movements, which are deviant groups, are "social movements that wish to cause or prevent change in a system of beliefs, values, symbols, and practices concerned with providing supernaturally based general compensators."[100] In other words, such movements are organized groups wishing to become religious institutions, that is, the dominant faith in their society. This relational and fluid definition of deviance helps to explain the myriad opposing views and groups in first-century Judaism as well as in the present. Within Judaism, Matthew's smaller group is viewed by the majority as deviant. Matthew's group has deviated from some of the culturally accepted ways of acting and thinking Jewishly, but it has not ceased to be Jewish in outlook, behavior, and identity. The author of Matthew hopes to convince the larger society to adopt its different behavior and outlook, so that it will become normative and no longer deviant.

Deviant groups are often evaluated as an (inevitable) evil, but deviance is crucial to culture and community. In studying the Jewish groups competing for power and influence in the first century, appreciation for their contribution to society and thus for the necessity of deviance is essential. What a society considers deviant is intimately related to its identity, shows where it draws its boundaries, and exposes key structures and values in its social and symbolic system.[101] What a society rejects is determinative of what it is.[102] In fact, deviants are a necessary part of society, and the tension between them and the dominant institutions is creative.[103] Thus consideration of the conflicts between Matthew's group and the dominant Jewish community will reveal how each conceives of and lives life. Matthew defends what is crucial to his interpretation of Judaism, and he attacks what is most important to his opponents' view of Judaism. Both groups share many

values and know each other's weak points. The Gospel of Matthew
cannot be compared or contrasted with Judaism because the gospel is
in a real sense a Jewish document, written within what the author and
his opponents understood as Judaism. They were debating the shape
of Judaism and forging competing identities in contrast to one another.
But they did this within the Jewish tradition, in Jewish categories,
concerning Jewish questions.

Deviance is a necessary part of a functioning society in several
senses. Every society has norms and patterns of behavior and thought,
but every society contains a great variety of behaviors and viewpoints.
If we picture society as a circle, behavior and thought which is considered normal and authoritative would be clustered in the center,
controlled and defended by those in power. Other social groups would
be scattered around the circle, all with a relationship to the center, but
all at the same time with a slightly different identity and pattern of organization and behavior. The line inscribing the circle would be the
boundary of the society. Groups outside the boundary may be related
to the society or parts of it, but they are not members. Many have con-
tended that the Gospel of Matthew and the group it was addressed to
were beyond the boundary of Judaism. However, further analysis of
group relations in this chapter and of Matthew's interpretation of biblical law and Jesus in the next two chapters will show that Matthew easily fits within the boundaries of first-century Judaism.

The argument over whether Matthew is *intra* or *extra muros* depends
on how groups are understood and boundaries defined. The boundaries of a society are more or less sharp depending on a variety of
factors. They are the ultimate definition of what is normative or deviant.[104] However, within the society, groups constantly differ from one
another, that is, engage in conflict over norms and boundaries. The
creation of boundaries and norms for discerning what is acceptable
and what is not is an intricate process requiring great social effort.
Much of our behavior is in itself ambiguous and indifferent. Thus setting boundaries and defining deviance are part of a struggle to bring
order to human activities and the meanings we see in them.[105] Defining behavior also helps a society limit the virtually infinite range of custom and attitude available to humans to a finite and coherent whole.
Deviance categories are a sign that a society has voluntarily restricted
itself to a constant and stable pattern of activity.[106] More important for
late first-century Judaism, deviance is also part of the larger social process associated with stability and change, continuity and adaptation.[107] It keeps a society from rigidifying and failing to fulfill its
necessary functions. In the present case, Jews in Israel and southern

Syria had to adapt, or perhaps better, reconstitute their symbolic and social-political worlds in the aftermath of the destruction of the Temple and its leadership. Jerusalem, the symbolic and political center of Judaism, was eliminated, with grave community consequences that had to be met with innovative solutions drawn from the tradition. Jewish literature of the period, including the Gospel of Matthew, testifies to several approaches adopted by different Jewish groups. Many groups competed for power by labeling others deviant, yet they all remained within the ultimate, somewhat hazy boundaries which defined Judaism.[108]

In any social system, especially one in crisis like the Jewish social system after the destruction of the Temple, what is within the boundaries of the society and what is not, what is deviant and what is accepted, is a matter of dispute. The competing rabbinic, apocalyptic, revolutionary, and Christian-Jewish movements are a rich field for analysis. The early rabbinic movement, with its emphases on Torah, purity, Sabbath observance, tithing, and so on, and its vision of a Torah-centered life, probably seemed strange and deviant to many loyal Jewish farmers in Judean and Galilean villages. Matthew's group had enough fundamental disputes with the majority of Jews to be classified as deviant in a deeper sense than many other Jewish movements, as we shall see. And Matthew's own narrative testifies to the heightened tension within Jewish society caused by his new teachings.[109]

The changes which Matthew has introduced into his interpretation of Judaism are typical of those found in social movements, deviant associations, and religious sects. Social movements which deviate from the majority usually originate because there are steering problems within a society. They respond to a lack of focus and direction, a decentering and loss of self and meaning. Movements such as these attempt to resolve contradictions among the social, political, religious, and economic orders and to revitalize the society through reinvigorated central symbols and patterns of behavior.[110] When large numbers of people have been labeled deviant by the dominant forces in society and have been rejected in some effective way, they may organize into voluntary associations aimed at defending and restoring respectability to their "deviant" behavior. Typically, they challenge the conventional standards by which community members are measured, seeking to delegitimate the societal leaders who control the definitions of deviance and ultimately to change the social order. In other words, they use the very techniques which were used to render them "deviant" in the first place in order to justify their deviance and turn the tables.[111] Matthew uses all the sources of Jewish teaching and authority to achieve legitimacy, and he constructs an alternative community story, centered on Jesus, to make a foundation for his group. The realities of Jewish history and life are rewoven into a new tapestry. At the same time, Matthew attacks the alternative views of his opponents throught the polemics against the scribes, Pharisees, priests, and other Jewish leaders who appear in the narrative.

Matthew's community engages in many of the functions of a deviant association. It recruits members, develops a coherent world view and belief system, articulates an ideology and rhetoric to sustain its behavior, and attacks competing social institutions and groups. The formation of such a voluntary association requires adjustment to a new situation, the need to assign new community functions and status rankings, and the creation of new community goals.[112] All of these activities are carried out in the narrative through the sermons and teachings of Jesus.

Types of Deviant Associations and Sects

More precision can be gained concerning Matthew's relationship to the larger Jewish community through a consideration of deviant groups, specifically, deviance associations and sects as understood in contemporary sociology. As was noted, deviance describes a relationship between the institutionally established groups in society and those groups opposed to them. Deviant groups often seek to become institutionalized and dominant in a society. In other cases, they seek to be left alone or to fend off the hostility and influence of the dominant group. Thus *deviance associations* can be classified into four types, using two criteria. Those which seek acceptance by society are conformative, and those which seek societal change are alienative. Those which focus on the needs of their own members are expressive, and those which seek to have an impact on society are instrumental.[113] Matthew identifies himself as part of Israel and still hopes to replace the Jewish leaders and their interpretation of Judaism in the community at large. Thus he is *instrumental* in his orientation. At an earlier stage in their history, before opposition had solidified and Matthew's group was expelled from the synagogue, these Jewish believers-in-Jesus were probably conformative-instrumental in their orientation. This means that they sought to change significantly the social order and world view of the dominant types of Jewish society.[114] But the Gospel of Matthew reads like the literature of a group with a stabilized deviant identity.[115] Because of the conflict, polemics, and resultant differentiation, the members of Matthew's group find their core identity and their "master status" in being believers-in-Jesus.[116] All other aspects of their Jewish life and world view are filtered through this central commitment, which has alienated them from many fellow Jews and colored all their activities and relationships. Thus the gospel shows Matthew's group to be *alienative-instrumental*. This means it is separated from the dominant Jewish assembly but still struggling to gain influence and power within it. It must be emphasized again that separation and deviance do not imply that Matthew's group is outside the Jewish community. Even though some leaders or members may have said that they are not Jewish any longer (just as various groups of Jews today declare other groups to be "not really" Jewish), socially, behaviorally, intellectually, and theologically, they are still within the Jewish world. The Matthean group offers its adherents a new Christian-Jewish world as an alternative to other ways of being Jewish. It defends and justifies its way of life against opposition and seeks to establish a firm and reliable identity. Though the Matthean group has its own assembly, it has not yet withdrawn from Jewish society as a whole, for it still operates within a Jewish world, following the interpretation of Judaism attributed to its prophetic teacher, Jesus, and seeking to recruit Jewish members to its program.[117] At the beginning of the second century, in the next generation, the "master status" of these believers-in-Jesus, or at least of some readers of the gospel, would crystallize into a Christian identity and lead them to drop their Jewish identity. Thus Matthew's gospel entered the mainstream of the non-Jewish, second-century Christian church soon after it was written, but not in the lifetime or intention of the author.

Further light on Matthew's group and the other groups and forces in Jewish society with which it competed can be gained from Bryan Wilson's typology of seven kinds of *sects*. Wilson seeks to classify corporate forms of deviance by an analysis of the positive goals of deviant communities. Since this typology proceeds from what the minority groups say and do, rather than upon the majority groups' negative evaluation of them, it responds more adequately to their identity and inner structure.[118] All deviant groups or sects respond positively, negatively, or in a qualified way to the world around them and develop a strategy for living in accordance with this response. Though Wilson's seven types cover a range of responses to the world, these are ideal categories. Few movements fit neatly into one category. Rather, at any one time, a group may be characterized more or less strongly by more than one category and over time may move from one to another.[119]

Wilson's seven types are determined by each group's relationship with and reaction to its host society.[120] Thus his classification procedure is roughtly parallel to that of Stark and Bainbridge, who measure tension with society. Wilson has created this typology in an attempt to categorize all corporate forms of deviance abstractly enough to be usable cross-culturally, but concretely enough to distinguish important defining characteristics.[121] The focus on the goals of groups allows us to understand their choices and activities. Sects are treated as active units of society not simply as groups with certain doctrinal views, and are seen to cause reactions among other groups and sometimes to effect changes in society.[122]

The first-generation Jesus movement (during and right after Jesus' life) was most probably, in Wilson's terms, a reformist movement within Israel. A reformist group seeks gradual, divinely revealed change in society that will lead to a more satisfying way of living the religious tradition. The Pharisees and the Jesus movement were probably competing reformist groups. Jesus' movement was also characterized by thaumaturgical and millennial hopes. Thaumaturgy seeks relief from specific ills by special (not general and continuing) divine intervention. Jesus' miracles fit this type of response to the ills of the world, but the doing of miracles died out early in the life of the Jesus movement.[123] The millennial (or revolutionist) response looks for the destruction of the evil social order by divine forces.[124] This outlook can be seen in apocalyptic literature. In the gospels, Jesus is pictured as promising and threatening divine intervention to establish an apocalyptically renewed society ruled by God (the kingdom of God). As the Jesus movement moved out of Israel, it took on more aspects of a conversionist movement, with the millennial/revolutionist emphasis left in the background. (The notable exception is the Book of Revelation.) Conversion changes the person through emotional transformation, with salvation presumed to follow in the future. Typically the converts form communities, which affirm the conversion and help members to endure the evils of the world.

The late first-century Matthean group was so closely related to the Jewish community that it functioned as a reformist movement or sect within Judaism.[125] It was not alone in its orientation. The early rabbinic group, which began to take shape and strive for influence in the late first century after the destruction of the Temple, was a reformist group which, like Matthew's, sought influence and power in the larger Jewish community. Over the next few centuries, the rabbinic way of practicing and understanding Judaism would prevail. However, in the first century, they were a small coalition composed of survivors of the war with Rome who were developing a new way of living Judaism. They were not yet recognized and powerful community leaders, but they sought to have influence on the people and their leadership and in some places probably achieved this. Matthew's polemics suggest that their teachings had influenced the community in which he lived. Matthew sought to counter that influence with his alternative program for Judaism, a program which was rejected by most. Gradually, his group became more alienated in response to the rejection of its program for the reform of Judaism. The group Matthew addressed seemed to be failing in its reformist goals and deemphasizing its immediate apocalyptic hopes. It retained the millennarian orientation of the Jesus movement as a cosmic grounding and ultimate goal. As is typical of religious movements and sects, although the Matthean group, and the Jesus movement generally, did not immediately achieve relief through divine intervention, its intellectual and emotional engagement with a vision of ultimate vindication gave the group a sense of hope for the future.[126] The Matthean group developed a restorative ethic and self-consciously constructed new social arrangements.

Matthew's group is thus a sect within first-century Judaism, in the widened sense of the term being used here. Matthew uses polemical and apologetic language that makes the boundaries between his group and other groups clear.[127] His quarrel is mainly with the leadership of the Jewish community and the emerging rabbinic group, which is influencing that leadership.[128] The Matthean group has created a counterorganization that is still reformist and millennarian/revolutionist but has deemphasized the thaumaturgical. The final commission to the disciples is to preach, teach, and baptize (28:19–20), not to exorcise and heal (contrast 10:7–8). Even prophets, though part of the community (10:41; 23:34), are treated with suspicion (7:15; 24:11, 24). Matthew's emphasis on bringing non-Jews into the group (28:19) and on the integrity of his own group (in contrast to the alleged hypocrisy of the leaders of the majority Jewish community) suggests that his group is becoming more conversionist in its orientation. For the author, the group is still Jewish and should adhere to the bulk of Jewish law and custom, but there is an increasing emphasis on personal integrity as a standard for the group and an increasing openness to bringing a mixture of people into the group (21:43). Matthew still has a hope that his fellow Jews will join him. However, soon the Matthean group will become isolationist vis-à-vis Jewish society, and it is already beginning to create a new community withdrawn from Judaism and from the empire as well.[129]

In summary, the goal of teaching Israel contained in the gospel narrative (see chap. 2 above) and the polemics against Israel's leaders (see chap. 3 above) can be best explained by envisioning Matthew and his group, not as former Jews outside the community, but as deviant Jews (in the technical, sociological sense) still within the community. They are an alienative-instrumental group that has been excluded from the local Jewish assembly (synagogue) but still seeks to gain influence and power over their opponents within the Jewish community. They can also be looked at as a reformist sect seeking to transform society gradually from within according to their understanding of the divine will revealed in Jesus.

Matthew's Assembly *(Ekklesia)*

At the beginning of chapter 2, it was noted that Matthew does not identify his group as a new Israel, nor does he have a distinctive name for his group. Unlike the other gospel writers, however, Matthew does have Jesus refer, once in 16:18, twice in 18:17, to "the *ekklesia*," a word usually translated as "church."[130] Many commentators have siezed on this common Greek word and attributed to it the technical Christian meaning which it has in Paul, Acts, Revelation, and subsequent Christian literature.[131] But *ekklesia* is a common Greek word for assembly with a wide range of meaning; its use in Matthew must be determined from immediate literary and social context and not by usage in other Christian literature. It is not completely clear that Matthew uses *ekklesia* as a proper name for his group; it is clear that the group meets in an assembly that is somewhat institutionalized, because it exercises disciplinary power (18:17) and has the authority to make decisions in God's name (16:19; 18:18–19). It has permanence because God promises to protect it against the "gates of Hades" (16:18). It is built by and belongs to Jesus (16:18), who is present when only two or three are gathered together in his name (18:20).[132] It is not clear, however, that this assembly thinks of itself as Christian rather than Jewish, or that an assembly of Jews who believe in Jesus is somehow a non-Jewish institution in the first century, as is assumed by so many New Testament interpreters. The meaning of *ekklesia* in Matthew should not be sought in a general Christian concept of church or in an amalgamation of the metaphors and narrative elements that can be attributed to Christian groups, but rather in the Greek, and especially the Hellenistic Jewish usage of the word, in Matthew's precise use of this term, and in the social context of the first century.

The Greek term *ekklesia* is primarily a political term and refers to any assembly of citizens duly summoned by the herald. It is also used, along with a number of other Greek terms, such as *synagōgē, syllogos, synodos,* for the meetings of various Greek voluntary associations.[133] These groups often met in private houses, as did Jewish assemblies (synagogues) and early Christian assemblies *(ekklesiai).*[134] These private organizations, along with public city assemblies, had a cultic aspect to them since civil and religious matters were thoroughly integrated. Thus meetings often involved prayer and invocations of various patron gods for protection and blessing. However, *ekklesia* was not a technical term for a cultic group.[135] It was an available term which could include a variety of communities and groups, including those involved in cultic activities.

Matthew's use of *ekklesia* for his group probably derives not only from general Greek usage, but proximately from the Septuagint, where it is used of the assembly of Israelites (e.g., Deut. 31:30) and very often translates the Hebrew *qāhāl.*[136] This term is found most frequently in postexilic writings, for example, Chronicles, Ben Sira, and 1 Maccabees. Thus, if Matthew has drawn the term from the Septuagint, he has used a familiar Greek term for the people of Israel and sees his and Jesus' group in relation to Israel, not as a new or different assembly.[137] The question is whether Matthew considers his group to be a replacement for Israel (a new Israel) or a reformed, authentic part of the concrete Israel of his experience.

Ekklesia, meaning church, is usually thought of as a Christian technical term for a clearly Christian institution, sharply differentiated from Judaism.[138] This institution is usually articulated and legitimated through a web of sophisticated theological concepts and affirmations. A brief look at the New Testament will show a variety of usages and will elucidate the implications of *ekklesia* in Matthew. Several New Testament books use *ekklesia* as a designation of the Christian assembly, especially Paul's Letters, Acts, and Revelation.[139] Paul's communities are outside Israel and Syria and are made up primarily of gentiles. Given Paul's position on the gentiles' exemption from obeying all of biblical law, it is safe to say that his communities are understood as distinct from (though not unrelated to) the Jewish assemblies (synagogues).[140] In Acts, the late first-century author uses *ekklesia* to denote several types of assembly of believers-in-Jesus, including the still very Jewish assembly of believers-in-Jesus in Jerusalem (5:11; 8:1), the Jewish-gentile group in Antioch (13:1), and Paul's gentile communities in the diaspora (14:23; 16:5). These multiple meanings mirror late first-century usage and are also consistent with the author's tendency to unify and harmonize developments within first-century "Christianity." Whether the *ekklesia* in Acts is to be polemically contrasted with the Jewish synagogue depends on how one understands the author's evaluation of Judaism. Some read him as very negative and rejecting of Judaism (because Jews have rejected Jesus) but others see him as positive because he seeks to relate gentiles to Jéws in one reformed group.[141] These debates over Luke's relationship to Judaism are still not settled.[142] At a minimum, the author of Luke-Acts sees the *ekklesiai* as different from and in tension with Jewish communities, yet also as outgrowths of that same group.

The late first-century Book of Revelation is addressed to seven *ekklesiai* in western Asia Minor. These assemblies (chaps. 2–3) are exhorted to remain separate from Roman and all other outside influences and to remain faithful to the message they have received from Jesus. Two of the churches, Smyrna and Philadelphia, are encouraged in the face of those who call themselves Jews but are not, who are in fact a synagogue of Satan, and who slander the church members (2:9; 3:9). These polemics suggest that the conflict with the Jewish community in these two cities is a live one; the charge that the Jewish communities are not truly Jewish carries an implied claim that the churches themselves truly confirm Judaism.[143]

What conclusions can be drawn from this broad and varied usage of the Greek word *ekklesia*? First, one cannot assume that a full-blown, corporate understanding of the Christian church is necessarily implied by the term in the first century. It is not a univocal, technical term. Second, literary context and the author's world view will be crucial for understanding its implications. Third, *ekklesia* is used most frequently of assemblies outside Israel and Syria. Only the author of Acts uses the term of mid first-century believers-in-Jesus in Jerusalem and Antioch, and his usage may be anachronistic. Fourth, *ekklesia* is a Jewish, biblical term and cannot be simply contrasted with *synagōgē* as though one were Christian and the other Jewish.[144] *Ekklesia* and *synagōgē* are both Greek words for an assembly. Both are frequently used in Greek literature, including Jewish and Christian literature, for a variety of gatherings. Neither Christian nor Jewish meaning nor any fixed content can be assigned to the word *ekklesia* without detailed argument from context.

In seeking to discern Matthew's meaning when he refers to *ekklesia*, we shall not focus on whether the sayings are redactional or reflect the pre-70 church but on how Matthew finally uses the word. The purpose of this brief treatment is to discern any hints which may be given to the identity and boundaries of the Matthean group, especially its relationship to fellow Jews who do not believe in Jesus.

Both uses of *ekklesia* in Matthew presuppose an identifiable, formal group.[145] In the first instance, Jesus promises that he will build his *ekklesia* on Simon, who is called a rock (16:18). The future reference and the metaphor of stability (cf. the parable of the house built on rock in 7:24) point to the endurance of the Matthean group. Its authority to teach and structure itself is given in the promise that things bound and loosed on earth will be ratified in heaven (16:19). The references to the gates of Hades and the keys to the kingdom of heaven give a cosmological and apocalyptic validity to the assembly on earth but do not imply that the assembly is an otherworldly, eschatological ideal. Matthew here, as always, speaks of the concrete group of believers-in-Jesus, which has God in its midst and is grounded in Israel's past and future under God's rule. Jesus is identified as a real human who, because he is the Messiah and the Son of God (16:16), has roots that go deeper and an identity that is wider than what is apparent in daily contact.[146] Similarly, the Matthean assembly, which is ostensibly a small, endangered, deviant Jewish group, has its roots and its future in God, its permanence in a guaranteed leader, and its authority validated in heaven. The second use of *ekklesia* (in 18:17 twice), which we saw above, denotes the assembled members of Matthew's group. The group tries to correct a member and has disciplinary power recognized by God (18:18–19). However, the power and relationship with God are not fixed and highly institutionalized because God is also authoritatively with two or three gathered together (*synegmenoi,* from the same root as synagogue).

Some commentators have claimed that Matthew's use of *ekklesia* and his polemical references to "their/your" synagogues prove that he and his group were totally separated from Judaism and institutionalized as a Christian community. This conclusion is based on inaccurate presumptions about Matthew's relationship with the larger Jewish community. Matthew probably used the word *ekklesia* to denote his group in order to differentiate himself from his opponents in the Jewish community. Since the leaders who rejected Matthew presided over assemblies designated in Greek as synagogues, he was reluctant to use that word. He may also have been influenced by the practice of other groups of believers-in-Jesus who called their assemblies *ekklesiai.* However, Matthew's avoidance of the term synagogue need not imply that he is no longer Jewish. Quite to the contrary, his use of the other Greek and biblical term for assembly, *ekklesia,* may have been a counterclaim against his opponents among the Jewish leadership. Just as they claimed to lead the assembly *(synagōgē)* of Israel, so Matthew claimed to lead the assembly *(ekklesia)* of Israel according to the teachings of Jesus. Tagawa notes that Matthew half-consciously identifies Israel and his own group as one: "[Matthew] is clearly aware of the fact that the people Israel and the Christian Church are not directly equal, but on the other hand, he confuses them because both are the milieu in which he finds his own existence. From this confusion arises the dilemma of the Jewish-Christian problem."[147] Various groups in Israel think that they are the people of God. This applies to so-called sects like the Essenes and Pharisees, and also to Matthew's group, which is a Jesus-centered form of Judaism.

Greek Voluntary Associations

Evidence from the text, especially the use of fictive kinship terminology, suggests that the Matthean group may have understood itself to some extent as a household. It is likely that the Matthean group met in a private dwelling or space, as did many synagogues in the first century. However, though the analogy with a household is helpful, it does not encompass all the relationships and goals which inform Matthew's narrative. The type of association postulated, one outside the bounds of close kinship and of geographical, political relationships, finds its cultural context and legitimation in the Greek voluntary association, so common in the Hellenistic and Roman periods. But such associations were so varied that they cannot define the Matthean group precisely, they simply provide a social context for such a development in a Greek-speaking city.

Formal or corporate voluntary associations, of which Greek associations are a type, have fixed goals, modes of action, and relations among members. They took many forms and existed for many purposes in the city and countryside, among wealthy and poor.[148] Their primary purpose could be worship of a particular deity or organization of a festival, provision of burial for members, scholastic activities, protection of a craft, fellowship within an ethnic group, or simple socializing. Many had multiple purposes. They might meet at occasional social gatherings, hold regular meetings for cult activities, or enjoy meals together. Most of them were probably very small, ranging from ten to twenty five members.[149] No generalizations about Greek associations can be used confidently to describe or define a group. However, non-Jews and non-Christians would have seen Matthew's group as a type of Jewish private association pursuing its own, mainly religious, interests amid some controversy.

Conclusions

The Matthean group is a new, deviant Jewish group which is not highly institutionalized with strong leadership roles. This makes the author argue that the group's authority to teach and rule is based on the strongest possible foundation. According to the narrative, Matthew's assembly *(ekklesia)* is not just a human arrangement to keep social order but derives its authority and legitimation from God through Jesus. Authority and legitimacy derive from the father-son relationship of God with Jesus. In its own self-understanding, Matthew's group poses a counterclaim to the traditional understandings of divine-human social arrangements within the Jewish community. What this little group decides is accepted by God, as Matthew's use of the traditional Jewish metaphor of binding and loosing shows (18:18; cf. 16:19). Since political and religious authority and power are inseparable in ancient society, Matthew's claim of authority to bind and loose is a claim to leadership, not just in his own group, but in the Jewish community at large.[150] Divine authority is so present that even the members of the group when gathered in two's or three's (18:19; cf. 18:16 also) have access to the Father in heaven.[151] Jesus the mediator is in their midst (18:20; cf. 1:23 and 28:19 for the importance of Jesus' presence), and Simon receives revelation which enables him (and presumably other members of the group) to recognize that Jesus is the Anointed One and Son of God (16:17). This tightly woven set of relationships transmits power and stability from God through Jesus to the group that he supports on earth (16:17).

Because Matthew's group can be known only from its imperfect reflection in Matthew's narrative, no clear and unambiguous categorization of it can be made. Several metaphors and relationships in the narrative provide data which can be interpreted with the help of ancient types of associations and modern sociological categories. Kinship is the dominant metaphor used by Matthew both for human and human-divine relationships. It is likely that Matthew's group assembled in households for worship and instruction. Because they had been expelled from the assemblies (synagogues) of their opponents, they had to form their own, which they called by another Greek word for assembly, *ekklesia.* Though the competing groups were in serious conflict, they all remained Jews and all operated within the world of Israel. Matthew's group continued to act like faithful Jews, worshiping God, studying and obeying God's law (in their case, according to the interpretations of Jesus), and keeping communal order. From the viewpoint of society at large, they were a deviant group, a reformist sect with millenarian tendencies, seeking to change Jewish society. The tension between Matthew's Jewish group of believers-in-Jesus and the majority of the Jewish community does not mean that Matthew's group is Christian in contrast to the Jewish community.

Matthew's group is still Jewish, just as the Essenes, revolutionaries, apocalyptic groups, and baptist groups all remain Jewish, though sectarian and deviant. Matthew's group has deviated from the majority position through its devotion to Jesus as a risen apocalyptic figure who is a divinely sent emissary. Like many other groups, including the early rabbinic group, Matthew's group seeks to reform Jewish society and influence the way it will live and interpret the will of God. Unlike the rabbinic group, it is in serious conflict with society as a whole. Thus it is alienative-instrumental in its orientation, seeking to influence society through conflict and confrontation. Such groups are an essential part of a living society, which must adapt and change to meet new circumstances. Certain aspects of the tradition are affirmed strongly and emphasized. Other parts receive less attention or are subordinated to the core values of the group. In addition, Matthew's group is conversionist in that it seeks the adherence of individual Jews and also gentiles to Jesus' teaching and way of life.

The teachings and actions of Jesus in Matthew's narrative serve to create and strengthen the group identity of those seeking justice and Godlike perfection. God's relationship with Israel and love for Jesus, his Son, serve as warrants for the promises made to the members of the group. By obeying Jesus and changing their lives, they hope to overcome the injustice and evil of the present, and triumph at the universal judgment at the end of the world. The group's identity is based on its confidence in God through faithfulness to Jesus and on its understanding of God's rule (kingdom) at work in the world, past, present and future. The author places great stress on teaching and the master-disciple relationship. Since such instruction was carried on in households, the master-disciple relationship was integrated into fictive kinship relationships, which bound the group together.

The gospel has a living relationship to the Jewish community and tradition. For the author, membership in the Jewish community was fundamental for the specific social identity he was trying to forge for his group. Matthew's group unsuccessfully sought to influence Jewish society as a whole to accept Jesus' teaching and high status before God. Though he failed in that goal, the author's narrative did help solidify his group's knowledge of itself and God and its commitment to Jesus and the kingdom he preached. Thus it completed part of its initial task and has repeated that function among many Christian communities in subsequent centuries. Christian apologists who separate the Gospel of Matthew from Judaism in order to safeguard Christian identity contradict the sociology of intergroup relations and Matthew's own biblical theology. Differentiated groups exist in mutual dependence. Their differences become intelligible and significant only if they relate to a shared and common symbolic universe of values, which make it possible for multiple groups to exist and be compared.[152] It has often been observed that Judaism in Israel was struggling to reappropriate and readjust its identity after the destruction of its limited political self-rule and its central symbol (the Temple) in the war against Rome (70 C.E.). Likewise, various groups of believers-in-Jesus who had belonged within or on the margins of Jewish communities were increasingly organizing their lives around Jesus and differentiating themselves from various Jewish practices and institutional structures. As one would expect, conflicts, apologetics, and polemics were common, especially on the part of the newer, minority movement that became Christianity. Even in the third and fourth centuries, Christian authors who are far from Judaism in their minds still identify Christianity by contrasting it to Judaism, making pejorative comparisons and devaluing certain symbols and behaviors important to Judaism. Later Jewish literature also defends its ownership of the Bible and its legitimacy as Israel, God's faithful people.

Christianity then, as today, shared a symbolic universe with Judaism and thus required clear criteria to maintain its identity. Similarly, the rabbis who gradually formed rabbinic Judaism in the late first and second centuries chose to emphasize certain themes from the tradition, including some improbable ones (in view of the destruction of the Temple), such as sacrifice and priestly purity, in order to protect Israel's holiness in relation to God and separation from the nations. The author of the Gospel of Matthew represents one of the small groups within the Jewish tradition which sought another way of defining and leading Israel, a way which was rejected by the larger Jewish community, but which had enormous influence on the growing number of gentile believers-in-Jesus and the emerging Christian church. To see how Matthew fits into first-century Judaism, a more detailed treatment of his view of the law and his understanding of the important roles of Jesus will be provided in the next two chapters. The law was an important symbolic center for the early rabbinic movement and other Jewish groups as well.[153] A fundamental allegiance to Jesus characterized a diverse network of communities, some of which were Jewish-Christian (or more accurately, Christian-Jewish), like Matthew's, and some of which were gentile or mixed Jewish and gentile. These core allegiances and symbols coexisted, albeit uneasily, as we shall see.

VI

Matthew's Torah

If the Gospel of Matthew comes from a deviant Jewish group which believes in Jesus but still identifies itself as part of Israel, it, like other Jewish sects and subgroups, should have developed its own interpretation of biblical law, articulating a particular vision of life under God. True to this principle, the gospel contains many interpretations of biblical law and Jewish custom that differ from those of other Jewish groups but fall within the broad boundaries of the Jewish community. Though some commentators have argued that the author supersedes Jewish law with a new Christian law or annuls it in favor of a new spirit of the law, in fact he carefully defends his *interpretation of Jewish law* and custom by establishing Jesus as the authoritative teacher of the law and by providing arguments to support his views.[1] Matthew's treatment of law fits comfortably within the context of first-century Judaism in Israel. The topics discussed, the positions affirmed and rejected, the sectarian apologetic and polemical stances, the competition for power and recognition, the maintenance of boundaries, and the creation of a world view and group identity are all similar to the agendas of numerous Jewish works found among the Dead Sea Scrolls, the apocalyptic writings, the pseudepigrapha, Josephus, and early layers of the Mishnah. Any attempt to portray Matthew as outside the Jewish discussion of how Jews ought to live ignores both Matthew's teaching of law and his presentation of Jesus.

In first-century Judaism, interpretation of the law was a political act in which the control of society was at stake. Disagreements among groups involved substantial conflicts over public laws and norms. Combatants over the interpretation of Scripture or the correct implementation of biblical law sought to delegitimize their opponents and establish their own views as the correct way for the Jewish community to think and act.[2] Thus Matthew's interpretations of law are part of his program to legitimize his group against the attacks of the community leaders who reject it.[3] Though the points of agreement among these

groups were extensive (monotheism, acceptance of the Bible as authoritative, the common observance of numerous commandments
and customs, hope for divine protection), the points of disagreement
were critical, no matter how small.[4] Small changes in behavior sig-
naled major changes in outlook. Seemingly unimportant customs
firmly marked out one group from another and symbolized substantive differences. Matthew's interpretation of law shows the contours of
his reform program for Judaism, a program which sought to neutralize
the powerful and ultimately successful program of the early rabbis.
Matthew and his competitors sought to meet the needs of the Jewish
community for a coherent world view and a concrete way of life responsive to the loss of political autonomy and the Temple as symbolic
center. The interpretations of biblical and traditional customs, norms,
rules, and laws proposed by Matthew and his opponents sought to give
social shape to the community and, more important, to mirror accurately God's will for Israel in a critical and confused time. Matthew,
more than any other gospel writer, told the story of Jesus as the teacher
par excellence, sent by God with an authority and status higher than
any other Jewish teacher. Within that story, he gathered extensive and
detailed teachings of Jesus with special emphasis on the interpretation
of biblical laws and the rebuttal of his opponents' views.

Jesus as teacher, messianic ruler of God's kingdom, and Son of God
in Matthew will be treated in the next chapter. Suffice it to say here that
Jesus and his disciples are always fully observant of the Jewish law, as it
is understood and interpreted by Matthew. In his frequent conflicts
with other teachers and authorities, Jesus gives more detailed and nuanced defenses of his positions than he does in the other gospels. In
Matthew's view, he does not reject any legitimate laws or interpretations, and he is innocent of the serious charges brought against him in
Jerusalem. His authority in the narrative comes directly from God and
is sanctioned apocalyptically. Those who believe in Jesus understand
that his teaching, his life's work, articulates his God-given power and
authority both now and in the future kingdom when God will rule
directly.

Matthew's Interpretation of the Law

The author of Matthew wrote a narrative about Jesus the Son of God
and Messiah, not an instructive discussion of the law like the Mishnah
or a commentary on Scripture like the midrashim. However, in his narrative on Jesus, he gave great prominence to Jesus' teachings and connected them with Jesus' life and with earlier narratives, laws, stories,

and instructions found in the Bible. Thus through Jesus' teachings, the author of Matthew reveals his interpretation of many parts of Scripture, including Jewish law and its practice in his day. Most significant for the argument of this study, all of the topics which Matthew addresses fit into the agenda of first-century Judaism, specifically, Sabbath observance, the payment of tithes and other taxes, the validity and appropriateness of various kinds of oaths and vows, and the scope of purity and dietary laws. The positions which Matthew takes on these issues are within the range of accepted discussion and similar to those taken by other groups. His arguments are detailed and sophisticated, showing that he knows the *status quaestionis* in first-century Judaism and is debating with his equals according to the assumptions and norms governing discourse in most of the Jewish community. The author presents Jesus as an informed, observant Jew who protests certain practices and interpretations and proposes certain reforms of attitude and practice in order to promote greater fidelity to God and God's teaching in the Bible. The figure of Jesus in the narrative enunciates the author's aspirations for himself and his group.

Sabbath Laws

Twice Jesus disputes with the Pharisees over Sabbath observance: once on whether the disciples can pick ears of grain to satisfy their hunger and once on whether Jesus may cure a man with a withered hand on the Sabbath (12:1–14). Jesus' quarrels reflect the author's disagreements with other Jewish leaders over Sabbath law. The author of Matthew makes clear the seriousness of his debate with his opponents by tightening up the arguments he inherited from Mark, eliminating a sweeping generalization which might lead to lax Sabbath observance and embedding the disputes in a context where Jesus' and his own teaching authority is defended against that of their opponents.[5] Thus the Sabbath controversies in chapter 12 reflect inner Jewish conflict in the late first century.[6]

The Sabbath was the premier Jewish practice in the Roman world and as such was both admired and satirized by Greco-Roman authors.[7] Some Christian commentators on Matthew 12 have identified with these satirists and argue that Matthew is rejecting a "legalistic" or "ritualistic" observance of the Sabbath. However, Matthew has no such problem because his group observes the Sabbath seriously. Their understanding of Sabbath observance does not allow them to flee the dangers and horrors of the end of the world because journeys are not allowed on the Sabbath. Thus the author has Jesus hope that these events do not occur on a Sabbath (24:20).[8] Matthew's position here is rigorous but well within the bounds of the ongoing debate over what is allowed on the Sabbath during war.[9]

A brief review of some Sabbath controversies will place Matthew in a proper setting. The biblical Sabbath commandment is admirably simple: no work is to be done by persons or animals on the Sabbath (Exod. 20:10; Deut. 5:14). People are to observe the Sabbath rest because it is a sign of the covenant, the day is holy and must be sanctified, and resting commemorates God's completion of creation (Exod. 31:13–17; Gen. 2:2–3). Since scattered Biblical laws and stories give limited guidance about what constitutes work, Israel went through a continuous process of defining work. The absence of manna on the Sabbath teaches that food may not be prepared on the Sabbath (Exod. 16:22–30). Fire may not be kindled (Exod. 35:2–3); a man caught just gathering firewood in the wilderness is stoned to death (Num. 15:32–36). Both Jeremiah and Nehemiah oppose the transportation of goods on the Sabbath because it means bearing a burden (Jer. 17:21–22; Neh. 13:15–22). Jeremiah specifically mentions bearing burdens through the gates of Jerusalem and out the doors of houses.[10] Nehemiah mentions bringing agricultural goods into Jerusalem for sale, the treading of winepresses, and commerce on the Sabbath. To prevent this, he closes the gates of Jerusalem on the Sabbath and drives merchants away. Earlier in the narrative, Nehemiah has the people take an oath not to buy from gentiles on the Sabbath (Neh. 11:31). These stories show that norms for observing the Sabbath were not clear and that nonobservance was at times common.

Sabbath observance still troubled Jewish society in the second century, B.C.E. The Book of Jubilees and the Covenant of Damascus put great stress on the Sabbath and promote their own peculiar norms for observance. Jub. 2:17–33 stresses the sanctity of the Sabbath because of the holiness of God, associating Israel's election by God with its being given the Sabbath to celebrate. Work defiles and pollutes the Sabbath (2:26–28). Specific prohibitions suggest common types of noncompliance with Sabbath law: drawing water, preparing food and drink, and carrying things in and out of houses. All these are normal domestic chores which would naturally be done by people to whom God gave the Sabbath "that they might eat and drink and keep the Sabbath."[11] The Book of Jubilees ends with a list of Sabbath commandments. In addition to biblical prohibitions, sexual intercourse is forbidden, along with discussing work that would violate the Sabbath (50:8), fasting, and making war (50:13).[12] The Covenant of Damascus, which is associated with the Qumran community and the Essenes, has a more extensive and stringent list of prohibitions (10:14–11:18).[13]

One should not engage in idle talk or mingle with others; one should not walk abroad to do business, or cause gentiles to do business for him, or discuss business, or rebuke a servant. One should not go more than a thousand cubits from town (two thousand to pasture a beast outside town). One may not carry a child from place to place, nor may one assist a beast to give birth or lift out an animal which falls into a pit. It is permitted, however, to use a ladder or rope to get a human out of water or fire. These rules show how a specific group promoted a detailed understanding of Sabbath observance, and at the same time, they testify to the variety of disagreements and practices which had arisen in the Second Temple period.

Later Rabbinic discussions of the Sabbath in the Mishnah and Talmuds deal with a plethora of cases.[14] In the most famous passage on work, m. Shab. 7:2 lists thirty-nine categories of forbidden work. These categories themselves then receive extensive exegesis in Tractate Shabbat and in many other tractates that discuss what may be done on festivals, but not on the Sabbath.[15] The regulations for the Day of Atonement are more stringent, since it is a day of fasting and penitence (m. Yoma 8:1). Exceptions are allowed for a good cause, of course. On the Day of Atonement, pregnant women, the sick, and the person who feels a ravenous hunger *(bŭlmôs,* from the Greek *boulimos)* are permitted to eat (m. Yoma 8:4–6).[16] Yoma (8:7) also allows for pulling a living person out from under the debris of a fallen house on the Day of Atonement (and implicitly on any Sabbath or festival). The opening or removal of the debris over a living person *(piqquah nefesh)* became the principle of overriding a Sabbath prohibition to save a life.[17]

Matthew argues the case for his interpretation of the Sabbath with great sophistication. In the first case, in which the disciples pick heads of grain to eat on the Sabbath, the setting—walking in a field on the Sabbath and being watched by the Pharisees—seems to contradict the prohibition against travel on the Sabbath. Yet travel on the Sabbath never arises as an issue. Perhaps in Galilee during the first century, strict limits on Sabbath travel were not established and so both Jesus and the Pharisees could legitimately be in the field. Or Jesus may be pictured as in a field contiguous to a village and thus within the Sabbath limit.[18] Most likely, the concise characterization of the setting is a formal stereotype rather than a historical account. Since Matthew is engaged in apologetic discourse, he begins with a disclaimer designed to defuse an obvious criticism. He gives a reason for the disciples' picking and eating heads of grain on the Sabbath: they were hungry (12:1).[19] This observation does three things. First, it argues that the disciples and Jesus were not engaged in wanton disregard of Sabbath law; they had a mitigating reason.[20] Second, their hunger forms a stronger connection with the story of David (adduced in vv. 3–4), long noted as a not very exact parallel.[21] Finally, it invokes human need as a principle for interpreting Sabbath law, a principle which will be legitimated through the citation of Hos. 6:6 in verse 7. The Pharisees object that the disciples should not be picking grain on the Sabbath. Though their reasons are not given, the scene implies that they judge picking grain as a kind of forbidden work. To Matthew's explanation that the disciples were hungry, they would probably invoke the rule that food for the Sabbath should be prepared the previous day (Exod. 16:22–30; Jub. 50:9).[22] What, then, is Matthew's argument? Matthew defends his interpretation of Sabbath law by citing a biblical example: David's taking the Loaves of the Presence from the sanctuary at Nob to feed himself and his men as they flee Saul.[23] Matthew draws a parallel between the hunger of David and his men and that of Jesus' disciples. In order to establish the parallel, he has added to Mark's account the explanation that the disciples were hungry, and he has changed Mark's description of David as "in need and hungry" (Mark 2:25) to simply "hungry." Though the solutions to the hunger (picking grain on Sabbath and eating the Bread of the Presence) are very different, Matthew argues that hunger justifies suspending the usual laws, namely, the Sabbath law prohibiting reaping and preparing food in the case of the disciples and the law which restricted the sacred bread to the priests in the case of David and his men.[24]

As the author of Matthew staked out his position in the first-century Jewish debates concerning Sabbath observance, he was aware that David's case, which had been given to him by the tradition, did not pertain to the Sabbath and was thus weak, so he added another argument based on the work priests do in the Temple to carry on worship (Matt. 12:5–6). Just as the priests "violate" the Sabbath rest in order to fulfill a more important task, the sacrifices mandated for the Temple, so Jesus' disciples pick grain to assuage human hunger and thus obey the commandment of mercy. Matthew's citation of arguments concerning what is allowed on the Sabbath fits first-century debates concerning the Sabbath.[25] The clash of the commandment to offer daily, Sabbath, and festival sacrifices with the commandment of Sabbath rest is fundamentally solved by the Bible, which says explicitly that certain offerings are to be made on the Sabbath (Num. 28:9).[26] However, in the Second Temple period, various groups were careful to restrict Sabbath work, even Temple service, to the bare minimum. The Covenant of Damascus taught that on the Sabbath only Sabbath offerings could be made, and that if some festivals fell on a Sabbath, their offerings should not be made.[27] In a tradition which probably dates from the Second Temple, period the schools of Hillel and Shammai disagreed on whether peace offerings could be made on a Sabbath or festival and on whether one could lay hands on them (m. Bez. 2:4).[28] In general, pre-70 discussions of Sabbath law revolved around what could be done on the Sabbath and what had to be done earlier.[29] Matthew's argument over what may be done on the Sabbath and his use of the Temple service as a precedent fit nicely into the first-century debates on Sabbath law.[30]

Matthew applies the Temple-service precedent to the case of the disciples in a strange way, by comparing Jesus to the Temple and finding him greater than the Temple.[31] Therefore, the disciples' actions, like those of the priests, are allowed. Though he uses the well-known principle of arguing from the lesser to the greater *(qal we-homer)*, Matthew's claim is not patently cogent. If Jesus is greater than the Temple, then the disciples might be justified in serving him the way priests serve the Temple. But the disciples serve themselves in their hunger; they do not feed Jesus. Perhaps the teaching and decision-making authority of Jesus is being invoked as great, as the saying in verse 8 says. But Jesus does not command his disciples to pick grain, and the warrants for this activity are the arguments presented rather than Jesus' authority to change divine law. First the Sabbath Temple service opens up the possibility of doing something normally forbidden on the Sabbath. Second, the whole thrust of Matthew's argument links hunger, the Bread of the Presence, and the Temple sacrifices, which are meals. Thus the sacrificial activities of the priests, food, Sabbath, and obedience to divine law are loosely linked and provide the matrix for Matthew's case.

The foundation of Matthew's teaching rests on the importance of mercy in Hos. 6:6, which is quoted in verse 7.[32] Hos. 6:6 was used by a variety of Jewish groups for different purposes. The Qumran community claims that, despite their separation from the Temple, their prayers will atone for sins (1QS 9:3–5). In the second or third century, the author of the Fathers according to Rabbi Nathan (version A, chap. 4) attributes to Johanan ben Zakkai the teaching (on the basis of Hos. 6:6) that acts of loving kindness replace the Temple sacrifices after the destruction of the Temple. Matthew is thus citing a very general principle of "mercy" *(eleos)* in order to justify the disciples' assuaging their hunger on the Sabbath by picking grain. The hunger is not life threatening, so the principle of saving a life cannot be invoked to supersede the Sabbath law. The comparison of the disciples' hunger to David's hunger and the precedent for working on the Sabbath provided by the Temple service are suggestive but loose parallels. Matthew needs a weightier

(23:23) commandment to supersede the important biblical commandment to rest on the Sabbath. The question is whether there is a divine
commandment which would justify meeting the disciples' real but not
life-threatening hunger on the Sabbath. The location of the disciples
and Jesus in a field outside of town implies that previously prepared
Sabbath food was not available to them. The only food available was
the grain in a neighbor's field, which Deut. 23:26 allowed them to eat
in casual hunger. In Matthew's view the principle of mercy overrides
the Sabbath rest enough to allow the disciples to pick some grain to
alleviate that hunger. The clash of laws is decided in favor of mercy.[33]
Matthew does not abolish or sweep aside Sabbath law as some kind of
legalism. Rather he affirms the binding force of Jewish law and then
argues for a modified interpretation consistent with the teachings of
Jesus.[34] He gives the principle of mercy in response to human need a
higher priority than his opponents do and thus authorizes assuaging
hunger on the Sabbath even if the food has not been previously
prepared.[35]

Matthew finishes his allusive arguments from Scripture with a confident Markan affirmation that "the Son of Man is Lord of the Sabbath" (12:8). Matthew is invoking the authority of the risen Jesus,
whom his late first-century group recognizes as judge and ruler. He
may also be alluding to Lev. 23:3, which says that the seventh day is a
"Sabbath to the Lord *(le-YHWH).*" The implication is that God is the
Lord of the Sabbath, a role which, along with many others, is given to
Jesus by Matthew.[36] Though Matthew invokes Jesus' teaching and ruling authority, he does so within the web of biblical law, which Jesus
has pledged to uphold (5:17–18).

Matthew's view could find further support in a saying of Jesus'
which Mark cites, but Matthew omits: "The Sabbath was made for
man, not man for the Sabbath" (Mark 2:27). Matthew avoids this saying because it might promote general laxity in keeping the Sabbath.[37]
Readers of Matthew might subordinate Sabbath observance to a variety of human needs and desires, and that would undermine its status
as a divine commandment incumbent on Israel. Matthew responds to
human need, not by abrogating the law, but by arguing from the law
and the prophets (5:17).[38] The Sabbath is not overridden directly by human need or decision, but by a correct understanding of the law of
mercy contained in Hos. 6:6: "If you had known what this means . . ."
(v. 7). Consistent with Matthew's acceptance of Jewish law, the Sabbath is overriden only in a limited and specific way for good reasons.

The second Sabbath controversy (12:9–14) continues the sophisticated legal argumentation of the first.[39] Matthew modifies Mark's nar-

rative and argument so that Jesus is presented as a legitimate teacher and serious interpreter of the law. Jesus meets the Pharisees in "their synagogue" (12:9), an expression which reflects the conflict between Matthew and rival Jewish leaders in the late first century (see chap. 3 above).[40] The hostility of the Pharisees is communicated through the editorial comment that they seek to entrap Jesus. The battle over interpretation of the law begins in scholastic fashion when the Pharisees ask Jesus whether it is permitted (*exestin* in Greek; *mutar* in Hebrew) to heal on the Sabbath, specifically, whether it is permitted to heal the withered hand of the man in the synagogue.[41] Matthew focuses the discussion on the precise point at issue in late first-century Judaism: what kinds of activity could override the Sabbath rest. As in the previous case, two principles of the law are in conflict, keeping the Sabbath and healing those in need. Mark's question, "Is it permitted on the Sabbath to do good or to do harm, to save life or to kill?" (Mark 3:4) is much too broad and imprecise for Matthew. There is no question of danger to the crippled man's life, so the principle of saving a life (m. Yoma 8:6) does not apply. Since the general principle is to put off or do in advance as much work as possible so as to safeguard the sanctity of the Sabbath, the question is whether one can heal on the Sabbath, that is, whether healing is to be defined as work that should be put off until the next day. If one follows a strict approach to avoiding Sabbath activity, Jesus' opponents have a prima facie stronger case.[42]

Jesus proposes to allow healing on the Sabbath by applying the practice of lifting a sheep out of a pit on the Sabbath to the case of the man with a withered hand. He argues from the lesser to the greater *(qal we-homer)*, as he did in the previous dispute: "Of how much more value is a human being than a sheep?" (12:12a). The argument depends upon the assumption that both Matthew and his opponents permitted raising an animal out of a pit on the Sabbath, a view which was probably accepted in Galilee during Jesus' time and Matthew's milieu, but which was not universally accepted. For example, in the second century B.C.E., the Covenant of Damascus ruled, "If [a beast] should fall into a cistern or pit, he shall not lift it out on the Sabbath (11:13–14).[43] This matter was still not resolved more than a hundred years after Matthew. In the Tosefta, during a discussion of what may not be done on a festival day, Rabbi Eliezer says that if a mother and young animal fall into a pit, the mother may be raised if she is to be slaughtered for the festival meal (meal preparation was permitted on festivals, but not on the Sabbath).[44] Matthew assumes but does not argue for the practice of lifting an animal from a pit on the Sabbath. He does not make a detailed application of this case to the cure of the man with a withered hand, but he invokes a very general principle: "So it is permitted to do good on the Sabbath" (12:12b).[45] Jesus' appeal is both ironic and polemical. No Jew would hold the opposite, that it is not permitted to do good on the Sabbath. The quarrel, then, is over exactly which types of good are permitted on the Sabbath when work is involved. If Matthew had allowed the Pharisees to speak in this dispute, they would have raised the succinct objection of the Lukan synagogue official who confronts Jesus after he cures a woman crippled for eighteen years on the Sabbath: "There are six days on which work ought to be done; come on those days and be cured, and not on the Sabbath day" (Luke 13:14). This is the principle of Sabbath observance explicitly operative later in rabbinic literature, that what can be done before or put off till after the Sabbath should be.[46] In the first century, the permissibility of medical or other treatment of sickness on the Sabbath had not been decided.[47] Matthew argues from an analogy between animal and human that healing should be done on the Sabbath. He is probably implicitly appealing to the principle of mercy in Hos. 6:6 (v. 7 in the previous conflict) and applying it to the suffering of the animal and then of the human. Doing good in this case and in general means acting mercifully in as full a way as possible because merciful actions override the Sabbath.[48] Thus Matthew enters into an open discussion concerning Sabbath observance with this very broad principle of doing good and of practicing mercy (23:23) even at the expense of the Sabbath rest. At the same time, he does not present Jesus as a provocative Sabbath breaker, for Jesus does nothing physical to cure the man. He merely tells him to stretch out his hand and the arm is cured.

In both Sabbath controversies, Matthew's arguments in favor of Jesus' interpretations are brief and debatable in many particulars. However, they are not attacks on Sabbath observance as such, but rather interpretations of Sabbath law based on Matthew's understanding of the Bible according to the teachings of Jesus. Arguments over Sabbath observance were common in Judaism, as can be seen in 1 Maccabees, the Covenent of Damascus, the Book of Jubilees, and early rabbinic material. Particularities of Sabbath observance probably differed according to local custom and certainly helped define the boundaries of various Jewish groups. Matthew defines his group partly by its Sabbath observance: they do good and act mercifully on the Sabbath in a self-conscious and deliberate way. Legitimate disputes about whether an action is forbidden are to be resolved in favor of a hungry, ill, or needy person. Though these principles are attractive, allowing work for these purposes compromises the Sabbath prohibition of work. Thus legitimate objections were raised to Matthew's teaching.

Matthew's stories of Jesus' disputes are polemical exchanges with his opponents, not learned discussions of legal principles and practices among respectful colleagues. These Sabbath controversies are set within the section of the gospel (chaps. 11–13) in which Jesus attacks the people who resist his message (11:16–24; 13:10–17; 34–35) and defends himself against Pharisaic charges of demonic possession (12:24–32). In these chapters, the opposition to Jesus takes shape, and in subsequent chapters he spends more time instructing his disciples and preparing them for his death. Even the seemingly pacific quotation from Isa. 42:1–4 in Matt. 12:18–21 has a polemical edge that is comprehensively related to the conflicts in chapters 11–13.[49] Matthew's position on Sabbath observance marks him out as a serious participant in the Jewish debate.

Purity and Dietary Laws

In the middle of the gospel, Matthew works out a crucial problem in his interpretation of Jewish law, clarifies his understanding of the principles underlying Jesus' teachings, and attacks his opponents' program. The core of the discussion is a saying which may go back to Jesus and which potentially threatens the whole of the biblical purity code (Matt. 15:1–20; see also Mark 7:1–23).[50] According to Mark (7:15), Matthew's source, the saying reads: "There is nothing outside a person that by going in can defile, but the things that come out are what defile." The potential impact of this saying can be seen in Mark's interpretive comments, the most striking of which claims: "Thus [Jesus] declared all foods clean" (7:19). Mark abrogates not only purity rules, but also all the dietary restrictions closely associated with purity. In addition, Mark ignores the original problem, handwashing, after it is stated at the beginning (Mark 7:2–5). Instead of explicitly deciding this issue, Mark denies the validity of all purity laws, a view which prevailed in his Christian community. Not surprisingly, Matthew suppresses this interpretation of Jesus' saying and understands Jesus' teaching as an affirmation and fulfillment of the biblical purity and dietary laws.[51] He treats handwashing more seriously than does Mark, bringing the debate to a conclusion by denying that eating with unwashed hands renders a person impure (15:20). Matthew supports the purity and dietary laws as part of biblical law but rejects traditions and practices which are not found in the Bible or only weakly supported there.[52] His opponents' reform program for Judaism stresses a number of purity and dietary customs which in Matthew's view detract from the observance of the Ten Commandments (5:19) and justice, mercy, and faith (23:23).

Matthew seeks to support his own readings of biblical law and to undercut the interpretive traditions and practices of his opponents. He begins the purity debate with clashing accusations. The Pharisees and scribes charge the disciples with transgressing "the tradition of the elders," specifically, with failing to wash their hands when they eat (15:2). In response, Jesus accuses the Pharisees and scribes of transgressing the commandment of God for the sake of their tradition (15:3). Matthew shifts the argument, for the time being, from handwashing to a more fundamental issue, the distinction between biblical law as a whole and particular human interpretations and customs. He understands his opponents' interpretations to be human and erroneous so that they miss the core message and values of the law. His opponents, by contrast, see their practices as ancient, authentic traditions based on God's will. By interpreting handwashing as human tradition, Matthew tries to rob it of its authority and divorce it from the commandments of God, which he consistently defends all through the gospel.[53]

Before following the stages of Matthew's argument, a few words on handwashing are necessary. In the twentieth century, it is all too easy to dismiss purity regulations as ancient and meaningless. In the first century, they were an important means of maintaining community boundaries and a holy relationship with God.[54] Within Judaism, purity was central, but also controversial. Handwashing is mentioned in three biblical passages, but it is not presented as a general obligation to be undertaken before meals. The extension of handwashing to other contexts can be found in the Mishnah and Talmud, but even there it is disputed and only loosely founded on biblical law. The three scriptural passages which mention handwashing have nothing in common. In the first, the Tent of Meeting has in front of it a laver of brass in which the priests are to wash their hands and feet before they enter the tent or offer sacrifice (Exod. 30:19–21). This is a typical rule of priestly purity associated with sacrifice. Another case concerns impurity caused by a bodily emission (Lev. 15). Among the rules for purification, handwashing is prescribed for the impure person so that he does not pass on uncleanness by touching others (Lev. 15:11). Finally, handwashing is one of several ritual acts performed by the elders who sacrifice a heifer at the place where a corpse has been found in the countryside in order to absolve themselves and their city from the guilt associated with the death (Deut. 21:6). Handwashing removes impurity in some cases, but is not required before meals.

Handwashing before prayer was practiced in the diaspora, but not handwashing before meals. Two Egyptian Jewish texts refer to handwashing.The Letter of Aristeas (305–6) explains that the elders who translated the Torah into Greek followed Jewish custom and washed their hands in the sea before praying. The Third Sibylline Oracle (591–95) testifies that Jews raise their arms in prayer at dawn, "always sanctifying their hands with water."[55] Various ablutions were common though not systematized or universally accepted in the diaspora.[56] In Israel, the second-century B.C.E. Book of Judith portrays the heroine praying each morning after bathing (Jth. 12:5–8). Recent archaeological excavations in Israel have uncovered many ritual purification pools.[57] Thus the use of water for purification rites was common, but not specifically for handwashing before meals.

Even a hundred years after Matthew, the Mishnah, which accepts handwashing as part of its purity system, indirectly concedes handwashing's debatable foundations. Eliezer ben Hanoch is reported to have been excommunicated because he cast doubt on the washing of hands (m. Eduy. 5:6). Since this passage is an apologetic for rabbinic rulings, handwashing in the late second century was a touchstone for the acceptance of the rabbinic system and authority—that is, it was integral to their views, but very arguable on the evidence and thus vigorously defended.[58] Much later the Babylonian Talmud still must warn that whoever makes light of washing of hands will be uprooted from the world; such threats usually support a problematic teaching.[59] The core teaching of the Mishnah presumes that hands ought to be washed before Sabbath and festival meals but argues over exactly when, based on differing theories of purity and impurity.[60] Though the disputes are attributed to the schools of Shammai and Hillel and relate to the pre-70 Pharisaic interest in meals and purity, the highly literary, memnotic lists of disputes between the schools in m. Ber. 8:1–8 most probably belong to the final redaction of the Mishnah about 200 C.E.[61] However, the dispute over whether to wash one's hands before or after mixing the cup turns on whether impure hands touching stray drops on the outside of the cup will render the contents inside unclean. The school of Shammai affirms this theory, and the school of Hillel denies it. The school of Hillel holds that the outside is always unclean but that this does not affect the inside.[62] The disputes over handwashing show that it was a debated issue, and the fact that rabbinic schools are differentiated according to their positions (m. Ber. 8:2–4; p. Kel. 8:11 [50b]) argues for its neuralgic importance in later Judaism and thus suggests its significance for the early Jesus movement and Matthew.

Matthew's attack on handwashing is indirect. Rather than debate the custom itself, he attacks its foundations. Handwashing is nonbiblical, based on human tradition, and actually detracts from a proper observance of divine law.[63] The analogous example used by Jesus to make his point is the clash between vowed property and the commandment to honor and support one's parents (15:3–6). Since this passage will be treated in detail below in relation to oaths and vows, only a few remarks will be made here. First, vows are allowed by the Bible, but making vows is not mandated by Scripture. Second, particular types of vows are customary and not explicitly sanctioned by Scripture. Matthew argues that such vows should be subordinated to the explicit commandments of Scripture. He charges that the Pharisees' teaching on vows allows a son to dedicate some property to God and thus to free himself of the obligation to use it to support his parents when they are old and in need. In Matthew's view, a human vow should not lead to an infraction of the biblical commandment to honor and support one's parents. Matthew supports his interpretation with a citation of Isa. 29:13, which in the Greek version contrasts human precepts with divine teaching.

After this confrontation with the Pharisees and scribes, Jesus addresses the people with his own teaching about purity in general (not about handwashing in particular): "Listen and understand: not what goes into the mouth defiles a person, but what comes out of the mouth, this defiles a person" (15:10–11). Matthew writes more precisely than Mark of what enters and leaves the *mouth*, not of what goes into and comes out of a person.[64] Thus he focuses on food, to which handwashing before meals is related. However, Matthew provides no explanation of Jesus' teaching, nor are the implications of this proverbial saying unpacked.[65] The author's main interest is in sharpening the conflict with the Pharisees, so he has Jesus' disciples tell him that the Pharisees are offended by his teaching.[66] Matthew keeps the conflict of interpretation in the foreground, both as a narrative element in Jesus' story and as a commentary on his relationships with his late first-century opponents. Note the imagery which Matthew uses to characterize the Pharisees: "Every plant which my heavenly Father has not planted will be rooted up" (15:13). The image of a plant is common for faithful Israel (Isa. 60:2). In sectarian writings, it is often used for the favored group, which is cultivated by God.[67] Matthew uses seed and growth imagery elsewhere to distinguish the faithful from the unfaithful (3:10; 7:16–20; 13), and his advice to the disciples to leave the Pharisees alone (15:14) because they are blind and will fall into a pit fits his polemic in chapter 23 and also the promise in the parables that the evil will be punished in the end (13:24–30, 36–43, 47–50).

The traditional Jesus saying which Matthew quotes could imply that food cannot become impure and that the dietary restrictions

which forbid certain animals, fish, and insects as well as animals im-
properly slaughtered were invalid. If so, the saying posed a major problem for Matthew's program, which emphasized and supported biblical
law. Both the Bible and community customs affirmed that some foods
were unfit for consumption and that eating them was an abomination
and made one unclean.[68] For example, either touching or eating a permitted animal which has died on its own requires that one wash one's
clothes, although the uncleanness remains until evening, when the
day ends (Lev. 11:39–40). The importance of purity and dietary restrictions is presumed in most Jewish literature and acknowledged by
non-Jewish authors. The strict Essenes defend the purity of their communities carefully. The Community Rule of Qumran protects its pure
meals (1QS 5:13–14) by prescribing a probationary period of one year
before a new member eats solid food with the community and two
years for liquids, which are more susceptible to impurity (1QS 6:13–
23). The Covenant of Damascus reaffirms and further interprets dietary and purity laws (CD12:12–22) and regulates purification with
water (CD10:11–13). The early Jesus saying concerning things entering from outside threatens to undermine dietary and purity regulations
which were long definitive for Jewish society.

Matthew defuses the dangerous edge to this saying by shifting its
focus to moral attitudes and behaviors and leaving the purity and dietary restrictions in a lesser, but still secure, position.[69] He contrasts the
passing effect of food with the permanent nature of moral evil. Food
passes into the stomach and is "passed on into the outhouse" (15:17).
Matthew does *not* say here, in contrast to Mark (7:18–19), that whatever goes into a person cannot render him unclean. He says only that it
passes through and is gone. He does not really make clear his exact
interpretation of Jesus' saying, but rather shifts the topic to his own
ground, as he did above in the questions about vows. Mark gives a reason for his devaluing of what comes from the outside: "since it enters
not [the] heart." Matthew does not; he keeps the saying gnomic and
vague, because he is not drawing the firm and reasonable conclusion
that purity is to be rejected. Matthew uses Mark's very unbiblical contrast between moral and purity rules to counter the Pharisaic program.[70] What comes out of the mouth shows what is in a person's
heart, and it is this that can render a person impure. Moreover, the
products of one's mouth are not just words, but all kinds of disobe-
dience to the commandments: "evil thoughts, murder, adultery, fornication, theft, false witness, slander" (15:19–20). But Matthew
pointedly omits other vices listed by Mark (7:21–23) and limits himself to biblical commandments, his main interest. Thus, Matthew's

reading does not take Jesus' saying to its fullest extent, blunting its sharp edge. Matthew is preserving but limiting and mitigating this traditional saying. He tones it down, but the implication that food is not determinative or important remains, and this implication is broader than handwashing. Matthew responds to this uncomfortable situation by distinguishing three things: handwashing (which he rejects), food purity (which he does not deny, contrary to Mark), and moral rectitude (which he emphasizes). Human agency and responsibility are stressed. By not fully interpreting the Jesus saying, Matthew qualifies it so that biblical laws are protected and affirmed. Biblical purity and dietary laws are not contradicted, the commandments are, as usual, placed first, and emphasis is on the inside rather than the outside, just as it was in the Sermon on the Mount.

Matthew's reasons for his nuanced support for purity laws can be seen in the series of cures in chapters 8–9. There Jesus is touched by a woman with a hemorrhage (9:20), touches a supposedly dead girl (9:25), goes into gentile territory (8:28), and eats with sinners (9:10–11). All of these contacts did or could render Jesus impure according to biblical law. However, he subordinates this concern to that of healing and teaching. The principles adduced for eating with "tax collectors and sinners" are two: the first is a proverb drawn from the tradition, that the sick need a physician. The second is a Matthean interpretation of Hos. 6:6 (a verse cited also in 12:7 in connection with Sabbath observance). Matthew has Jesus command, "Go and learn what this means: 'I desire mercy, not sacrifice.' For I came not to call the righteous but sinners" (9:13). Both here and in chapter 12, the author interprets Hos. 6:6 as support for a principle of mercy that allows real human need (hunger in chap. 12; moral need here) to take precedence over observance of laws which protect God's and Israel's holiness.[71]

These same interests continue in Matthew's other attack on the Pharisees and scribes' purity rules in his seven curses (23:13–36).[72] Matthew refers to a first-century debate over the purity of *containers:* "Woe to you, scribes and Pharisees, hypocrites! For you clean the outside of the cup and of the plate, but inside they are full of greed and self-indulgence. You blind Pharisees! First clean the inside of the cup, so that the outside also may become clean" (23:25–26).[73] The inside is contrasted with and valued over the outside, impurity is associated vice, and a clean interior is seen as the key to a clean exterior, in both the purity and moral senses. Matthew has made an analogy between a pre-70 Pharisaic purity teaching and his own emphasis on the interior and on obedience to the commandments. Mishnah Kelim, which concerns the purity of various containers and utensils, has an understanding of the purity of cups and plates that is presumed by Matthew (and the Q collection of sayings from which he draws the core saying).[74] Debates among late first-century and early second-century rabbinic sages found in Mishnah Kelim (25:7–8; 25:1) presume that a container is divided into three parts—the inside, the outside, and the "holding place" (handle or finger hole, etc.)—and that each of these parts has an independent purity status. Thus Matthew's distinction of the inside from the outside fits Jewish thought about purity in the first century. However, nothing is said in Mishnah Kelim about the inside determining the purity of the whole cup or container. Rather, Kelim argues that each part is independent. However, Mishnah Berakot (8:2–4) implies that the school of Hillel thought that the outside of the cup was always unclean, in contrast to the school of Shammai, which held that the outside could be clean and the inside unclean.[75] Thus the Hillelites, who regard the outside of a cup as always unclean, must take the status of the inside (clean or unclean) as determinative of the cup as a whole. The Q saying (mid first century) takes up this controversy among Pharisees and criticizes the Shammaite view.[76] It supports the Hillelites' view that the inside determines the overall status of a cup, and from this interpretation of the purity rules, it teaches a moral lesson. The charge against the Pharisees in both Q and Matthew presumes that the early followers of Jesus and Matthew understood and participated in ongoing debates over Jewish purity law.

The dispute over purity and dietary restrictions is used by Matthew in chapter 15 as a dramatic final confrontation of Jesus with the Pharisees and scribes in Galilee and (since the Pharisees and scribes are from Jerusalem) as a foreshadowing of the Jerusalem conflicts (chaps. 21–23), which lead to Jesus' arrest and execution. Thus chapter 15 is a climax to the conflicts which began in earnest in chapters 11–12 over the teachings of John the Baptist and Jesus, Sabbath law, and the source of Jesus' power. The discussion of food purity is embedded in a complex of miracles and teachings concerned with food. Before and after the controversy, Jesus feeds the multitudes by multiplying loaves and fish (14:13–21; 15:30–38).[77] The teaching of the Pharisees and Sadducees, which Jesus warns his disciples to avoid (16:5–12), is compared to food (leaven). The purity issues are also connected to contact with and incorporation of gentiles and Jewish sinners. The discussion of food purity is immediately followed by an encounter with a (ritually impure) Canaanite woman, who asks for Jesus to cure her daughter and who convinces him to do so with the analogy of dogs eating crumbs from the table (15:21–28). In this story, Jesus goes to (toward) gentile (unclean) territory, that is, Tyre. The use of the biblical term

"Canaanite" (in contrast to Mark's "Syrophonecian") accentuates the separation of Jesus the Jew from this woman. Jesus does not enter her house, and the Matthean phraseology makes it ambiguous whether Jesus even enters gentile territory.[78] Yet significant contact is made, and the boundaries that purity rules define and defend have been breeched, even though no law has been broken. Earlier, to cure the centurion's paralyzed servant, Jesus offered to enter a gentile house (8:7), but this proved unnecessary. Twice Jesus is censured by his opponents for eating with tax collectors and sinners, who presumably eat food without great care for purity rules (9:11; 11:19). In all these cases, Matthew does not deny the validity of purity or dietary rules, but subordinates them to a higher good, healing the sick and sinners.

Matthew assumes the reality and validity of normal dietary and purity regulations. He argues against a certain interpretation of them (the Pharisaic/rabbinic), and he deemphasizes them in favor of the Ten Commandments, the love commandments, justice, mercy, and other Biblical themes emphasized by his movement. Concretely, he focuses his disagreement over purity regulations on a nonbiblical custom, washing hands before meals. No biblical law is infringed, nor is its validity denied. Rather, Matthew distinguishes his opponents' traditions and interpretations from his own, as he has done in previous cases, and attacks their views as unfaithful to the biblical commandments, which reflect God's will.

Tithes and Taxes

Taxes, lamentably, are an essential and universal part of complex societies. The Gospel of Matthew treats taxes three times. The author mentions tithes once, supporting their payment but deemphasizing their importance: "Woe to you, scribes and Pharisees, hypocrites! For you tithe mint, dill, and cummin, and have neglected the weightier matters of the law: justice *(krisis)* and mercy *(eleos)* and faith. These it is necessary to do and those not to neglect" (23:23). This passage, which was interpreted in chapter 3 along with the other six curses, is a climactic polemic by Matthew against his opponents. Three observations are crucial in considering tithes as part of Matthew's legal teaching. First, Matthew is opposing the reform program of his opponents (probably early proponents of what will become rabbinic Judaism), which includes a heavy emphasis on tithes. Second, even after the destruction of the Temple, the author of Matthew, along with other Jews, affirms the validity of tithes. Third, the author explicitly argues for his interpretation of the most important laws, those concerning justice, mercy, and faith. His position concerning the relationship of broad legal obligations to particular, limited laws was implicit in the Sabbath controversies, but it is made plain here where he characterizes the Pharisees and scribes' lack of proportion with the striking metaphor of "straining out a gnat and swallowing a camel" (23:24). This kind of polemic was common to sectarian Jews. The Community Rule of Qumran affirms the goal of abstaining from evil and holding fast to the good in order that the members "may practice truth, righteousness *(se-daqah),* and justice *(mishpat)* upon earth" (1QS 1:5). As the attacks on nonobservant Israel in the first two columns of the Community Rule show, the Qumran community claims for itself these central biblical values and attributes to its opponents the opposite vices.

The tithing system was not fixed and stable. Biblical tithes were imposed on grain, wine, oil, fruit, and animals (Deut. 14: 22–23; Num. 18:12; Lev. 27:30). The rules for tithes found in the Bible show evidence of development and change in tithing practices (cf. Lev. 6–7; Num. 18; Deut. 18). The latest stage of redaction reflects postexilic practices when there was no king to support the Temple and when the Levites had been subordinated to the priests.[79] In the Hasmonean and Roman periods, the Pharisees made scrupulous tithing of their food a distinctive characteristic of their program for reform, thus indirectly testifying to general laxity in this area (as is often the case in the payment of taxes).[80] The Mishnah, like Matthew, testifies to an expansion of tithing to include all growing things, including vegetables and herbs (m. Ma'as. 1:1; 4:5), like mint, dill, and cummin, which are herbs used as spices in food.[81] The Mishnaic Order of Agriculture continued the Pharisees' interest in tithing by devoting ten treatises to working out ambiguities in the tithing system.

Paying tithes should not be pictured merely as a pious religious practice. Tithes were a tax used to support the central religious and political institutions of Israel, the Temple and its priests. Both the Pharisaic support of tithing and the early Christian deemphasis of tithing were fraught with economic and political consequences for Jewish society. The Pharisees desired a strong Temple as an anchor for Jewish identity and society. The early Christian communities were in conflict with the leaders and institutions of Judaism. Even in Matthew's time, tithing was real in Galilee and adjacent areas. The priests did not disappear after the destruction of Jerusalem, nor did they immediately lose their power. Both Josephus and rabbinic literature provide evidence of the continuing influence and power of some priests.[82] It is very likely that priests continued to collect and people continued to donate certain tithes for their support. If this is so and if Matthew's group is to be located in Galilee or its environs, then he is encouraging his Jewish group, along with the larger Jewish community, to continue its practice of paying tithes to the priests.[83] If paying tithes is not a widespread practice any longer, he remains faithful to his premise that the law has not changed and must be upheld in principle and in practice as much as possible (5:17–19). However, the law must be interpreted with due weight to the most important things (5:21–6:18; 12:1–14; etc.), and for Matthew tithes are secondary, though still necessary.[84] Matthew's opponents, on the other hand, emphasized tithes as an integral and central part of their program for reorganizing the Jewish community, an approach which Matthew and the followers of Jesus rejected.[85]

Matthew supports the payment of another Temple tax, the yearly half-shekel tax owed by each adult male (17:24–27).[86] Coming after the second prediction of Jesus' death (17:22–23), his argument in favor of the Temple tax is one of a series of conflicts which prepare for Jesus' arrest. As we shall show, it is also connected to the third story of conflict over taxes, which follows (22:15–22). The history of this tax is pertinent to the position Matthew takes on it. The biblical basis for it is usually found in a half-shekel levy collected once by Moses during a census (Exod. 30:11–16).[87] This passage was soon combined with others to support taxes for the sacrifices and upkeep of the Temple.[88] In fact, the empire often paid for the sacrifices and upkeep of the Temple (Ezek. 45:17; Darius in Ezek. 6:8ff; Artaxerxes in Ezek. 7:17). However, government support might be insufficient and taxes or donations would be needed (e.g., 2 Kings 12:4–16 [Heb. 5–17]). Postexilic authors assumed the existence of a tax for the upkeep of the Temple during the preexilic reign of Josiah (2 Chron. 24:1–14). During the governorship of Nehemiah, (Neh. 10: 32–33 [Heb. 10:33–34]) a third shekel tax was collected to pay for the offerings and upkeep of the Temple. There is no evidence that this type of tax for a set amount was continually in force in the postexilic period, and many authors think it came into force as a regular tax during the Hasmonean period.[89] It certainly was not accepted without dispute, because protests against the tax were still current in the Second Temple period. The Qumran community, who disapproved of the Temple administration, limited their support and contact with the Temple to a once-in-a-lifetime contribution: "Concerning . . . the money of valuations which they give, each man as a ransom for his life, it shall be half [a shekel]; only one [time] shall he give it all his days."[90] The spotted history of the tax left room for various Jewish groups, including the Jesus movement and Matthew's group, to challenge its applicability.

In Greco-Roman and Greek Jewish literature, the two-drachma tax (in Greek, *didrachma*, roughly equivalent to a half shekel) was the best

known of the Jewish taxes because it was paid by all Jews, including
those in the diaspora. Roman authors complained at the amounts of
money donated.[91] After the Temple was destroyed in 70 c.e., the yearly
tax was collected by the imperial government for the support of the
Temple of Jupiter Capitolinus in Rome.[92] Rabbinic literature treated
the Temple tax as part of its system of support for the Temple but did not
acknowledge that it was being paid to the empire.[93] In sum, the Temple
tax was widely paid to the Temple in the first century, but still needed to
be defended as a legitimate tax. After the destruction of the Temple, the
tax was paid to Rome, though the legitimacy of this levy was not acknowledged by Jewish sources.

By inserting a story concerning the Temple tax, not found in the
other synoptic gospels, the author of Matthew is addressing a problem
which faces his Jewish community in the later first century. The Temple
no longer stands, and Matthew's group is estranged from the Jewish
community leaders. But the Romans still collect the tax from all Jews,
including Jews who believe in Jesus.[94] The highly compressed Matthean story about the Temple tax involves a conflict, a teaching by
Jesus, and the report of a miracle. When the tax collectors inquire of
Peter whether his teacher pays the half-shekel tax, he affirms that Jesus
observes normal Jewish practice. And at the end of the story, Peter's
answer is proved correct: Jesus and Peter keep the law, as they always
do in Matthew, though a miracle provides them with money to pay the
tax collectors. However, in the interim, Jesus challenges his need to
comply with the tax law. Matthew has Jesus argue that he is exempt
from the tax because he is the son of the king (God), and the sons of
kings do not pay taxes. This analogy assumes the predestruction designation of the tax for the Temple and its service; the Temple tax is paid to
God the King, and God's Son, Jesus, is exempt from paying. In the context of Second Temple Judaism, the narrative furthers Matthew's claim
for Jesus' unique status and special relation to God as Son of the Father.
But to avoid offense, Peter catches a fish with a stater in it to pay both
his and Jesus' tax.[95] Jesus thus remains firmly within the Jewish community as a loyal, tax-paying Jew.

The story of the Temple tax functions most pointedly as instruction
for the Matthean group in the late first century when the Temple tax
has become the *fiscus Judaicus* paid to the Roman government. The terminology used in the story is telling: not just any king and his son, but
the "kings of the earth" (cf. Ps. 2:2); and not a tithe or specifically Jewish tax, but tolls *(telē)* and tribute *(kēnson)*. These are taxes collected by
the imperial government and local rulers, and the tribute is what is at
issue in the story of Caesar's Coin (22:17). Thus Jesus' analogy about

the king and his sons fits the reality of the Jewish community in the late first-century; Israel, the son of God the king, should be exempt from tolls and tribute, the taxes levied by foreign rulers. But Israel is under the domination of Rome, and so to avoid trouble, Matthew's group is to pay the half-shekel tax to Rome.[96] Matthew's group is still part of the Jewish community, and community officials are still responsible for collecting the tax from all Jews, including Matthew and his adherents. Consequently, Matthew's Jesus teaches by example. He and his disciples (symbolized by Peter) pay, even though they oppose the authorities, both Roman and Jewish, who collect it.

The Temple tax story is beset by a number of well-known exegetical problems, which have produced a welter of interpretations concerning what Jesus taught, how the early Jewish-Christian church understood the teaching, and how Matthew used it. Whether the teaching comes from Jesus is disputed. Davies and Allison argue for the authenticity of the key exchange (17:25–26) as Jesus' teaching about the Father.[97] There was room in first-century Judaism for opposition to this tax, a position Jesus may have held.[98] Daube's recent attempt to argue that Jesus claims priestly prerogative as a basis for exemption from the tax has little foundation in other Jesus materials.[99] Montefiore and Horbury have Jesus taking a position between the schools of Shammai and Hillel concerning who should pay for the daily sacrifices.[100] Jesus might have opposed the paying of the Temple tax by all Jews, against Pharisaic teachings that all Israel should pay the tax—even priests, according to Johanan ben Zakkai (m. Shek. 1:4)—so that they all participate in the daily sacrifice. This interpretation is uncertain because we cannot date the Mishnaic controversies to the first century. Finally, Horsley argues that the teaching goes back to Jesus and that the sons are all Israel, whom he exempts from taxation by an unjust Temple establishment.[101]

Lack of a clear context in the life of Jesus leads Gnilka to treat the teaching as almost certainly nonhistorical, while Luz can imagine no context for this teaching in the time of Matthew and so reads the passage as a record of past conflicts of the Jewish-Christian community.[102] But Matthew is not an archivist, gathering outdated teachings. The disagreements over interpretation are caused by Jesus' enigmatic analogy that as the king's sons are free from taxation, so he is not obligated to pay the Temple tax to God, his Father. Because Jesus and Peter are paired, some claim that Jesus and his disciples are exempt, and that the disciples symbolize the early Jewish-Christian community or the Matthean group, understood as Israel or as a separate (gentile) Christian community in opposition to Judaism. A few observations may help to sort out these difficulties. First, the analogy contrasts a king's sons to tax-paying citizens and not to foreigners. Thus the analogy does not support the interpretation that Israel is being contrasted with the gentiles.[103] Second, the "others" who pay taxes (v. 26) are deliberately vague; they do not clearly symbolize any theologically significant group. Third, Gnilka is correct that the story makes a christological claim for Jesus in Matthew's narrative; Jesus is the Son of God and has special prerogatives.[104] However, Gnilka undercuts his position concerning Jesus' uniqueness by trying to claim that the story also includes the disciples as sons exempt from the tax, reflecting the separation and superiority of Christianity to Judaism and the Temple. But nowhere are the disciples called sons. Strangely, Thompson makes the same kind of argument that Matthew is abrogating allegiance to the Temple and Judaism and proclaiming the superiority of his Christian community to Judaism.[105] No such general claim is made. Jesus is superior to the Temple, but neither the Temple nor Judaism is rejected.[106]

If the teaching does come from Jesus, he was either claiming exemption from the Temple tax because of his relationship with the Father or, more probably, taking the position that the Temple tax was illegitimate for all Israel.[107] In the narrative, Matthew keeps up the fiction that the tax is paid to the Temple, but of course by his day, the Temple tax has become a tax levied by Rome. It is highly probable that Matthew uses the story of the Temple tax to argue that Israel ("the sons"), which includes his group, is exempt in principle from the Temple tax and (implicitly) that Israel is not obligated by divine law to pay the half-shekel tax to the Roman government. But Matthew and the rest of the Jewish community must compromise and pay the Romans to avoid destruction. Thus Matthew has Jesus pay to avoid offense.[108]

The question about paying *imperial tribute* (22:15–22) is set among a series of bitter disputes with the Jerusalem authorities after Jesus enters the city (21:1ff).[109] In this episode, the Pharisees plot against Jesus by setting their disciples and the Herodians on him with the avowed purpose of entangling him in his talk (v. 15).[110] As in so many other cases, they ask Jesus a formal legal question: "Is it permitted to pay taxes to Caesar or not?" (v. 17). The issue here is the hostility of Jesus' opponents and their desire to trick Jesus into a politically compromising statement that will result in his arrest. Matthew makes very clear the ill will of Jesus' opponents—they seek to entrap him (v.15); they have malice toward him (v. 18)—and accuses them of hypocrisy (v. 18), a theme which reaches its climax in the next chapter. The author of Matthew implicitly parallels the intensely personal conflict of the

Pharisees with Jesus to his own with the leaders of the Jewish community in his day.

Jesus' simple but subtle answer evades his opponents' trap: since
the coins have Caesar's image and name on them, they ought to be paid
to Caesar in tribute.[111] Matthew is one with other New Testament
writers in encouraging compliance with imperial and local authorities
and laws (Rom. 13:1–7; 1 Pet. 2:13–17; Titus 3:1). This was presumably the position of the Jewish community among whom Matthew
lived in the late first century. To refuse to pay the imperial tribute was
an act of revolt. The lack of extended argumentation and distinctions in
Jesus' reply reflects the pragmatic agreement on this issue within the
Jewish community and the impossibility of openly debating the tax
issue.[112]

In summary, the author of Matthew affirms the validity of biblical
taxes (tithes) for the Temple and priests but subordinates their payment to more important social virtues: justice, mercy, and faithfulness.
He judges Jesus as in principle exempt from the Temple tax, but accepts
the (now-Roman) half-shekel tax as a pragmatic obligation for his
group. He avoids the question of imperial taxes in the only way possible, by subtly advising their payment. Matthew's positions on tithes
and taxes fit into the mainstream of Jewish teaching in the first century.
His arguments are more simple than in the cases of Sabbath and purity
laws because he was closer to the consensus of his contemporaries and
danger from the Roman authorities was great.

Observance of Sabbath restrictions on work, purity, and tithes never
became important topics for Christian theology or practice. These
topics were ignored in Paul's letters, written mostly in the fifties, and in
later exhortations to good behavior, such as the Letters of James and 1
Peter. Their presence and emphatic importance in Matthew bespeak a
Jewish context in which a vigorous debate is in progress over the way
Jewish life, laws, and customs are to be interpreted and emphasized.
This part of Matthew's agenda fits the early layers of the Mishnah and
what we know of the Pharisees' interests and suggests that Matthew's
opponents and competitors may have been the post-70 founders of the
rabbinic movement.[113] The details of his arguments and his perceptions of this opponents' positions show that Matthew was certainly
part of the first-century discussion of how Judaism was to be lived and
that he took the outcome of these debates very seriously.

Divorce

Twice the Gospel of Matthew affirms the early Christian prohibition of
divorce (5:31–32; 19:3–9). This unusual and early teaching, which

may stem from Jesus, is found also in Paul (1 Cor. 7:10–11), Q (Luke 16:18), and Mark 10:2–12). In the Sermon on the Mount, the teaching to avoid lust as well as adultery (5:27–30) leads naturally into a more specific rule prohibiting divorce. Some commentators have argued that the biblical law of divorce is changed or abrogated, but that is not exactly correct. The Bible takes for granted the possibility that a man may divorce his wife (but not vice versa) and that he will give her a legal document of divorce, which leaves her free to marry (Deut. 24:1–4; Jer. 3:8).[114] Divorce is not encouraged or regulated in any detail, nor is it clearly a positive command.[115] Deuteronomy gives a general reason for a husband divorcing his wife: "if then she finds no favor in his eyes because he has found some indecency in her" (24:1). Deuteronomy does not give detailed regulations concerning divorce, as if divorce were an aspect of life to be regulated by divine command. It legislates only that the original husband may not *remarry* his divorced wife if in the meantime she had married another man and then become widowed or divorced. Jesus' new rule clearly goes beyond first-century Jewish and Greco-Roman practice, and thus Jesus is in conflict with other interpreters of the Bible. Is he in conflict with the Bible? By the criteria of twentieth-century literal, historical exegesis, yes; the Bible allows divorce and Jesus does not. But by the critieria of the first century, not necessarily, and in Matthew's view, certainly not. Matthew argues on a biblical basis (19:3–9), using and modifying earlier Markan material, that Jesus teaches the true will of God concerning marriage. His teaching is very compressed, however, and not all issues are clear.[116]

In the Sermon on the Mount, Matthew summarizes current Jewish divorce practice based on Deuteronomy 24: "Whoever divorces his wife, let him give her a certificate of divorce" (5:31). He then condemns the husband's divorce action and rules that remarriage while a former spouse lives is adultery.[117] No reason is given for this understanding of the commandment against adultery; Matthew simply assumes, on the basis of Jesus' teaching, that marriage is indissoluble (except in the case of *porneia,* to be treated below). In his second, more extended instruction on divorce and marriage (19:2–12), Matthew has the Pharisees ask Jesus a very precise and controversial first-century question: "Is it lawful to divorce one's wife *for any cause?*" (19:2).[118] Matthew has added the phrase "for any cause" to Mark's simple question about divorce in order to discuss the precise intentions and warrants of the biblical teaching and its subsequent interpretations. Matthew grounds his argumentation on creation and the institution of marriage, not on divorce practices. Humans were made male and female in order to be joined to one another as one flesh (Matt. 19:4–5; Gen. 1:27; 2:24). From this, Matthew generates a rule which is prior to and more important than divorce both logically and temporally.[119] The divinely commanded and effected union of male and female allows Matthew to qualify divorce practices sharply. In the style of a scholastic dispute, Jesus' opponents bring up current divorce practice, which is based on Deuteronomy 24 (Matt. 19:7) and which they say Moses "commanded" (*eneteilato*, ενετειλατο). Matthew's Jesus replies that Moses "allowed" them to divorce their wives because of their hardness of heart.[120] However, "from the beginning it was not so," and Matthew implies that the permanent union of husband and wife is the proper reading of the Bible and God's will. Then Jesus teaches the proper interpretation of the Bible, as he did more concisely in chapter 5, that remarriage after divorce is adultery.[121] Matthew thus ends his scholastic dispute over biblical interpretation in the technically proper way: Jesus the authoritative teacher, having presented his evidence and refuted his opponents, articulates his rule governing marriage and divorce.

That this precision in argumentation is not a fluke can be seen in the exception to the divorce teaching which Matthew alone among the gospel writers allows.[122] Matthew's Jesus teaches that remarriage after divorce is not allowed, except if the divorce is for "unchastity" (19:9), and he argues in classic case-law fashion: "Whoever divorces his wife, except for unchastity, and marries another, commits adultery."[123] In enunciating this rule, Jesus answers the question which began the dialogue, "Is it lawful to divorce one's wife for any cause?" (19:2). But what is this single cause for which divorce is allowed? The meaning of *porneia*, "unchastity," has been argued at length with little agreement.[124] *Porneia* can be used for a wide variety of sexual infractions, including fornication, prostitution, and incest. The most common interpretation of this passage has been adultery. Recently, an argument has been made on the basis of a number of hints in Second Temple documents that any sexual irregularity (adultery or rape) required divorce.[125] Either of these interpretations would explain Joseph's decision to divorce Mary, his betrothed, when he found her pregnant by some other agency than himself (Matt. 1:18–19).[126] In addition, on the basis of the prohibition of marriage within certain degrees of consanguinity and the labeling of such unions as prostitution *(zenut)* in the Covenant of Damascus, Joseph Fitzmyer has suggested that Matthew, too, forbids these unions and thus allows the dissolution of certain consanguinous marriages among gentile converts.[127]

Matthew's terminology and concern about *porneia* is consistent with what the later Mishnah and midrashim report was the view of the school of Shammai, transmitted in the Mishnah Gittin (9:10), that one could divorce one's wife for "indecency" (*'erwat dabar* [Dt. 24:1], literally, "indecency of a matter").[128] The school of Hillel held that one could divorce for any, even trivial, cause. They interpreted the Hebrew word *dabar* ("thing, matter, word") separately from the word for "indecency," with which it belongs grammatically. Thus any "matter" which estranged a husband from his wife was grounds for divorce. Specifically, the school of Hillel said that a man may divorce his wife "even if she spoiled his dish of food." Underlying this exegesis was probably the principle that marriage had to be voluntary, and if one party (the man in traditional Judaism) wanted to separate, then it was better to do so. This Mishnah dates from about 200 c.e., and the midrash on Deuteronomy, which has further arguments supporting the Hillelite side, is probably later.[129] The context of the debate between the houses does not help the dating because the debate is the final Mishnah of Tractate Gittin (Writs of Divorce). Chapters 8–9 of Gittin concern improprieties which render a writ invalid, concluding with Mishnah 9:9, concerning rumors of divorce. The final Mishnah of the tractate (9:10) treats grounds for divorce after all aspects of writing and delivering a writ have been covered. This final comment is in no way dependent on the previous, sophisticated discussions of agency and stipulations necessary for a valid writ of divorce. The dispute on the grounds for divorce is based on Deut. 24:1 and cannot be dated from context. An additional comment in that Mishnah, however, does suggest a date contemporary with Matthew. Rabbi Akiba, who was killed during the Bar Kosiba War (132–35), comments on the dispute by offering a further interpretation of Deut. 24:1 that supports the Hillelite position. "Rabbi Akiba says, 'Even if he found another prettier than she, as it says, "If she find no favor in his eyes."'" Note that Akiba's view is not a free-standing opinion, but presumes that the matter of divorce has already been raised by the schools of Hillel and Shammai. Thus Akiba attests to the prior existence of the dispute over the grounds for divorce.[130] On the basis of Akiba's and Matthew's attestations to the debate concerning grounds for divorce, it is likely that the Shammaite view (that divorce should be initiated only for sexual impropriety) was known in the late first century and that Matthew was influenced by it. The nature of this debate is further elucidated by a difficult passage in the Covenant of Damascus (CD 4:12–5:14) and a rule concerning the king in the Temple Scroll (11QTemple 57:17–19), concerning which Fitzmyer has argued that both polygamy and remarriage while the divorced spouse lived were forbidden by the Qumran community.[131]

Even if the texts are interpreted to refer to polygamy only, or if the Temple Scroll's rule is taken to be valid only for the king and to have no implications for the ordinary people, it is clear that marriage issues were a fertile field for discussion in the Second Temple and early rabbinic periods. Matthew's formulation of Jesus' teaching, whether it reports or modifies what Jesus taught, fits firmly within the first-century debates on divorce law and is part of a lively and ongoing controversy.[132]

Matthew's particular interest in divorce can be seen by the place he gave it in the Sermon on the Mount. The teaching on divorce comes as the last of a triad of teachings concerned with family and social stability (5:21–32). Likewise, chapter 19 treats marriage, divorce, celibacy, and children.[133] Harmony in family and social relations, fidelity in male-female relations, and permanence in marriage are all crucial to the health and stability of a small community that is new and under pressure from outside forces. If the members nurse resentments or fail to achieve stable family relationships, then their group will dissolve. An established group can use its traditions and structures to withstand a reasonable amount of conflict, but a small vulnerable social unit has nothing to fall back on. The members must actively create and maintain the relationships which form the substance of the group; if they do not, the group ceases to exist.

Oaths and Vows

The second triad of teachings presented by Matthew in the Sermon on the Mount (5:33–48) concerns public rather than family issues: oaths, legal recourse to solve disputes, and relations with one's enemies and "outsiders." These teachings articulate further Matthew's vision of the relationships which bind the group together and give it its identity and boundaries. The prohibition against taking oaths (5:33–37) is an early teaching of the Jesus tradition, found also in James 5:12. Matthew supports his teaching by an attack on the criteria used to assess the validity of oaths (23:16–22) and on certain vows (15:3–6). The cultural context of the prohibition is threefold, a critique of the excessive use of oaths, an attack on the misuse of oaths, and an exhortation to simple truthfulness.

As was noted in chapter 3, oaths and vows were very common in ancient society and were taken very seriously. Writers and teachers sought to preserve the sanctity and seriousness of oaths, to prevent people from making frivolous oaths, and to distinguish valid from invalid commitments. In the Bible, oaths are presumed to be part of the judicial and social system (Deut. 6:13; 10:20) and are regulated as such. One is not to "take the name of the Lord God in vain," especially when testifying in legal proceedings (Exod. 20:7, 16; 23:1; Deut. 5:11, 20). These and other biblical passages show a special interest in legal proceedings and a more general concern for the sanctity of God's name, which is not to be used "vainly or emptily." The purpose of these prohibitions is just social relations. A concise set of instructions in Leviticus 19 expands much of the content of the Ten Commandments and includes the command to love one's neighbor (v. 18). It associates swearing falsely and profaning God's name (v. 12) with stealing, dealing deceitfully, lying, defrauding, robbing, and withholding a laborer's wages (vv. 11–13). In general, oaths and vows were to be scrupulously fulfilled for the sake of justice and God's name (Num. 30:3).

Matthew's resistance to oaths and vows has many precedents. Reluctance to make oaths and warnings against false or excessive swearing are common in Jewish and Greco-Roman literature.[134] The Covenant of Damascus warns against using certain forms of God's name in taking oaths (CD 15:1) though it affirms the importance of binding oneself to the covenant by a solemn oath (CD 15:5). The Temple Scroll regulates some cases of vows and repeats the biblical rule that vows must be kept.[135] True to most Jewish literature, it does not encourage vows. Josephus portrays the Essenes as refusing to take oaths (in the public sphere) because their word was to be binding and the appeal to God cast doubt on one's probity.[136] In listing the proofs for the Essenes' love of God, Philo mentions among many virtues the "abstinence from oaths" and "veracity."[137] Philo elsewhere urges avoidance of oaths in order to maintain truthfulness in all speech and protects the sanctity of God by suggesting that euphemisms rather than God's name be used.[138] The Covenant of Damascus prohibited all oaths using divine names or the Torah and ordered that all oaths be taken on the "curses of the covenant."[139] These regulations preserved the sanctity of God's name because infractions against the curses associated with the covenant were violations of an oath, not profanation of the divine name, a greater crime. Later rabbinic literature expended much effort in regulating and controlling oaths and vows, especially in Tractates Shebuot and Nedarim.[140] Mishnah Nedarim 1–9 reviews an imaginative tangle of vows that were common in the late second century, and this bears testimony to the continuing popularity and variety of vows. Excessive or trivial use of oaths, disrespect for the divine name, imprudent or erroneous vows, and the use of deceitful oaths are all of concern in rabbinic literature, as they were in Greco-Roman literature.[141]

Matthew's criticism of oaths in 5:31–32 and 23:16–22 and of vows in 15:3–6 are part of this broader discussion. Like his contemporaries, Matthew treats as real oaths those which use substitutes for God's name (23:16–22) and at the same time discourages them. The examples Matthew gives are all known from Jewish literature in late antiquity. Oaths by "heaven and earth" are found in Philo and the Mishnah.[142] Oaths in the name of Jerusalem and vows by the life of one's head are known to the compilers of the Mishnah a century later.[143] They, too, are to be avoided. Matthew's teaching on validity of oaths taken with euphemisms and his mockery of excessive oath-taking is in alignment with the views of other teachers in the first and second centuries. However, the mockery of oaths (chap. 23) presumes that people take oaths and does not explicitly forbid them.[144]

In the Sermon on the Mount, Matthew explicitly forbids taking oaths.[145] First, he correctly summarizes the biblical teaching on oaths: "You have heard that it was said to those of ancient times, 'You shall not swear falsely, but shall perform to the Lord what you have sworn'" (5:31). Then he has Jesus teach his followers to avoid oaths: "Do not swear at all. . . . Let what you say be "Yes, yes" or "No, no"; anything more than this comes from the evil one [or evil]." Grammatically, the repetition of yes or no is a strong affirmation or denial, not a substitute oath formula.[146] Thus Matthew seems to be advocating simple truthfulness and trustworthiness.[147] Matthew forbids swearing oaths, but nothing is said about invalidating oaths and vows. Presumably if one makes an oath or vow, it must be kept, since it has been sworn in God's name. In teaching this, Matthew is close to the Covenant of Damascus and the Temple Scroll.

A similar prohibition appears in the Letter of James, an ethical, wisdom treatise. "Do not swear, either by heaven or by earth or with any other oath, but let your yes [be] yes and your no [be] no, that you may not fall under condemnation" (Jas. 5:12). This saying is disconnected from its immediate context, and thus we learn no more from James than we do from Matthew concerning the origin of the early Christian reluctance to take oaths. The nature of James' exhortation is to encourage simple truthfulness.[148] Certainly this is an object of Matthew's injunction also, but is more intended in Matthew? Matthew is recommending to his group that the members relate to one another with truthfulness and that they avoid oaths, which imply an adversarial relationship in the courts or marketplace. The brevity of his instruction in chapter 5 precludes knowing his full meaning, but the tendency of the saying is against all oaths, and this interpretation is supported by both the narrative and the mockery of vows in chapter 23.[149]

Matthew's negative attitude toward oaths matches the failure of oaths to substantiate truth in his passion narrative. The use of both juridical and personal oaths there leads, not to the uncovering of the truth and the doing of justice, but to falsehood and injustice. In his desire to convict Jesus, the high priest is said to suborn witnesses (26:59). At the same time, when Peter is identified as a follower of Jesus by members of the high priest's household, he first takes an oath that he is not with Jesus and then swears and curses against the accusation (26:72, 74). Thus Jesus is both abandoned and condemned to death through false oaths. But between these false oaths, Jesus is adjured to speak truthfully under oath by the high priest and to say whether he is the "Messiah, the Son of God" (26:62−64). He responds truthfully but without taking an oath. He simply affirms that he is what the high priest has suggested and that he is also the apocalyptic Son of Man. The function of oaths in the passion narrative substantiates Matthew's earlier distrust and prohibition of them.

Oaths and vows were often treated similarly in antiquity because in both instances a diety's name and power were invoked. Vows are promises to dedicate something to a diety and thus to remove it from one's own use. One could dedicate something of value to a temple, or vow not to enjoy the use of something in honor of a diety, or vow to undertake some action. Vows were usually conditional on receiving some favor from the diety or performed to win favor. The making of a vow was voluntary, but once made, its fulfillment was obligatory. The Bible does not mandate the making of vows, but regulates them once they are made and demands that they be carried out (Deut. 23:21−23; Num. 6, 30). Many sacrificial offerings were in payment of vows (Lev. 22:17−25; Num. 15:1−10). Various biblical figures made vows. For example, Jacob promises to worship and tithe if he is protected (Gen. 28:20; 33:13), and Hannah vows her son Samuel's service in return for his conception (1 Sam. 1:11). Vows were a normal part of ancient life, but the biblical tradition did not greatly encourage them.

In the first century, vows dedicating property to the Temple were common. Consequently, the Temple treasury was called the *Korban* (Matt. 27:6) because the formula for this type of vow used the biblical expression for "offering," *qŏrbān* (found in Lev. 1:2, etc.). *Korban* was well known in Greek as a Jewish oath (not vow) formula.[150] Josephus attests that Theophrastus (fourth century B.C.E.) refers to it as a foreign oath forbidden by the Tyrians.[151] Josephus uses *qorban* in the correct sense to designate a vow when he is explaining the vows found in Lev. 27:1−9, namely, that people would declare themselves *qŏrbān* to God and then fulfill their vow by paying the priests a fixed sum of money (*Ant.* 4.4.4 §73). The Gospel of Mark (7:11, parallel to Matt. 15:3−6) uses *qŏrbān* of property dedicated to God or the Temple and thus not available for parental support. The Hebrew or Aramaic expression *qŏrbān* is inscribed on a fragment of a stone vessel with birds on it, excavated from Herodian Jerusalem, and the Aramaic is also known from an ossuary inscription which warns that the contents of the ossuary are dedicated and thus should not be stolen.[152] The Mishnah testifies to the continued use of this terminology for vows through the second century.[153]

Matthew takes up the discussion of vows (15:3–6) in a very polemical attack on the Pharisees and scribes which he received from Mark (Mark 7:1–23; Matt. 15:1–20). As we saw above, this complex discussion wrestles with reliance on tradition, handwashing, ritual and moral purity, bearing fruit, and understanding of God's law. Matthew attacks both the Pharisees' concrete interpretations of certain biblical laws and their more general approach to law. Along with the Sermon on the Mount and the polemic in chapter 23, this series of teachings is a major Matthean statement of how God's law is to be interpreted and obeyed. Matthew charges the Pharisees with supporting vows which result in the neglect of one's parents, and thus with subverting biblical law by their tradition.[154] In Matthew's view, because the Pharisees misinterpret the law and lack inner integrity (15:6–9), their understanding of purity and handwashing is false also (15:10–20). From the opposite perspective, the Pharisees and scribes from Jerusalem formally challenge Jesus' authority as a teacher on the basis of his disciples' misbehavior: they do not wash their hands when they eat (15:2). Jesus accepts the challenge to interpret the law, but he moves the debate onto a question from which he can attack the authority and accuracy of his opponents.[155] As in the Sabbath controversies (12:1–14), Jesus poses a clash of two laws: that vows should be kept and that parents in need should be supported by their children. No Jewish teacher would deny either law; the question is how the two are to be reconciled when a conflict occurs.

The dilemma posed by a vow to support the Temple to the detriment of the commandment to support one's parents engages several aspects of the Jewish tradition. The tradition counsels against imprudent vows which cause problems, yet it provides few resources for release from vows. In the Bible, Jephthah's rash and inhumane vow, which required him to sacrifice his daughter, was carried out (Judg. 11:29–40). Fathers and husbands may void a woman's vow under certain circumstances, but that is because the woman is seen as insufficiently independent to make a vow (Num. 30). The Mishnah improved the situation somewhat by distinguishing types of invalid vows (m. Ned.

2:1–2) and various grounds for releasing people from vows (m. Ned. 3:1–4). But the Mishnaic authors recognized a serious problem: "[Rules for] release from vows hover in the air and do not have anywhere upon which to land" (m. Hag. 1:8).[156] It is likely that in the late-first century, before the Mishnaic laws were developed, the problem of release from vows was acute.[157] It is this ongoing problem which Matthew addresses.

Because of his polemical broadside against both his opponents' teaching and their integrity, Matthew's account of their views is unreliable.[158] Yet the issue raised by Jesus fits into the development of Jewish teaching on vows and the clashes among various schools of thought. "Why do you transgress the command of God for the sake of your tradition?" is a charge typical of sectarian strife. One party accuses the other of abandoning Scripture and substituting human teaching, viewing its own interpretations and traditions as simple and correct understandings of Scripture.[159] As always, Matthew is careful to preserve Scripture as authoritative. The contrast is between what they say, which is inadequate, and what Scripture says.[160] Implicit in this charge is an accusation of misplaced priorities (similar to that found in 23:23) that lead the opponents away from Scripture. The author then builds a case against certain vows as a groundwork for his attack on handwashing. In the conflict between devoting vowed property to the purpose for which it was vowed and using the property to support one's needy parents, the opponents opted for fidelity to the vow, probably because it was a clear and specific commitment, difficult to evade.[161] Baumgarten suggests with some plausibility that the Pharisees (in Matthew's situation, possibly the early rabbinic group) had developed only very restricted grounds for releasing people from vows.[162] Even the Mishnah struggles with whether a person can be released from a vow for the honor of his parents (m. Ned. 9:1). Matthew disagrees with a group which stresses the fulfillment of vows, and he pleads that fidelity to Scripture demands keeping the commandments in preference to a human vow, even though vows invoke the divine name and are supposed to be fulfilled.

Circumcision

Circumcision is not mentioned as a problem in Matthew. The gospel's silence on this issue implies that circumcision was not controversial in Matthew's community. Most commentators, if they even take up the problem at all, assume that by the late first century the Pauline view, that circumcision was not necessary for gentiles who believed in Jesus, had prevailed and circumcision had died out among Christians, except among Jewish-Christians, who were rapidly becoming an insignificant minority.[163] Several aspects of the development of Christianity and Judaism argue against this assumption. First, Christianity and Judaism were both made up of diverse groups and communities in the first centuries, so blanket statements meant to characterize adequately the whole of Judaism or Christianity are very suspect. Second, many believers-in-Jesus in Israel and greater Syria remained socially and intellectually part of Judaism for a long time. Third, the influence of Pauline thought on the author of Matthew and his group is very doubtful.[164] Finally, the Gospel of Matthew, as we have seen above, debates concrete interpretations of law with Jewish opponents. If circumcision were not practiced, Matthew would have had to defend his position on the basis of Jesus' teaching and reading of Scripture. However, no Jesus traditions challenge circumcision. The fact that it is not brought up in the gospel suggests that Matthew and his opponents agree on the importance of circumcision.[165]

What about circumcision of the gentile members of Matthew's group? Gentiles appear in the narrative as marginal figures who are interested in and impressed by Jesus, but who do not become faithful followers (see chap. 4 above). The final scene of the gospel, in which Jesus exhorts his disciples to go forth to teach all nations, is most probably Matthew's call to his mostly Jewish followers to include gentiles within their number. Thus at the time the gospel was written, not many gentiles were members of Matthew's group and those who had joined may have been circumcised so they could participate in communal life fully, without conflict over Sabbath observance, dietary and purity regulations, and so on. Whatever the position on circumcision may have been, the final scene of the gospel also shows that the early Christian practice of baptism was decisive for membership in the group.

However, since the argument is from silence, the opposite may be true. Matthew's group may indeed have accepted gentile members without demanding circumcision. Usually commentators assume that this would mean that the group was no longer Jewish. If circumcision is treated as a sine qua non of being a Jew, then this is true. But there is ample evidence that the sharp boundary between Jew and gentile found in talmudic literature was much more fuzzy in the first century than it was to become later. First, though circumcision was an ancient and continuous practice in Israel, it was emphasized as a crucial identity marker only during the Maccabean period, when Antiochus IV sought to suppress the Jewish way of life by forbidding circumcision, promoting idolatry, and destroying the Torah (1 Macc. 1:44–63). From then on, circumcision was considered by many Jews and non-Jews as one of a complex of practices and symbols crucial to Jewish identity. The resistance to Antiochus made circumcision all the more important.

However, there is another side to the emphasis on circumcision. Some of the Jewish leaders in Jerusalem during the second century tried to cover the marks of circumcision through epispasm so they could live as Greeks and exercise naked (1 Macc. 1:11–15; 2 Macc. 4:11–17). Presumably they stopped circumcising their children as well. Though they are censured for their behavior in Maccabees and labeled as apostates, sociologically they did not cease to be Jews when they dropped circumcision. They lived in Israel, had power and standing within the nation, were identified as Jews by gentiles, and indeed by their Jewish opponents who called them apostates—for as we have discussed, an apostate is a deviant from a community, and the label "deviant" or "apostate" sociologically reaffirms one's membership (no matter how compromised) in the group doing the labeling, despite efforts to expel the offending member. At various points in history, many Jews, as well as members of other religions and ethnic groups, have been nonobservant of many laws and customs. Emphasis on circumcision was not universal for Jews in the ancient world. Much of Greek-Jewish literature, especially the works which sought to enhance the status of Jews in the Greek world by emphasizing similarities rather than differences, omits mention of circumcision.[166] The Third and Fifth Sibylline Oracles and the Letter of Aristeas promote worship of the one God (whom they claim gentiles actually worship) with proper sacrifices and moral behavior. Aristeas defends separatist laws by allegorizing them and relating them to Greek values, but among them it does not mention circumcision. The Egyptian story of Joseph and Aseneth recounts the conversion of Aseneth and her marriage to Joseph in such a way that Jews may live in close relationship with gentiles and yet defend the superiority of Judaism.[167] Emphasis is placed on rejection of idolatry, observance of dietary laws, and purity. Circumcision is not mentioned, perhaps because the convert is a woman. Yet the avoidance of the problem of circumcision by creating a female convert may be deliberate.[168] In all of these works, avoidance of idolatry is much more important than circumcision. Refusal to participate in Greco-Roman worship separated Jews much more decisively from the rest of the Mediterranean world than dietary laws or circumcision.[169] For their part, some Jewish authors emphasized the worship of one God and praised the rejection of false gods. They stressed that gentiles could worship the true God without circumcision. This evidence does not deny that circumcision was practiced by Jews and ordinarily required of converts. It shows, however, that it was not demanded in all circumstances.

Among some Jews, circumcision may have been omitted in certain cases.[170] The evidence is slight and controversial, but it cannot be ignored. In his explanations of circumcision, Philo stresses its moral meaning and does not use it as a defining characteristic of Jewish identity.[171] Yet he affirms the necessity of physically observing the commandment to circumcise. This kind of defense of this and other laws has led scholars to infer that there were some Alexandrian Jews who did not observe the commandments, including the commandment to circumcise.[172] Surprisingly, the Mishnah does not use circumcision as a taxonomic index of who is and is not a Jew, though it presumes that a Jew will be circumcised.[173] Even so, the question of circumcision is still discussed. Talmudic authors debated the necessity of circumcision in ambiguous cases and on the relative importance of immersion and circumcision in the conversion process. R. Joshua is reported to have held that immersion alone made one a legitimate convert (b. Yeb. 46b) and that if the situation required, circumcision could be delayed. The discussion assumes, however, that a man will be circumcised, and the majority opinion, representing the talmudic period, is that both rituals are needed for a proper conversion.[174] Such discussions show that in the talmudic period, and certainly earlier in the first century, practices surrounding circumcision were, like many other practices and laws, local and varied. The uniform code of law and practice promoted by the Talmud did not have its effect on many Jewish communities for several centuries.

Talmudic passages which discuss circumcision treat Israelites who have not been circumcised, probably because of hemophilia (b. Pes. 96a; b. Hul. 4b; b. Yeb. 64b), and of gentiles who have just been converted and want to eat the Passover meal (m. Pes. 9:5; b. Pes. 92b).[175] The case of Izates, who wished to become a Jew but was advised to refuse circumcision because he would have lost his crown (Josephus, *Ant.* 20.2.3 §34–46), suggests that there was a legitimate difference of view concerning the necessity of circumcision in extreme cases.[176] The story shows clearly that not fulfilling the commandment of circumcision is something undesirable, but God will grant forgiveness (42) although Jewish law requires circumcision (43). But the story also supports Izates' course of action, which is to keep Jewish law without circumcision. It teaches, following good Hellenistic, diaspora Jewish ethics, that keeping the ancestral customs of the Jews is more important than circumcision. This implies that Izates is doing what is essential to be a Jew, submitting to God's will and keeping the command-ments. He does not become circumcised because if he does, his subjects will regard him as a Jew and may revolt.[177]

This ambiguity over obeying God's will and becoming a Jew in the full sense can also be seen in the controversy over the so-called God-fearers. Both Jewish and Greco-Roman authors testify that many gen-tiles were attracted to synagogue worship and to observance of Jewish customs.[178] They were often mocked and treated as Jews by their own groups; they certainly supported and related closely to the Jewish community. Gentile followers of Jesus, especially if they were few in number, may have related to the Matthean group in the same way, without compromising its Jewishness.[179]

The evidence for Jews who thought that circumcision was not nec-essary for membership in Israel is weak, but granted the lack of data on diaspora communities, not to be dismissed. These peculiar cases sup-port two highly probable conclusions. First, circumcision was not a central theme to all Jewish writers. Rejecting other gods, keeping Jew-ish customs, worshiping in the synagogue, observing dietary laws, and keeping the commandments were considered laudable and important, even without circumcision. Second, the status of uncircumcised gen-tiles who attached themselves to the synagogue and kept Jewish law was not sharply defined. This is meant in two senses. They were not an official class of "semi-proselytes" or "God-fearers," but neither were they just gentiles with no relationship to Israel or God. Gentiles in Matthew's group were probably accepted on the same basis: some may have been circumcised and some not. The relationship each had with God in faith through Jesus was the central focus of their commitment.

Matthew's Torah

The characters in Matthew's narrative do not conduct legal discussion as a dispassionate search for truth in a school. Legal disagreement is a mode of polemic here and in much of first-century Jewish litera-ture.[180] The underdogs in social and religious disputes typically used differences in interpretation and practice of law to discredit commu-nity leaders who were their opponents. An appeal to a "true" under-standing of the law supplies to the protester the authority he lacks in society as a whole and seeks to undermine the authority and veracity of the established leaders.[181] In addition, changes in laws, which sup-port community identity and boundaries, cause deep social and inter-nal changes in a group's outlook and practices. Changes in purity and dietary laws affect the group's perception of its holiness and relationship to both God and the world. Changes in marriage laws, oaths, and vows affect internal relationships that bind members together. Changes in Sabbath observance reflect changes in the perception of God and of relationships between heaven and earth. The changes in practice and understanding which Matthew proposes, though thoroughly Jewish, aim to reorientate and reform the Jewish community deeply and comprehensively.

But how does Matthew arrive at his teachings and what warrant does he give for their veracity? Though Matthew does not set forth his legal or hermeneutical philosophy thematically in a preface or discursive chapter, a number of comments and his placement of legal discussions in the narrative give clues to his outlook. The importance of Matthew's teaching can be seen in the number of sermons and the intensity of Matthew's conflicts with the Pharisees and scribes. After a general report concerning Jesus' activities, the Sermon on the Mount (chaps. 5–7) provides an elaborate and detailed account of Jesus' teaching and the way of life he proposes. His teaching is also the cause of the conflict with the scribes and Pharisees, which begins in chapters 11–12 and reaches a climax in Galilee in the dispute over purity, handwashing, and vows in chapter 15. Finally, just before his arrest, Jesus systematically attacks the scribes and Pharisees' whole program for the Jewish community (chap. 23). Throughout all this, Jesus continues to teach his understanding of God and his kingdom in the sermons (chaps. 10, 13, 18, 24–25), culminating in the commission to his followers to teach all nations (28:19–20). Thus Matthew relates both his group's teachings and their ostracism by the leadership of the Jewish community to Jesus' life and teachings. Jesus' teachings are of crucial importance, according to Matthew, because they have an effect on life, come from God and the Bible, and are essential to the welfare of the Jewish community and the world.

In places, Matthew affirms certain key components of his understanding of God's law and the relative importance of various commandments. The law is not to be changed but "fulfilled" in two ways: in Jesus' life, which corresponds to God's promises in the Bible, and in Jesus' teachings, which lay bare the true meaning and requirements of the law (5:17–19). Matthew means for his group to obey fully the demands of the law as they are understood through Jesus' teaching.[182] He makes no distinction between the law and the prophets, but sees the law as prophetic (11:13; 9:13; 12:7) and prophecy as teaching the law, that is, the will of God (5:17; 7:12). Fulfillment of the law does not mean replacement of the law with Jesus or abrogation of the details of Torah through the love commandment. Rather, the commandments of the law, including the love commandments, are to be understood and obeyed in dynamic relationship with one another.[183]

The core of the law is the Ten Commandments, which are assessed as more fundamental than purity regulations (15:17–19), as categorically binding over sectarian traditions (15:3–6, 20), and as the foundation of Jesus' special emphases in his teaching (5:21–30). Other core values which Matthew singles out are justice, mercy, faith(fulness), and Godlike perfection (5:20, 48; 9:13; 12:7; 23:23). These qualities override Sabbath observance in the face of human need (12:1–14), subordinate tithing to larger virtues (23:23–24), give sinners access to Jesus (9:9–13), and reshape social relations. According to the Sermon on the Mount, Jesus' greater justice (5:20) will suppress anger and lust and stabilize human relationships so that neither divorce nor oaths nor legal retaliation will be necessary (5:21–42). Rather, people will mean what they say, be generous with one another even in the face of wrong, and love their enemies (5:43–47).[184] In thus transforming social relations and the attitudes which underlie them, the members of Matthew's group will be characterized by a righteousness greater than that of their rivals, the scribes and Pharisees, and they will be perfect, like God (5:48).[185] Matthew's interpretation of biblical law is neither an abrogation nor a surpassing of that law, but a correct understanding and fulfillment of it. The six so-called antitheses (5:21–48) are not understood by Matthew as changes in God's law, but as a more penetrating appreciation of and obedience to the law.[186] The actions encouraged are not violations of any biblical law; they uphold the law. Though from a strictly logical point of view, some of the six antitheses could be seen as changes in the law, scholars do not agree on which ones. Given Matthew's framework and consistent teaching, it is unlikely that he would admit to changes in Scripture. Instead, he has Jesus teach authoritatively the true meaning of the law and at the same time refute his (Matthew's) opponents' views.[187]

The two greatest commandments, to love God and neighbor (Matt. 22:34–40; Deut. 6:5; Lev. 19:18), summarize the teaching of Matthew's Jesus. The double commandment near the end of Jesus' life balances the teaching on love for enemies at the beginning of his career (5:43–48) and gives further definition to the notion of just social relations and attitudes promoted by Matthew. The demands of the law and the prophets can be summarized by the golden rule (7:12), and they depend on the love commandments (22:40). The love commandments are alluded to elsewhere (19:19; 24:12), along with closely related values such as mercy and justice. The weightier things in the law must be given precedence (23:23), though the lesser things may not be neglected or voided (23:23; 5:19). Though many Christian interpreters have understood this emphasis as a rejection of Jewish law (which is understood as legalistic and meaningless), Matthew is more concrete and demanding. Love *(hesed)* cannot be directly legislated, so its framework must be outlined with laws.[188] The love commandments serve as the center of the law, giving to the Bible and Jesus' teachings an order and thrust that distinguish Matthew's group from other Jewish communities and movements.[189] Thus the emphasis on the love commandments, mercy, and justice, like the particular interpretations of other laws in Matthew, serve both to give the community its internal orientation and to identify it in contrast to other groups..

The authority for Matthew's teaching comes from its author in the narrative, Jesus. Thus Jesus' relationship with God, high status, and divinely given knowledge and mandate (3:13–17; 11:25–27) are crucial to Matthew's claims and will be taken up in the next chapter. Jesus' own authority is passed on to Peter and the community he leads (16:16; 18:18–20). His followers may bind and loose in God's name and God will be in their midst. The author of Matthew envisions his own teaching authority as that of a scribe (13:52; 23:34) who, along with the prophets and sages, guides the followers of Jesus and, potentially, all of Israel. Matthew's scribal authority is in continuity with that of Israel because he brings forth from the storeroom things old and new (13:52), that is, he affirms Israel's tradition as taught and interpreted by Jesus.

Both life in the kingdom of God and the discernment of good from evil depend on the law in Matthew. A person who is faithful to God understands God's commandments, that is, his self revelation, and obeys them sincerely and often without public notice. Since Matthew is the leader of a reform group in the Jewish community, understanding of and obedience to God's commands cannot be derived from generally accepted community practices or from the teachings of its established leaders, who are judged to be blind guides and hypocrites. Jesus and his designated followers (Matthew) provide guidance for those who seek God faithfully. The guidance is not simply the general injunction to love God and neighbor, though this double command is foundational and important. Faithful adherence to an interpretation of all the commandments that stresses justice and mercy is the core of Jesus' message and of the Matthean way of life. These central emphases qualify the rigid enforcement of the law: Human need can override observance of the Sabbath in certain circumstances, and stable human relationships built on love will obviate the need for divorce and oaths. Legal retaliation will not be necessary, and love of enemies will repair broken relationships. Tithing, purity, and dietary laws are affirmed but firmly subordinated to justice, mercy, faithfulness, and love. Matthew thus envisions his little group of believers-in-Jesus influencing Jewish society to become an ideal community ruled by God, that is, the "kingdom of heaven."

VII

Jesus, Messiah and
Son of God

Thus far in this study, the social relationships of Matthew's group to the Jewish community and the group's place in Jewish tradition have dominated the discussion. The claims Matthew makes for Jesus in the narrative, especially his high status and divinely given power, have not been thematically treated. Since Jesus is the main character and dominant interest in the gospel, we must explain how the author understood Jesus and his importance within the context of late first-century Judaism. Usually theological reflections on Matthean Christology emphasize the decisive separation between Judaism and belief in Jesus. As we have seen, however, the boundaries between Judaism and emerging Christianity were not firmly drawn in the late first century, especially in Matthew's milieu. Many believers-in-Jesus understood Jesus as a thoroughly Jewish figure completely consistent with Jewish tradition and life. Thus the proper setting for a study of Jesus in Matthew is theology in its literal sense, that is, a consideration of God and God's activity through Jesus.[1] Modern Christians tend to read the New Testament as a primitive or incomplete Christology on its way to classical formulation in the third through sixth centuries. But early believers-in-Jesus sought to understand Jesus of Nazareth, the prophetic teacher and wonderworker, in his relationship with God. To do so, they used all the resources provided in their traditions and cultures.[2] Because the task was new and complex, their understandings of Jesus and evaluations of his life and teaching varied greatly. The object of this brief treatment is to grasp what one of those followers, the author of Matthew, was saying to a Jewish group who had accepted Jesus as Messiah and Son of God and to appreciate his claims and commitments without reference to later christological developments.[3]

Jesus as Son of God and Messiah can be understood as a Jewish figure because Matthew's Christology is completely embedded in his theology, which is itself explicitly and deeply rooted in the Bible as it was understood by much of first-century Judaism. Matthew's claims for Jesus' high status and special roles in the narrative are based on Jesus' close relationship with God, his participation in the biblical traditions of Israel, and his fulfilling of God's will in bringing the kingdom of God. The author of Matthew, in telling the story of Jesus, is making something more out of Jesus than he does of other figures in Israel. But his claims for Jesus' special, high status and roles are based on very concrete, traditional, Jewish warrants. Jesus has a special relationship with God as God's Son; "son of God" is a traditional title for divinely approved Jewish leaders. Jesus' authority and power come from God, who legitimizes him at his baptism (3:17) to teach, heal, preach repentance, and command. According to Matthew, Jesus has a special relationship with Israel as the fulfillment of its traditions. His ultimate victories over his opponents, namely, overcoming suffering and death through resurrection and the judgment of evil at the end of the world, are a concretization of Jewish apocalyptic hopes. Matthew called his listeners to involve themselves in a "participatory Christology," which would transform the believer into a follower of Jesus.[4]

Though the characterization of Jesus derives from first-century Jewish teaching, the intense focus on him and the high claims made for him imply a new divine intervention and revelation to Israel. The author of Matthew builds a case for an intense commitment to Jesus and his way of life. Matthew claims that Jesus is God's presence with humans (1:23; 18:20; 28:20) to save them from their sins (1:21; 20:28). Jesus' goal is achieved by his teaching and healing and preeminently by his death, which leads to his resurrection (chaps. 26–28) and the ultimate vindication of the just at the final judgment (25:31–46).

Jesus' place in Matthew's world is communicated by his roles in the narrative and his titles.[5] The narrative is centered on Jesus' activity, his teaching, his relationships with his contemporaries, and his death and resurrection. All are presented as significant indicators of his relationship with God, his authority, power, underlying goals, and future roles. Even Jesus' most transcendent roles are intimately linked with his birth as a Jew, his life in Galilee as a teacher, and his conflict with the national authorities in Jerusalem.[6] The titles attributed to Jesus by the author of Matthew significantly affect the reader's evaluation of Jesus. The relationships among the titles and their relative importance and "doctrinal content" will not occupy us here. Rather, the interplay of the names, titles, and roles assigned to Jesus by Matthew and the interaction of different characters in the narrative will make clear his complex understanding of Jesus and his relationship to God.[7]

All the activities, names, and relationships attributed to Jesus are thoroughly Jewish. Matthew uses native categories, metaphors, images, and patterns, but the particular emphases in the narrative, the relationships among Jesus' deeds and words, and Matthew's claims for Jesus—all these give a particular cast to Jesus in Matthew.[8] We shall work from the introductory scenes and statements about Jesus at the beginning of the gospel and see how Matthew weaves his understanding of Jesus into the whole narrative.[9] Since a full exposition of Matthew's view of Jesus would itself require a book, our focus will be on the emergence of Matthew's views from his Jewish context and their function in his narrative.

Jesus the Christ, Son of David, Son of Abraham

Matthew introduces his narrative as "The book of the genealogy [or origins, *geneseos*][10] of Jesus Christ, son of David, son of Abraham" (1:1), and it is with these names we will begin. Jesus' personal name suggests the complexity of Matthew's views. "Jesus" derives from the Hebrew name Joshua, which is from the verb root *ys'*, meaning "save." Jesus receives his name from God through an angelic messenger, who commands Joseph: "You shall call his name Jesus, for he will save his people from their sins" (1:21). The narrator habitually refers to Jesus by his personal name, which is seldom used by other characters in the story, and never by Jesus himself.[11] The people in this highly charged narrative never relate to Jesus simply as a Galilean Jew. He is sometimes called "Lord" by his disciples (14:38; 17:4; 18:21; 26:22), though more often no vocative address is used. Nondisciples call Jesus "Lord" when seeking a cure (9:27–31; 15:21–28; 20:29–34). Sincere questioners and opponents address him as "teacher" (8:19; 9:11; 12:38, etc.). Only Judas, the disciple who betrays Jesus, calls him "Rabbi" (26:25, 49), perhaps because this title was used by the author's opponents (23:8). The false witnesses at his trial refer to him as "this man" (26:60), and during the trial, the Sanhedrin has no designation for him (26:55). After the trial, the Sanhedrin mockingly refers to him as "Messiah" (26:68), and later the Roman soldiers mock him as "king of the Jews" (27:29). He refers to himself as the Son of Man (8:20; 9:6; 11:19, etc.). In none of these cases is Jesus simply a person with a name. He is a special figure who possesses positive or negative valence for those who come in contact with him.

Jesus' special role in Matthew is communicated by the title *Messiah*. As early as Paul (the 50s, c.e.), Jesus is referred to frequently as Jesus Christ, not Jesus the Christ. The understanding of Jesus as Messiah was probably the earliest and most central heavenly role attributed to Jesus by his followers.[12] But the interpretation of this title is fraught with dangers and misunderstandings. Christian interpreters have often attributed to first-century Judaism a univocal belief in an eschatological, political, nationalistic Messiah. In reality, not all Jews believed in an afterlife or an apocalyptic ending to the world. Of those who did, some expected a "messianic" figure and some did not. Of those who expected such a figure, that figure varied greatly in name, roles, and relationship to God. In Ethiopic Enoch, angelic intermediaries act in God's stead.[13] At Qumran, two anointed ones are expected, a priestly, Aaronic messiah correlative to the priestly class of the community and a Davidic messiah for the rest of Israel (e.g., 1QS 9:11). Elsewhere a prophet like Moses (cf. Deut. 18:15) and an angelic Melchisedek figure are mentioned.[14] The Samaritans also awaited a prophet like Moses. The Testament of Levi (chap. 18) envisions a new priest who will bring justice at the end. The Book of Daniel speaks of an angelic figure who is "like a son of man" (Dan. 7:13) and who will rule over God's kingdom. The Similitudes of Enoch (1 Enoch 37–71, from the first century C.E.) await a figure called "Son of Man" and "the Chosen One" as judge at the end of the world. Expectations for God's intervention at the end of the world were thus varied at the time of Jesus.

The early believers-in-Jesus had a number of uses for these beliefs and combined them creatively. The opening title and the genealogy claim that Jesus is descended from David and is the anointed king, the Messiah (1:1, 16–17). After the intervention of God at the birth of Jesus, when the Magi come inquiring into the whereabouts of the "king of the Jews" (2:1–12), Herod, the chief priests, and scribes tell them that the Christ is to be born in Bethlehem. The Magi, who seek the Messiah, find him, but Herod, who seeks to kill a rival king, does not. Though Herod fears a political threat to himself, Matthew's Jesus is not an earthly political leader, neither in the infancy narrative nor in the rest of the gospel, nor on the cross, where he is ironically identified as "king of the Jews" by another group of threatened leaders (27:37). Other messianic roles emerge in the narrative. John the Baptist hears in jail about the deeds of the Christ and sends to Jesus asking whether he is the one who is to come (11:2–6). Jesus replies by referring to his healing and teaching as messianic activities. Later Jesus asks Peter to identify him, and when Peter says he is Messiah and Son of God, Jesus attributes his judgment to divine revelation (16:16–17). For Matthew, contrary to Mark (8:27–30), Jesus is not adequately identified as the Messiah only, but must be recognized as Son of God.

Matthew raises the question of Jesus as Messiah when the acceptance or rejection of Jesus' messianic identity is at issue.[15] Those who reject the claim or misuse it are outsiders to Matthew's group; so messianism is a boundary-setting mechanism. It allows further understanding if accepted, and if rejected, it cuts one off. False messiahs illegitimately claim Jesus' roles (24:5, 23; 23:10). Herod (2:7–12, 16–18), the high priest (26:63), the soldiers (26:68), and Pilate (27:17–22) all reject Jesus by misunderstanding his status as Messiah and king. They think of the Messiah as a triumphant king in an earthly sense (2:2; 27:11–37, 42) and either fear or mock or attack Jesus accordingly. But Matthew's Jesus is a humble king (21:5), though as the apocalyptic Son of Man, he will be the king judging all the nations (25:34, 40). Matthew does not dwell greatly on the role of Jesus as Messiah. He assumes the currency of this early Christian claim and uses it as a touchstone for those who are inside or outside the orbit of believers-in-Jesus. To be the savior of Israel and judge at the end of the world, Jesus must be the Messiah, but other roles, activities, and titles occupy a more central place in Matthew's development of Jesus' character.

Matthew follows the identification of Jesus as Christ with the claim he is *son of David*. These two designations are closely intertwined because King David was the divinely chosen and anointed king par excellence. "Son of David" has multiple connotations, which unfold in the narrative. In the genealogy Jesus is traced back to David, and thus he is established as part of the royal family and a legitimate contender for the kingship.[16] The apocalyptic messiah, who is God's anointed and appointed ruler at the end of the world, must also come from the house of David.[17] Thus the family identification with David reinforces Matthew's initial claim that Jesus is the Messiah. This claim is acknowledged twice by the people, once when the crowds acclaim Jesus as the son of David as he enters Jersualem (21:9) and again when the children acclaim him in the Temple after he has driven out the merchants and moneychangers and cured the blind and lame (21:15). In Matthew, the son of David is preeminently a healer.[18] The two blind men in Galilee (9:27), and the two in Jericho (20:30–31) call him "son of David" and "Lord" when they seek to be healed. The Canaanite woman seeking a cure for her possessed daughter (15:23) addresses him as "Lord, son of David" (15:22). When Jesus cures a blind, mute, possessed person, the crowd wonders if he is the son of David (12:23). Near the end of the gospel, the two strands of Matthean messianism, the kingly and the healing, come together in the Temple, the seat of

Israel's government, where the healing Messiah cures the sick and is recognized by some of the people (21:15).

But Matthew's claim that Jesus is son of David is not without its problems. Both the first and last occurrences of "son of David" are ambiguous, the first subtly and the last explicitly. The genealogy which begins with Abraham includes David and continues unbroken to Jacob, the father of Joseph. Here the pattern is broken, for Joseph is not the father of Jesus but only the husband of Mary, who bore Jesus (1:16). Thus the final link of the genealogy that leads to Jesus, the supposed son of David, the Messiah, does not fit into the patterns of father begetting son. That break in the pattern is justified by Joseph's dream, which explains that God has intervened in the birth of Jesus.[19] The story of the virginal conception, which makes clear that Jesus is Son of God, undercuts the claim that he is son of David through his legal and social father, Joseph. But reciprocally, the claim that Jesus is Son of God, as it is developed in the narrative, supports the claim that Jesus is Messiah.[20] Just as David was divinely appointed and anointed as king, so is Jesus the divinely chosen and prepared Messiah, son of David, and king.

The implications of the claim that Jesus is Messiah, son of David, are explored at the end of the narrative, just before Jesus' arrest and death. Jesus himself raises the question of David's son by asking the Pharisees whose son the Messiah is (22:41–42). They answer, as most Jews would, "David's son."[21] Matthew then has Jesus make the argument that he has higher status than David and thus is more than his son. On the basis of Psalm 110, often cited in early Christian literature, Jesus is David's Lord, that is, superior to David in kingly authority.[22] Matthew does not reject the claim that Jesus is son of David, but tries to relate it to the claim that Jesus is also Lord.[23] He builds on the title "son of David" in order to argue that Jesus has the ultimate authority in Israel's tradition. He implies, on the basis of Psalm 110, that if Jesus is David's Lord as well as son, then he is not adequately and fully described as David's son.[24] Matthew implies that Jesus must be God's Son (22:45; cf. the same implication of divine sonship in the birth story in 1:18–25). Matthew neither denies that Jesus is David's son nor says explicitly that he is God's Son. Rather, he asks two troubling questions concerning the application of Psalm 110 to Jesus, neither of which his interlocutors can answer. The inability of the Pharisees to answer these questions concerning Jesus' identity is climactic and final in the narrative because they do not dare to ask him any more questions (22:46). The disciples and readers, however, understand the answer to the questions through divine revelation (16:17); Jesus is Son of God and thus David's Lord at the same time that he is David's son in conventional terms.

In the first sentence of the gospel, Matthew identifies Jesus, finally, as a *son of Abraham*. In its simplest meaning, "son of Abraham" means a Jew. However, even this common denotation has deeper implications, though not as many as "Christ" and "son of David." Matthew more than any gospel writer stresses the Jewishness of Jesus' teaching and work.[25] Yet he opens up the community boundaries to those of non-Jewish ancestry. Just as he includes gentiles in Jesus' ancestry, he also makes them sons of Abraham.[26] John the Baptist challenges the Pharisees and Sadducees to repentance with an apocalyptic threat of judgment (3:8–10). John counteracts overconfidence in being sons of Abraham by the claim that God can raise up children to Abraham from stones (3:9), a metaphor that is not a rejection of Israel, as we have seen, but a prophetic threat against behavior inappropriate to God's people, Israel. Jesus similarly challenges his fellow Jews with the faith of the centurion (8:10–12) and predicts that the banquet in the kingdom of God will have many non-Jews in attendance with the patriarchs and will lack many of the "sons of the kingdom." The relationships of gentiles to Jesus is hinted at and implied in many places, beginning with the story of the Magi (2:1–12), and it reaches its climax at the end of the gospel when Jesus instructs his disciples to teach all nations (28:19–20). Thus Jesus' status as son of Abraham has implications for Jesus' work and those who follow him. These implications are suggested in the scenes following the genealogy and worked out in the course of the narrative.

In introducing Jesus as Messiah, son of David, and son of Abraham in the first sentence of the gospel, the author taps the core of his Jewish tradition. He develops these descriptions of Jesus throughout the narrative and uses them to make Jesus' identity, relationship to God, activities, and goals intelligible to his audience. In no case does he simply assimilate Jesus to a traditional role or category. Rather, the use of each designation in the narrative suggests modifications and hidden possibilities in the Jewish tradition, which Matthew exploits to develop Jesus as a special intermediary sent by God. Within the narrative, Matthew most often presents Jesus in three ways, as the Son of God, teacher, and healer. That he is Son of God is communicated by the story of Joseph's reaction to his conception and by a number of passages which emphasize the title "Son of God." The narrative action between Jesus' birth and death oscillates between the teaching and healing of Israel. Thus it is to these three roles we turn next.

Son of God

Though Jesus is introduced as a son of Abraham, a royal son of David, and God's anointed, the final line of the genealogy and the subsequent story of Jesus' birth point to Jesus' most important role in Matthew, Son of God. The odd notation at the end of the genealogy, that Jesus is son, not of Joseph, but of his wife, Mary (1:16), is immediately explained in the story of Jesus' birth (1:18–25). Jesus' mother is discovered to be pregnant before she has begun to live with Joseph, her betrothed. A divine message from an angel in a dream reassures Joseph that the birth is "legitimate" and that Jesus will have a special role in regard to Israel. Though the conclusion is unstated, clearly Jesus, who is not Joseph's son, is the Son of God. Matthew's point is confirmed by his frequent use of "Son of God" in the narrative.[27] Equally important, God is frequently portrayed as Father of Jesus in Matthew.[28] God the Father and Jesus his Son form the center of the web of kinship relations which hold the community of Matthew together as brothers and sisters.[29] The relationships of love and mercy which permeate Matthew's teaching to his group are supported by the close relationship that binds God to Jesus. That father-son relationship, in turn, rests on God's relationship with the Judean royal house in the Bible and contrasts starkly with the tensions that separate God from the Herodian family ruling in Judea in Jesus' time. At crucial moments God reveals that Jesus is his Son, especially at the baptism and transfiguration (3:17; 17:5). In turn, Jesus acknowledges the importance of the Father's revealing this relationship to his followers (11:25–27), especially when Peter, who speaks for the disciples, calls Jesus "Messiah and Son of God" (16:16–17). Others testify to Jesus' sonship as a result of divine communication. The apocalyptic phenomena at the death of Jesus make clear to the centurion and the guard, who are "neutral" observers, that Jesus, though executed on a cross, is the Son of God (27:54). Satan (3:17) and demons (8:28–29), who have otherworldly knowledge, know that Jesus is Son of God. Paradoxically, the high priest who does not accept his claim (26:63) and the people and leaders who mock him while he is hanging on the cross (27:39–43) misunderstand what they see and so reject Jesus' claim to be Son of God.[30]

The closeness of the kinship relations between God the Father, Jesus the Son and Jesus' followers is communicated by a prophetic promise at the beginning of the gospel and by Jesus' promise at the end. The author summarizes the story of Jesus' birth with Isa. 7:14, which says that a virgin (LXX: *parthenos*) will conceive and bear a son and that the child's name will be Emmanuel ("God with us"). The double naming of God's Son as Jesus and Emmanuel highlights two of his roles, to save his people from their sins (1:21) and to be with his people (1:23). Similarly, at the end of the gospel (28:19–20), Jesus tells his disciples to teach and baptize all nations and that he will be with them until the end of the age. The names and functions assigned to Jesus in these two passages form a literary inclusion so that they reinforce and illuminate one another. In both passages, Jesus' "royal lineage" lies in the background. Isaiah seems to expect a royal prince, and in the final scene of the gospel Jesus appears as a reigning monarch, empowered by God, sending out his followers.

Because the title "Son of God" carries with it connotations of Trinitarian theology for modern Christians, it is important to review the first-century Jewish understanding of this term, which Matthew mobilized in his narrative.[31] The royal and apocalyptic atmosphere of these scenes fits both the biblical and first-century usages of the term "son of God." The Judean kings, preeminently David, were the sons of God in a special way. God promised to treat David's son as his own son and not reject him (2 Sam. 7:14). This stress on royal kinship merges divine with human rule in Israel. Ps. 2:7 extends the hope of divine and Israelite rule over all the earth: "The Lord said to me, 'You are my son. . . . I will give you the nations for an inheritance.'" That the hopes found in these two passages were alive among Jewish groups in the first century can be seen in the Qumran midrash on the Last Days, which quotes 2 Samuel 7 and Psalm 2 together.[32] Psalm 110, cited often in the New Testament, links royal rule ("Sit at my right hand") with the priesthood of Melchisedek. The Greek translation of this Psalm (LXX 109) interprets an obscure clause in verse 3 as God's acknowledgment of the king-priest as son: "I have begotten you from the womb before the morning star." The themes of divine election, sonship, and eschatological royal power are also found in the so-called Son of God text found at Qumran.[33] A king is being addressed and promised that his son "shall be hailed [as] the son of God, and they shall call him son of the Most High." The text promises that after war and rule by foreigners, this son shall rule and a people of God arise. Fitzmyer interprets this text as apocalyptic in orientation. All these biblical and Second Temple texts envision in one way or another a divinely sent leader who is accepted by God as his son and is granted extraordinary powers to rule.

The "son of God" is not limited to the heir of the Davidic throne. Second Temple literature recognizes the righteous person as a son of God, and this too fits Matthew's stress on the way of righteousness in responding to God. The righteous one who is a son of God helps his

fellow humans, endures suffering from the unjust, and in the right circumstances rules wisely as God wills. Ben Sira advises his student to be
"as a father to the fatherless and to help the widow as a husband
would"; as a result, "God will call you son" (Sirach 4:10 [Heb.]).[34] The
reward for caring for a needy family is proportionate; one becomes a
member of God's family and thus presumably will receive God's care.
God's care for the just, like his care for the king, is expressed in kinship
terms and transcends the present. The Book of Jubilees has God predict
to Moses that Israel will return to God and keep the commandments.
Then "I shall be a father to them and they will be sons to me. And they
will all be called 'sons of the living God.' And every angel and spirit will
know and acknowledge that they are my sons . . . and I shall love
them" (Jub. 1:24–25). The first-century B.C.E. Psalms of Solomon use
the same expression when the psalmist promises that God "will gather
a holy people whom he will lead in righteousness. . . . He will not tol-
erate unrighteousness [even] to pause among them. . . . For he shall
know them that they are all sons of their God" (Pss. of Sol. 17:26–27).
When the just sin, they—like David's descendants in 2 Sam. 7—are
disciplined by God like sons: "[God] will admonish the righteous as a
beloved son and his discipline is as for a firstborn" (Pss. of Sol. 13:9). In
the Wisdom of Solomon (100 B.C.E.–100 C.E.) the enemies of the just
man challenge this common idea of God's faithfulness to his sons. The
wicked say, "[The just man] calls the last end of the righteous happy,
and boasts that God is his father. Let us find out what will happen to
him. For if the just one be the son of God, he [God] will defend him and
deliver him from the hand of his foes" (Wisd. of Sol. 2:16–18). When
the just man is vindicated by God at the Last Judgment, the unjust marvel at "how he [the just person] is numbered among the sons of God
and how his lot is among the holy ones" (Wisd. of Sol. 5:5). Similarly,
in the early part of the gospel, Matthew implicitly equates Jesus the
Son of God with Israel.[35] The relationship of son to God is clear in
Second Temple Judaism. The son obeys God faithfully and can depend
on God for favor, protection, or in the case of persecution, vindication.

The son of God as a faithful and just Jew can be found in other diaspora literature besides the Wisdom of Solomon. Philo reflects the
common theme that correct behavior makes one a son of God when he
argues that natural kinship bonds are of a lesser significance than fidelity to God.[36] To prove his argument, he connects Deut. 13:18 with
Deut. 14:1, so that those who keep God's commandments are sons of
the Lord their God: "If you obey the voice of the Lord your God by
keeping all his commandments . . . You are sons of the Lord your
God." One becomes a son of God doing "what is pleasing to nature and

what is good" and as a result God "will think fit to protect and provide for you as would a father."

The romance "Joseph and Aseneth" from Egypt (100 B.C.E.–100 C.E.) demonstrates the varied meanings of "son of God." It uses this metaphor to signify both Joseph's high (royal) status in Egyptian society and his favored position before God, both of which derive from his justice and faithfulness to God.[37] When Aseneth first sees Joseph, she compares him to the sun coming down from heaven in its chariot and calls him a son of God (6:2–6). When she prays in repentance of her faults, including speaking blasphemous words against her Lord Joseph, she refers to him as God's son, not just as a shepherd's son from the land of Canaan (13:10). Thus Joseph's appearance manifests his status as one favored by and in close relationship to God. Joseph's status before God is recognized by others as well and is the basis for his powerful position in Egyptian society. When Aseneth is about to marry Joseph, Aseneth's foster father says with great pride, "The Lord God of heaven has chosen you as a bride for his firstborn son, Joseph" (18:11).[38] Pharoah likewise refers to Joseph as the firstborn son of God, and to Aseneth, his bride to be, as a daughter of God because of her marriage to Joseph (21:4). Later, Joseph's brother Levi tells Joseph's enemy, the Pharoah's son, that his father Jacob is a friend of the Most High God and Joseph is like God's son (23:10). Metaphors of kinship with God match the social standing and relationships of people on earth. Those who are just and faithful to God are referred to as sons of God (19:8), and those who eat of the mysterious honeycomb are identified as the angels, "the chosen of God" and the "sons of the Most High." This expression may refer to angels or to the righteous dead in paradise or to God's children on earth.[39] In sum, the expression "son of God" in "Joseph and Aseneth" serves a flexible series of purposes, including the identification of those who are close to and favored by God, in particular, Joseph, who is preeminent and appointed by God to save his family and provide leadership for both Israel and Egypt.

The traditional link between obedience to God and sonship was maintained in rabbinic literature and associated with Deut. 14:1 as it was in Philo above. Mishnah Abot (3:14) attributed to Akiba the argument that Israel was loved by God because the people were called sons of God (Deut. 14:1 is cited) and because they were given Torah. In a long, complex exegesis of the prohibition against making a "baldness between the eyes for the dead" (Deut. 14:1) the Palestinian Talmud cites Rabbi (E)leazar (ben Pedat), a late third-century Palestinian Amora, interpreting the word "sons" in Deut. 14:1: "When Israel does the will of the Holy One, blessed be he, they are called sons; when Israel does not do the will of the Holy One, blessed be he, they are not called sons."[40] Fidelity to Torah and being a son of God are closely linked, as one would expect in rabbinic literature. A number of other rabbinic texts speak of various favored rabbis and charismatics, like Honi the Circle Drawer and Hanina ben Dosa, as sons of God.[41] Though these rabbinic texts do not reliably testify to late first-century usage, they do demonstrate the continuous use of the term "son of God." The image of the son of God as one who is obedient to and favored by God is durable indeed, from the Davidic kingship through the Talmud. It can be used of kings, wise men, and the just. Those in power who are favored by God are sons of God, and the just who are persecuted by the powerful are likewise sons of God and will be vindicated in the end. The son of God can be a king on earth or the king at the apocalyptic transformation of the earth. In all cases, a close relationship with God results in high status, divine care, and the availability of divine power.

The author of Matthew drew upon this rich and varied tradition when he stressed God the Father of Jesus in the birth narrative (chap. 1). At the same time, he brought a variety of titles, roles, and scriptural passages to bear on Jesus in order to establish him firmly within the biblical world and further mark him out as a special figure in Israel (chaps. 1–2). Since David was king, anointed one, and son of God, Jesus is presented as the son of David, born in Bethlehem, David's ancestral home. Jesus' kingship enters the dramatic action when the Magi come to Herod seeking the newly born king of the Jews and subsequently honor Jesus as king, even as God (2:1–12). Herod ironically testifies to Jesus' kingly power by seeking to kill him to protect his own position (2:16). Jesus' royal status is again confirmed ironically at the end of the gospel, during the interrogation that leads to his execution for claiming to be king of the Jews (27:11, 29, 37, 42). Jesus' royal power is manifested decisively in the final scene, when he appears to his disciples claiming that all power in heaven and on earth has been given to him (28:18). This final revelation of Jesus' high position has been prepared for by the gradual revelation during the narrative that Jesus is the preeminent Son of God who reveals God's will (11:25–30), controls nature (14:33), and has God's approval (17:5), and by the exposition of the ultimate role of the Son of Man as judge (chaps. 24–25; see below).

Jesus is also presented as the just, wise, and faithful Son of God who is persecuted by evil and powerful opponents. Jesus' persecution by the authorities both in the birth narrative and at the end of the gospel parallels the hostility shown the just man in the Wisdom of Solomon, chapters 2–5. He faithfully observes God's law and teaches it authoritatively. He is given power by God over disease and demons. In conflicts with the leaders of Israel, he shows himself superior because he has wisdom from God. The associations of Jesus with the traditional just and wise man shows how themes from Jewish wisdom, prophecy, and royal theology interpenetrate in the Matthean narrative.

Jesus as Teacher

Matthew presents Jesus as an observant Jew who teaches others by word and example to observe faithfully the will and law of God. Jesus speaks as an authoritative teacher. When he opposes other Jewish teachers, he is neither a revolutionary nor the founder of a new religion, but a reformer within the Jewish community. The intricacies of Jesus' teaching, presented in the previous chapter, fit within the legal debates of first-century Judaism. In his frequent conflicts with other teachers and authorities, Matthew's Jesus gives more detailed and nuanced defenses of his positions than he does in the other gospels. Like any recognized teacher, Jesus observes the law carefully.[42] With other repentant Jews, he seeks baptism from John the Baptist (3:13–17). Both Jesus and John recognize that Jesus has greater authority than John, but Jesus insists on being baptized because "it is proper for us [Jesus and John] in this way to fulfill all righteousness" (3:15). "Righteousness" in Matthew refers to acts which are in agreement with God's will, and "fulfill" refers to fulfilling Scripture.[43] Thus Jesus' first act, baptism by John (3:13–17), affirms his obedience to God and commitment to a total program of reform. He maintains his commitment to God by resisting three temptations from the devil and dismissing him with the declaration that God alone is to be worshiped (4:10).

After beginning his teaching, preaching, and healing in Galilee (4:23–25), Jesus gives an inaugural instruction (the Sermon on the Mount, chaps. 5–7), in which he both affirms (5:17–19) and reinterprets (5:21–6:18) the law. Jesus teaches a zealous observance of the Ten Commandments, which includes avoiding anger and lust and giving up wealth (5:21–30; 19:16–30). He affirms and praises traditional Jewish practices such as sincere almsgiving (6:2–4), prayer (5:44; 6:5–15; 21:22), and fasting (6:16–18); he himself prays (14:23; 19:13; 26:36–44) and fasts (4:2).[44] Immediately after the Sermon on the Mount, Matthew shows Jesus' fidelity to biblical law by making his next action the cleansing of a leper (8:1–4), who is then told to show himself to the priest and make the required offering (Lev. 13–14). Jesus supports the paying of tithes (23:23) even while criticizing the scribes and Pharisees' way of teaching about them. Jesus has tassels on his garments, which the woman with a hemorrhage (9:20) and the sick in Gennesaret (14:36) touch to be cured, but he opposes ostentatious display of them (23:5).[45] He instructs his disciples to prepare for the Passover sacrifice and meal in the appropriate fashion (26:18), and he tries to prevent them from using violence against the established authorities during the feast (26:51–53).

Jesus does not reject any laws or advocate any interpretations which would cause his ostracism or execution.[46] In the view of Matthew, Jesus is innocent of all the more serious charges brought against him. The charge of blasphemy at Jesus' trial is trumped up, and the witnesses perjure themselves (26:57–66). Earlier charges by the scribes that Jesus blasphemes by forgiving sins are unsubstantiated in the narrative (9:3), and the "witchcraft accusation" that Jesus derives his power from the ruler of demons is refuted (12:24–32). According to Matthew, the cause of Jesus' execution was a conflict over authority and power with the Jerusalem officials (21:23–27), manifested in a series of conflicts in chapters 21–22.[47] But even these conflicts are within the bounds of first-century Judaism. The atmosphere and tone of Matthew's narrative assumes that Jesus is a Jew living among Jews and accepting their customs and laws, unless his teaching varies from common custom for good reason.

The teachings of Jesus and the person of the teacher are inseparable in the narrative. Jesus' authority is not that of a learned scribe or Pharisee, nor is it that of a later rabbi.[48] His authority in the narrative comes directly from God and is sanctioned apocalyptically. From the genealogy and birth narrative, in which Jesus is identified as a descendant of David, as Son of God and as "God with us," to his final appearance as a risen apocalyptic figure, in which he instructs the disciples to teach others to obey him and promises to be with them until the end, Jesus is presented as a divinely warranted teacher who is messianic ruler and eschatological judge. Jesus' status and access to God, according to Matthew, transcend any authority found elsewhere in the Jewish community. As he begins to face opposition from other Jewish leaders, Jesus thanks God for revealing hidden things, which the wise do not understand, and claims that all things have been delivered to him by the Father and that no one knows the Father except through the Son (11:25–27). To those who accept him, Jesus promises rest. As Davies and Allison put it, "11:25–30 is a capsule summary of the message of the entire gospel. In this passage, Jesus reveals that he is the revealer. That is, he reveals that, as the meek and humble Son of the Father, he fulfils the calling of Israel, embodying in his own persona Torah and

Wisdom and thus making known the perfect will of God."[49] Israel's ancient and central concern with wisdom and fidelity to God's law are gathered up into Matthew's presentation of Jesus as teacher par excellence.

Scholars have long noted that in the Gospel of Matthew Jesus is called "teacher" only by outsiders, not by the disciples who believe in him. Thus the title has been treated as secondary in importance.[50] This approach is misleading. Though Matthew stresses Jesus' *titles* as Son of God, Son of Man, and Messiah, the *role* of teacher is neither subordinate nor discontinuous with these titles.[51] Those who believe in Jesus understand that his teaching, his life's work, implies and articulates his God-given power and authority both in life and in the future kingdom when God will rule directly.[52] The relationship to the outsiders, who know Jesus as teacher but do not fully understand or accept him, is crucial for Matthew, for these people are the potential members of his group. For example, Jesus identifies himself as teacher and the disciples as "my disciples" in a message he addresses to the man in whose house he will celebrate Passover (26:18). (This is the only place Jesus identifies himself as teacher.) Though the man is, as usual, an outsider, he is also one of the "many" (26:28) on whose behalf Jesus is about to die and to whom his disciples are supposed to teach "all that I have commanded" (28:20). The role of teacher is passed on to the disciples, who are scribes instructed in the kingdom of heaven to bring forth old and new things from their storeroom (13:52), that is, biblical, Jewish tradition understood through the teachings of Jesus.

Jesus as Healer

After teaching, Jesus' most frequent activity in the gospel is healing.[53] Matthew twice summarizes Jesus' activities as "proclaiming the good news of the kingdom and curing every disease and every sickness among the people" (4:23; cf. 9:35). The Sermon on the Mount (chaps. 5–7) and the ten healings (chaps. 8–9) which follow thoroughly introduce the reader to Jesus the teacher and healer. Healing includes exorcism (4:24; 8:16) and providing leadership to the oppressed (9:36).[54] Jesus' role as healer is authenticated by a formula quotation from Isaiah: "He took our infirmities and bore our diseases" (Isa. 53:4; Matt. 8:17). His teaching and healing activities, which bring help to the needy, characterize his role as Messiah. In response to John the Baptist's inquiry whether he is the Christ, Jesus refers to his activities as the "deeds of the Christ" and enumerates them by paraphrasing Isaiah that the "blind receive sight, the lame walk, the lepers are cleansed, and the deaf hear, the dead are raised and the poor have the good news brought to them" (Isa. 28:18–19; 35:5–6; 61:1; Matt. 11:5). When Jesus cures the crowds who follow him (12:15), Matthew applies to him another formula quotation from Isaiah that stresses the chosenness and gentleness of God's servant (Isa. 42:1–4; Matt. 12:17–21). Matthew's summaries of Jesus' healing activities continue through the gospel (14:13–14, 35–36; 15:30–31; 19:2). Finally Jesus cures the blind and lame in the Temple (21:14), provoking the opposition of the Temple authorities.[55]

Jesus' healing is integrally connected to his roles as Messiah, son of David, son of Abraham, and teacher. Healing and teaching characterize Jesus' life from beginning to end. A series of prophecies (cited above) show that Jesus is fulfilling God's will, just as he is teaching it in his instructions. The references to messianic activity (11:2–6) and to the coming of the kingdom—"If it is by the Spirit of God I cast out demons, then the kingdom of God has come upon you" (12:28)—give Jesus' activities deep roots in Israel's traditions. Jesus sends his disciples to Israel (10:5–6) and, for the most part, confines his own work to his fellow sons of Abraham. In Jerusalem, Matthew has the children in the Temple recognize Jesus as Messiah after he has cured people (21:15). Matthew suggests, by his choice of formula quotations, that the Messiah must cure the ills of his people as part of his leadership. Twice people in Jerusalem acclaim Jesus as the actual son of David (21:9, 15). In some traditions, Solomon, who was the son of David, is associated with powers of healing, exorcism, magic, and miracle.[56] Thus, by allusion to Scripture and popular tradition, Matthew gradually builds a picture of Jesus as an authentic healer in Israel's tradition with access to the amplitude of divine power.

Since the programmatic essay of Hans-Joachim Held, emphasis has been placed on the way Matthew retells the miracles and integrates them into his theology and narrative.[57] As he does with many Markan narratives, Matthew frequently abbreviates the miracle stories, omits thaumaturgical action (e.g., Mark 7:33–36) or even an entire miracle (e.g., Mark 8:22–26). Held claims that Matthew has deemphasized the miraculous and changed the nature of many miracle stories so that they become controversies or pronouncement stories.[58] However, J. P. Heil has argued convincingly that Matthew's accounts remain miracle stories even after thorough editing to Matthew's purposes.[59] Matthew uses Jesus' manifestation of God-given powers to undergird Jesus' teaching authority.[60] Miracle working is also closely related to Jesus' messianic activity, to his high status as God's Son and as Lord, and to his relationship with his community of believers.[61] The disciples, too, are pictured as replicating Jesus' mission of teaching and healing during Jesus' lifetime (10:1, 7–8). Throughout the narrative, Matthew puts more emphasis on teaching, as can be seen in the final instruction to the disciples (28:18–20), which mandates teaching but not healing.[62]

Jesus as healer fulfills a common role in first-century Judaism and in the eastern Roman Empire. The Near Eastern "holy man" or "divine man" *(theios anēr)* who gathered a popular following was expected to manifest divinely given powers through wise teaching and powerful deeds. This type of leadership can be seen in Jewish charismatic leaders, in Greco-Roman religious leaders, and in later Christian figures. People sought personal, powerful, and local religious leaders and mediators to intercede for them with the gods and to help them reap the benefits of divine power. The role of holy man should not be seen as a fixed, institutionalized function. The Hellenistic concept of the divine man is varied and often vague in its meaning. The term "divine man" can refer to an inspired man or to someone related to God in some special sense or just to an extraordinary man.[63] Thus it is not a fixed, explanatory category, but a usage that requires precise definition when it is used.

Within the Jewish tradition, biblical figures are presented as divine mediators, messengers, and heavenly figures much more frequently and consistently in apocalyptic literature than in Greek Jewish literature. In the rabbinic tradition, the activities of miracle workers are acknowledged but controlled and tamed. Vermes has gathered the fragments of information attributed to Hanina ben Dosa, a first-century figure, and suggests that he represents a Galilean, charismatic type of Judaism with which Jesus, too, was associated.[64] Vermes's acceptance of later rabbinic sources about Hanina and Honi the Circle Drawer as evidence for the first century is questionable, and his attempt to describe this type of Judaism is too hypothetical to be determinative. All the rabbinic stories of charismatics and miracle workers serve the ends of later rabbinic authorities who seek to integrate or submerge other trends in Judaism. Thus the stories of Honi and Hanina rabbinize them.[65] These texts do show, however, that miracle working continued within the culture and could easily be accepted. The Babylonian Talmud (third century on) shows a renewed interest in the rabbi as wonderworker, probably in response to cultural interest in these roles.[66] This is consistent with social developments in the Greco-Roman world in general. The Greco-Roman literary figure of a wandering, charismatic with miraculous powers was a product of the second and third centuries, not the first.[67] In writings of the first century C.E., the wise man proved his authenticity by virtuous actions. For

Jewish writers, Moses was the archetypal wise man. In addition, Jewish writers did not stress miracle working as a criterion for authenticity or divine approval.[68]

The presentation of Jesus as a miracle worker in all the gospels fits into a long and complex tradition in Judaism and the Near East. Matthew's particular emphasis is on Jesus' healing of the people as part of his larger role as Messiah and the healing is subordinate to and supportive of Jesus' role as teacher. Nevertheless, Jesus as a healer and powerful representative of God stands out in the narrative.

Biblical Roles

The Gospel of Matthew is noted for its sophisticated and extensive use of Scripture, especially its theory of the fulfillment of Scripture expressed in the dozen formula quotations. In addition to explicit quotations, the narrative is undergirded by a web of allusions to the Bible and its characters and events. Biblical figures, roles, and events that were culturally familiar to Matthew's readers are mobilized in the background, language, and style of the narrative and give it a familiar sound and cultural legitimacy. Three of these figures and roles will be explored briefly: Moses, personified wisdom, and the prophet.

Moses

Jesus is associated with Moses, the Exodus, and Israel itself in the introductory stories and throughout the narrative.[69] Matthew utilizes the unrivaled stature of Moses within Judaism to support his comprehensive claims for Jesus. He suggests that Jesus is a prophet like Moses (17:4–5; Deut. 18:15).[70] He explicitly parallels the marvelous births of Moses and Jesus as well as their escapes from mortal danger. Moses' mother is barren, and Jesus' mother conceives through God's power. Moses is threatened by Pharoah's decree to kill all Jewish male children (Exod. 1:16; 2:2–3), and Jesus by Herod's attempt to kill any rival king (Matt. 2:3, 12, 16–18). Jesus, like Moses, lives in Egyptian exile and then returns toward the land of Israel. Jesus' baptism and forty days of temptations (chaps. 3–4) recall Moses' passage through the sea and forty years in the desert (Exod. 14–16, etc.). Moses' central role as recipient and teacher of divine revelation and as leader of Israel is replicated in Jesus by Matthew. Just as Moses went up to Mount Sinai and brought down the commandments, Jesus teaches on a mountain (5:1; 8:1). Jesus quotes and interprets Scripture (chap. 5), a task he can fulfill because he receives and teaches revelation from God (11:25–27), just as Moses did (Exod. 33:12–14).[71] Jesus, like Moses, leads the people to rest through his many healings (11:28; cf. Exod. 33:14) and in addition heals them on the mountain (15:29). Jesus sends his disciples forth in his place (28:16–20) as Moses sent Joshua forth to lead Israel in his place (Josh. 1:5, 7, 17). The echoes from Moses and the Exodus are constant. Since the Exodus was formative for Israel as a nation and Sinai is the archetype for authoritative divine teaching, Jesus' interpretation of the Bible and Jewish tradition is put on a par with the original biblical revelation itself and becomes part of it, especially in the Sermon on the Mount (7:28–29). In establishing Jesus as the unique teacher and master (23:8–12) by association with the tradition's most authoritative teacher, the narrative inclines the reader to accept the extensive teachings of Jesus contained in the sermons upon which Matthew puts such emphasis.

Wisdom

Wisdom and wise men are mentioned in only a few passages in Matthew (11:19; 12:42; 13:54 for wisdom; wise men in 11:25; 23:34). Wisdom motifs can be found in longer Matthean passages, especially 11:16–30 and 23:29–39. Granted that wisdom is a common biblical theme, one would expect to find it in Matthew. However, its role and influence on Matthew have been disputed. Maximalist positions have been taken by Felix Christ and Suggs.[72] Suggs, who is more restrained than Christ, sees the identification of Jesus with the figure of wisdom as central to Matthew's Christology. But Suggs has been criticized by Marshall and to a lesser extent by Pregeant and by Davies and Allison, who admit that Matthew identifies Jesus with wisdom but point out that he does not emphasize this identification.[73]

Several passages are crucial. The rejection of Jesus by his contemporaries is symbolized by the children taunting one another in the marketplace (11:16–19); Matthew changes the probable original Q saying, "Wisdom is justified by all her children" (found in Luke 7:35) to "Wisdom is justified by her deeds" (11:19). The insertion of "deeds" is a reference to the "deeds of the Messiah," cited by Jesus in answer to John the Baptist at the beginning of the chapter (11:2).[74] These deeds include both the teachings and miracles found in chapters 5–9 and they implicitly identify Jesus with the Messiah and with wisdom. Later, in the diatribe against the scribes and Pharisees, Matthew charges their ancestors with killing the prophets (23:30–31) and them with killing the prophets, wise men, and scribes sent by Jesus (23:34). This attack reflects the hostility prevalent between the teachers and leaders of Matthew's group and those of the Jewish community at large (see chap. 3 above). This pattern of rejection and persecution fits the rejection of wisdom in Israel's earlier wisdom tradition.[75] Luke (11:49) says, "The wisdom of God said: I will send you prophets and apostles." Matthew changes the speaker to Jesus who says: "I send you prophets, wise men, and scribes" (23:34). If Luke represents the original form of the saying in Q, then Matthew here identifies Jesus with wisdom. However, paradoxically, he also suppresses a clear reference to wisdom in favor of having Jesus as the authoritative speaker in the narrative. Matthew's dependence on the wisdom tradition and his modeling of Jesus on wisdom is clear, but he does not underscore the connection. Rather, he leaves wisdom in the background to enrich and interpret his portrait of Jesus.

When Matthew begins to portray the opposition to Jesus in chapters 11–12, he subtly presents Jesus as wisdom who has come to earth, only to be rejected.[76] "This generation," symbolized by the children in the marketplace, rejects wisdom (11:16–19), just as the towns northwest of the Sea of Galilee rejected Jesus (11:20–25). In response, Jesus affirms the gift he brings, its positive effects, and his authenticity as a messenger who knows the mind of God and has been divinely commissioned (11:25–30). The Father has given revelation to "infants" *(nepioi)* through his son; those who accept Jesus will find rest.[77] Jesus the Son is associated with wisdom and also, as Davies and Allison have pointed out, with Moses, who had an intimate relationship with God, received revelation, and passed it on to Israel (Exod. 33:12–14).[78] The allusions to the figure of wisdom, like those to Moses are subtle and implied. Matthew draws upon several streams of biblical imagery in order to give Jesus a dominant standing as messenger and revealer.

Prophet

Matthew values the testimony of the prophets greatly, both in the formula quotations which claim that Jesus fulfills the prophets and in the many references to individual prophets. The author himself never explicitly refers to Jesus as a prophet, though he does implicitly compare and associate Jesus with them. People are reported to be saying that Jesus is John the Baptist, Elijah, Jeremiah, or one of the prophets (16:14). The crowds at the Temple during Passover take Jesus to be a prophet (21:11, 46), as well as son of David (21:9, 15), and the council of leaders invokes this popular view of Jesus when they mockingly challenge the blindfolded Jesus to prophesy (26:68). Matthew's presentation of popular sentiment toward Jesus accurately reflects the first century, since prophets frequently arose as popular leaders and influential figures and since apocalyptic expectations often centered on a prophet like Moses (Deut. 18:15–20).[79]

Though a later rabbinic teaching claimed that prophecy ended in the sixth century with Haggai, Zechariah, and Malachi, prophecy was common in the first century.[80] Josephus reports that a number of Essenes were notable as prophets during the Second Temple period, including Judas, who predicted the murder of Antigonus by his brother Aristobulus, Menahem, who predicted Herod would be king, and Simon, who interpreted a dream for Archelaus.[81] Similar phenomena were found among unnamed Pharisaic prophets and their leaders Samias and Pollion, who predicted Herod's reign.[82] Josephus himself predicted Vespasian's accession to the throne and recognized John the Baptist as a prophet.[83] Jesus ben Hananiah, a peasant, lamented the destruction of Jerusalem in the Temple for four years before the beginning of the war against Rome.[84] The phenomenon of oracular prophecy seems to have been taken for granted and attributed to popular figures who possessed foresight.

Many other prophets led popular uprisings and these Josephus consistently condemns.[85] The prophet Theudas led a large group of people to the Jordan and promised to part the waters in 44–45 C.E.[86] An Egyptian urged the crowds to go to the Mount of Olives, from where they would take possession of Jerusalem.[87] Later, an unnamed "charletan" promised the people deliverance if they followed him into the wilderness.[88] Finally, according to the testimony of the Dead Sea Scrolls, there was some, though not extensive, expectation of an apocalyptic prophet before the end of the world.[89] There is sufficient first-century evidence from Qumran, the New Testament, and Josephus to show that the traditional category "prophet" was still current and multivalent.[90]

Granted that the category prophet lurks in the cultural background, how does the author of Matthew use it? He does not directly call Jesus a prophet, because for him, Jesus is the Messiah and the Son of God, as Peter the spokesperson for the disciples confesses (16:16). Though Matthew pushes his readers beyond the figure of the prophet, he does not deny its validity and usefulness, nor does he disconnect Jesus from prophecy. His qualified acceptance of the term "prophet" can be seen also in the case of John the Baptist. The crowds recognize John as a prophet (14:5; 21:26), but Jesus says that he is more than a prophet (11:7–9). However, being "more" than a prophet means being like Elijah (11:10–14; 17:10–13). The "more" is a prophetic status higher than that of other prophets: Elijah was seen as the forerunner of the Messiah. Though Matthew does not explicitly name Jesus as a prophet, he subtly identifies Jesus with the prophets. Jesus' rejection by his own townspeople (13:54–58) is explained by a proverb that a prophet is not without honor except in his native place and in his own house. Matthew, alone among the gospel writers, refers to Jeremiah by name (2:17; 16:14; 27:9) and associates him with Jesus.[91] Just as Jeremiah opposed the Jerusalem leadership at the time of the first destruction of the Temple and was persecuted by them, so Jesus opposes them and is persecuted. In addition, the Matthean group shares these experiences after the second destruction. Thus Jesus, the author of Matthew, Jeremiah, and the prophets of the Bible (23:29–36, 37) endure a similar fate: rejection, persecution, and often death. The persecution of Israel's heroes is a common polemical theme in first-century Judaism, one mobilized by Matthew and the early Christian tradition.[92] Matthew thus identifies Jesus with the most admired ancient Jewish heroes, the prophets, and at the same time explains the rejection and execution of Jesus by the national leaders. In doing so, he affirms the authority and standing of Jesus in Israel as teacher and holy man.

Lord

"Lord" is an amorphous title and depends on usage and context for meaning.[93] In general, the honorific title "Lord" signifies a relationship between a superior and inferior. Thus it is used in Matthew's gospel of both God and Jesus in relationship with the other narrative characters. The Greek term *kyrios* (κύριος) and its Aramaic equivalents (*mārēh, mārēy, mārē'; determinative māryā'*) had a wide idiomatic usage. In daily life, it was the equivalent of "Sir" or "Mr." It often designated people of high station, even the emperor. In the New Testament and some Jewish literature, "Lord" is used for God's proper name, the Tetragrammaton, probably following oral usage in the reading of the Hebrew Scriptures.[94] In earlier studies of New Testament Christology, which made a sharp distinction between Semitic and Greek contributions to the thought of the early church, "Lord" was long thought to be a Hellenistic Jewish or gentile title for God, which was also applied to Jesus.[95] However, the Dead Sea Scrolls have given unambiguous evidence of the use of the absolute form "Lord" *(mr')* in parallelism with "God" *('lh')*.[96] The use of this title for God in the determinative state is also found in Dead Sea Scroll fragments of the Book of Enoch: "And to Gabriel the Lord *([m]ry')* said . . ."[97] The Hebrew equivalent *('dwn)* is found in Psalm 151 (11QPs^a 28:7–8). Evidence from Aristeas, Josephus, and some passages in Aquila's translation of the Bible indicate that such usage was generally known. Thus the use of "Lord" for God and for anyone of high status or great power is thoroughly established in both Aramaic and Greek of the first century. It was available to express the high status accorded Jesus by his followers, who believed him to be risen from the dead and expected him to come as judge at the end of the world.

Matthew uses the title "Lord" for God numerous times.[98] He also uses it as a conventional mark of respect to mean "Sir" (27:63) and to indicate the relationship between a slave and his master (10:24). Most frequently "Lord" is used as a form of direct address to Jesus by his disciples or those seeking his help.[99] In some cases "Lord" connotes "teacher." Peter addresses Jesus as Lord when he inquires how often he must forgive his brother (18:21), and "another of the disciples" addresses him as Lord when he responds to Jesus' call by saying that he must first bury his father. (In a parallel exchange, a scribe addresses Jesus as "teacher," 8:19.). In the majority of cases when Jesus is addressed as Lord both by the disciples and others, they are seeking help or responding to his more-than-human powers. In the two stories of the disciples caught in a storm on the lake, the disciples (8:25) and Peter (14:28, 30) ask to be saved, addressing Jesus as Lord. The second story climaxes with the highly symbolic recognition by the disciples in the boat that Jesus is the Son of God (14:33).[100] When Jesus is transfigured into a "divinelike" figure, Peter addresses him as Lord (17:4). When he predicts the future, for example, that he will die, Peter rebukes him, addressing him as Lord (16:21–22). When he predicts that a disciple will betray him, the disciples each sorrowfully ask the Lord if the traitor is himself (26:21–22). Those seeking cures from Jesus, both Jews and gentiles, often address him as "Lord." The leper (8:2), the man with a possessed son (17:15), and the two sets of blind men, who call him son of David (9:27–28; 20:29–34), also call him "Lord" when they seek help. Similarly, the centurion (8:6, 8) and the Canaanite woman (15:22, 25, 27) address Jesus as Lord when seeking help for their loved ones. In all cases, the speakers look to Jesus for the exercise of more than human powers to help them in their need. Matthew also refers to the apocalyptic judge, who is the Son of Man, as "Lord." The audience is instructed to watch: "For you do not know on what day your Lord is coming" (24:42). The "Lord" who is coming is clearly the Son of Man (24:39, 44). Similarly, when the Son of Man sits in judgment, those before him address him as "Lord" (25:37, 44). In a brief allusion to judgment, the false followers of Jesus will plead with him on the Last Day, addressing him as "Lord, Lord" (7:21–22).

The early Christians used the title Lord to suggest Jesus' transcendence as Son of God, as judge at the end of the world, and as ruler.[101] In Matthew all these usages appear. Lord is the form of address most often used, but it is just as often linked with another, more substantial characterization, which gives content to the speaker's attitude. Peter calls Jesus Lord and Son of God (14:28, 33; 17:4, 5). People seeking to be cured call him Lord and son of David (9:28; 15:22; 20:31). Those facing judgment meet Jesus as Lord and Son of Man (chaps. 24–25). In general, those who address Jesus with petitions for help or mercy call him Lord, the traditional term for a patron, for a powerful or authoritative person to whom one is subordinate, or for God. Implicit in the title is recognition of the power and authority of the person being addressed and the hope that that power will be used for the benefit of the petitioner. Since Jesus is God's agent to heal and teach and takes on transcendent aspects of a divine intermediary, the uses of "Lord" for God and Jesus often overlap. However, the meanings of "Lord" are so protean that no precise claims for a divine status for Jesus can be based on it.

Son of Man

In Greek, the common gospel expression "the son of [the] man" is unidiomatic and would most plausibly mean "the man's son." Thus most scholars agree that the expression and title the "Son of Man," comes from the Aramaic used by the early followers of Jesus or from Jesus himself. Surprisingly the meaning of "son of man" *(bar ['ě]nāsh[ā'])* in first-century Aramaic is also uncertain because the expression is uncommon in the surviving Aramaic of the Second Temple period. It is common in third-century and later Palestinian Aramaic as a way of saying both "I" and "human being," but how pertinent this later dialectical usage is for first-century Aramaic is disputed.[102] The only occurrence of the phrase son of man *(bar 'enosh)* in Official and Middle Aramaic of the Second Temple period is Dan. 7:13, where "one like a son of man" appears in the heavens to receive from God authority over the universe. Further, both here in Daniel and in Old Aramaic (e.g., the Sefire Inscription) "son of man" means "human being" in the generic sense and has no theological or figurative sense. Vermes has argued vigorously that the phrase means "I."[103] It certainly means that in later Aramaic, but attestation for this usage in the first century is weak.

Within first-century Judaism, "son of man" is not a developed title or figure.[104] Some of the gospel uses of Son of Man" for Jesus obviously depends on the heavenly, royal figure in Daniel who is decribed as "one like a son of man" (Dan. 7:13; Mark 14:62; Matt. 26:64). The "one like a son of man" found in Dan. 7:13 reappears and fulfills eschatological roles as a redeemer, ruler, or judge in apocalyptic contexts in 4 Ezra 13, the Similitudes of Enoch (Enoch 37–71), the Apocalypse of Abraham (A 12–13, B 8), and the synoptic gospels. But these figures are identified by many other titles, and it is clear that "son of man," insofar as it has a content beyond the meaning "human," derives its meaning from Daniel or from its immediate context.

The designation of Jesus as Son of Man is so ambiguous that its meaning and connotations have been greatly disputed in New Testament studies.[105] It is used in the New Testament only twice outside the gospels, in Rev. 1:13 and Acts 7:56. Later Christian writers dropped this expression when referring to Jesus, probably because it had so little specific content that it could not stand on its own.[106] Attempts to derive Christian usage from an earlier Jewish apocalyptic Son of Man figure, proposed by Bultmann, have foundered. Thus the "Son of Man" must be understood in individual gospels. Perrin's linking of the Son of Man with Mark's theology of the suffering Messiah is an excellent example of this project.[107] And yet, the problem of the meaning of the "Son of Man" persists, as a review of some article titles shows: "The Apocalyptic Son of Man: A Theological Phantom"; "Exit the Apocalyptic Son of Man"; "Re-enter the Apocalyptic Son of Man"; "The End of the Son of Man?"; "Is the Son of Man Problem Insoluble?"; "Is the Son of Man Problem Really Insoluble?" Hundreds of books, chapters, and articles devoted to this expression and its gospel use have appeared without the emergence of a consensus. Two of the most recent treatments by Hare and Davies and Allison reach diametrically opposite conclusions on crucial issues. Though both suggest that the odd expression derives from Jesus' own usage, Hare says that "Son of Man" was a modest self-reference used by Jesus when speaking of his own vocation, destiny, and death, and Davies and Allison argue vigorously that Jesus was alluding to Daniel 7 and prophesying his own fate.[108] Hare concludes that at no stage of the New Testament tradition is "Son of Man" a title with a clear theological content or broad traditional connotations, while Davies and Allison argue for a titular use of this expression.[109] With these complex, presently unresolvable difficulties as a context, we will make a few cautious comments about Matthew's use of Son of Man in his narrative and its contribution to his presentation of Jesus in a Jewish context.

Matthew carried over the "Son of Man" from Mark but developed a number of additional uses of this expression, mostly apocalyptic in nature (esp. 13:41; 16:28; 19:28; 24:30; 25:31).[110] Matthew uses the phrase "Son of Man" thirty times, thirteen in reference to the future coming of the Son of Man, ten with reference to his death and resurrection, and seven with reference to his earthly activity.[111] Hare tries to

minimize Matthew's apocalyptic use of "Son of Man" by saying that
Matthew is generally interested in Jesus' future role but has no consistent pattern in his dropping and adding uses of "Son of Man." Hare
concludes that Matthew always uses "Son of Man" to mean "human,"
albeit often "human par excellence." Matthew never uses "Son of
Man" to reveal Jesus' nature or significance, but only to refer to his
destiny.[112] However, Davies and Allison have the better of the argument in claiming that in some cases Matthew consciously links "Son of
Man" with Daniel 7 and apocalyptic roles.[113] Even so, it remains true
that the designation or title "Son of Man" remains strangely multivalent and thus paradoxically lacking in specific content.[114] The dynamics of the narrative and its associated titles, allusions, and
metaphors are needed to give shape to the meaning of "Son of Man."
All the significant experiences and roles of Jesus are connected to passages that use the expression. These sayings serve as a reminder and
call to his disciples to be like Jesus, the Son of Man.[115]

In Matthew, Jesus uses the expression "Son of Man" of himself, but
the author never uses it to denote Jesus. After Jesus has been introduced (chaps. 1–4) and has begun to teach (chaps. 5–7), he finally refers to himself as the Son of Man, telling a scribe about the difficulties
disciples face in following him (8:20).[116] This theme is picked up in
two of the predictions of Jesus' suffering and death, where his fate is
implicitly linked with the disciples' fate (17:22; 20:18), and is also implied in his giving of his life (20:28).[117] The second occurrence of this
expression stresses Jesus' authority: the Son of Man has authority to
forgive sins and the power to cure (9:6). Later he is described as Lord
of the Sabbath (12:8). It is noteworthy that in both these contexts
Matthew's Jesus cites Hos. 6:6 in reference to God's desire for mercy
from human beings in their mutual relations, using the principle of
mercy to decide a rule for behavior. Thus Jesus' authority is based on
Scripture, derives from God, but is exercised by a human. Jesus seems
to be referring to himself as Son of Man in contexts where his humanity, special functions, and closeness to God are at issue. The third time
Matthew mentions the Son of Man, he is a figure who comes at the end
of the world (10:23). This figure appears again (24:27), usually to
judge (13:41; 19:28; 24:30, 39; 25:31). Consistent with this usage, the
last time the expression is employed (26:64), Jesus identifies himself as
the Son of Man who will come in the future by quoting Dan. 7:13 to
the high priest during his hearing. Thus Matthew's usage, like Mark's,
covers a wide range of roles and claims for Jesus and stresses his power
and authority, even when he suffers.

The identification of the Son of Man as an apocalyptic figure seems fundamental to Matthew's view of Jesus and consistent with his stress on judgment, as well as with his presentation of Jesus' death and resurrection as apocalyptically significant. Kingsbury suggests with some plausibility that in Matthew Jesus is viewed as Son of Man in public roles, that is, when he is in contact with outsiders who do not accept him and when he appears in apocalyptic roles before the whole world.[118] As we have seen, the predominance of this theme in Matthew is consistent with the late first-century Jewish apocalyptic tradition in which Matthew stands.[119] The multiple allusions to Daniel 7 and the "son of man" in late first-century Jewish texts, along with Matthew's emphasis on this figure, suggest that the expression and image were current in some Jewish groups of this period. These observations do not recreate Bultmann's independent apocalyptic Son of Man, but rather take note of a probable first-century Jewish linguistic usage that found its way into the gospels. Matthew uses Son of Man in connection with Jesus' tasks, which he fulfills in obedience to the Father; with Jesus' power and authority given to him by God; and with his apocalyptic roles at the end of the world. However, the expression "Son of Man" gains meaning only through its association with other traditions and its unfolding use in the narrative.

Jesus Crucified and Risen

Just as Jesus was presented as Messiah, son of David, king, Son of God, savior, and "God with us" at the beginning of the gospel, the same cluster of traditions and titles are used to illuminate the meaning of his final experiences.[120] Upon his arrival in Jerusalem, Jesus engages in a series of symbolic actions and polemical exchanges with the national leaders of Israel. These attacks have the dual effect of explaining why the rulers had Jesus arrested (21:45–46; 26:3–5) and of showing Jesus' superior authority and status. Thus Jesus is identified as messianic king (21:5), son of David and prophet (21:9, 11, 15), healer (21:14), Son of God (21:37), and Lord of David and all other Jewish authorities (22:45). In the controversies with his Jerusalem opponents (chaps. 21–23) and in his hearing and trial (26:59–68; 27:11–26), Jesus is shown to be right and innocent, and his opponents erroneous and corrupt. (Herod was similarly shown to be devious and evil in chapter 2.) At the Last Supper with his disciples Jesus, who will save his people from their sins (2:21), uses the cup of wine to symbolize his death and his (sacrificial) blood, "which will be poured out for many for the forgiveness of sins" (26:28).[121] In the hearing before the high priest and the council, Matthew presents Jesus as the Messiah, Son of God, and Son of Man

(26:63–64). Pilate and his soldiers ironically misunderstand him as a
false, aspiring king of the Jews (27:11, 27–31, 37) and would-be messiah (27:22). The Jerusalem leaders mockingly call him a prophet
(26:68), king (27:42), and Son of God (27:43). The people also mock
him (27:40), in contrast to the centurion and guards, who acknowledge the dead Jesus as Son of God (27:54) on the basis of nature's response to his death. Finally, Jesus' triumph over death is revealed by
miraculous phenomena (earthquake and light, 28:2–3) and a heavenly messenger. He reappears as apocalyptic ruler and Son of God
(28:16–20, 9–10), as he said he would in chapters 24–25. Thus the
climax and end of the narrative brings to completion many of the symbolic claims made for Jesus in the opening chapters. The thematic
threads woven through the narrative are tied into a unity by the para-
doxical and ironic death of Jesus on the cross, a death that is not an
end, but a fulfillment of all that was promised at the beginning.

Conclusion

After nineteen centuries of interpretation of Matthew, centuries which
separate us from the original context of Matthew, it is difficult to say
what he said about Jesus without adding the reflections of later centuries or losing the resonances of the first century.[122] All the categories
and titles Matthew uses to explain Jesus were native to Judaism in the
first century and were immediately comprehensible to his Jewish community.[123] None of them is precise and univocal in its meaning, but all
are part of the rich tradition of Israel based on the Bible and developed
in the literature of the Second Temple period. The claims that Jesus is
Messiah, son of David, Son of God, and Lord anchor Matthew's presentation of Jesus as a powerful representative of God who came to
teach and heal; not only Israel, but all who would believe in Jesus and
accept God. The narrative tells the story of Jesus' special origin, of his
teaching and healing, and finally of his significant death and resurrection. The narrative's meaning depends on Israel's traditions but is generated by the original and compelling use the author of Matthew
makes of those traditions of prophecy, wisdom, the figure of Moses,
and the Davidic kingship. Through the life and work of Matthew's
Jesus, believers can gain a close, kinship relation with God, come to
know God and God's will with unprecedented clarity, and participate
with Jesus in his battle against evil, a battle which will be won in the
end when the Son of Man judges the good and evil. No one text, title,
or allusion proves Matthew's case, but the mass of them woven into the

deeds and teachings of Jesus urge the listener to accept Jesus and thus God's manifestation in Jesus: "God with us" (2:23).

Though Matthew draws his interpretation of Jesus from Jewish tradition, the emphasis on Jesus and the high status accorded him make the gospel different from other Jewish literature. Second Temple literature contains accounts of biblical figures and their final testaments, but none gives as important and unique a role to its central figure as that given to Jesus by Matthew. Heavenly intermediaries and messengers are common in apocalyptic literature and rewritten biblical accounts, but Jesus' roles are more humanly intimate and enduringly effective than those of angelic messengers or returned biblical figures. By the creative combination of many of the archetypal figures, leaders, and roles found in the Bible, Matthew turned Jesus into *the* transcendent teacher, revealer, ruler, and savior authorized by God for Israel and humanity.

To say that Matthew, because he accords Jesus such a high status, is not Jewish, but Christian, in his teaching about Jesus, anachronistically imposes on the late first century the clear identity that most Christians created for themselves during the second century, often in contrast to Judaism. To say that Matthew's emphasis on Jesus as Son of God is incompatible with Judaism in the first century is to ignore the varieties of Judaism current in the first century. Granted the apocalyptic, mystical, political, sectarian, revivalist, and reformist movements within Palestinian and diaspora Judaism in the first century, Matthew's Christology makes claims that fit within the broad parameters of Judaism as it actually existed. Matthew did not claim for Jesus divinity in the way that Greek Christian theologians two centuries later did. He struggled to express his community's experience of Jesus using all the images, traditions, and words at his disposal. In all cases, however, Jesus is understood in his relationship with the God of Israel, known in the Bible, and in the experience of the community. Though Matthew's narrative would later be used to support ontological theories of the Son's relation to the Father, Matthew remains firmly in the orbit of Judaism.

VIII

Conclusions

We shall conclude this study with a review of the argument and a further consideration of the relationship of the Gospel of Matthew to Judaism, using the categories deviance, sect, and community. This review of the evidence will also give special attention to the passages most often cited by those who say that Matthew is a non-Jew or a Jew who has broken decisively with Judaism. Finally, we shall outline some of the consequences of this study for Matthean studies, the history of early Christianity, the history of early Judaism, for Christian theology and Jewish thought, and for Jewish-Christian relations.

Review of the Argument

Many studies of early Judaism and Christianity have erroneously retrojected later, classical forms of Judaism and Christianity into the first two centuries. To a greater or lesser degree, such treatments have denied the variety of form and expression found in each tradition and supported a harmonized picture of emerging orthodoxy that devalues minority views. Both Judaism and Christianity have sought to reaffirm clear and separate identities, often at the expense of the other. Christians have denigrated Jews as legalistic, effete, and unfaithful to God. Jews have dismissed Christians as misguided deviants from the Jewish tradition and sought to dissociate rabbinic Judaism from Christianity as early in history as possible. With these tendencies at work in theology and scholarship, common traditions have been treated as secondary and accidental in favor of a supposed essence of each religion. Contrary to this idealized picture of mutually exclusive salvation histories, most mid first-century believers-in-Jesus were Jews, and even at the end of the first century a substantial minority still were. Even after most Christians were non-Jewish in background, Jews and Christians rubbed shoulders, fought with one another for acceptance and status, and sometimes cooperated. As the two communities gradually separated in the second and following centuries, intellectual and social contacts remained close, as the hostility of some Christian writers to Judaism paradoxically demonstrates. Christians continued to use Jewish exegesis and ethics in their thought and teaching. In the cosmopolitan milieu of the Roman Empire, Jews, Christians, and other peoples constantly interacted with one another. In the East, Jewish-Christian groups endured, often overlapping the Jewish communities and sometimes indistinguishable from them to outsiders.

Christians inevitably had to relate themselves to Judaism because they read the Bible (their Old Testament), practiced many modified Jewish traditions, and cherished the deeds and teachings of Jesus, who lived as a Jew in Israel. They did so with varying degrees of sympathy, defensiveness, and hostility. Many who were born Jewish remained so, even when marginalized or rejected by one or both communities. In the first two centuries, most Jewish believers-in-Jesus probably found an acceptable place within the diverse groups, movements, and local communities that made up the larger Jewish community. A variety of diaspora groups, Near Eastern villages, apocalyptic movements, and political parties pulled the Jewish community in various directions during the centuries before rabbinic Judaism gained effective control of the leadership. Believers-in-Jesus made up a small part of this complex mix.

When we look closely at Matthew's terms for the people of Israel and their land—"Israel," "people," "Jews," "crowds," "this generation"—and examine their narrative roles in relationship to Jesus (and to the Matthean group), it seems clear that he sees himself and his group as part of Israel and that he hopes to attract members of the larger Jewish community to his form of Judaism, just as Jesus did. Contrary to many commentators on the gospel, Matthew's narrative is not a general indictment of Israel, nor does his presentation of the people imply that the Jewish nation as a whole rejected Jesus or that the Jewish mission of early Christianity has ended. Rather, condemnations of Jesus' opponents, such as the crowd/people who call for his crucifixion in 27:20–25, is limited to specific subgroups within Judaism. Matthew attacks only those who reject Jesus definitively, especially those in authority who lead the people away from Jesus. The crowds and the Jewish people as a whole remain, in the eyes of the author of Matthew, fertile ground for sowing the teachings of Jesus concerning Judaism.

Jesus' opponents in the gospel narrative are symbolic neither of Jews in general nor of Israel as a corporate entity, but of the leaders of the Jewish community in both Jesus' and Matthew's time. Not only

the leaders, but the institutions they control and the interpretations of
Jewish law and custom that they propose, are subject to constant and
systematic attack. Jesus is not pictured as hostile to the Temple itself,
much less to Jewish (that is, biblical) law. Rather, he is against business
as usual at the Temple. Through Jesus, the author of Matthew directs
his own polemics against rival leaders and their competing programs
for understanding and living Judaism in the late first century. He alleges that they have misunderstood and rejected God's will and so they
will be replaced by a new group of leaders (the *ethnos* producing
the fruits of the kingdom in 21:43). Matthew and his group are in a
struggle for the hearts and minds of their fellow Jews. They propose
their teacher and leader, Jesus, and their understanding of God's will as
the appropriate response to God, the law, and the prophets and as a
viable response to the loss of the Temple and the execution of Jesus by
hostile Jerusalem authorities. The people of Israel are condemned in
the narrative only when they blindly follow the community leaders
and firmly reject Jesus (and Matthew's teaching about him). For the
most part, Israel is portrayed as neutral or positively disposed toward
the teachings of Jesus.

The author of Matthew has varied evaluations of non-Jews who
appear as actors in the narrative. The same is true of references to
non-Jews in general. Thus there is no uniform category "gentile" in
Matthew that can be opposed to Jews. However, Matthew does sometimes reproduce cultural biases against outsiders. At other times, he
takes the gentiles' presence for granted as part of his social world, treating them neutrally and without any great interest. Of most interest are
the non-Jews who recognize and accept Jesus, especially the Magi, the
centurion with a sick servant, the Canaanite woman with a sick
daughter, and the centurion and guards at Jesus' execution. Though
none of them becomes a true follower of Jesus, they foreshadow an
emerging goal of the Matthean community in the late first century, to
teach and baptize the gentiles.

Though no simple, categorical definition of the Matthean community can be defended, attention to ancient forms of association, modern sociological categories, gospel data concerning positive and
negative relationships and the varieties of Jewish groups make it possible to understand Matthew's group of believers-in-Jesus as a part of
the larger Jewish community. The conflict between Matthew's group
and other Jews, including the community authorities, suggests that
the larger community sees Matthew's group as deviant. That is, they
are not outside the Jewish community, but they are objectionable to
the majority of the community. If sects are understood as deviant

groups that respond to their social and political context in a variety of ways (not just by withdrawal), then Matthew's group is a sect. As a sect or deviant group, Matthew's group is alienated from the larger Jewish community, but is still seeking to reform it and gain power.

Within Greco-Roman society, Matthew's group would have been understood as a private, voluntary association. Matthew's assembly probably met in a house and modeled itself on the household. The frequent use of kinship terminology for relationships among members and with God and Jesus reflects this household context. The frequent reference to disciples suggests, not a formal school, but household schooling and the close teacher-student relationship. In the Greco-Roman world, the philosophical teacher was expected to live a virtuous life, even to the point of dying for his beliefs, and he was thus someone to be admired and imitated. Matthew's household assembly followed the Jewish teacher, Jesus, and his interpretations of Jewish law and life. In order to promote this program, Matthew fostered close, communal relationships and a form of leadership which stressed community control rather than hierarchical relationships.

The gospel's teachings and disputes about observance of the law shows that its author was an informed participant in a number of first-century Jewish legal debates. Second Temple Jewish documents, such as the Book of Jubilees, the Temple Scroll, and the Covenant of Damascus, as well as the early strata of the Mishnah, show that Jewish sects and reform movements disagreed concerning many points of interpretation. They argued over tithing duties, the validity and suspension of oaths and vows, the conditions for divorce, the exact requirements of the Sabbath and the interpretation of purity and dietary laws. Matthew joins in this debate as a serious defender and teacher of his group's understanding of how one should live Judaism according to the teachings of Jesus. His arguments are based on Scripture and the types of reasoning found in Jewish literature of the first century. Matthew's polemics against his opponents and their positions are typical of sectarian conflict. His accusations of hypocrisy against his opponents are an attack on their integrity. In matters of substance. Matthew claims for himself the high ground, stressing love, mercy, justice, and faith, as though his opponents neglect or oppose these fundamental principles of biblical life and theology. Needless to say, these polemics do not give a fair picture of Matthew's opponents, but they do testify to the intensity of the struggle for control in late first-century Judaism.

Matthew's teaching about Jesus is rooted firmly in the larger Jewish tradition of the first century. Many commentators have treated Matthew's Christology as so decisively contradictory to Jewish teaching that it would have ipso facto placed him outside the Jewish community. But Matthew grounds his teaching about Jesus on an irreproachable biblical theology, that is, its teaching about God and God's activity among his people Israel. Jesus fits comfortably within first century Jewish understandings of how God guides and acts in human affairs through divinely empowered agents. The figures of an anointed one and son of David appointed to rule and care for Israel originated in the Bible and are developed in various ways in Second Temple literature. Jesus' roles as authoritative teacher and powerful healer fit the expectations of the culture and time. Typological associations of Jesus with Moses, personified wisdom, and the prophets resonate deeply with first-century Jewish understandings of their history and heroes. The rich and ambiguous meanings of "Lord" and "Son of Man," two common designations for Jesus, and the constant reference to Scripture to validate Jesus' life and teachings support the extensive claims Matthew makes for Jesus as God's presence among his people. More than the titles and the biblical quotations and allusions, the pattern of Jesus' life and divine approval—along with his powerful deeds—convey Matthew's understanding of Jesus' importance for Israel and the nations.

Deviance, Sect, and Community

This study concludes that the Gospel of Matthew addresses a deviant group within the Jewish community in greater Syria, a reformist Jewish sect seeking influence and power (relatively unsuccessfully) within the Jewish community as a whole. This sectarian stand and deviant label explain the harsh polemics and sharp disagreements that lead some commentators to identify the author as a Christian and not a Jew, to postulate a complete separation between Matthew and Judaism, and to brand him as anti-Jewish. Quite to the contrary, the Gospel of Matthew and its author are Jewish to the core; the gospel's polemics and disputes prove its Jewishness. Conflicts among groups within a religion, nation, or tradition arise from their cultural, political, or geographical proximity and are fed by the substantial relationships that bind them to one another even as they fight. Heated exchanges take place, metaphorically speaking, within the same house, in this case, within the house of Israel, which includes the separate assemblies of Matthew and his rival Jewish leaders (Matthew's *ekklesia*/church and "their synagogues"). The separate assembly and "house" of the Qumran community (1QS 8:4–10) and their diatribes against those who reject their teaching and way of living Judaism (e.g., 1QS 2:4–10) illustrate the kind of sectarian disagreement found in the Gospel of Matthew.

Throughout this study, I have referred to what is usually called the Matthean community as a "group" because group is the most general and neutral sociological designation available for the gospel writer's audience. I have reserved the more rich designation "community" for the Jewish community as a whole, including in this designation the whole Jewish tradition and the full variety of Jewish groups and sub-traditions in Israel and the diaspora during the first century. In choosing this terminology, I have stressed the continuing membership of Matthew's group in Israel and argued against the usual implications of the term "Matthean community," namely, that this community is separate from Judaism and is markedly Christian, not Jewish. Can one legitimately refer to Matthew's group as a community? Yes, if community is defined correctly. The modern use of "community" carries with it individualistic, romantic notions of interpersonal relationships contrasted with modern bureaucratic social structures. But the Jewish community in the Roman Empire integrated religious, cultural, political, bureaucratic, and personal aspects of life into a communal whole. With its history, literature, strong social organization, and rich cultural life, the Jewish community was the matrix within which both Christianity and the Matthean group originated. The Matthean group had a strong sense of identity and a common set of deeply held values and perceptions, which resulted in close, supportive, loving contact among the members. Since the fundamental beliefs and practices of the Matthean group spring from and are consistent with those of the larger Jewish community, it can be understood as a sect or deviance association within the larger Jewish community and also as a Jewish community of a particular kind, a Christian-Jewish community.

But how does the Matthean group relate to the nations, to whom Matthew cautiously opens the boundaries of his community, and how does it fit into the network of Christian communities which had arisen in Syria, Asia Minor, Greece, Rome, and elsewhere by the end of the first century? First, the gentiles. As we have seen, Matthew does not replace Israel with the gentiles, contrary to the views of many commentators. The replacement or supercessionist theory was developed by second-century Christian writers, for example, Barnabas and Justin, and was then projected back on Matthew, usually through the construction of a theology of salvation history foreign to Matthew. Matthew does open his doors to non-Jews, but he expects them to observe the law revealed in the Bible. He does not treat all gentiles alike, but rather uses the words *ethnē* and *ethnikoi* with a variety of

meanings, positive and pejorative. His usage matches the complex social and religious situation he finds himself in. The argument that
Matthew's inclusion of gentiles automatically moves his group beyond
the bounds of Judaism ignores the complex and varied relationships
between Jews and gentiles in many Jewish communities and writings.
The thematic proclamation that the followers of Jesus are to be a "light
to the world" (5:14) does not hint at the emergence of the church out
of Judaism and its transformation "in a worldwide Christian community of which he and his readers are members," but points in the opposite direction.[1] Picking up on the Isaianic themes of a gathering of the
gentiles to acknowledge and worship at the Temple in Jerusalem (Isa.
2:2; 56:1–8; 60:1–22; 66:18–21), Matthew envisions his group
attracting gentiles to Israel. In this hope, he is at one with many parts
of the Jewish community which received converts and welcomed
gentiles (the so-called God-fearers) to synagogue services and instructions.

Defense of the thesis that Matthew does not reject Israel or replace
Israel with the church requires a careful and, in this author's view,
more even-handed interpretation of several passages in Matthew that
are often read as a rejection of Israel in favor of the gentiles. A number
of these passages have been treated in the course of the argument in
this study; a brief reminder will suffice here. John the Baptist's threat
that God can raise up children of Abraham from stones is not a rejection of Israel or Israel's special relationship with God (3:9). This prophetic threat addresses the leaders, the Sadducees and Pharisees. Like
biblical prophetic oracles, it presumes Israel's chosenness and urges Israel to a full commitment to and observance of the covenant and God's
law. Relativizing the value of birth as a Jew is not a Christian attack on
Judaism, but a Jewish polemic against injustice in Israel. The juxtaposition of those from the east and west who eat at the heavenly banquet and the "sons of the kingdom" who refuse to attend (8:11–12) is
often interpreted as a contrast of the gentiles who make up the Matthean group with (all) Jews who have rejected Jesus. But as we saw in
chapter 2 above, those who come from the east and west may have
originally been diaspora Jews; even if Matthew is referring to gentiles,
they attend a Jewish banquet presided over by the Jewish patriarchs.
The "sons of the kingdom" who refuse to attend are not all Jews, but
only some, especially the leaders who oppose Jesus. For the others, the
"crowds" in the narrative, Matthew has hope; thus he envisions a
gathering of both Jews and gentiles.

Many commentators have noted that Jesus, after teaching in chapters 5–7 and doing miracles in chapters 8–9, engages in a series of con-

flicts and begins to be rejected in chapters 11–12. In chapter 13 he instructs his disciples privately about the meaning of the parables after the crowds have not fully understood, and he continues this instruction in subsequent chapters. Some commentators see this section of Matthew as a reflection of the total rejection of Jesus and Matthew's community by Judaism.[2] But Matthew's treatment of Israel is much more nuanced than this view allows, for he treats Israel from the inside as a member. He distinguishes leaders from people, followers of Jesus from those who are interested or neutral, the people of Jerusalem from the Galilean crowds, and so on. The process of appealing to Israel and distinguishing different responses continues from the time of Jesus to that of the author of the gospel. Thus the historicizing of Matthew's narrative and the relegation of any positive statements and attitudes about Judaism to the past is unwarranted.[3] Those in Israel who have rejected Jesus are lost in Matthew's eyes, but those who have not are still available to his teaching. Thus the *ethnos* bearing the fruits of the kingdom to which the vineyard is to be given (21:43) is not the gentiles conceived of as a new nation, but the Matthean group conceived of as new leaders of Israel. The Matthean group replaces the chief priests and Pharisees (21:45), not all of Israel, because the crowds (Israel) support Jesus as a prophet (21:46). During Jesus' trial before Pilate the crowd, spurred on by the chief priests and elders, call for Jesus' execution, and finally the people say, "His blood be on us and on our children" (27:25). But even here Matthew is not using "people" in a highly theological sense to condemn all of Israel. As always, he is speaking concretely of part of Israel, the people in Jerusalem who allowed themselves to be manipulated by the leaders into calling for Jesus' death. Matthew has them utter an *ex eventu* prophecy that looks forward to the destruction of Jerusalem in 70, a disaster which Matthew attributes, not to the sins of Israel in general (2 Baruch, 4 Ezra), but to the crowds who sought Jesus' death. Finally, the author of Matthew comments in his own voice on the slander that Jesus' body was stolen from his tomb by his disciples, noting that "this story has been spread among the Jews to this day" (28:15). As was shown in chapter 3, the use of "Jews" does not mean that Matthew is gentile or that he no longer considers himself part of Israel. Rather, this outsiders' term for Israel is a calculated polemical attack by a Christian-Jewish author speaking of those members of Israel who are beyond reach because of their denial of the foundations of faith in Jesus.

Commentators who interpret these crucial passages as manifestations of the author's distance from Israel ignore the sociological relationships which bind groups to one another within a tradition.

Matthew's attacks are vivid and vituperative because he is a member of Israel who still hopes to influence his fellow Jews to accept Jesus and reject their traditional (mis)leaders. Matthew does not reject Israel or oppose Christianity to Judaism; he hopes to unite all within a Jesus-centered Israel. Christian commentators who have read later Christian conflicts into Matthew's polemics seek to defend the position that Matthew teaches the rejection of Israel or the replacement of Israel by the gentiles. In order to support this view, they find themselves connecting symbolic parables and sayings with issues and problems these texts do not explicitly address. They subsume nuanced and concrete Matthean attacks on his contemporaries under an alleged Matthean theology, a complex, detailed system or salvation-history scheme, according to which Matthew's narrative encodes a history of the development of early Christianity. Expressions and tactics typical of inner-Jewish polemic are attributed to the anti-Judaism of an outsider.[4] I would argue, in contrast, that Matthew speaks directly to his Christian-Jewish group about specific disagreements, opponents, and rejections that were taking place in the late first-century Jewish community.

Just as Matthew's group lives as part of the Jewish community, albeit as a deviant group, so it is also part of the network of Christian communities dotting the shores of the Mediterranean Sea in the late first century. The variety of religious movements and the flow of people encouraged frequent crossing of boundaries. Matthew's mostly Jewish group welcomed gentiles and was being urged by Matthew to welcome them more. In doing this, they acted like many diaspora Jewish communities that had patrons, followers, and members from the gentile world. Since Christian communities varied greatly in the late first century, there was still room for very Jewish communities of believers-in-Jesus alongside Pauline, gentile communities, Johannine sectarian groups, the inclusive groups addressed by Luke-Acts, and so on. In a climate of great spiritual and social ferment, the opportunities for keeping Judaism and Christianity together were very real. Fifty years later, in the middle of the second century, the borders of both Judaism and Christianity were less permeable, but still not closed. Only in subsequent centuries would the identities of Judaism and Christianity harden decisively.

Consequences

Insofar as the conclusions reached in this study are accepted, what are their consequences for Matthean studies, the history of early Christianity and the history of early Judaism, for Christian theology and Jewish thought, and for Jewish-Christian relations? Matthean scholars have long admitted the tensions in Matthew, especially the contrast between his zealous interest in and fidelity to Jewish tradition and his hostility to certain Jewish teachings and Jewish leaders (often interpreted inaccurately as hostility to the people). The dominant interpretive paradigm has treated Matthew as a faithful Christian tradent who preserved earlier Jewish-Christian traditions, to which he no longer adhered, either in order to reconcile a gentile community to the Jewish origins of Christianity or in order to mediate between Jews and gentiles in his own community. Understood this way, Matthew is derivative and inconsistent. The seriousness with which he takes biblical law has been ignored by some. Others have valued Matthew less than Paul because of his partiality toward Jewish traditions and laws. In the Great Church tradition, Matthew became the spokesperson for structure and ethics because of the abundance of his teachings and biblical interpretations. He has also become an embarassment for Christians well disposed toward Judaism because of the way his polemics against his contemporaries have been used against Jews. But if, as is argued here, Matthew is a Jew who believes in Jesus, then his love for biblical teachings and interpretations, his zeal for the "lost sheep of the house of Israel" (10:6), and his passionate polemics all make sense and can aid Christian theology as it begins a new millennium.

If Matthew is read as a Christian-Jew of the late first century still seeking to influence the Jewish community, then he fits more readily into the newly emerging paradigm of Christian origins according to which Christian theological, social, and institutional identity took shape only gradually during the first two centuries. The many small Christian communities in the Roman Empire varied greatly in their views and practices. The universal characteristics attributed to Christians two centuries later are inappropriate for defining Christianity in the first century. The "identity" of Christianity was not a fixed center, but a moving complex of beliefs and practices. The boundaries of Christianity and Judaism overlapped, and multiple religious participation was more the norm than the exception. Christian-Jews and Jewish-Christians were numerous in the East and continued to exist in various local forms for centuries. Thus Matthew's group as part of the Jewish community is not an anomaly, but one of many predecessors in the gradual evolution of a more universal form of Christianity.

Similarly, the history of early Judaism is being rethought, and this view of Matthew's group aligns with most recent evidence. The discovery of the Dead Sea Scrolls, a resurgence of scholarship on the so-called

apocrypha and pseudepigrapha, and critical study of rabbinic literature have all worked to illuminate the diversity of Judaism (or Judaisms) in Israel and the diaspora during the Second Temple period and
its immediate aftermath. Earlier interpretations of this period were derived from talmudic retrojections of rabbinic Judaism into the Second
Temple period. This led Jewish scholars to treat Second Temple Judaism as an immature form of rabbinic Judaism. Christian interpreters
tended to denigrate this Judasim as inferior to Christianity or as a theologically outdated and divinely rejected religion.[5] Needless to say, one
hopes that the understanding of Second Temple Judaism as a vigorous
and creative religion and communal way of life will foster respect for its
achievements, which led to the later development of both Christianity
and the Talmuds.[6]

Both Christian theology and Jewish thought can profit from a more
nuanced reading of Matthew and similar documents of the first two
centuries. Both traditions have tended to obliterate minority views and
"deviant" positions in favor of a dominant "orthodox" theology and
practice, making exclusive claims to truth and authority.[7] Giving serious attention to different, dissident views forces each community to
cherish and integrate its variety of views and ways of living and to develop a more critical grasp of what it takes for granted. Christian theology has often responded to the modern emphasis on individuality by
deemphasizing fidelity to God's commandments. The discipline and
practice of Christianity necessary for the actualization of God's gifts
and the effective communication of the gospel have been ignored. In
its modern eagerness to avoid the evils of so-called legalism, many
churches have lost Matthew's emphasis on a well-rounded faith and
practice of God's will founded on a deep acceptance of God's love and
presence.

Modern Jewish thought has emphasized the independence and integrity of the Jewish tradition in the face of persistent attempts by anti-
Semites and anti-Jewish Christian theology to denigrate it. Though
people often speak of the Judeo-Christian tradition of the West, some
Jewish writers have denied the substantial unity of the tradition and
stressed the essentially independent religious and cultural core of Judaism, which differs substantially from Christianity.[8] According to this
position, despite many common intellectual and social roots, Judaism
and Christianity today share only an arm's-length and often negative
relationship. This view does justice to the unique achievements of each
tradition over the past nineteen centuries and gives full weight to the
history of hostility and oppression against Judaism that has characterized Western Christianity. Nevertheless, Jewish and Christian tradi-

tions still share many of the same cultural contexts and problems. Christianity and Judaism interacted often in their efforts to establish themselves in the late Roman Empire.[9] During the Middle Ages, Jewish and Christian scholars interacted significantly with both positive and negative results. Both communities shared the fertile world and culture which led to modernity. In the modern period, traditional Judaism in the West, like traditional Christianity, has struggled to respond effectively to the Enlightenment. In philosophy, theology, and practice, Jews and Christians have involuntarily and often unwillingly shared a common political and cultural world, as they did in Matthew's time. Further productive relationships are possible, and given the flow of world history, desirable.

But we do not live in the world of pretend. Even though the Gospel of Matthew was written for Jews within the first-century Jewish community, it has had its effect and its home among gentiles for the last nineteen hundred years.[10] The gospel's polemics have been used again and again by gentile Christians as a club to beat the whole Jewish tradition, marginalizing the Jewish community and threatening its existence. The actual history of the gospel thus ironically includes a large measure of anti-Semitism along with its honorable role in promoting a healthy communal life within the Christian churches. The checkered history of the Gospel of Matthew corresponds to the tensions that commentators have found in the text; Matthew is at once the most Jewish of gospels in its traditions and interpretations and the most critical of gospels in its attacks on certain forms of Judaism. Matthew is an authentic witness both to the shared traditions that unite and to the deep hostilities that divide the Jewish and Christian communities. Most important, though, this gospel forces Christians to confront again and again their Jewish roots and rules out Marcion's expedient of obliterating the Jewish foundations of faith in Jesus as Messiah and Son of God. For Jews, the Gospel of Matthew understood positively testifies to the turbulent relations among various Jewish groups in the late first century and to the creative matrix that eventually produced rabbinic Judaism as the dominant tradition and way of living according to Torah.

As for the future, a healthy appreciation for human limitations counsels moderation in utopian hopes for peace and understanding. Jews and Christians have been thrown together because of their common origins in the Middle East, their common religious traditions (however differently interpreted), and the course of history in the West. The increasingly smaller world of instant communication and swift travel guarantees that Jews and Christians will continue to argue over their traditions, history, political relationships, and ultimate goals.

From a Christian point of view, narratives like that of Matthew may be of help, but only if fully understood and maturely appropriated. Rhetorical attacks and one-sided arguments, uprooted from their living, first-century contexts and hypostatized into eternal truths, endanger the fundamental understandings, convictions, and commitments which underlie Christian life.[11] The Gospel of Matthew, understood as a Christian-Jewish attempt to unite Jews and gentiles, may serve as a vital witness to the gentile search for God and as a deeply Jewish interpretation of God's work in the world.

Abbreviations

Books of the Bible

Acts	Acts of the Apostles
Bar.	Baruch
Chron.	Chronicles
Col.	Colossians
Dan.	Daniel
Deut.	Deuteronomy
Eccles.	Ecclesiastes
Eph.	Ephesians
Esd.	Esdras
Exod.	Exodus
Ezek.	Ezekiel
Gal.	Galatians
Gen.	Genesis
Heb.	Hebrews
Hos.	Hosea
Isa.	Isaiah
Jer.	Jeremiah
Josh.	Joshua
Jth.	Judith
Judg.	Judges
Lev.	Leviticus
Macc.	Maccabees
Matt.	Matthew
Mic.	Micah
Neh.	Nehemiah
Num.	Numbers
Pet.	Peter
Phil.	Philippians
Prov.	Proverbs
Ps. (Pss.)	Psalm(s)
Rev.	Revelation
Rom.	Romans
Sam.	Samuel

Thess.   Thessalonians
Tim.   Timothy
Wisd. of Sol.   Wisdom of Solomon

Orders and Tractates in Mishnaic and Related Literature

The same tractate names are used for the Mishnah, Tosefta, Palestinian Talmud, and Babylonian Talmud. The tractates are distinguished by a prefixed "m," "t," "p," or "b."

Bab. Bat.   Baba Batra
Bab. Met.   Baba Metzia
Bek.   Bekorot
Ber.   Berakot
Bet.   Betsa
Bik.   Bikkurim
Eduy.   Eduyot
Hag.   Hagiga
Hul.   Hullin
Kel.   Kelim
Kidd.   Kiddushin
Ma'as   Ma'aserot
Ma'as. Shen.   Ma'aser Sheni
Mak.   Makkot
Naz.   Nazir
Ned.   Nedarim
Pes.   Pesahim
Shab.   Shabbat
Shek.   Shekalim
Sot.   Sota
Taan.   Taanit
Yeb.   Yebamot

Dead Sea Scrolls

Numbers before the letter "Q" refer to the Qumran cave in which the document was found.

CD   Covenant of Damascus
Gen. Apoc.   Genesis Apocryphon
p   pesher
Q   Qumran
tg   targum
1QapGen   Genesis Apocryphon
1QPHab   Pesher on Habakkuk
1QS   Community Rule

4QFlor	Florilegium or Eschataological Misrashim
11QMelch	Melchisedek text
11QTemple	Temple Scroll
11QtgJob	Targum of Job

Other Texts

Ant.	*Jewish Antiquities* (Josephus)
Apoc. of Abr.	Apocalypse of Abraham
ARNA, ARNB	Abot de Rabbi Nathan, Versions A and B
Enoch	1 Enoch or Ethiopic Enoch
Jub.	Book of Jubilees
LXX	Septuagint
Num. Rab.	Numbers Rabbah
Sifre Deut.	Sifre Deuteronomy
Sib. Or.	Sibylline Oracles

Notes

Introduction

1. Richard B. Hays, *Echoes of Scripture in the Letters of Paul* (New Haven: Yale University Press, 1989), ix, protests a review by Steiner which casually refers to Paul's hatred of the Jews. His book is a refutation of that position. But Hays himself commits the same fault when he casually remarks that Steiner's comment "might be applied, with some justice, to the Evangelists Matthew and John." (p. x).

W. D. Davies, *The Setting of the Sermon on the Mount* (Cambridge: Cambridge University Press, 1963), 286, notes the complex attitude toward Judaism found in Matthew.

2. The unknown author of the Gospel of Matthew will sometimes be referred to as the author and sometimes by the abbreviation "Matthew." This usage does not imply acceptance of the traditional position that this gospel was written by the apostle Matthew (9:9; 10:3). It is merely a convenient shorthand.

3. The charge that Jesus' marvelous birth was really illegitimate is answered in Matt. 1:18–25, and the charge that his disciples stole his body in 27:62–66 and 28:11–15. Charges that followers of Jesus reject the law are probably being refuted in chapter 5 and attacks on the legitimacy of the Matthean leadership in chapter 23.

4. The tension between deviance as destructive and as formative for society is brought out well by Nachman Ben-Yehuda, *Deviance and Moral Boundaries: Witchcraft, the Occult, Deviant Sciences and Scientists* (Chicago: University of Chicago Press, 1985), 3–7. On the positive effects of deviance, see Kai T. Ericson, *Wayward Puritans: A Study in the Sociology of Deviance* (New York: Wiley, 1966), 3–5. For the necessity of deviance see Emile Durkheim, especially *The Rules of Sociological Method* (Glencoe, Ill.: Free Press, 1958), 67, and *The Division of Labor in Society* (Glencoe, Ill: Free Press, 1960), 102. See also George H. Mead, "The Psychology of Punitive Justice," *American Journal of Sociology* 23 (1918): 577–602, esp. 591.

5. For a review of modern positions on Matthew's group in relation to Judaism, see Graham N. Stanton, "The Origin and Purpose of Matthew's Gospel: Matthean Scholarship from 1945–1980," in H. Temporini and W. Hasse, eds., *Aufstieg und Niedergang der Römischen Welt* 2.25.3 (Berlin: deGruyter, 1985), 1889–1951, esp. 1911–21.

6. See Stanton, "Origin," 1914–16, 1921. See also Sean Freyne, "Oppression from the Jews: Matthew's Gospel as an Early Christian Response," *Concilium* 200 (1988): 47–54, for an analysis of the Matthean group's search for identity vis-à-vis its parent religion.

7. Luke T. Johnson, "Borgen's *Philo, John, and Paul,*" *Jewish Quarterly Review* 79 (1989): 386, points out the variety of positions in Judaism and then summarizes accurately: "Within this already variegated Judaism, the messianic cult based on Jesus was, from the time of his death until approximately the last decade of the first century, one of the competing voices. . . . The study of Christianity in its formative period, therefore, requires taking seriously its claim to an authentic Jewish identity."

8. The endurance of these categories is phenomenal. See, for example, Hans Dieter Betz, *Essays on the Sermon on the Mount* (Philadelphia: Fortress, 1985), 22, who claims that the Sermon on the Mount is Jewish and pre-Matthean in contrast to the gospel itself, which is gentile and universal. This is also the thesis of his commentary on the Sermon on the Mount due to appear in the Hermeneia series.

9. See Adolf Harnack's *What Is Christianity?* New York: Harpers, 1957). Originally published as *Das Wesen des Christentums* (1900).

10. Alfred Loisy, *The Gospel and the Church* (Philadelphia: Fortress, 1976). Originally published as *L'Évangile et l'église* (1902).

11. The story is in b. Ber. 28b. The Birkat Ha-Minim is invoked by W. D. Davies, *Setting,* 256–315, to explain the composition of the Gospel of Matthew, and by J. Louis Martyn, *History and Theology in the Fourth Gospel,* 2d ed. (Nashville: Abingdon, 1979), chap. 2, to explain John's social situation.

12. Adolf Harnack, *The Mission and Expansion of Christianity in the First Three Centuries,* 2d ed., (London, 1908), 18. See Robert Wilken, *John Chrysostom and the Jews: Rhetoric and Reality in the Late Fourth Century* (Berkeley: University of California Press, 1983), 44–46. David Rokeah, *Jews, Pagans, and Christians in Conflict* (Jerusalem: Magnes; Leiden: Brill, 1982), 46–48, substantially affirms Harnack's thesis of the withdrawal of Judaism and the dominance of Christianity.

13. For example, Wilken, *John Chrysostom,* 152–53, suggests that Chrysostom may have engaged in actual disputes with Jews. For further data, see chap. 1 of this volume.

14. This position refers to redaction criticism, which followed on form criticism after the Second World War. The pioneering essays in Matthean studies are found in G. Bornkamm, *Tradition and Interpretation in Matthew* (Philadelphia: Westminster, 1963). More recent literary critical and social scientific approaches to the gospels presume redaction criticism. See also the focus on the narrative as a whole found in "composition criticism" as practiced by William Thompson in "An Historical Perspective on the Gospel of Matthew." *Journal of Biblical Literature* 93 (1974): 243–62 and *Matthew's Advice to a Divided Community (Matt. 17:22–18:35),* AnBib 44 (Rome: Biblical Institute, 1970).

15. G. Barth, "Matthew's Understanding of the Law," in Bornkamm, *Tradition and Interpretation,* 111; R. Hummel, *Die Auseinandersetzung zwischen Kirche*

und Judentum im Matthäusevangelium (Munich: Kaiser, 1963), 154; Douglas R. A. Hare, *The Theme of Jewish Persecution of Christians in the Gospel according to St. Matthew,* SNTSMS 6 (Cambridge: Cambridge University Press, 1967), 81ff.; E. Schweizer, *Matthäus und seine Gemeinde,* Stuttgarter Bibelstudien 71 (Stuttgart: KBW, 1974).

16. Georg Strecker, *Der Weg der Gerechtigkeit: Untersuchung zur Theologie des Matthäus,* 3d ed. (Göttingen: Vandenhoeck, 1971; orig. ed. 1962), is the major proponent of this theory. He is followed by John Meier, *Law and History in Matthew's Gospel,* AnBib 71 (Rome: Biblical Institute, 1976), 14–21, who reviews all the positions and arguments. Strecker has been often attacked. See the review by H. B. Green in *Journal of Theological Studies* 5 (1964): 361–65, and the sharp attack by Martin Hengel, in "Zur matthäischen Bergpredigt und ihrem jüdischen Hintergrund," *Theologische Rundschau* 52 (1987), 327–400, esp. 341–48. Hans Dieter Betz, "The Sermon on the Mount in Matthew's Interpretation," in Birger Pierson et al., eds., *The Future of Christianity: Essays in Honor of Helmut Koester* (Minneapolis: Fortress, 1991), 258–75, again attempts to overcome this tension between Judaism and Matthew's orientation toward gentiles by postulating that Matthew incorporated a preexisting, Jewish-Christian sermon into his very Christian gospel.

17. See Hare, *Persecution;* David E. Garland, *The Intention of Matthew 23* (Leiden: Brill, 1979). Contrary to Garland, chapter 23 is a Matthean redactional unit which expresses in a most fervent way the author's engagement with the Jewish authorities.

18. This view comes out most clearly in Justin Martyr's *Dialogue with Trypho* (123; 135), where Christians are said to be Israel and the true Israelite race *(genos).* For a thematic development of such theses, see Marcel Simon, *Verus Israel: Étude sur les relations entre Chrétiens et Juifs dans l'Empire Romain* (Paris: de Boccard, 1948); translated as *Verus Israel: A Study of the Relations between Christians and Jews in the Roman Empire, 135–425* (New York: Oxford University Press, 1986).

19. Steven Fraade, *From Tradition to Commentary: Torah and Its Interpretation in the Midrash Sifre to Deuteronomy* (Albany: SUNY Press, 1991), 5, 174 n. 18, correctly notes that Matthew and the Covenant of Damascus use Scripture to tell their stories and claim that biblical prophecy is fulfilled in their community experience.

20. Joseph B. Tyson, *The Death of Jesus in Luke-Acts* (Columbia: University of South Carolina Press, 1986), 168, observes concisely that when an author uses a source, it is his own.

21. Donald A. Hagner, "The *Sitz im Leben* of the Gospel of Matthew," *SBL Seminar Papers 1985* (Atlanta: Scholars, 1985), 243–69, esp. 256.

22. For the argument that Matthew's opponents were early representatives of what would become rabbinic Judaism, see J. Andrew Overman, *Matthew's Gospel and Formative Judaism: The Social World of the Matthean Community* (Minneapolis: Fortress, 1990).

23. Peter Richardson, *Israel in the Apostolic Church,* SNTSMS 10 (Cambridge: Cambridge University Press, 1969), 194, despite an anachronistic

use of the term "Christian," correctly characterizes the sectarian conflict in Matthew thus: "In so far as he works toward a theory of the Church as 'true Israel,' he does it as a Jewish Christian for a Jewish Christian community, as a part of a dispute with a pharisaic Synagogue which is also claiming to be 'true Israel.' In the post-Jamnian situation where a Jewish Christian church might stand alongside a synagogue, each has a deep need to clarify its thinking about its relationship to the cultus and the law. Each is forced to move beyond the attitude before the fall of Jerusalem towards these matters, and in doing so each is tempted to claim that it fully represents 'Israel.' The pharisaic community rested its claim basically on continuous tradition; the Christian on the fulfillment of the old and better obedience through the Messiah." It should be noted that the claims both to continuous tradition and to fulfillment are equally artificial. They are creative, sectarian initiatives seeking to adapt Jewish tradition to new circumstances.

24. This is contrary to the thesis that Matthew's group is mostly or completely gentile (and that the Jewish mission is in the past). For the gentile thesis, see Strecker, *Weg der Gerechtigkeit*, 34–35; Hare, *Persecution*, 153; Meier, *Law and History*, 14–21; Rolf Walker, *Die Heilsgeschichte im ersten Evangelium*, FRLANT 91 (Göttingen: Vandenhoeck, 1967); Lloyd Gaston, "Messiah of Israel as Teacher of the Gentiles: The Setting of Matthew's Christology," *Interpretation* 29 (1975): 24–40. Wolfgang Trilling sees the gospel community at midpoint, separated from Israel, but claiming to be the true Israel (hence all the Jewish traditions). See *Das Wahre Israel: Studien zur Theologie des Matthäus-Evangelium*, SANT 10, 3d ed. (Munich: Kosel, 1964); orig. ed., Erfurter Theol. Stud. 7 (Leipzig: St. Benno-Verlag, 1959). For vigorous rejections of Strecker's position on the gentile nature of Matthew's community, see Hengel, "Bergpredigt," 341–48, and Benno Przybylski, "The Setting of Matthean Anti-Judaism," in Peter Richardson, ed., *Anti-Judaism in Early Christianity, Paul and the Gospels* (Waterloo: Laurier, 1986), 1:181–200.

25. Shaye J. D. Cohen, "The Significance of Yavneh: Pharisees, Rabbis, and the End of Jewish Sectarianism," *Hebrew Union College Annual* 55 (1984): 27–53, has proposed that after the destruction of the Temple, Jews no longer broke into sects, but rather argued matters of practice and thought under the aegis of the emerging rabbinic movement. However, the rabbis gained control over Jewish society in the Mediterranean and the East only slowly over the next several centuries. The variety of Jewish literature, the revolt under Trajan, and the Bar Kosiba War all argue to great diversity within Jewish society.

26. *Logoi kata Ioudaion* [Homilies against the Jews], most recently translated into English by Paul W. Harkins as *Discourses against Judaizing Christians*, vol. 68 of *The Fathers of the Church*. (Washington, D.C.: Catholic University, 1979).

27. For the literary influence of Matthew in the second century, see E. Massaux, *Influence de l'evangile de Matthieu sur la litterature chretienne avant saint Irénée* (Louvain: Publications Universitaires, 1950); reprinted with a review of subsequent scholarship in the Leuven University BETL series (no. 75; Leuven: Peeters, 1986), and translated as *The Influence of the Gospel of Saint Matthew on*

Christian Literature before St. Irenaeus, ed. Arthur J. Bellinzoni, 3 vols. (Leuven: Peeters; Macon, Ga: Mercer, 1990–93); and *Die Rezeption des Matthäusevangeliums in der Zeit vor Irenäus,* ed. Wolf-Dietrich Köhler, WUNT 2, no. 24 (Tübingen: Mohr, 1987). For the milieu of Matthew and later developments, see Graham N. Stanton, "5 Ezra and Matthean Christianity in the Second Century," *Journal of Theological Studies 28* (1977): 67–83, and Ulrich Luz, "The Disciples in the Gospel according to Matthew," in Graham N. Stanton, ed., *The Interpretation of Matthew* (Philadelphia: Fortress; London: SPCK, 1983), 115–19.

28. Edwin M. Schur, *The Politics of Deviance: Stigma Contests and the Uses of Power* (Englewood Cliffs, N.J.: Prentice-Hall, 1980), 13; *Labeling Deviant Behavior* (New York: Harper, 1971), 69–81. For more on deviance, see chap. 5 of this volume.

Chapter One

1. Though the gospel never says this, it is susceptible to that interpretation. Benno Przybylski, *Righteousness in Matthew and His World of Thought,* SNTSMS 41 (Cambridge: Cambridge University Press, 1980), 81, shrewdly observes that Matthew did not intend to teach a new law (much less a new Israel) but that he did communicate something that led people to interpret him that way.

2. The materials in this chapter appeared in another form in "Jews and Christians in the First Two Centuries: The Changing Paradigm," *Shofar* 10 (1992): 16–34.

3. The classic affirmation of diversity is found in Walter Bauer's older study, translated as *Orthodoxy and Heresy in Earliest Christianity* (Philadelphia: Fortress, 1971).

4. For critiques of Christian and Jewish scholarship on Judaism, see A. T. Kraabel, "Synagoga Caeca: Systematic Distortion in Gentile Interpretations of Evidence for Judaism in the Early Christian Period," in Jacob Neusner and Ernest S. Frerichs, eds., *"To See Ourselves as Others See Us": Christians, Jews, "Others" in Late Antiquity* (Chico: Scholars, 1985), 219–46; and Jack Lightstone, "Christian Anti-Judaism in its Judaic Mirror: The Judaic Context of Early Christianity Revised," in Stephen G. Wilson, ed., *Anti-Judaism in Early Christianity,* vol. 2: *Separation and Polemic,* Studies in Christianity and Judaism 2 (Waterloo: Laurier, 1986), 103–32, esp. 103–12.

5. For a broad bibliographic survey of Judaism from 70 to 200, see Baruch Bokser, "Recent Developments in the Study of Judaism, 70–200 c.e.," *Second Century* 3 (1983): 1–68. For basic works and texts, see H. L. Strack and G. Stemberger, *Introduction to the Talmud and Midrash* (Edinburg: Clark, 1991 [revision of the 1982 German revised edition]).

6. For an analysis of the Jewish leadership and Roman policy before and after the war see Seth Schwartz, *Josephus and Judean Politics,* CSCT 18 (Leiden: Brill, 1990).

7. Martin Goodman, *State and Society in Roman Galilee, A.D. 132–212* (Totowa, N.J.: Rowan and Allanheld, 1983), 104, 123–24.

8. For a review of synagogues, see the articles in Lee I. Levine, ed., *Ancient Synagogues Revealed* (Jerusalem: Israel Exploration Society, 1981).

9. For the limited roles of rabbis in the third century, see Lee I. Levine, *The Rabbinic Class of Roman Palestine in Late Antiquity* (Jerusalem: Yad Izhak Ben-Zvi Press; New York: Jewish Theological Seminary, 1989), 127–33.

10. For a recent defense of the position that Gamaliel II was appointed by Rome, see David Goodblatt, "The Origins of the Roman Recognition of the Palestinian Patriarchate" [in Heb.: *Reshit shel Hanesi'ut Ha-'Eretzyisraelit Hamukeret*], *Studies in the History of the Jewish People and the Land of Israel* 4 (1978): 89–102. Goodblatt's position has been criticized by Daniel Schwartz, "Josephus and Nicolas on the Pharisees," *Journal for the Study of Judaism* 14 (1983): 167–68. Goodman, *State and Society,* 116–17, notes that only in the fourth century do we have proof that the patriarch was legally recognized by the empire. Goodman stresses the patriarch's lack of general authority in the second century, until Judah the Prince. Even then the Nasi's secular power was severely limited (pp. 113–16).

11. For a critical study of the Johanan ben Zakkai stories, see Jacob Neusner, *Development of a Legend: Studies on the Traditions concerning Yohanan ben Zakkai,* SPB 16 (Leiden: Brill, 1970); Peter Schäfer, "Die Fluct Johanan b. Zakkais aus Jerusalem und die Gründung des 'Lehrhauses' in Jabne," in H. Temporini and W. Haase, eds., *Aufstieg und Niedergang des Römischen Welt* (Berlin: deGruyter, 1979), 43–101; Anthony J. Saldarini, "Johanan ben Zakkai's Escape from Jerusalem: Origin and Development of a Rabbinic Story," *Journal for the Study of Judaism* 6 (1975): 189–204. For a critical view of the limited role of Jamnia, see Peter Schäfer, "Die Sogenannte Synode von Jabne: Zur Trennung von Juden und Christen im ersten/zweiten Jh. n. Chr.," *Studien zur Geschichte und Theologie des Rabbinischen Judentums,* AGAJU 15 (Leiden: Brill, 1978), 45–64; G. Stemberger, "Die sogenannte Synode von Jabne," *Kairos* 19 (1977): 14–21; Shaye J. D. Cohen, "The Significance of Yavneh: Pharisees, Rabbis, and the End of Jewish Sectarianism," *Hebrew Union College Annual* 55 (1984): 27–53. For an analysis of Jamnia and Johanan within the context of imperial politics, see Schwartz, *Josephus,* 200–208.

12. For canonization, see Sid Z. Leiman, *The Canonization of Hebrew Scripture: The Talmudic and Midrashic Evidence* (Hamden, Conn.: Archon, 1976). Reuben Kimelman, "Birkat Ha-Minim and the Lack of Evidence for an Anti-Christian Jewish Prayer in Late Antiquity," in E. P. Sanders et al., eds., *Jewish and Christian Self-Definition, Vol. 2: Aspects of Judaism in the Graeco-Roman Period* (Philadelphia: Fortress, 1981), 226–44, refutes the common view that a universal, first-century measure was promulgated against Christians.

13. Ithamar Gruenwald, *Apocalyptic and Merkavah Mysticism* (Leiden: Brill, 1980); David Halperin, *The Faces of the Chariot: Early Jewish Responses to Ezekiel's Vision* (Tübingen: Mohr, 1988).

14. Peter Schäfer, *Synopse zur Hekhalot-Literatur,* TSAJ 2 (Tübingen: Mohr, 1981); *Geniza Fragmente zur Hekhalot-Literatur,* TSAJ 6 (Tübingen: Mohr, 1984).

15. Anthony J. Saldarini, "Apocalyptic and Rabbinic Literature," *Catholic*

Biblical Quarterly 37 (1975): 348–58, and "The Uses of Apocalyptic in the Mishna and Tosepta," *Catholic Biblical Quarterly* 39 (1977): 396–409. Rabbinic law and exegesis tamed apocalyptic visions into hopes based on fidelity to Torah and severely limited participation in mystical exercises.

16. See Jacob Neusner, *Judaism: The Evidence of the Mishnah* (Chicago: University of Chicago Press, 1981), for the development of the rabbinic world view. Representative essays may be found in Neusner's *Method and Meaning in Ancient Judaism*, BJS 10 (Missoula: Scholars, 1979), and *Formative Judaism*, 5 vols. (Chico: Scholars, 1982–85).

17. Goodman, *State and Society*, 110–13.

18. The Mishnah records only two decisions (m. Shab. 16:7; 22:3). In p. Shab. 16:8, the Amora Ulla interprets the lack of decisions by Johanan ben Zakkai as evidence for the Galileans' lack of devotion to Torah. This often-repeated inference, that the Galileans were not Torah-observant, is groundless, as is shown by Sean Freyne, *Galilee from Alexander the Great to Hadrian* (Wilmington: Glazier; Notre Dame: Notre Dame University Press, 1980), chap. 8.

19. Freyne, *Galilee*, 344–91; Goodman, *State and Society*, 88–89, 128.

20. Goodman, *State, and Society*, 67, citing t. Meg. 3(4):13 (Lieberman, 356) and 2:6 (Lieberman, 349). Lieberman noted the differences in the talmudic tractates written in Caesarea in "The Talmud of Caesarea: Jerusalem Tractate Nezikin" (in Hebrew), *Tarbiz* 2 no. 4; (1931): i–viii, 1–108. Lee I. Levine, *Caesarea under Roman Rule* (Leiden: Brill, 1975), 106, argues that the Palestinian Jewish community was acculturated to the Roman Empire.

21. Goodman, *State and Society*, 110–11; Levine, *Class*, chap. 4.

22. *Peri Archon* 4.3.

23. Michael R. Greenwald, "The New Testament Canon and the Mishnah: Consolidation of Knowledge in the Second Century C.E. (Ph.D. diss., Boston University, 1989). For the Second Sophistic, see Glenn Bowersock, *Greek Sophists in the Roman Empire* (Oxford: Clarendon, 1969).

24. For the third-century fortunes of the patriarchate, see Lee I. Levine, "The Jewish Patriarch (Nasi) in Third Century Palestine," in H. Temporini and W. Haase, eds., *Aufstieg und Niedergang des Römischen Welt* 2.19.2 (Berlin: deGruyter, 1979), 649–88. For the limited powers of the patriarch and loss of power in the third century, see esp. 676–78 and 680–85. See also Goodman, *State and Society*, 111–18.

25. Philo, *De Legatione ad Gaium; In Flaccum*.

26. A. T. Kraabel, "Social Systems of Six Diaspora Synagogues," in Joseph Guttmann, ed., *Ancient Synagogues: The State of Research* (Chico: Scholars, 1981), 79–91, and "The Diaspora Synagogue: Archaeological and Epigraphic Evidence since Sukenik," in H. Temporini and W. Haase, eds, *Aufstieg und Niedergang des Römischen Welt* 2.19.1 (Berlin: deGruyter, 1979), 477–510. On misunderstandings of the diaspora, see A. T. Kraabel, "The Roman Diaspora: Six Questionable Assumptions," *Journal of Jewish Studies* 33 (1982): 445–64 (Yadin Festschrift). For the overlap of diaspora and Palestinian Judaism, see J. Andrew Overman, "The Diaspora in the Modern Study of Ancient Judaism," in J. Andrew Overman and Robert MacLennan, eds., *Diaspora Jews and Juda-*

ism: Essays in Honor of and in Dialogue with A. Thomas Kraabel (Minneapolis: Fortress, 1992), 1–17.

27. H. J. Leon, *The Jews of Ancient Rome* (Philadelphia: Jewish Publication Society, 1960).

28. Robert L. Wilken, *John Chrysostom and the Jews: Rhetoric and Reality in the Late Fourth Century* (Berkeley: University of California Press, 1983), 47–55.

29. Ibid., 53–54.

30. Menahem Stern, *Greek and Latin Authors on Jews and Judaism* (Jerusalem: Israel Academy of Sciences and Humanities, 1980), 2:580–99, esp. 595–96.

31. Wilken, *John Chrysostom,* 63–64.

32. John Chrysostom, *Discourses against the Jews* 1.3.

33. Bernadette J. Brooten, *Women Leaders in the Ancient Synagogue: Inscriptional Evidence and Background Issues,* BJS 36 (Chico: Scholars, 1982).

34. Justin Martyr, *Dialogue with Trypho* 38.2; 48:2. In the *Dialogue* 112.5, Justin notes that the Jewish teachers wish to be called "Rabbi." This charge is based on Matt. 23:7–8 rather than on observation of the Jewish community. It should also be noted that "Rabbi" is an honorific title with a wide range of usage.

35. John J. Collins, *Between Athens and Jerusalem: Jewish Identity in the Hellenistic Diaspora* (New York: Crossroad, 1983), esp. chaps. 4–6.

36. Jack N. Lightstone , *The Commerce of the Sacred: Mediation of the Divine among Jews in the Graeco-Roman Diaspora,* BJS 59 (Chico: Scholars, 1984). For an abbreviated account of some of this evidence, see Lightstone, "Christian Anti-Judaism." For an account of the development of the world view of Judaism during and after the Second Temple period, see Lightstone, *Society, the Sacred, and Scripture in Ancient Judaism: A Sociology of Knowledge,* SCJ 3 (Ontario: Laurier 1988).

37. Justin *(Dialogue,* 46) has a list of practices observed after the destruction of the Temple: Sabbath, circumcision, observance of months, and washing after touching forbidden things and after sexual intercourse. John Chrysostom mentions circumcision, food laws, ritual baths, celebrating festivals, including dancing on the Day of Atonement *(Discourses against the Jews* 1.2; cf. m. Taan. 4:8), building sukkot, and phylacteries. See Wilken, *John Chrysostom,* 64–65. Greco-Roman literature often mentions Sabbath, circumcision, and dietary rules as strange Jewish practices.

38. See the Sefer Ha-Razim for magic (and mysticism and liturgy): M. Margolioth, ed., *Sefer HaRazim* (Jerusalem: Yediot, 1966). Lightstone, "Christian Anti-Judaism," 107–9 and 116–21, correctly emphasizes the importance of this evidence. On the rabbis, miracles, and magic, see Levine, *The Rabbinic Class,* 105–9, and Lightstone, *Commerce of the Sacred.*

39. For patristic and rabbinic understandings and uses of heresy, see M. Simon, "From Greek Hairesis to Christian Heresy," in William R. Schoedel and Robert L. Wilken, eds., *Early Christian Literature and the Classical Intellectual Tradition,* R. M. Grant Festschrift, Théologie Historique 53 (Paris: Beauschesne, 1979), 101–16; and Shaye J. D. Cohen, "A Virgin Defiled: Some Rabbinic and

Christian Views on the Origins of Heresy," *Union Seminary Quarterly Review* 36 (1980): 1–11.

40. Justin, *Dialogue* 80. For a study of this passage, see M. Simon, "Les sectes juives d'après les témoinages patristiques," *Studia Patristica* I, TU 63 (Berlin: Akademie, 1957), 526–39.

41. The presence of Pharisees on Justin's list has often perplexed authorities since Justin says that they would not be recognized as Jews. (They are listed as a sect by Josephus, but hardly one to be rejected.) Adolf Harnack, *Judentum und Judenchristentum in Justins Dialog mit Trypho*, TU 39, no. 1 (Leipzig, 1913), 57ff., assumed that the Pharisees and the chiefs of the synagogue (*Dialogue* 137.2) were one, so he treated them as an interpolation in *Dialogue* 80. But Justin does not say the Pharisees are leaders of the synagogue. Since the original text has Baptists immediately preceding Pharisees (with no *kai* ["and"] between, contrary to some emendations), some commentators understand "Baptist Pharisees" as the object of Justin's comment. See Matthew Black, "The Patristic Accounts of Jewish Sectarianism," *Bulletin of the John Rylands Library* 41 (1958–59): 288–89. But the presence of Pharisees is not surprising. The rabbinic authorities seldom used the word Pharisee and did not connect themselves with the Pharisees until the middle ages (Cohen, "The Significance of Yavneh," 40). In rabbinic literature, seven kinds of Pharisees are named, most, if not all pejoratively (ARNA, chap. 37; ARNB, chap. 45; p. Ber. 9:5 [13b]; b. Sot. 22b). Finally, Justin evaluates all schools, sects, and groups negatively, as corruptions of the original, unified truth (see Simon, "Les sectes," 530–31).

42. Nachman Ben-Yehuda, *Deviance and Moral Boundaries: Witchcraft, the Occult, Deviant Sciences and Scientists* (Chicago: University of Chicago Press, 1985), 1–20, esp. 3 and 19–20.

43. Kai T. Ericson, *Wayward Puritans: A Study in the Sociology of Deviance* (New York: Wiley, 1966), 22–23. For example, Elisha Ben Abuya, nicknamed Aher, "the other," is a perfect case of the difficulties of boundary maintenance. Elisha apostasized, yet he was born a Jew and was learned in Torah. Thus he could not simply be ignored, the way gentiles could. His Jewish birth and especially his enduring knowledge of Torah are prime values in the rabbinic world. Elisha retained a certain value and presented a permanent challenge, which had to be answered by the rabbis. See William S. Green, "Otherness Within: Toward a Theory of Difference in Rabbinic Judaism," in Neusner and Frerichs, *"To See Ourselves,"* 49–69.

44. Cohen, "The Significance of Yavneh," claims that after 70 the rabbis encouraged disagreement and debate within the group, but discouraged sects (35–36). "Yavneh was a grand coalition of different groups and parties, held together by the belief that sectarian self-identification was a thing of the past and that individuals may disagree with one another in matters of law while remaining friends" (50). He dismisses Justin Martyr's list of sects and also m. Nid. 4:2 and parallels on the Sadducees (32–36). At the same time, Cohen claims that those who would not accept this compromise were expelled. This idyllic picture is doubtful. That the rabbis should discourage divisions is normal for a small group (sect) seeking power and influence in society

at large. However, Cohen goes too far when he envisions this actually happening in the second century. Rather, there were multiple Jewish groups and movements after 70, though we have only hints about some of them. In the first half of the second century, the rabbinic groups could justly be said to be one of those groups or sects. Naturally rabbinic literature supresses the other groups and enlarges the roles and prestige of its own group.

45. For further analysis of patristic accounts, see Cohen, "The Significance of Yavneh," 51–52, and Black, "Patristic Accounts," 290–303.

46. For analysis of the position of the Sadducees, see Cohen, "The Significance of Yavneh," 32–34.

47. For a review of recent work in this area, see James D. Purvis, "The Samaritan Problem: A Case Study in Jewish Sectarianism in the Roman Era," in Baruch Halpern et al., eds., *Tradition in Transformation* (Winona Lake, Ind: Eisenbrauns, 1981), 323–50. The history of relationships with and attitudes toward Samaritans is sketched out in Ferdinand Dexinger, "Limits of Tolerance in Judaism: The Samaritan Example," in Sanders et al., *Jewish and Christian Self-Definition*, 2: 88–114.

48. For a study of the manifold opponents gathered under the category of "those who affirm two powers in heaven," see Alan Segal, *Two Powers in Heaven: Early Rabbinic Reports about Christianity and Gnosticism*, SJLA 25 (Leiden: Brill, 1977).

49. Because Christian censors often mandated that anti-Christian passages be changed to refer to other opponents, specified or unspecified, polemical passages are hard to interpret in context. See Burton L. Visotzky, "Prolegomenon to the Study of Jewish-Christianities in Rabbinic Literature," *Association of Jewish Studies Review* 14 (1989): 63–70.

50. Gary Porton, *Goyim: Gentiles and Israelites in Mishnah-Tosefta* (Atlanta: Scholars, 1988).

51. E. E. Urbach, "Self-Isolation or Self-Affirmation in Judaism in the First Three Centuries: Theory and Practice," in Sanders et al., *Jewish and Christian Self-Definition*, 2:269–98, claims to speak of the first three centuries, but he draws upon a wide range of sources from many places and periods and so really shows that the rabbis remained in lively contact with their surrounding culture over the course of many centuries.

52. Adolf Harnack, *The Mission and Expansion of Christianity in the First Three Centuries*, 2d ed. (London, 1908), 18. See Wilken, *John Chrysostom*, 44–46. David Rokeah, *Jews, Pagans, and Christians in Conflict* (Jerusalem: Magnes; Leiden: Brill, 1982), 46–48, substantially affirms Harnack's thesis of the withdrawal of Judaism and the dominance of Christianity.

53. Reuben Kimelman, "Birkat Ha-Minim and the Lack of Evidence for an Anti-Christian Jewish Prayer in Late Antiquity," in Sanders et al., *Jewish and Christian Self-Definition*, 2:226–44, establishes the lack of evidence for the Birkat Ha-Minim as a universal, first-century measure. Lawrence Schiffman, *Who Was a Jew? Rabbinic and Halakhic Perspectives on the Jewish-Christian Schism* (Hoboken: Ktav, 1985), 53–61, defends the traditional position and attempts to refute Kimelman. Steven T. Katz, "Issues in the Separation of Judaism and

Christianity after 70 c.e.: A Reconsideration," *Journal of Biblical Literature* 103 (1984): 43–76, defends Kimelman's position against Schiffman. William Horbury, "The Benediction of the *Minim* and Early Jewish Christian Controversy," *Journal of Theological Studies* 33 (1982): 19–61, defends a first-century date for the "blessing" (23), but says that the blessing did not cause the break with Judaism; it merely gave formal liturgical expression to it (61). However, Horbury adduces evidence from as late as the Middle Ages to understand the development of the "blessing," much of it hardly relevant to the first century.

54. For a sustained Christian theology of Israel, see Paul Van Buren, *A Theology of the Jewish-Christian Reality,* 3 vols. (San Francisco: Harper, 1980–88).

55. The texts on Jesus and heretics have been collected several times, most recently in German by Johann Maier, *Jesus von Nazareth in der Talmudischen Überlieferung* (Darmstadt: Wissenschaftliche Buchgesellschaft, 1978), and *Jüdische Auseinandersetzung mit dem Christentum in der Antike* (Darmstadt: Wissenschaftliche Buchgesellschaft, 1982). Extensive bibliography and notes are provided, but the analyses of texts are relatively brief. In English the earlier analysis of Travers Herford, *Christianity in Talmud and Midrash* (London: Williams and Norgate, 1903), is seriously defective. A better but still apologetic analysis may be found in Morris Goldstein, *Jesus in the Jewish Tradition* (New York: Macmillan, 1950). Some of the comments of Jacob Z. Lauterbach are also helpful: "Jesus in the Talmud," in *Rabbinic Essays* (Cincinnati: HUC Press, 1951), 473–570. See also David Rokeah, "*Ben Stada' Ben Pantîra' hû'*" [Ben Stada is Ben Pantera: Towards the clarification of a philological-historical problem] *Tarbiz* 39 (1969): 9–18.

56. For a review of trends in rabbinic polemics, see Michael Chernick, "Some Talmudic Responses to Christianity, Third and Fourth Centuries," *Journal of Ecumenical Studies* 17 (1980): 393–406; and Moshe David Herr, "The Sages' Reaction to Antisemitism in the Hellenistic-Roman World," in Shmuel Almog, ed., *Antisemitism through the Ages* (Oxford and New York: Pergamon, 1988), 27–38.

57. Eugene Mihaly, "A Rabbinic Defense of the Election of Israel: An Analysis of Sifre Deuteronomy 32:9," *Hebrew Union College Annual* 35 (1964): 103–43. For the role of covenant in Sifre's commentary on Deuteronomy 32, see Steven Fraade, *From Tradition to Commentary: Torah and Its Interpretation in the Midrash Sifre to Deuteronomy* (Albany: SUNY Press, 1991), ch. 4. For the commentary on Deut. 33 as a response to the postwar situation, see Reuven Hammer, "A Rabbinic Response to the Post Bar Kochba Era: The Sifre to Ha-Azinu," *Proceedings of the American Academy of Jewish Research* 52 (1985): 37–53.

58. Norman J. Cohen, "Analysis of an Exegetical Tradition in the *Mekhilta DeRabbi Ishmael:* The Meaning of *'amanah* in the Second and Third Centuries," *Association of Jewish Studies Review* 9 (1984): 1–25, on Be-Shallah, para. 7.

59. Lou H. Silberman, "Challenge and Response: Pesiqta DeRab Kahana, Chapter 26, as an Oblique Reply to Christian Claims," *Harvard Theological Review* 79 (1986): 247–53.

60. Leivy Smolar and Moshe Auerbach, "The Golden Calf Episode in Post-biblical Literature," *Hebrew Union College Annual* 39 (1968): 91–116.

61. Nicolas R. M. deLange, *Origen and the Jews: Studies in Jewish-Christian Relations in Third-Century Palestine* (Cambridge: Cambridge University Press, 1976).

62. Reuven Kimelman, "Rabbi Yohanan and Origen on the Song of Songs: A Third-Century Jewish-Christian Disputation," *Harvard Theological Review* 73 (1980): 567–95.

63. Jacob Neusner, *Judaism in Society: The Evidence of the Yerushalmi* (Chicago: University of Chicago Press, 1983); *Judaism in Scripture: The Evidence of Leviticus Rabbah* (Chicago: University of Chicago Press, 1986); and *Judaism and Christianity in the Age of Constantine: History, Messiah and Israel, and the Initial Confrontation* (Chicago: University of Chicago Press, 1987).

64. See Judith R. Baskin, "Rabbinic-Patristic Exegetical Contacts in Late Antiquity: A Bibliographical Reappraisal," in William S. Green, ed., *Approaches to Ancient Judaism, vol. 5: Studies in Judaism and Its Greco-Roman Context,* BJS 32 (Atlanta: Scholars, 1985), 53–80, and Baskin's thematic study, *Pharoah's Counselors: Job, Jethro, and Balaam in Rabbinic and Patristic Tradition,* BJS 47 (Chico: Scholars, 1983).

65. Though serious disagreement has arisen over the status of God-fearers as a social role and category, the phenomenon of non-Jews being attracted to the Jewish community cannot be doubted. See an attack on the concept of God-fearers by A. T. Kraabel, "The Disappearance of the God-fearers," *Numen* (28 1981): 113–26, which served to correct the overconfident appeal to a supposed social category. J. Andrew Overman has reaffirmed, however, the evidence for gentiles sympathetic to Judaism being associated with synagogues in "The God-Fearers: Some Neglected Features," *Journal for the Study of the New Testament* 32 (1988): 17–26.

66. See the history of conversion by Shaye J. D. Cohen, "Conversion to Judaism in Historical Perspective: From Biblical Israel to Post-Biblical Judaism," *Conservative Judaism* 36, no. 4 (1983): 31–45. For Jews in Roman law, see Amnon Linder, *The Jews in Roman Imperial Legislation* (Detroit: Wayne State University Press, 1987). For definitions of a Jew, see Shaye J. D. Cohen, "Crossing the Boundary and Becoming a Jew," *Harvard Theological Review* 82 (1989): 13–33.

67. Martin Goodman, "Proselytizing in Rabbinic Literature," *Journal of Jewish Studies* 40 (1989): 175–85. See also Shaye J. D. Cohen, "The Rabbinic Conversion Ceremony," *Journal of Jewish Studies* 41 (1990): 177–203.

68. Wilken, *John Chrysostom,* 90–92.

69. Recently David Rokeah, *Jews, Pagans,* has argued that actual Christian-Jewish debate died out in the mid second century and that both Christians and Jews used references to Judaism as a way of attacking each other. Using different evidence, Robert S. MacLennan, *Early Christian Texts on Jews and Judaism* (Atlanta: Scholars, 1990), argues that Christian anti-Judaic texts were not attacking real Jews. But the relationships of religious and ethnic groups in the empire makes it much more likely that Jews were active participants in the intellectual, religious, cultural, and political life of the empire until persistent anti-Semitism and imperial legislation impeded contact in the fifth, sixth, and later centuries.

70. This study accepts the priority of Mark as the most probable solution to the literary relationship of Matthew to Mark.

71. The case for Matthew is argued concisely in Anthony J. Saldarini, "The Gospel of Matthew and Jewish-Christian Conflict," in David L. Balch, ed., *Social History of the Matthean Community: Cross-Disciplinary Approaches* (Minneapolis: Fortress, 1991), 36–59.

72. For recent reviews of New Testament attitudes toward the Jewish community, see Richardson and Wilson, *Anti-Judaism in Early Christianity,* and Alan T. Davies, ed., *Anti-Semitism and the Foundations of Christianity,* (New York: Paulist, 1979).

73. Mid first-century relationships between believers-in-Jesus and Judaism varied. Raymond Brown has suggested a useful four-part typology in "Not Jewish Christianity and Gentile Christianity but Types of Jewish/Gentile Christianity," *Catholic Biblical Quarterly* 45 (1983): 74–79.

74. Urban C. von Wahlde, "The Terms for Religious Authorities in the Fourth Gospel: A Key to Literary Strata," *Journal of Biblical Literature* 98 (1979): 231–53, and "The Johannine 'Jews': A Critical Survey," *New Testament Studies* 28 (1982): 33–60, examines the multiple meanings of terms for Jewish leaders. R. Alan Culpepper, *The Anatomy of the Fourth Gospel: A Study in Literary Design* (Philadelphia: Fortress, 1983), 126, suggests that from a literary point of view John is using "Jews" with multiple, connected meanings. For the various opponents of the Johannine community, see Raymond Brown, *The Community of the Beloved Disciple* (Ramsey, N.J.: Paulist, 1979).

75. See the suggestive comments by Jerome Quinn, *The Letter to Titus,* AB 35 (New York: Doubleday, 1990), 106–12, 244–48.

76. Ignatius, *Philadelphians* 5–9; *Magnesians* 8–10. For commentary, see William R. Schoedel, *Ignatius of Antioch,* Hermeneia (Philadelphia: Fortress, 1985), ad loc. For a review of literature on this question, see C. K. Barrett, "Jews and Judaizers in the Epistles of Ignatius," in R. Hamerton-Kelly et al., eds., *Jews, Greeks, and Christians: Essays in Honor of W. D. Davies,* SJLA 21 (Leiden: Brill, 1976), 220–44. On Ignatius' social situation, see most recently William R. Schoedel, "Ignatius and the Reception of the Gospel of Matthew in Antioch," in Balch, *Social History of the Matthean Community,* 129–77.

77. For the text of Barnabas, see Robert A. Kraft and P. Prigent, *Épître de Barnabé,* SC 172 (Paris: Cerf, 1971) and for an English translation see Robert A. Kraft, *Barnabas and the Didache,* vol. 3 of Robert M. Grant's *The Apostolic Fathers: A New Translation and Commentary* (New York: Nelson, 1965). Both volumes have introductions and notes.

78. Justin Martyr, *Dialogue with Trypho* 1:2, 16:4, 17:1, 92, 108.

79. Justin, *Dialogue* 11, 123, 135. For a full development of this theme, see Peter Richardson, *Israel in the Apostolic Church* (Cambridge: Cambridge University Press, 1969), esp. chap. 2 on Justin.

80. Harold Remus, "Justin Martyr's Argument with Judaism," in Wilson, *Anti-Judaism in Early Christianity,* 2:67–68; Dimitrius Trakatellis, "Justin Martyr's Trypho," in G. W. E. Nickelsburg and G. W. MacRae, eds., *Christian*

among Jews and Gentiles, K. Stendahl Festschrift, (Philadelphia: Fortress, 1986), 287–97; MacLennan, *Jews and Judaism,* 85; Jon Nilson, "To Whom Is Justin's *Dialogue with Trypho* Addressed?" *Theological Studies* 38 (1977): 542; and H. P. Schneider, "Some Reflections on the Dialogue of Justin Martyr with Trypho," *Scottish Journal of Theology* 15 (1962): 175.

81. Nilson, "Justin's *Dialogue,*" 541.

82. For an interpretation of 5 Esdras (or Ezra), see Graham N. Stanton, "5 Ezra and Matthean Christianity in the Second Century," *Journal of Theological Studies* 28 (1977): 67–83. Stanton plausibly argues for a mid second century-date. He thinks that 5 Esdras brings out some implicit views of Matthew (73, 74, 82), an argument which is not well founded or proven. Rather, 5 Esdras is a clear change in thinking from Matthew.

83. Theophilus of Antioch, *Ad Autolycum,* text and translation by Robert M. Grant (Oxford: Clarendon, 1970). Theophilus was the bishop of Antioch from 169–77, if Eusebius' dates are correct. See Robert M. Grant, *Greek Apologists of the Second Century* (Philadelphia: Westminster, 1988), 143 and in general, chaps. 16–19.

84. Grant, *Ad Autolycum,* xvii–xix.

85. Grant, *Ad Autolycum,* xvii–xix; *Greek Apologists,* chap. 19; "Jewish Christianity at Antioch in the Second Century," *Recherches de science religieuse* 60 (1972) 97–108. Grant holds that Christian Jews of Antioch brought to the church the apologetic, historical, liturgical, and theological insights that we find in Theophilus' work.

86. This is the thesis, ably established, of Robert Wilken's *John Chrysostom.* See esp. xvi–xvii and chap. 3.

87. Lightstone, *Commerce of the Sacred,* 125–58; David A. Fiensy, *Prayers Alleged to be Jewish: An Examination of the Constitutiones Apostolorum,* BJS 65 (Chico: Scholars, 1985), 217–19; Wilken, *John Chrysostom,* 66–73.

88. Fiensy, *Prayers.*

89. Jewish-Christian is used with a wide variety of meanings, usually dependent on each author's understanding of Christian origins. For recent attempts to bring order out of the varied usages, see Bruce J. Malina, "Jewish Christianity or Christian Judaism," *Journal for the Study of Judaism* 7 (1990): 46–57; R. A. Kraft, "In Search of 'Jewish Christianity' and its 'Theology,'" *Recherches de science religieuse* 60 (1972): 81–92; S. K. Riegel, "Jewish Christianity: Definitions and Terminology," *New Testament Studies* 24 (1978): 410–15. For a concise review of the study of Jewish-Christianity, see A. F. J. Klijn, "The Study of Jewish Christianity," *New Testament Studies* 20 (1973–74): 419–31, and Visotzky, "Prolegomenon." There is broad agreement that groups of believers-in-Jesus, who were ethnically Jewish or kept the Jewish law or had a low Christology or identified strongly with Judaism persisted in the East for several centuries. However, they did not form one movement, but were independent and varied. See Klijn, "Study of Jewish Christianity," 431, and J. E. Taylor, "The Phenomenon of Early Jewish Christianity: Reality or Scholarly Invention," *Vigiliae Christianae* 44 (1990): 313–34. For a review of Jewish Christianity which stresses continuities, see Jesús María Velasco and Leopold

Sabourin, "Jewish Christianity of the First Centuries," *Biblical Theology Bulletin* 6 (1976) 5–26.

90. For the sources and a brief analysis, see A. F. J. Klijn and G. J. Reinink, *Patristic Evidence for Jewish-Christian Sects* (Leiden: Brill, 1973).

91. Gerard P. Luttikhuizen, *The Revelation of Elchasai: Investigations into the Evidence for a Mesopotamian Jewish Apocalypse of the Second Century and Its Reception by Judeo-Christian Propagandists,* TSAJ 8 (Tübingen: Mohr, 1985).

92. Georg Strecker, "Appendix I: On the Problem of Jewish Christianity," in Bauer, *Orthodoxy,* 257.

93. See Georg Strecker, "The Kerygmata Petrou," in Edward Hennecke and Wilhelm Schneemelcher, eds., *The New Testament Apocrypha,* 2 vols. (Philadelphia: Westminster, 1965), 2:102–27, esp. 210–22 and 270–71. For the complex history of scholarship concerned with the source problems plaguing the Pseudo-Clementines, see F. Stanley Jones, "The Pseudo-Clementines: A History of Research," *Second Century* 2 (1982): 1–33, 63–96. The most influential modern treatment in the tradition of the Tübingen school is Georg Strecker, *Das Judenchristentum in den Pseudoklementinen,* TU 70, no. 2 (Berlin: Akademie, 1958; rev. ed., 1981). Hans-Joachim Schoeps reopened the Pseudo-Clementine question with a modified form of the Tübingen thesis. However, his attempt to synthesize a single, coherent Ebionite tradition probably conflates a number of diverse groups. See his *Theologie und Geschichte des Judenchristentums* (Tübingen: Mohr, 1949), and his later abbreviated synthesis, *Jewish Christianity: Factional Disputes in the Early Church* (Philadelphia: Fortress, 1969; orig. German, 1964).

The Ascents of James is another hypothetical source of the Pseudo-Clementines, specifically Recognitiones 1.33–71 (omitting an interpolation at 1.44.4–1.53.3). It was from a law-observant Jewish-Christian community with a high Christology. See Robert E. van Voorst, *The Ascents of James: History and Theology of a Jewish-Christian Community,* SBLDS 112 (Atlanta: Scholars, 1989).

94. Wilken, *John Chrysostom,* 94.

95. Robert Murray, *Symbols of Church and Kingdom: A Study in Early Syriac Tradition* (Cambridge: Cambridge University Press, 1975), 8. On the close relations between Aphrahat and Judaism, see Jacob Neusner, *Aphrahat and Judaism* (Leiden: Brill, 1971).

96. A. P. Hayman, "The Image of the Jew in the Syriac Anti-Jewish Polemical Literature," in Jacob Neusner and Ernest S. Frerichs, eds., *"To See Ourselves as Others See Us": Christians, Jews, "Others" in Late Antiquity,* (Chico: Scholars, 1985), 440.

97. Van Voorst, *Ascents of James,* 164; Strecker, "Appendix I," 274.

98. Ray Pritz, *Nazarene Jewish Christianity: From the End of the New Testament Period until Its Disappearance in the Fourth Century* (Jerusalem: Magnes; Leiden: Brill, 1988), 108–9.

Chapter Two

1. The term *ekklesia* (church), which occurs in 16:18 and 18:17, will be treated in chap. 5, where I argue that this word does not have a technical,

Christian, "non-Jewish" meaning in Matthew. The term "Christian" occurs only three times in the New Testament writings (never in Matthew), and each time it is used by outsiders, not by believers-in-Jesus as a self-designation. See Acts 11:26 and 26:28; in 1 Pet. 4:16, judicial authorities are presumed to penalize members of the community because of the charge they are Christian. Wolfgang Trilling, *Das Wahre Israel: Studien zur Theologie des Matthäus-Evangelium*, SANT 10, 3d ed. (Munich: Kosel, 1964), 61, notes with astonishment the fact that the term "people" is not used by Matthew for his group and then tries to explain it away. His book identifies Matthew's community with the people of God and calls it (even in the title of the book) the "true Israel." The inappropriateness of this interpretation, which is contrary to Matthew's explicit usage, was noted by G. Barth in a review of Trilling in *Theologische Literatur Zeitschrift* 86, no. 10 (1961): cols. 756–59.

2. See, for example, 1 Enoch 39, 58, 91; 4 Ezra 7.

3. Justin Martyr, *Dialogue with Trypho*, 123, 135, first says that the Christians are born of God and are the "true Israelite offspring [*genos*]."

4. Many commentators automatically interpret the words "people" and "Israel" theologically, understanding by these terms those who are called by God to be his special people and are given the promises and covenants. They then contrast the old covenant people with the new people, or new Israel or church. See Hubert Frankemölle, *Jahwe-Bund und Kirche Christi: Studien zur Form- und Traditionsgeschichte des "Evangeliums" nach Matthäus*, NTAbh 10; 2d ed. (Münster: Aschendorff, 1984; orig. ed. 1974), 191–218, esp. 195. Frankemölle sees "people" as an Old Testament theological category taken over by Matthew. Trilling, *Wahre Israel*, 61–79, interprets several key passages with a strong theological overlay. More recently, P. Beauchamp, "L'evangile de Matthieu et l'heritage d'Israël," *Recherches de science religieuse* 76 (1988): 5–38, argues that the lost sheep of Israel are received by a new people. We will argue that this salvation-history scheme, with its tendentious reading of words and its use of non-Matthean categories, distorts the gospel.

5. Similarly, in the story of John the Baptist's death, Herod (Antipas) is said to have let John live because he feared the crowd, which held John to be a prophet (Matt. 14:5).

6. The Pharisees occur only here in the passion narrative. The author probably makes them characters in this scene concerning claims of resurrection because they believe in resurrection.

7. Ulrich Luz, *Matthew 1–7* (Minneapolis: Augsburg, 1989; orig. German, 1985), says that here and throughout the gospel "people" refers to "the Old Testament people of God, Israel" (ad loc.). W. D. Davies and Dale C. Allison, *The Gospel according to St. Matthew*, vol. 1: *Chapters 1–7*, ICC (Edinburgh: Clark, 1988), following the majority of commentators, identifies "people" with "the ekklesia of both Jew and Gentile" (ad loc.). Frankemölle, *Jahwe-Bund*, 217, reads 1:21b as a dogmatic faith statement. Kenzo Tagawa, "People and Community in the Gospel of Matthew," *New Testament Studies* 16 (1969–70): 159, suggests that 1:21 is a free citation of LXX Ps. 129 (130):8, which reads "And he [the Lord] shall redeem Israel from all its iniquities *(anomiōn)*" and that

it refers to both Israel and the Matthean group. Tagawa comes closest to Matthew's thought.

8. Davies and Allison, *Matthew 1–7*, 1:243, correctly note that the interpretation which supposes that Israel has been supplanted by the Matthean church is highly improbable.

9. For a detailed presentation of Matthew's polemic against the Jewish community leaders, see chap. 3 of this volume.

10. Though the references to "their synagogues" often symbolize the Matthean group's distance from the Jewish assemblies in the late first century, here Matthew's use of the expression seems nonpolemical He follows Mark 1:39 and merely indicates that Jesus went to different assemblies in the villages of Galilee to teach the people.

11. For hypocrites, cf. Matt. 6:1–18, 7:5, 22:18, 23:13–16, 24:51. Hypocrite originally meant an actor behind a mask.

12. Joachim Gnilka, *Die Verstockung Israels: Isaias 6:9–10 in der Theologie der Synoptiker*, SANT 3 (Munich: Kosel,1961), esp. 94–102, argues that Matthew uses the hardening theme to explain and justify Israel's loss of its special status and that this is one of the major goals of the gospel. See also Gnilka, "Das Verstockungsproblem nach Matthäus 13:13–15," in W. P. Eckert et al., eds., *Antijudaismus in Neuen Testament?* (Munich: Kaiser, 1967), 119–28. Jack Dean Kingsbury, *Matthew as Story* (Philadelphia: Fortress, 1986; 2d ed., 1988), 75, sees Matt. 13:13–15 as Jesus' declaration that Israel has become hard of heart. This is followed by an address to the people in parables, which they cannot understand. Kingsbury stresses the people's misunderstanding in contrast to the disciples' understanding and confession of Jesus (75, 77). Kingsbury and many other commentators treat Israel as an undifferentiated whole and stress its rejection of Jesus (though Kingsbury does see the Jewish mission as still open). Matthew's view of the crowds and Israel is more complex and differentiated, as this chapter will show. For Second Temple Jewish literature which criticizes Israel, threatens punishment, but affirms its salvation, see Dale C. Allison, "Gnilka on Matthew," *Biblica* 70 (1989): 536–37. However, W. D. Davies and Dale C. Allison, *The Gospel according to St. Matthew*, vol. 2: *Chapters 8–17*, ICC (Edinburgh: Clark, 1991), 294–96, 642, understand Matt. 11:1–12:50, esp. 11:20–24, as a rejection of Jesus by corporate Israel. Why the towns mentioned in 11:20–24 are symbolic of corporate Israel and where the concept of corporate Israel can be found in Matthew is not explained.

13. In Mark 4:12 and Matt. 13:13 this Isaianic verse is alluded to. Acts 28:23–28 uses Isa. 6:10 as a rejection of those Jews who reject Paul's teaching. John 12:40 uses this verse in a similar way. Krister Stendahl, *The School of St. Matthew* (Philadelphia: Fortress, 1968; orig. ed., 1954), 131, suggests that the full quotation was added to Matthew at a late stage of redaction.

14. Jacques Dupont, "Le point du vue de Matthieu dans le chapitre des paraboles," in M. Didier, ed., *L'Évangile selon Matthieu: Rédaction et théologie*, Bib. Eph. Theol. Lov. 29 (Gembloux: Duculot, 1972), 249, notes that the crowd never symbolizes Judaism rejecting the gospel.

15. Mark 4:10–12 lacks the full quotation from Isaiah and refers to "those

outside," a more generic term, which might refer to gentiles as well as Jews who rejected Jesus. Matthew refers to the crowds specifically and in the quotation from Isaiah, the people.

16. Later anti-Semitic Christian writings have read the verse as a permanent condemnation of the whole Jewish people. This verse has a long history in anti-Semitic literature and has been used as the primary justification for accusing Jews of the murder of Jesus and of deicide. These charges have been a stimulus for many persecutions. K. H. Rengstorf, "Das Neue Testament und die nachapostolische Zeit," in I. Rengstorf and K. von Kortzfleisch, eds., *Kirche und Synagoge: Handbuch zur Geschichte von Christen und Juden* (Stuttgart: Klett, 1968), 33–34, notes that only in the fifth century did this verse receive an anti-Semitic interpretation in conjunction with social hatred of Jews. John Chrysostom in his *Homilies on Matthew*, ad loc., says that the curse against all the people did not take effect because many in Jerusalem and in the next generation (their children) repented and became Christians. At the same time, he accuses Jews of crucifying Jesus in his *Discourses against the Jews* (1.5.1; 6.1.7). For a full exposition of the Latin patristic interpretation of this verse, see Rainer Kampling, *Das Blut Christi und die Juden: Mt 27,25 bei den lateinischsprachigen christlichen Autoren bis zu Leo dem Grossen*, NTAbh, n.s. 16 (Munich: Aschendorff, 1984).

17. Blood is an idiom for life. In the Bible, one swears by taking one's blood on one's head or one's self (2 Sam. 1:16) or one is responsible for one's own loss of life ("their blood is on them," Lev. 20:9–16). It is noteworthy that Joab and his seed are cursed forever for Joab's killing of Abner and Amasa: "Their blood will return on the head of Joab and the head of his seed forever" (1 Kings 2:33). Matthew does not use "forever," and pace Trilling, *Wahre Israel*, 71, the use of *ta tekna* for descendants does not imply *all* succeeding generations. The theme of the spilling of innocent blood is found in the Bible, and its use here associates Jesus with the righteous heroes of the Bible. Further reference to the just in Israel can be found in Matt. 23:29–36 and 27:52. This is a common theme in Jewish literature of the period (2 Baruch 64; 4 Ezra 15:22) and is carried over into Christian literature (5 Ezra 1:32). See H. G. Reventlow, "Sein Blut Komme über Sein Haupt," *Vetus Testamentum* 10 (1960): 311–27; and J. Andrew Overman, "Heroes and Villains in Palestinian Lore: Matthew's Use of Traditional Jewish Polemic in the Passion Narrative," *SBL Seminar Papers 1990* (Atlanta: Scholars, 1990), 592–602. Recently T. B. Cargal, "'His Blood Be upon Us and upon Our Children': A Matthean Double Entendre?" *New Testament Studies* 37 (1991): 101–12, has argued that 27:25 refers both to partial Jewish responsibility for Jesus' death and to the forgiveness offered them by the blood of Jesus' death. This intriguing suggestion seems less probable in the light of Matthew's whole narrative and treatment of Israel.

18. David Hill, *The Gospel of Matthew*, NCBC (Grand Rapids: Eerdmans, 1972), ad loc., correctly notes that 27:25 functions as a Matthean prophecy of the judgment which will fall on the Jews in the future.

19. Contrary to Alan H. McNeile, *The Gospel according to St. Matthew* (London: Macmillan, 1952), 413. McNeile's reference to 27:64 and its use of "the

people" as being from the same tradition is neither coherent nor convincing. Joachim Gnilka, *Das Matthäusevangelium*, HTKNT, 2 vols. (Freiburg: Herder, 1986, 1988), 2:458, adopts McNeile's position that the author deliberately and significantly shifts from the amorphous crowd to "all the people," meaning God's people, Israel, in its entirety. Both Gnilka and McNeile mistakenly think that Matthew contrasts Israel with the church and sees the church as replacing Israel. This view is common in the literature. Trilling, *Wahre Israel*, 72–73, says that this verse is a theologoumenon, that the people are representatives of all Israel, and that responsibility for Jesus' death is placed on all Israel. Gnilka, *Matthäusevangelium*, 2:459; Frankemölle, *Jahwe-Bund*, 210–11, and Georg Strecker, *Der Weg der Gerechtigkeit: Untersuchung zur Theologie des Matthäus*, (3d ed. (Göttingen: Vandenhoeck, 1971; orig. ed. 1962), 116–117, say that this verse and 21:43 (treated in chap. 3 of this volume) signify the loss of Israel's prerogatives in salvation history and its replacement by the church. These interpretations read later Christian theology into Matthew. Here "people" is used in a restricted, ordinary sense.

20. Douglas R. A. Hare, "The Rejection of the Jews in the Synoptic Gospels and Acts," in Alan Davies, ed., *Antisemitism and the Foundations of Christianity* (New York: Paulist, 1979), 38. Jeremiah has a similar threat against his opponents, the priests and prophets (Jer. 26:10–12), in which he warns the princes and the people, who are judging between them: "If you put me to death, it is innocent blood you bring on yourselves, on this city and its citizens" (Jer. 26:15). Matthew alone among the New Testament writers mentions Jeremiah's name (2:17; 16:14; 27:9). The fulfillment quotation in 27:9 is really from Zechariah, but Matthew is using the first destruction of the Temple, of which Jeremiah is the preeminent prophet, to discuss the death of Jesus and the second destruction of the Temple. Thus, blood, the blood guilt of Judas and the people of Jerusalem, and the destruction of Jerusalem are all part of one symbolic complex.

21. F. Lovsky, "Comment comprendre 'Son sang sur nous et nos enfants'?" *Etudes théologiques et religieuses* 62 (1987): 343–62, restricts the representative character of the people to the crowd in Jerusalem at the time of Jesus' death. It might also be noted that in Matthew's view because the high priest and people in Jerusalem reject Jesus as king (messiah), they interrupt the proper political, religious order and thus bring disorder to the city, the next generation, and relations with Rome.

22. Nils Dahl, "The Passion Narrative in Matthew," in *Jesus in the Memory of the Early Church* (Minneapolis: Augsburg, 1976), 47.

23. On Matthew's treatment of the trial of Jesus, see Trilling, *Wahre Israel*, 73–74; Gnilka, *Matthäusevangelium*, 2:454; E. Lohmeyer, *Das Evangelium des Matthäus*, ed. W. Schmauch, KEK, 2d ed. (Göttingen: Vandenhoeck, 1958), 382.

24. It is an exaggeration to ascribe a confessional character to the verse as Trilling does (*Wahre Israel*, 74).

25. Joseph A. Fitzmyer, "Anti-Semitism and the Cry of 'All the People' (Mt 27:25)," *Theological Studies* 26 (1965): 670–71. Fitzmyer also assumes that

many gentiles have already entered the community and that the church is fully aware of its own separate identity, assumptions not shared by this study. Frankemölle, *Jahwe-Bund*, 210, suggests that this story is an etiology for the end of Israel. But we will argue that Matthew does not take such a position.

26. See chap. 4 of this volume for the exegesis of the passage on Israel and the nations.

27. Josephus, *The Jewish War* 2.14.1–15.6 §277–332. In Matthew, the leaders persuade the crowd to go along with them.

28. Ibid., 4.3.1–3 §121–37.

29. In over 1,700 Jewish inscriptions, "Jew" occurs less than fifty times, according to Ross S. Kraemer, "On the Meaning of the Term 'Jew' in Greco-Roman Inscriptions," *Harvard Theological Review* 82 (1989): 37–38. The exact meaning of the term and the reason for its use is often ambiguous, but it is probable that the term is used by proselytes (or by their families in burial inscriptions) to affirm their adopted community (38–48). The term is also used as a proper name (48–51) and as an indicator of geographic origin (= Judean). Cf. A. Thomas Kraabal, "The Roman Diaspora: Six Questionable Assumptions," *Journal of Jewish Studies* 33 (1982): 445–64. The messy boundaries of the Jewish community and the ambiguity and variety of words used to mark communities is stressed by Jonathan Z. Smith, *Imagining Religion: From Babylon to Jonestown* (Chicago: University of Chicago Press, 1982), 17–18.

30. Contrast the Gospel of Matthew with the Gospel of John in which "the Jews" is a frequent designation for Jesus' (and the Johannine community's) opponents.

31. Strecker, *Weg der Gerechtigkeit*, 15–35, makes the strongest case for a gentile redactor. See a summary of views in John Meier, *Law and History in Matthew's Gospel*, AnBib 71; (Rome: Biblical Institute, 1976), 14–21.

32. Strecker, *Weg der Gerechtigkeit*, 116, and Frankemölle, *Jahwe-Bund*, 211, both claim that after their rejection of Jesus in 27:25 the Jewish people are no longer the covenant people in Matthew's eyes, a judgment signified by the use of the term "Jews." See also Frankemölle, *Jahwe-Bund*, 206, and Rolf Walker, *Die Heilsgeschichte im ersten Evangelium*, FRLANT 91 (Göttingen: Vandenhoeck, 1967), 47 n. 19, for the equation of Jews with all of Israel. However, this interpretation ignores the relationship of the editorial comment to the narrative sequence. In addition, Matthew does not drop the term "people" after they call for Jesus' death in 27:25, but uses it again in the ordinary sense of people who might be convinced by Jesus' disciples that he has risen (27:64). Thus "people" is not a technical term with one theological meaning, but a common, ambiguous word with many meanings.

33. Josephus, *War* 2.18.9 §499–503.

34. Ibid., 2.18.9 §506; 2.18.11 §510–11.

35. Ibid., 2.19.1 §513–14; 2.19.2 §517–19.

36. Ibid., 2.19.2 §520. See also the comment of H. St.-J. Thackeray in the Loeb edition.

37. Ibid., 2.19.3 §523; 2.19.5 §533; 2.19.5 §536.

38. It has been suggested that *Ioudaioi* in Matt. 28:15 is a geographical

term, meaning "Judeans." See, for example, Bruce Malina, in a review of A.-J. Levine's *Social and Ethnic Dimension,* in *Biblical Theology Bulletin* 19 (1989): 130. Since the guards at the tomb are located in Judea, this is possible. However, the polemical use of the term "Jews" by Jews against each other is more likely. In addition, 28:15 is a comment in the author's own voice, referring to his opponents within the larger Jewish community of the late first century.

39. In many passages Matthew follows Markan usage.

40. See Peter Richardson, *Israel in the Apostolic Church,* SNTSMS 10 (Cambridge: Cambridge University Press, 1969), 193; A.-J. Levine, *The Social and Ethnic Dimension of Matthean Salvation History* (Lewiston, N.Y.: Mellen, 1988), chap. 1 and passim; Michael Wilkins, *The Concept of Disciple in Matthew's Gospel,* Suppl NovT 59 (Leiden: Brill, 1988), 170–71; Kingsbury, *Matthew as Story,* 23–27.

41. Wilkins, *Disciple,* 157, suggests that because in Matthew (contrary to Mark) only the crowds, not the disciples, are mentioned as gathered around the epileptic boy, Matthew is simplifying the scene and contrasting the disciples and the father with the crowd. The teaching on faith is an attempt to draw the disciples and the man away from the crowd, which does not have faith. Certainly Matthew is presenting the disciples in a more positive way than Mark, but it seems that all the characters are included in Jesus' frustrated lament concerning their lack of faith.

42. Wilkins, *Disciple,* 157.

43. Paul S. Minear, "The Disciples and the Crowds in the Gospel of Matthew," in M. H. Shepherd and E. C. Hobbs, eds., *Gospel Studies in Honor of S. E. Johnson,* AThR Suppl., ser. 3 (1974), 28–44, sees the crowds as true followers of Jesus and suggests that the disciples represent the leadership and the crowds the laity in Matthew's church (31). But the narrative does not present the crowds as committed followers and the disciples as "clergy," especially in the light of Matt. 23:1–12.

44. Matthew follows Mark (14:43, 48) in having the crowd come to arrest Jesus. Luke changes the arresting officers to chief priests, officers of the Temple, and elders (22:52), who are accompanied by a crowd (22:47). Thus Jesus' rebuke (that they had a chance to arrest him in the Temple every day) makes more sense in Luke.

45. One other hostile group, which is not denoted by the word "crowd," is the inhabitants of Jesus' "own country" *(patridi),* presumably Nazareth (Matt. 13:54; cf. Mark 6:1). Elsewhere, Matthew recounts that Jesus' mother and brothers wanted to speak with him and Jesus instead chose his disciples (12:46–50), but he omits Mark's earlier comment that his family wanted to seize him, presumably to take him home (Mark 3:21).

46. For the structure of Palestinian society, see Anthony J. Saldarini, *Pharisees, Scribes, and Sadducees in Palestinian Society* (Wilmington: Glazier, 1988; Edinburgh: Clark, 1989), chap. 3. See also John D. Crossan, *The Historical Jesus: The Life of a Mediterranean Jewish Peasant* (San Francisco: Harper, 1991).

47. See Richard A. Horsley and John S. Hanson, *Bandits, Prophets, and Messiahs: Popular Movements at the Time of Jesus* (Minneapolis: Winston-Seabury,

1985); and Richard A. Horsley, *Jesus and the Spiral of Violence: Popular Jewish Resistance in Roman Palestine* (San Francisco: Harper, 1987).

48. Hans Toch, *The Social Psychology of Social Movements* (Indianapolis: Bobbs-Merrill 1965), 5.

49. John D. McCarthy and Mayer N. Zald, "Resource Mobilization and Social Movements: A Partial Theory," *American Journal of Sociology* 82 (1977): 1217–19.

50. Some commentators put great stress on the exclusion of the crowds in Matthew 13 as a sign that Jesus now concentrates solely on the disciples, and that this literary turn symbolizes Matthew's estrangement from the whole Jewish community of his own day: "Repudiated by *all segments of Israel*, Jesus reacts by declaring that Israel has become hard of heart (13:13–15). Moreover, he gives public demonstration of this by addressing the crowds in parables, that is, in speech they cannot comprehend (13:2–3, 10–13)" (Kingsbury, *Matthew as Story*, 75; italics added). Hill (*Matthew*, 227) has a similar interpretation. But the narrative is more complex. The crowds continue to gather around Jesus and he continues to teach them. The parables, which are the standard way of teaching in traditional Near Eastern society, continue both to make plain and to hide the truth. Jesus also continues to heal and feed the crowds and to care for them. The condemnation in chapter 13 is for those who specifically reject Jesus' teaching. In the narrative, the crowds are on the whole ambiguous and uncertain. As Hill notes, it is the Pharisees who actually reject Jesus in Matthew. Thus, the polemic in chapter 13 does not symbolize the break between Matthew's group and the Jewish community in the late first century, but rather the struggle for the allegiance of the bulk of the Jewish people. The judgment made by Jesus makes clear the stakes and explains also why most Jews did not accept Jesus during his lifetime and have not accepted his teaching from Matthew's group. It does not pronounce a final judgment on them or end the Matthean group's obligation to appeal to fellow Jews.

51. Wilkins, *Disciple*, 171.

52. See chap. 3 of this volume.

53. Davies and Allison, *Matthew 8–17*, 260–61, note that "this generation" always refers to the contemporaries of Jesus and Matthew and never to all Jews. The fault of "this generation" is rejection of Jesus.

54. The reference to "this generation" in the final discourse (24:34) is a temporal statement with no positive or negative evaluation expressed.

55. In the Lukan parallel (7:31–35), the context suggests that the Pharisees are the critics. See O. Linton, "The Parable of the Children's Game. Baptist and Son of Man (Matt. xi. 16–19 = Luke vii. 31–35): A Synoptic Text-Critical, Structural, and Exegetical Investigation," *New Testament Studies* 22 (1976): 159–79. Here there is an implicit link to the Pharisees in the charges brought. John is said to have a demon; this charge is brought against Jesus by the Pharisees (9:34). Jesus is charged with not fasting; the question of fasting was raised by John the Baptist's disciples (9:14–15), who do, like the Pharisees, fast.

56. For this theme in early Christianity, see O. H. Steck, *Israel und das gewalt-*

same *Geshick der Propheten: Untersuchungen zur Überlieferung des deuterono-mistischen Geschichtsbildes im Alten Testament, Spätjudentum, und Urchristentum,* WMANT 23 (Neukirchen: Neukirchener Verlag, 1967). See the treatment of 27:25 above for the importance of this theme to Matthew.

57. Frankemölle, *Jahwe-Bund,* 172–74; he also sees, incorrectly, a dog-matic message that Israel has squandered its prerogatives (313–14).

58. Wayne Meeks, "Breaking Away: Three New Testament Pictures of Christianity's Separation from the Jewish Communities," in Jacob Neusner and Ernest S. Frerichs, eds., *"To See Ourselves as Others See Us": Christians, Jews, "Others" in Late Antiquity* (Chico: Scholars, 1985), 112, argues for the progres-sive alienation of "the whole people" from Jesus in the gospel. He cites 8:11 as a prediction of the rejection of the Jews and says, "The implication of this dark saying works its way through the rest of the gospel," until Israel is ultimately replaced. Dale C. Allison, "Who Will Come from East and West? Observations on Matt. 8:11–12; Luke 13:28–29." *Irish Biblical Studies* 11 (1989): 158–70, argues that this saying originally referred to diaspora Jews. Carl R. Kazmierski, "The Stone of Abraham: John the Baptist and the End of Torah (Matt 3, 7–10 par. Luke 3, 7–9)," *Biblica* 68 (1987): 22–40, argues that this saying originally arose among charismatic Jewish preachers who had been rejected and were defending themselves against their opponents.

59. Note that in this and the previous saying Abraham is mentioned.

60. There is probably a word play on the Hebrew *banim* (בנים, sons) and *'ebanim* (אבנים, stones). Isa. 51:1–2 speaks of Israel quarried from Abraham. The defining of true Abrahamic descent on something other than a physical basis is found in Paul and John as well (Rom. 2:17–29; 4:12; Gal. 3:7; John 8:39).

61. Davies and Allison, *Matthew 1–7,* 309.

62. The view that the mission to Israel is in the past and is now closed is like the view that Matthew periodizes history in such a way that Jesus was sent to Israel, was rejected, and sent his disciples to the gentiles. See Strecker, *Weg der Gerechtigkeit,* 184–88; Walker, *Heilsgeschichte;* Douglas R. A. Hare, *The Theme of Jewish Persecution of Christians in the Gospel according to St. Matthew,* SNTSMS 6 (Cambridge: Cambridge University Press, 1967), 147–48; William Thomp-son, "An Historical Perspective on the Gospel of Matthew," *Journal of Biblical Literature* 93 (1974): 243–62. It is based on understanding *ethnē* in 28:19 as referring exclusively to non-Jews, on a periodization of chaps. 24–25 that as-sociates the destruction of Jerusalem with the end of the Jewish mission, on a reading of chapter 10 that places the Jewish mission in the past, and similar exegetical arguments. For a similar position, see J. Lambrecht, "The Parousia Discourse. Composition and Content in Mt., XXIV–XXV," in Didier, ed., *L'Évangile selon Matthieu,* 309–42. For recent acceptance of the thesis that Is-rael has been rejected in Matthew, see Lloyd Gaston, "Messiah of Israel as Teacher of the Gentiles: The Setting of Matthew's Christology," *Interpretation* 29 (1975): 32; Meeks, "Breaking Away,"112–13; and Sean Freyne, "Vilifying the Other and Defining the Self: Matthew's and John's Anti-Jewish Polemic in Focus," in Neusner and Frerichs, *To See Ourselves,* 123. Other recent inter-

preters hold that the Jewish mission is still open, or at least not closed in princi-
ple. See John Meier, "Nations or Gentiles in Matthew 28:19?" *Catholic Biblical
Quarterly* 39 (1977): 94–102; Kingsbury, *Matthew as Story,* 154; Tagawa,
"People," 160; E. A. Russell, "The Image of the Jew in Matthew's Gospel,"
Proceedings of the Irish Biblical Association 12 (1989):51; Graham N. Stanton,
"Aspects of Early Christian-Jewish Polemic and Apologetic," *New Testament
Studies* 31 (1985): 388–89; Benedict T. Viviano, "Social World and Commu-
nity Leadership: The Case of Matthew 23:1–12, 34," *Journal for the Study of the
New Testament* 39 (1990): 3–21; and Levine, *Dimensions.* Levine argues that
Matt. 28:19 does mean "gentiles," but that the gospel as a whole leaves the
Jewish mission open. R. Hummel, *Die Auseinandersetzung zwischen Kirche und
Judentum im Matthäusevangelium* (Munich: Kaiser, 1963), 156 n. 72, 157–61,
correctly stresses the close relationship between Matthew's group and other
Jewish communities.

63. Richardson, *Israel,* 193.

64. To repeat the interpretation of Matt. 27:25, "people" there refers to the
Jerusalem leadership and people and is post eventum prophecy, that is, a response to the actual destruction of Jerusalem and its leaders and people in 70.
The crowds in chapters 26–27 are the crowds in Jerusalem and seem to be a
subset of, or different from, the crowds in Galilee.

Chapter Three

1. Hostility to the leadership within the Jewish community is common in
Jewish literature. See J. Andrew Overman, *Matthew's Gospel and Formative Judaism: The Social World of the Matthean Community* (Minneapolis: Fortress,
1990), 19–23, 141–47.

2. For the leaders as a corporate character in the plot, see Jack Dean Kingsbury, *Matthew as Story* (Philadelphia: Fortress, 1986; 2d ed. 1988), 17–23. See
also his study "The Developing Conflict between Jesus and the Jewish Leaders
in Matthew: A Literary-Critical Study," *Catholic Biblical Quarterly* 49 (1987):
57–73. I have not seen Mark Allan Powell, "The Religious Leaders in
Matthew: A Literary Critical Approach" (Ph.D. diss., Union Theological Seminary in Virginia, 1988).

3. For a complete account of their characterization in Matthew, their
agendas, and the historicity of Matthew's account, see Anthony J. Saldarini,
Pharisees, Scribes, and Sadducees in Palestinian Society (Wilmington: Glazier,
1988; Edinburgh: Clark, 1989), 157–73.

4. Bruce Malina and Jerome Neyrey, *Calling Jesus Names: The Social Value of
Labels in Matthew* (Sonoma: Polebridge, 1988), chaps. 1–2, esp. chap. 1, an-
alyze the traditional nature of this type of attack and its desired effects in detail.
The legal disputes are interpreted in detail in chap. 6 of this volume.

5. As we saw in chapter 2 above, the expression "this generation" refers to
the Jewish leaders in several cases (12:38–45; 16:1–4).

6. David E. Garland, *The Intention of Matthew 23* (Leiden: Brill, 1979), holds
that the scribes and Pharisees serve as a negative example of leadership for

Matthew's group. This is a goal of the chapter, but it is secondary to the attack on the Jewish leadership. For another attempt to apply this chapter to Christian leaders, see M. Limbeck, "Die nichts bewegen wollen! Zum Gesetzesverständnis des Evangelisten Matthäus," *Theologischer Quartalschrift* 168 (1988): 299–320. See also Hubert Frankemölle, "'Pharisaismus' in Judentum und Kirche: Zur Tradition and Redaktion in Matthäus 23," in H. Goldstein, ed., *Gottesverachter und Menschenfeinde: Juden Zwischen Jesus und frühchristlichen Kirche* (Dusseldorf: Patmos, 1979), 123–89; E. Haenchen, "Matthäus 23," *Zeitschrift für die neutestamentliche Wissenschaft* 48 (1951): 38–63, reprinted in *Gott und Mensch* (Tübingen: Mohr, 1965), 29–54; W. Pesch, "Theologische Aussagen der Redaktion von Matthäus 23," in P. Hoffmann et al., eds., *Orientierung an Jesus: Zur Theologie der Synoptiker,* for J. Schmid (Freiberg: Herder, 1973), 286–99.

7. A similar approach to these materials has been taken recently by Benedict T. Viviano, "Social World and Community Leadership: The Case of Matthew 23:1–12, 34," *Journal for the Study of the New Testament* 39 (1990): 3–21.

8. In reality, scribes were found at every level of society and did not form a cohesive group. Some of them were surely officials and teachers and thus had contact and conflict with Jesus. Since the Hasmonean period, the Pharisees had had a program for reform of Jewish society and had won influence and sometimes power in society. Neither group was in control of society; the Roman government, the chief priests and families in Jerusalem, and Herod Antipas in Galilee had that role. The author of Matthew describes the scribes and Pharisees as lower-level officials, that is, as just the type of Jewish leader who would have interacted with Jesus and the small, new Christian-Jewish group. Scribes, Pharisees, and the leaders of the Jewish community in Matthew's day had recognized power and status in the community and sought to preserve it by receiving public honor and titles and by controlling the interpretation of community custom and justice. See Saldarini, *Pharisees.*

9. For a more extended treatment of Matthew 23, see Anthony J. Saldarini, "Delegitimation of Leaders in Matthew 23," *Catholic Biblical Quarterly* 54 (1992):659–80.

10. Peter Berger and Thomas Luckmann, *The Social Construction of Reality: A Treatise in the Sociology of Knowledge* (Garden City: Doubleday Anchor, 1967), 92–128.

11. Berger and Luckman, *Construction of Reality,* 61–62, 93. Berger and Luckmann effectively describe the social processes of legitimation at a very abstract level. The neo-Kantian presuppositions of their epistemology are not being utilized or espoused here.

12. Ibid., 93.

13. Ibid., 106–9.

14. Ibid., 94–95.

15. The attack on the scribes and Pharisees is made by Jesus in Jerusalem as a climax to his attack on the Jerusalem authorities in chapters 21–22. The narrative place, Jerusalem, and the time of the attack, just before Jesus' arrest, in

dicates that Matthew is opposing the highest Jewish authorities in their entirety.

16. Note that at the beginning of the Sermon on the Mount, in which Jesus teaches authoritatively, he sits.

17. Commentators typically assign these verses to the Jewish Christian stratum of tradition and then depict Matthew as preserving but disagreeing with them. In these types of interpretations, commentators have difficulty showing why Matthew would preserve them and what use he makes of them. See Joachim Gnilka, *Das Matthäusevangelium*, HTKNT, 2 vols., (Freiburg: Herder, 1986, 1988), 2:271–72, for sharply differing views on the tradition history of 23:1–12.

18. Garland, *Intention*, 53–54.

19. Classically, sects have been contrasted with church, for example, by Troelsch. For a modern, broad typology of sects and their characteristics, see Bryan Wilson, *Magic and the Millennium: A Sociological Study of Religious Movements of Protest among Tribal and Third-World Peoples* (London: Heinemann, 1973), Introduction and chaps. 1–2.

20. Woe oracles are found frequently in prophetic literature, either individually (Amos 5:8; 6:1; Isa. 1:4; 3:11; 10:5) or in series (Isa. 5:8–24). The woe is usually followed by a participle describing the criticized action or by a noun giving a negative characterization of the person. Appended to the woe may be a variety of forms, such as rhetorical questions or threats. A woe oracle is a mild form of curse, which functions as a public denunciation. Woe's may have been adapted from wisdom literature. Lief E. Vaage, "The Woes in Q (and Matthew and Luke): Deciphering the Rhetoric of Criticism," *SBL Seminar Papers 1988* (Atlanta: Scholars, 1988), 603, 605, relates the woes to Greek rhetorical contrasts between appearances and reality and shows how this type of critique of human blindness and untempered zeal has been transformed into a polemic that serves to justify Matthew's group.

The "woe" in Matt. 23:14 is rejected by most textual critics. It is missing from many manuscripts, interrupts the topical arrangement of the woes, and increases the number of woes from seven to eight.

21. The Sermon on the Mount (chaps. 5–7) and the woes against the scribes and Pharisees are respectively the first and last lengthy public teachings of Jesus. For the correlation of eschatological blessings and curses, see W. D. Davies and Dale C. Allison, *The Gospel according to St. Matthew*, vol. 1: *Chapters 1–7*, ICC (Edinburgh: Clark, 1988), 432–33. In both passages, Jesus is said to teach both the crowds and disciples (5:1; 23:1). The Beatitudes, like the woes, stress the inner attitudes of the group and the patterns of its behavior. Its members should be merciful, meek, pure of heart, and peacemakers; they mourn and seek justice; they know suffering, for they are poor in spirit and persecuted (the beginning and end of the series). The sense one has of this group is that it is neither powerful nor established. It seeks to make the best of its minority, deviant status. The reward offered at both the beginning and end of the Beatitudes (5:3, 10) is the kingdom of heaven, that is, life under the rule of God rather than that of the unreliable Jewish authorities excoriated in chapters 6, 23, and

elsewhere in the gospel. Those who adhere to Jesus' code will see God, possess the land, and enjoy justice, mercy, peace, and comfort. This is in direct contradiction to the society promoted by the scribes and Pharisees, which, according to Matthew's tendentious view, neglects justice and mercy (23:23), places burdens on people (23:4), keeps cups and dishes pure, but not hearts (23:25), appears just, but is hypocritical (23:28), and kills God's messengers (23:31–32) rather than creating peace and harmony. Thus Matthew brackets his account of Jesus' deeds and teaching with a vision of a new society (chaps. 5–7) and an attack on an alternate program (chap. 23). It should be noted that both have succeeded quite well for almost 2,000 years.

22. As mentioned before the term "hypocrite" originally referred to a mask used in the theater. It then became used for insincerity and pretense. It also is used of the misplaced and mistaken zeal of the scribes and Pharisees. See Garland, *Intention*, 96–116. This kind of an attack on the hypocrisy of Jewish leaders is found in Pss. of Sol. 4. Hypocrisy makes it difficult to know the actual commitment of a person to a culture, religion, or system, and so it inhibits strong relationships among people. Hence it is despised. See Hans Mol, *Identity and the Sacred: A Sketch for a New Social-Scientific Theory of Religion* (Oxford: Blackwell; New York: Macmillan, Free Press, 1977), 216–17.

23. For a complete exposition of Matt. 16:18–19 against its apocalyptic background, with attention to the teaching authority claimed for the group by Matthew, see J. Marcus, "The Gates of Hades and the Keys of the Kingdom (Matt. 16:18–19)," *Catholic Biblical Quarterly* 50 (1988): 443–55. See also W. D. Davies and Dale C. Allison, *The Gospel according to St. Matthew*, vol. 2: *Chapters 8–17* (Edinburgh: Clark, 1991), 621–41.

24. Though Judaism ceased trying to win converts during the Byzantine period because of Christian laws and the development of rabbinic Judaism, during the Roman period Judaism was very attractive to many members of the empire (Josephus, *Contra Apionem* 2 §39; *War* 7.3.3 §45). Greeks and Romans admired Jewish monotheism, its strict sexual ethic, and its ritual, especially Sabbath observance and synagogue worship. Roman writers parodied and attacked Jewish customs adopted by Romans (e.g., Juvenal, *Satire* 14). The limited evidence available suggests that synagogues welcomed converts and those interested in Judaism. Male converts had to be circumcised, and they and female converts perhaps had to undergo immersion (as later regulations required). Other non-Jews participated in some Jewish rituals and practices. It is doubtful that there was a recognized, named category of "God-fearers" (Acts 13:16, 26) or "semiproselytes," but the phenomenon of gentiles attached to synagogue communities in some way is very probable. See A. Thomas Kraabel, "The Disappearance of the God-fearers," *Numen* 28 (1981): 113–26; J. Andrew Overman, "The God-Fearers: Some Neglected Features," *Journal for the Study of the New Testament* 32 (1988): 17–26.

25. "Child of Gehenna" is the opposite of "sons of heaven" (8:12; 13:38), that is, those who do not versus those who do believe in Jesus.

26. Oaths and vows were very common in ancient society and were taken seriously, since the threat of divine punishment for broken oaths and vows was

perceived as a present danger. An oath or vow was secured by a curse on the speaker in case of nonfulfillment. Traditionally, an oath (Heb. *shevu'ah*) was a commitment to do something, and a vow (Heb. *neder;* Latin *votum*) was the dedication of something to the divinity and thus a commitment not to use or benefit from it. However, the two were often used interchangeably. Both Greek and later talmudic literature testify to the variety of oaths and vows sworn by all classes of people. Great effort was expended on (1) preserving the sanctity and seriousness of oaths; (2) preventing people from swearing frivolous oaths or making imprudent vows; and (3) distinguishing valid from invalid vows. Some of the distinctions Matthew mocks, for example, between a vow by the Temple (cf. t. Ned. 1:3) or by the gold of the Temple, are found in other literature. Thus an oath sworn by the king is distinguished from one by the life of the king (Sifre Num. 153). The reasons for these distinctions are often unknown, except that some less sacred object might be used to preserve the sanctity of the more sacred. In rabbinic literature, these substitute oaths are called handles. See Saul Lieberman, *Greek in Jewish Palestine: Studies in the Life and Manners of Jewish Palestine in the II–IV Centuries* (New York: Jewish Theological Seminary, 1942), 115–43.

27. A tithe is one tenth (or some other determinate portion) of produce, animals, money, and so on, which is to be given to God, usually through a temple. Biblical tithes were on grain, wine, oil, fruit, and animals (Deut. 14: 22–23; Num. 18:12; Lev. 27:30). The Mishnah, like Matthew, reflects an expansion of tithing to include all growing things, including vegetables and herbs (m. Ma'as. 1:1). "Mint, dill and cummin" are herbs used as spices in food. Dill and cummin were also used for medicinal purposes. Tithing of dill is mentioned later in m. Ma'as. 4:5. Cummin is transliterated into Greek from Hebrew (Isa. 28:25). Matthew selected three commonly used herbs. See D. Correns, "Die Verzehntung der Raute. Lk xi 42 and M. Schebi ix 1," *Novum Testamentum* 6 (1963): 110–12.

Tithes were a form of tax to support the Temple, and through it, the central governmental institutions of Israel. The rules for tithes found in the Bible show evidence of development and change in tithing practices (cf. Lev. 6–7; Num. 18; Deut. 18). The latest stage of redaction reflects postexilic practices, when there was no king to support the Temple and priests and when the Levites had been subordinated to the priests. In the Hasmonean and Roman periods, the Pharisees made scrupulous tithing of their food a distinctive characteristic of their program for reform, testifying to general laxity in this area (as is often the case in the payment of taxes). The Mishnaic Order of Agriculture continued the Pharisees' interest in tithing by devoting ten treatises to working out ambiguities in the rules for tithing. Paying tithes should not be pictured as a pious religious practice. Tithes were a tax used to support the central religious and political institution of Israel, the Temple and its priests. Both the Pharisaic support of tithing and the early Christian (and Jesus'?) deemphasis on tithing were fraught with economic and political consequences for Jewish society. The Pharisees desired a strong Temple as an anchor for Jewish identity and society. The early Christian-Jewish communities were in conflict with those leaders and institutions of Judaism.

Disputes over the ritual cleanliness of the outside and inside of cooking and eating dishes and utensils and over the various sources of impurity were based on biblical injunctions (Lev. 11:29–35; 15:1–12; Num. 31:19–24). According to Jacob Neusner, "'First Cleanse the Inside': Halakhic Background of a Controversial Saying," *New Testament Studies* 22 (1976): 486–95, the earliest layer of the Mishnah contains a dispute over distinguishing the outer part of a dish or cup from the inner part and the handles; the schools of Hillel and Shammai are presented as disagreeing about whether the inside and outside could affect one another (m. Kel. 25:1, 7–8). Thus Matthew is taking a position on a live first-century controversy, not just making a metaphoric point. See further analysis of this in chap. 6 of this volume.

28. Since corpses and tombs were sources of ritual impurity (Num. 6:6; 19:16), the later Mishnah says that graves were marked with whitewash, especially at times of feasts, so that people would not stray over them and become ritually unclean (m. Ma'as. Shen. 5:1; m. Seqal. 1:1). The suggestion that decorated ossuaries are being referred to is less probable.

The whitewashing of tombs and the building of monuments to the dead were two elements of Jewish funerary practices. Every culture has rituals and customs for dealing with the death of loved ones, the disposal of the corpse, and the remembrance of those who have died. Because the corpse was considered ritually impure, burial took place the day of death. Burial in trench or shaft graves was the common mode, and these were the types of graves that had to be marked by whitewashed stones so that people would not walk on them and contract ritual impurity. Another common form of burial in the first century was cave burial; usually the body was placed in a wall niche, and after the flesh had decayed, the bones were gathered in a box (ossuary). The famous or wealthy deceased might be buried in a stone sarcophagus or in a monumental tomb, such as those found in the Kedron Valley east and south of Jerusalem. Though these tombs are Hellenistic and Roman, they were preceded by tombs to kings and prophets, referred to by Matthew.

For a later but similar use of inside-outside imagery, see b. Ber. 28a concerning genuine and false rabbinical students.

29. The literal meaning of the Greek word *anomia* is "lawlessness," but in its various forms *anomia* connotes wickedness and godlessness and generally the opposite of justice. For example, those who do not do the will of God are designated, in the words of Ps. 6:9, "doers of lawlessness" (cf. Matt. 7:23). G. Barth, "Matthew's Understanding of the Law," in G. Bornkamm, G. Barth, and H. J. Held, *Tradition and Interpretation in Matthew* (Philadelphia: Westminster, 1963), 159–64, held that Matthew was polemicizing against antinomian Christians. This view has been effectively refuted by A. Sand, "Die Polemik gegen die 'Gesetzlosigkeit' im Evangelium nach Matthäus und bei Paulus," *Biblische Zeitschrift* 14 (1980): 112–25; and J. E. Davison, "*Anomia* and the Question of an Antinomian Polemic in Matthew," *Journal of Biblical Literature* 104 (1985): 617–35. Davies and Allison, *Matthew 1–7*, 718–19, stress the eschatological dimensions of this word, and Overman, *Matthew's Gospel*, 98, associates its Matthean usage with the sectarian language in Matthew. Matthew

accuses of *anomia* those who do not do God's will and who are not bearing fruit (7:21–23).

30. The mention of tomb links this woe oracle with the previous one. Tombs in honor of leaders and heroes were common. For David's tomb, see Josephus, *Jewish Antiquities* 7 §393–94; 16 §179–83. The prophets and righteous (Matt. 13:17) designate those who are faithful to God and are likely to be persecuted and killed (Matt. 23:30). Matthew's apocalyptic heightening of Jesus' death has the tombs of the "saints" opening and the saints walking about (27:52).

31. Abel is the first "martyr" in the Bible and Zechariah, who is associated with the prophets, is the "last" (2 Chron. 24:20–22). Abel is designated as just *(dikaios)*. The identity of Zechariah has long been a problem. The text says "Zechariah, son of Berachiah," one of the minor prophets (Zech. 1:1), but Matthew probably means to refer to Zechariah, son of Jehoiada the priest (2 Chron. 24:20), who along with the prophets (2 Chron. 24:19) opposed the leaders' and people's idolatry. By the king's order, he was stoned in the court of the Temple (2 Chron. 24:21). Matthew may also have had in mind Zechariah, son of Baris, murdered by two Zealots in the Temple during the Roman war (Josephus, *War* 4.5.4 §334–44). For the use of this theme in early Christian literature, see O. H. Steck, *Israel und das gewaltsame Geshick der Propheten: Untersuchungen zur Überlieferung des deuteronomistischen Geschichtsbildes im Alten Testament, Spätjudentum, und Urchristentum*, WMANT 23 (Neukirchen: Neukirchener Verlag, 1967). For later Jewish interpretations, see S. H. Blank, "The Death of Zechariah in Rabbinic Literature," *Hebrew Union College Annual* 12–13 (1937–38): 327–46.

32. The author is referring to the missionaries and teachers of his own movement when he speaks of prophets, wise men, and scribes. His group uses traditional terms for its officials, but not rabbi, master, and teacher, rejected earlier in the chapter (vv. 8–12). Matthew contrasts Jewish scribes in the seven woes to true scribes. See the earlier rejection of "their scribes" (7:29) and praise of the scribe trained for the kingdom (13:52).

33. Deut. 25:3 limits lashes to forty; in order not to exceed this number, one less lash was given. Cf. m. Mak. 3:10.

34. For the redactional coherence of chapters 21–25, see E. Schweizer, "Matthäus 21–25," in P. Hoffmann et al., eds., *Orientierung an Jesus: Zur Theologie der Synoptiker, Festschrift for J. Schmid* (Freiberg: Herder, 1973), 364–71.

35. For the activities of some prophets during the first century and an explanation of the Israelite traditions which gave them legitimacy, see Richard A. Horsley, "'Like One of the Prophets of Old: Two Types of Popular Prophets at the Time of Jesus," *Catholic Biblical Quarterly* 47 (1985): 435–63. For messianic movements, see Horsley, "Popular Messianic Movements around the Time of Jesus," *Catholic Biblical Quarterly* 46 (1984): 473–80. These roles are treated more fully in chap. 7 of this volume.

36. Matthew reorganized the materials he found in Mark 11:1–17 so that the entrance into Jerusalem is separated from the cleansing of the Temple.

37. It should be noted that the changing of money for offerings and the sell-

ing of sacrificial animals were legitimate and necessary parts of Temple activities. The early Jesus tradition presents these practices in a highly prejudicial and polemical manner as an excuse to reject the Temple or its guardians and the type of worship going on there. For the problems of historicity and the importance of this incident for Jesus' restoration eschatology, see E. P. Sanders, *Jewish Law from Jesus to the Mishnah* (London: SCM; Philadelphia: Trinity, 1990), 61–76.

38. Mark 11:17 continues the quotation to include the gentiles: "a house of prayer for all the nations." (The Hebrew has "all peoples.") The context in Isaiah concerns the stranger *(nekar)* who joins Israel. Isaiah also includes a critique of the watchmen and shepherds (Isa. 56:10–11), that is, the leaders of Israel at the Temple, who are compared to greedy dogs. Matthew seems to pick up the critique of the Temple leadership from Isaiah to support his main concern in chapters 21–23, but he does not develop the gentile theme. In fact, he suppresses it by omitting the Isaianic and Markan "for all the nations," perhaps, as Daniel J. Harrington argues, because after 70 such a claim for the Temple made no sense for his group and goals. See Harrington's *The Gospel of Matthew,* Sacra Pagina (Collegeville, Minn.: Liturgical Press, Glazier, 1991), 294. The dropping of the phrase is also testimony to Matthew's emphasis on inner Jewish reform.

39. Isaiah 56, along with chapters 60 and 66, envisions the gentiles worshiping in the Temple. Pss. of Sol. 17:30–34 envisions a purified Temple and a king who prevails without war; the gentiles are expelled from the Temple and serve Israel. R. H. Hiers, "Purification of the Temple: Preparation for the Kingdom of God," *Journal of Biblical Literature* 90 (1971): 82–90, associates such an expectation with the historical Jesus' preaching.

40. Figs are fully ripe only from June to August. All one would find at Passover season would be unripe, green fruit. Mark 11:13 notes that it was not the season for the tree to have fruit. Matthew omits this, probably because it gives the impression that Jesus' act was unreasonable. He also makes the miracle instantaneous, in contrast to Mark, who has the tree wither by the next day. The interpretation of this parable is very uncertain. Many commentators have tried to ascertain the original meaning underlying all the gospels. See W. R. Telford, *The Barren Temple and the Withered Tree: A Redaction-Critical Analysis of the Cursing of the Fig-Tree Pericope in Mark's Gospel and Its Relationship to the Cleansing of the Temple Tradition* (Sheffield: JSOT, 1980); H. Giesen, "Der verdorrte Feigenbaum—eine symbolische Aussage?" *Biblische Zeitschrift* 20 (1976): 95–111; G. Münderlein, "Die Verfluchung des Feigenbaums," *New Testament Studies* 10 (1963–64): 89–104.

41. See Matt. 3:8, 10; 7:16–20; 12:33; 13:8, 26; 21:19, 34, 41, 43. See also Hos. 9:16; Isa. 27:6; Jer. 12:2; 17:8; Ezek. 17:8–9, 23, for bearing fruit as a sign of life, prosperity, and divine favor and not bearing fruit as a sign of the opposite.

42. See Telford, *Temple,* 69–94, for a treatment of Matthew. Telford notes that Matthew attacks the leaders but not the institutions of Judaism.

43. Matthew follows Mark in drawing from the withered fig tree a lesson

on faith and prayer, but he emphasizes the didactic aspects more than Mark. Luke solves the problem by omitting the incident.

44. This application of the fig tree story to faith and prayer is awkward and extrinsic to the story. Yet this is the central focus in Matthew. See E. Lohmeyer, *Das Evangelium des Matthäus*, 2d ed., W. Schmauch, KEK, (Göttingen: Vandenhoeck, 1958), 302; W. Grundmann, *Das Evangelium nach Matthäus*, THK 1 (Berlin: Evangelische Verlagsanstalt, 1968), 452; Telford, *Temple*, 80–81. Luke omitted the withering of the fig tree and told the story of the fig tree as a parable, though he too connects it with Jerusalem (13:1–9). Matthew may be encouraging his own minority group to persevere against the established majority in the Jewish community and to trust in their own faith and prayer (cf. 6:5–15, 25–34). He may also be affirming his Judaism's relationship with God after the destruction of the Temple.

45. Jesus is sovereign over the Temple in Matthew, not antagonistic to it. He competes for authority with the Temple leaders in chapters 21–23 and in Matthew's view, defeats them. See Telford, *Temple*, 83–84; R. S. McConnell, *Law and Prophecy in Matthew's Gospel* (Basel: Reinhardt, 1969), 72–75.

46. For an attempt to see what these parables meant in the context of Jesus' life, see Philip Culbertson, "Reclaiming the Matthean Vineyard Parables," *Encounter* 49 (1988): 257–84.

47. The leaders' reluctance to express publicly their rejection of John the Baptist because they feared the crowd is another example of Matthew's central charge against them—hypocrisy.

48. The challenging of the wise man or philosopher with trick questions and the clever reply that refutes the question without giving anything away is well known from wisdom materials and Greco-Roman literature.

49. Richard A. Horsley, *Jesus and the Spiral of Violence: Popular Jewish Resistance in Roman Palestine* (San Francisco: Harper, 1987), 306–17. The coin may be Caesar's, but the "things of God" include more than money and Temple taxes. The things of God include the kingdom and all of human life. Thus, in the end, the "things of Caesar" are nothing.

50. For the contrast of Pharisees, Sadducees, Essenes, and the fourth philosophy, see Josephus, *War* 2.8.2–14 §119–66; *Ant*. 18.1.2–6 §11–25. On the Sadducees, see Saldarini, *Pharisees*, 107–23 and chap. 13.

51. Dan. 12:2; Enoch 62:13–16; 104:4; 2 Bar. 51:10. In these texts, humans become like divine beings (stars, angels) in heaven with God.

52. In the psalm, the speaker is an official acclaiming his Lord, the king, who has himself been called by his Lord, God.

53. See D. M. Hay, *Glory on the Right Hand: Psalm 110 in Early Christianity*, SBLMS 18 (Nashville: Abingdon, 1973), for a complete treatment of the exegesis of Psalm 110 in early Christianity. See also R. Hummel, *Die Auseinandersetzung zwischen Kirche und Judentum im Matthäusevangelium* (Munich: Kaiser, 1963), 121; A. Suhl, "Der Davidssohn im Matthäusevangelium," *Zeitschrift für die neutestamentliche Wissenschaft* 59 (1968): 57–81; J. M. Gibbs, "Purpose and Pattern in Matthew's Use of the Title 'Son of David,'" *New Testament Studies* 10

(1963–64): 461; Hay, *Glory,* 116–17; Jack Dean Kingsbury, *Matthew: Structure, Christology, Kingdom* (Philadelphia: Fortress, 1975), 101–2.

54. Some recent work has reversed this traditional emphasis. A. Ogawa, "Paraboles de l'Israel véritable? Reconsidération critique de Mt 21,28–22,14," *Novum Testamentum* 21 (1979): 121–49, understands them as a warning to the church, and Culbertson, "Reclaiming," argues that they are a message of comfort to repentant Israel.

55. This parable of the two sons and the following parables of the vineyard and wedding guests are linked thematically by the references to "son" in each, though they make different use of this metaphor.

56. This is another example of duplicity and hypocrisy, the ultimate sin for Matthew. See W. L. Richards, "Another Look at the Parable of the Two Sons," *Biblical Research* 23 (1978): 5–14; and A.-J. Levine, *The Social and Ethnic Dimension of Matthean Salvation History* (Lewiston, N.Y.: Mellen, 1988), 204–6.

57. Joachim Jeremias, *The Parables of Jesus* (New York: Scribner, 1963), 70–77; Hubert Frankemölle, *Jahwe-Bund und Kirche Christi: Studien zur Form- und Traditionsgeschichte des "Evangeliums" nach Matthäus,* NTAbh 10, 2d ed. (Münster: Aschendorff, 1984; orig. ed. 1974), 247–56; R. Walker, *Die Heilsgeschichte im ersten Evangelium,* FRLANT 91 (Göttingen: Vandenhoeck, 1967), 79–83; Georg Strecker, *Der Weg der Gerechtigkeit: Untersuchung zur Theologie des Matthäus,* 3d ed. (Göttingen: Vandenhoeck, 1971; orig. ed. 1962), 110–11; 169–172; Wolfgang Trilling, *Das Wahre Israel: Studien zur Theologie des Matthäus-Evangelium,* SANT 10, 3d ed. (Munich: Kosel, 1964), 55–65. For a review of interpretations and methods, see Klyne Snodgrass, *The Parable of the Wicked Tenants,* WUNT 27 (Tübingen: Mohr, 1983).

58. Jeremias, *Parables,* 70, has a concise summary. "The vineyard is clearly Israel, the tenants are Israel's rulers and leaders, the owner of the vineyard is God, the messengers are the prophets, the son is Christ, the punishment of the husbandmen symbolizes the ruin of Israel, the 'other people' (Matt. 21:43) are the Gentile Church." There are several problems with this summary. Why the punishment of the husbandmen (leaders) is equivalent to the ruin of Israel is unclear. The expression "other people" is a conflation of "to others" in Mark 12:9 (paralleling Matt. 21:41, "other tenants") with "an *ethnos* [nation, group] bearing fruit" (Matt. 21:43). In neither case is *another people* spoken about. Finally, no implicit or explicit mention is made of gentiles. Problems with this type of interpretation led E. Lohmeyer, "Das Gleichnis von den bösen Weingärtnern (Mark 12, 1–12)," *Zeit. Syst. Theol.* 18 (1941): 242–59, to argue that in Mark the vineyard stands for the Temple and cult. He abandoned this interpretation in his commentary on Matthew. Snodgrass, *Tenants,* 74, responds to confusion over the referent of the vineyard by suggesting that the vineyard does not refer to Israel but to the kingdom, understood as the business or concerns of God. But the weight of Jewish tradition in favor of the vineyard as a symbol of Israel is irresistible.

59. Alan H. McNeile, *The Gospel according to St. Matthew* (London: Macmillan, 1952), 311, already suggested that the parable and quotation imply that pious Jews who were "oppressed and misused by their religious leaders

will be advanced to honour." Robert H. Gundry, *Matthew: A Commentary on His Literary and Theological Art* (Grand Rapids: Eerdmans, 1982), 430, though he does not agree with the complete interpretation here, accurately notes that the leaders, not all Israel, are rejected by this parable. Jack Dean Kingsbury, "The Parable of the Wicked Husbandmen and the Secret of Jesus' Divine Sonship in Matthew: Some Literary-Critical Observations," *Journal of Biblical Literature* 105 (1986): on 645–46, aptly grasps the orientation of the parable toward the leaders, but then confuses them with Israel as a whole: "This parable portrays God as choosing Israel to be his people and entrusting it to the care of its leaders. Through his prophets and, at the last, his Son Jesus, God has called Israel's leaders to do his will. The leaders, however, have continually repudiated and killed the prophets, and they also conspire to kill the Son. In consequence of their wickedness, God will severely punish them, destroying Jerusalem and taking his kingdom and giving it to the church, his eschatological people called to do his will." Somehow in this interpretation Israel (the vineyard) has been pushed aside, though Matthew makes no negative comments about the vineyard itself. Kingsbury and many others seem to identify the leaders as a metonym for Israel and thus their rejection of Jesus as Israel's rejection. Kingsbury (655) cites Matt. 21:37–38 (the tenants' rejection of the son) as proof that "Israel has repudiated" the claim of Jesus that he is Son of God. As I have argued in chap. 2, in Matthew's narrative Israel, the crowds and the people as a whole are the object of Jesus' attention, are generally interested in and well disposed toward him, and are never rejected. Jesus previously hoped and Matthew now hopes to attract Israel to the kingdom of God.

60. Jeremias, *Parables*, 76, holds that the parable was originally an attack on Israel's leaders in favor of the "poor." Snodgrass, *Tenants*, also argues that the parable in a different form comes from Jesus (cf. esp. 108). H. Merkel, "Das Gleichnis von den 'ungleichen Söhnen,'" *New Testament Studies* 20 (1974): 254–61, argues that it is completely redactional. For an argument that the unallegorical version of the parable in the Gospel of Thomas 65 is earlier than the synoptic version, see Helmut Koester, "Three Thomas Parables," in A. H. B. Logan and A. J. M. Wedderburn, eds., *The New Testament and Gnosis: Essays in Honour of Robert McL. Wilson* (Edinburgh: Clark, 1983), 195–203. Snodgrass, *Tenants*, 52–54, argues that the Gospel of Thomas version is late. For a review of the literature associated with the parables in the Gospel of Thomas and their relationship to the New Testament, see Francis T. Fallon and Ron Cameron, "The Gospel of Thomas: A Forschungsbericht and Analysis," in H. Temporini and W. Haase, eds., *Aufstieg und Niedergang des Römischen Welt* 2.25.6 (Berlin: deGruyter, 1988), 4209–13.

61. Pluralism has become the hallmark of defining nations. See, for example, Benedict Anderson, *Imagined Communities: Reflections on the Origins and Spread of Nationalism* (London:Verso, 1983); John Breuilly, *Nationalism and the State* (New York: St. Martin, 1982); Ernest Q. Campbell, *Racial Tensions and National Integration* (Nashville: Vanderbilt, 1972).

62. See chap. 4 of this volume for a treatment of the passages which mention the nations.

63. The subdivision of an *ethnos* was often designated a *genos*, that is, a clan (Latin *gens*). In the Aphrodisias reliefs of the various *ethne* conquered by the Romans, each relief is identified by an inscription using the word *ethnos*, for example, *ethnous Ioudaion*. Here *ethne* is translated into Latin as *gentes*). See R. R. R. Smith, *"Simulacra Gentium:* The *Ethne* from the Sebasteion at Aphrodisias," *Journal of Roman Studies* 78 (1988): 50–77.

64. H.G. Liddell, R. Scott, H.S. Jones, and R. MacKenzie, *A Greek-English Lexicon,* 9th ed. (Oxford: Clarendon Press, 1940), 682a, citing the Petrie papyri of the third century B.C.E. For the classic study of these associations, see Franz Poland, *Geschichte der Griechischen Vereinswesens* (Leipzig: Teubner, 1909), who traces a wide variety of terms and types of association. See also Marcus N. Tod, *Sidelights on Greek History* (Oxford: Blackwell, 1932), 71–96, and Saldarini, *Pharisees,* 67–68.

65. G. W. Bowersock, *Hellenism in Late Antiquity* (Ann Arbor: University of Michigan Press, 1990), 10–11. Bowersock notes that in patristic literature both *ethnikos* and *hellenikos* came to refer to non-Christians. Consult also W. G. H. Lampe's *A Patristic Greek Lexicon* (Oxford: Clarendon, 1961).

66. Douglas R. A. Hare, "The Rejection of the Jews in the Synoptic Gospels and Acts," in Alan Davies, ed., *Antisemitism and the Foundations of Christianity* (New York: Paulist, 1979), 38–39, takes this verse as a rejection of "Israel according to the flesh." Note his use of Pauline language (1 Cor. 10:18), which is not appropriate to Matthew's categories. Hare also holds (153) that the kingdom of God is being transferred to another people *(ethnos),* not to a new or true Israel. Trilling earlier had argued that Matthew's group saw itself as a true Israel, still associated with unfaithful Israel (*Wahre Israel,* 95, 224, passim). See Levine, *Social Dimension,* 206–11, for a discussion of the passage and references to other authors.

67. See Graham N. Stanton, "The Gospel of Matthew and Judaism," *Bulletin of the John Rylands Library* 66 (1984): 269, for the suggestion that the stone which is rejected (21:42) refers to the rejection of the Matthean group by the leaders of the Jewish community.

68. In 1 Macc. 1:29–40, the Mysarch sent by Antiochus IV plundered Jerusalem and built the Akra (a citadel). In it he stationed a "sinful *ethnos,* lawless [*paranomous*] men" (1:34) who kept Jerusalem subjugated. This *ethnos* is a group of people left in charge of Seleucid interests. They are judged by the author of 1 Maccabees to be an evil leadership group, much like the group condemned in Matthew 21. Commentators identify this "sinful *ethnos*" (variously translated as "breed, race, people") as Jews loyal to the Seleucids. This interpretation also fits biblical usage. See Jonathan Goldstein, *1 Maccabees,* AB 41 (Garden City, N.Y.: Doubleday, 1976), 123–24, 219–20.

69. Lohmeyer, *Matthäusevangelium,* 315, argues that *ethnos* refers to a portion of the historical people Israel. He suggests that it refers to a community living among the Jewish people and knowing itself as the true eschatological Israel. For a similar usage of *ethnos,* see Acts 21. Paul brings alms to the Jewish community of believers-in-Jesus and offers sacrifices at the Temple. Defending his actions after his arrest, he says that he was bringing alms and sacrificial gifts

to his *ethnos* in Jerusalem (24:17). His *ethnos* is both the whole Judean Jewish community and a subgroup of those Jews, the followers of Jesus.

70. See, for example, Jeremias, *Parables*, 70–71.

71. The grapes are said to be foul, literally, "stinking," rather than the usual translation "wild." The two pairs of virtues and vices are similar sounding words in Hebrew. Judgment *(mîshpāt)* may refer to upholding the rights of the needy (Isa. 1:17). Justice *(sĕdāqāh)* is, of course, a crucial concept for Matthew.

72. Davies and Allison, *Matthew 8–17*, 642, speak of the kingdom being taken from its Jewish custodians and given to the church. It is unclear whether the church is seen as another part of Israel.

73. The root is *rîb*, the technical term for a lawsuit.

74. Similar imagery is used in Jeremiah (12:7–13), where God laments that he has forsaken his house (Judah) and abandoned his heritage and given it into the hands of her enemies. Specifically, "many shepherds have destroyed my vineyard, they have trampled down my portion" (12:10).

75. In Matt. 23:13, the leaders are said to have shut the kingdom off from the people. The implication is that the people would willingly enter the kingdom if not prevented.

76. The image of fruitfulness is used elsewhere to similar effect. In the allegory of the eagles (Ezek. 17), the royal house of Judah is compared to a vine (17:8) and a twig (17:22). In one case it will not bear fruit (17:9), and in the other it will (17:22). Snodgrass, *Tenants*, 25–26 and 77–78, notes that in later rabbinic literature Tanhuma (Buber), *Beshelah* 7 (29a), has a parable in which the Canaanites are likened to tenants who kept the land of Israel while the people of Israel were in a foreign country (Egypt). Snodgrass's inference on the basis of this late parable, that first-century Jews would have thought of the Romans as the tenants, is of course, invalid. But the consistent use of this imagery shows how fundamental and enduring it is.

77. This verse, taken over from Mark 12:10 (paralleling Luke 20:17), is also cited in Acts 4:11 and 1 Pet. 2:7. In Acts, Ps. 118:22–23 is used to refer to the resurrection.

78. John R. Donohue, *Are You the Christ? The Trial Narrative in the Gospel of Mark*, SBLMS 10 (Missoula: SBL, 1973), 124, interprets Mark similarly. In Mark, the verse is part of an anti-Sanhedrin and anti-Temple polemic.

79. This is brought out by Kingsbury, "Wicked Husbandmen," 652–53, and linked to the revelation of Jesus as Son throughout the whole Matthean narrative. Both here and in the trial at 26:63 (Kingsbury, 654), Jesus reveals his sonship to the Jewish leaders and is rejected. Strangely, Kingsbury draws the conclusion that Israel, not its leaders, rejects Jesus (655).

80. The parable of the workers in the vineyard (20:1–16) is often bundled with the parables of the two sons ordered to work in the vineyard and of the evil tenants who refuse to pay rent on the vineyard. These vineyard parables are seen as a group and as a rejection of Israel. In this interpretation, the first and last are understood as Israel and the gentiles; that is, the early morning workers are Israel and the late afternoon workers, the gentiles. But the context concerns rewards for those who believe in Jesus. In addition, all the workers

receive their pay (reward for service), and no one is rejected. The point of the parable seems to concern equality among the believers-in-Jesus no matter when they became followers. Whether one is a Jew or gentile is immaterial.

81. For an argument that this passage does not specifically refer to the destruction of Jerusalem, see K. H. Rengstorf, "Die Stadt der Mörder (Mt 22, 7)," in Walther Eltester, ed., *Judentum, Urchristentum, Kirche,* Festschrift J. Jeremias, BZNW 26 (Berlin: Töpelmann, 1960), 106–29. Though the destruction of a city is a rhetorical *topos,* Matthew's interest in explaining the destruction of Jerusalem (e.g., 27:25) and the fact that this verse does not really fit the parable make it very likely that Matthew has the destruction of Jerusalem in mind.

82. Jeremias, *Parables,* 64; Joseph A. Fitzmyer, *The Gospel according to Luke,* AB 28, 28A (Garden City: Doubleday, 1981–85), 1053.

83. Even the prediction of destruction is not a final rejection of Judaism or even of Jerusalem, as many commentators claim. Matthew's threats and condemnations are similar to those of the prophets. Graham N. Stanton, "Aspects of Early Christian-Jewish Polemic and Apologetic," *New Testament Studies* 31 (1985): 386–89, shows that a sin-exile-return pattern is operative and that Matt. 23:39 implies hope for Jerusalem.

84. For a complete treatment of the Pharisees, scribes, and Sadducees in Matthew, see Saldarini, *Pharisees,* 157–73.

85. One "ruler" *(archōn)* appears in a positive relationship with Jesus, seeking a cure for his daughter who has just died (9:18). Presumably he is a Jewish leader, but no explicit role or social location is given. Because Matthew has hostile relations with the synagogue authorities, he changed Mark's (5:21) identification of the man as a leader of the synagogue *(archisynagōgōs).*

86. "Synagogue" in Israel during the first century refers primarily to assemblies of Jews for reading Scripture and prayer. They probably met in the public square, a public building, or in a large house. Synagogue *buildings* become common in the third century. Claims to find first-century synagogue rooms or buildings are ambiguous. See Lee I. Levine, ed., *The Synagogue in Late Antiquity* (Philadelphia: American Schools of Oriental Research, 1987), and *Ancient Synagogues Revealed* (Jerusalem: Israel Exploration Society, 1981), for essays on recent research.

87. For an analysis of the passages, see G. D. Kilpatrick, *The Origins of the Gospel according to St. Matthew* (Oxford: Clarendon, 1946), 110–11. Kilpatrick shows that the usage "their/our synagogues" is characteristically Matthean. (The appearance of this phrase in Mark 1:23, 39, is textually suspect and may have originated from Matthean influence on copyists.)

88. Many commentators have taken references to "their synagogues" as an indication that Matthew's group is completely separated from Judaism. See, for example, Strecker, *Weg der Gerechtigkeit,* 30. Ulrich Luz, *Matthew 1–7* (Minneapolis: Augsburg, 1989; orig. German 1985), 203, says that the Matthean group has its own place outside the synagogue and posits a complete break with the synagogue (88). Douglas R. A. Hare, *The Theme of Jewish Persecution of Christians in the Gospel according to St. Matthew,* SNTSMS 6 (Cambridge: Cam-

bridge University Press, 1967), 104–5, argues that Matthew's inconsistency in his usage indicates that the synagogue has become a separate institution. But community relationships are complex and cannot be covered by the categories "united" and "separate." For further analysis, see chap. 5 of this volume.

89. One other, similar polemical usage should be mentioned. At the end of the Sermon on the Mount, the crowds were astonished at Jesus' teaching because he taught with authority and not as "their scribes" (7:29).

90. This relationship between the Matthean group and other Jewish communities will be developed fully in chap. 5.

Chapter Four

1. Frank J. Matera, *Passion Narratives and Gospel Theologies: Interpreting the Synoptics through Their Passion Stories* (New York: Paulist, 1986), 137–39, gathers together a number of passages often attributed to Matthew's orientation toward the gentiles.

2. Schuyler Brown, "Universalism and Particularism in Matthew's Gospel: A Jungian Approach," *SBL Seminar Papers 1989* (Atlanta: Scholars, 1989), 390, notes that outsiders are often scapegoated in Matthew, but no one group consistently. Gentiles appear as both good and bad in the narrative.

3. Luke, as we have seen, links Jesus with Adam and thus with all humanity (3:23–38).

4. There is no biblical support for Matthew's contention that Rahab married Boaz. Later rabbinic tradition has her marrying Joshua.

5. For changes in ethnic identity and the absorption of unrelated people into ethnic groups, see the essays in Fredrik Barth, *Ethnic Groups and Boundaries* (Boston: Little, Brown, 1969).

6. See Raymond E. Brown, *The Birth of the Messiah* (New York: Doubleday, 1977), 71–74, for a detailed discussion of various proposals and the problems associated with them.

7. Mark has only the centurion testify that Jesus is the Son of God. In Matthew, the testimony of the centurion and his men counters the later perjured testimony of the tomb guards that the disciples stole Jesus' body (28:11–15).

8. Jack Dean Kingsbury, *Matthew: Structure, Christology, Kingdom* (Philadelphia: Fortress, 1975), 54–77, shows the importance of this title for Matthew. It is used by the guards also because "king of the Jews" would not be appropriate in a Roman soldier's mouth.

9. The story of Herod's attempt to kill Jesus and the flight into Egypt is built on both Jacob/Israel and Moses/Exodus typology. For our purposes, the salient point is the irony of Jesus' fleeing death *toward* Egypt, in contrast to the Hebrews' fleeing death out of Egypt (Exod. 11–15).

10. The work he uses for his boy, *pais*, can mean son, child, servant or slave.

11. See the partial analysis of Matt. 8:11–12 in chap. 2 above. See also Georg Strecker, *Der Weg der Gerechtigkeit: Untersuchung zur Theologie des Matthäus*, 3d ed. (Göttingen: Vandenhoeck, 1971; orig. ed. 1962), 99–101; Wolfgang Trilling, *Das Wahre Israel: Studien zur Theologie des Matthäus-*

Evangelium, SANT 10, 3d ed. (Munich: Kosel, 1964; orig. ed. 1959), 88–90; Ulrich Luz, *Das Evangelium nach Matthäus (Mt 8–17)* EKK (Zurich: Benzinger; Neukirchen-Vluyn: Neukirchener, 1990), 15–16. See the analysis of R. Hummel, *Die Auseinandersetzung zwischen Kirche und Judentum im Matthäusevangelium* (Munich: Kaiser, 1963), 146–53, for a critique of this position. David Hill, *The Gospel of Matthew,* NCBC (Grand Rapids: Eerdmans, 1972), 159, says that this passage does not even imply a gentile mission before the end, though he associates those from the east and west as gentiles coming at the end who replace recalcitrant Israel.

12. See Ben F. Meyer, *The Aims of Jesus* (London: SCM, 1979), 137, 211, 219, 247; E. P. Sanders, *Jesus and Judaism* (Philadelphia: Fortress, 1985), 118–19. This passage may have originally concerned the gathering of diaspora Jews to Israel according to Dale C. Allison, "Who Will Come from East and West? Observations on Matt. 8:11–12; Luke 13:28–29," *Irish Biblical Studies* 11 (1989): 164, and may even here in Matthew refer to the judgment of the faithless in contrast to the faithful in Israel (167). W. D. Davies and Dale C. Allison, *The Gospel according to St. Matthew,* vol. 2: *Chapters 8–17* (Edinburgh: Clark, 1991), 27–29, associate those from the east and west with diaspora Jews and identify the dispossessed sons of the kingdom with the Jewish leaders who reject Jesus, not with all Israel.

13. Note that the gentiles come to the table in the end, in contrast to the Canaanite woman, who only asks for scraps from the table now (15:21–28). Note also that both the centurion and woman have their loved ones cured but do not become followers of Jesus or enter into the group of disciples. This is reserved for the future. The question remains, Does the Matthean group have a large gentile membership or are they just now turning to the gentiles in the hope that they will join? On balance, the latter seems more likely. Matthew is justifying the integration of non-Jews into his Christian-Jewish group on the basis of their faith in Jesus.

14. Davies and Allison, *Matthew 8–17,* 31, note the prophetic mode of expression here.

15. See the comments on this passage above in chap. 2.

16. Matthew is careful to have Jesus obey Jewish law and provide a justifying interpretation if he departs from normal custom. In this story, Matt. 8:7 is probably best interpreted as a question expressing surprise or annoyance: "Am I supposed to come [to your house] and cure him?"

17. Matthews Greek is ambiguous in two places. He speaks of Jesus withdrawing toward or into *(eis)* the district of Tyre and Sidon. Then a Canaanite woman "comes out from that region," or a Canaanite woman "from that region comes out." Matthew may be suggesting that Jesus remained within Jewish territory because he envisions Jesus' work as confined to Israel. See Davies and Allison, *Matthew 8–17,* 546–48, and Daniel J. Harrington, *The Gospel of Matthew,* Sacra Pagina (Collegeville, Minn: Liturgical Press, Glazier, 1991), 235, for commentators inclined to see Jesus within Israel. Luz, *Matthäus (Mt 8–17),* 433, rejects this as a less probable interpretation.

18. Some commentators suggest that the daughter is present because

Matthew does not say (as Mark does in 7:30) that the woman went home and found her daughter healed. But it is more natural to understand that the woman came alone, since there is no account of Jesus touching the daughter or confronting the demon.

19. G. D. Kilpatrick, *The Origins of the Gospel according to St. Matthew* (Oxford: Clarendon,1946), 132, and Luz, *Matthäus (Mt 8–17)*, 432, present some evidence that Canaanite might have been used for Phoenician in the Roman period, but the case is far from certain.

20. Davies and Allison, *Matthew 8–17*, 556.

21. Contrary to many commentators who see the story of the Canaanite woman as affirming the gentiles and rejecting Israel, Davies and Allison, (ibid., 543–44) point out forcefully that the story raises many questions without answering them.

22. Ibid., 557.

23. Gadara is six miles inland from the southeast shore of the Sea of Galilee.

24. W. D. Davies and Dale C. Allison, *The Gospel according to St. Matthew* vol. 1, *Chapters 1–7*, ICC (Edinburgh: Clark, 1988), 379. For the birth narrative, see Krister Stendahl, *"Quis et Unde?* An Analysis of Mt 1–2," in W. Eltester, ed., *Judentum, Urchristentum, Kirche,* Festschrift J. Jeremias, BZNW 26 (Berlin: Töpelmann, 1964), 94–105.

25. Davies and Allison, *Matthew 1–7*, 384–85, following Ulrich Luz, *Matthew 1–7* (Minneapolis: Augsburg, 1989), 195, accepts the symbolic allusion to the mission to the gentiles.

26. Harrington, *Matthew,* 71. Harrington notes correctly that the main point of the quotation at this point in Matthew is Galilee, not the gentiles.

27. Davies and Allison, *Matthew 1–7*, 383–84, make this point well. See chap. 1 above, also.

28. The summary of Jesus' Galilean ministry is parallel to the summary of his ministry at the end of the chapters containing miracles stories (9:35). Both these summaries are generally agreed to be redactional. In addition, they are part of a literary frame around the the Sermon on the Mount (Luz, Matthew 1–7, 204).

29. Davies and Allison, *Matthew 1–7*, 417. It is unlikely he means the whole Roman province of Syria extending to the Euphrates and the Arabian Desert. Kilpatrick, *Origin,* 131, suggests that this singular mention of Syria signals that the author lives in Syria. See also Luz, *Matthew 1–7*, 206 n. 16. Harrington, *Matthew,* 73–74, suggests that Matthew lives in Galilee, or near Galilee in Syria. J. Andrew Overman, *Matthew's Gospel and Formative Judaism: The Social World of the Matthean Community* (Minneapolis: Fortress, 1990), 158–61, and Anthony J. Saldarini, "The Gospel of Matthew and Jewish-Christian Conflict in Galilee," in Lee I. Levine, ed., *Studies on Galilee in Late Antiquity* (New York: Jewish Theological Seminary, 1992), 23–38.

30. H. D. Slingerland, "The Transjordanian Origin of St. Matthew's Gospel," *Journal for the Study of the New Testament* 3 (1979):18–28, argues that this verse and 19:1 presuppose a Transjordanian perspective and thus the Matthean group was located east of the Jordan. However, the verse fits the usual

biblical perspective, looking east across the Jordan. See Davies and Allison, *Matthew 1–7*, 142 and 420.

31. Note that Matthew omits Idumea, Tyre, and Sidon from the Markan parallel (3:8). Tyre and Sidon were never part of the biblical Israel, though the territory which became Idumea was part of the territory of Judah (Simeon originally). Note that Samaria, also part of the biblical Israel, is omitted because Samaritan Judaism was hostile to Jerusalem-oriented Judaism and does not seem to have been part of Matthew's world (nor of Jesus' in the synoptic gospels) except as something foreign.

32. The crowds are present in 5:1 as the Sermon on the Mount begins, they are astonished at the end (7:28), and they follow Jesus when he comes down the mountain (8:1).

33. Davies and Allison, *Matthew 8–17*, 369–70.

34. *Ethnikoi* can refer to the common people or to less cultured rural folk, in contrast to the cultured; but in Matthew, non-Jews seem to be referred to with the implication that they are not fully civilized or do not do things properly.

35. The burning cities refer, of course, to the destruction of Jerusalem by the Romans. Understood allegorically, the king is God punishing Jerusalem. But concretely and historically for Matthew, the model for kings who beseige and detroy cities is Rome.

36. For biblical distinctions between *'am* as cohesive, unified people and *goy* as a group with territory and government, which were lost in the Hellenistic period, see Aelred Cody, "When Is the Chosen People called a Gôy?" *Vetus Testamentum* 14 (1964): 1–6.

37. See recently, Shaye J. D. Cohen, "Crossing the Boundary and Becoming a Jew," *Harvard Theological Review* 82 (1989): 13–33, for a listing of the types of relationships non-Jews had with the Jewish community and the ambiguity concerning membership. The Egyptian Jewish story of Joseph and Aseneth, for example, seems to have less rigorous requirements for membership than the more polemical Fifth Sibylline Oracle. Scot McKnight, *A Light among the Gentiles: Jewish Missionary Activity in the Second Temple Period* (Minneapolis: Fortress, 1991), 110–113, has a balanced discussion of the relationship of Jewish communities to God-fearers and gentiles. See also chap. 1 above.

38. The Qumran community rejected many of its fellow Jews as not faithful to the covenant. Various sections of Ethiopic Enoch and other apocalyptic works make the same distinction among truly faithful Jews and those who will be condemned for their wickedness.

39. Alan F. Segal, *Paul the Convert: The Apostolate and Apostasy of Saul the Pharisee* (New Haven: Yale University Press, 1990), chap. 3, argues that gentiles could be functionally Jews without circumcision. Later rabbinic rules and sharp boundaries were not yet in force, and many Jewish communities had indistinct borders. See also David Balch, "The Greek Political Topos περι νομων and Matthew 5:17, 19, and 16:19," in David Balch, ed., *Social History of the Matthean Community: Cross-Disciplinary Approaches* (Minneapolis: Fortress, 1991), 81, on universalism within first-century Judaism and the possible presence of gentiles in Matthew's Jewish community.

40. Segal, *Paul*, 113–14, 263, 272, etc., argues that Paul wished to unite Jews and gentiles into one community, not create a third entity, the church.

41. See the literature cited in chap. 3 above.

42. A.-J. Levine, *The Social and Ethnic Dimension of Matthean Salvation History* (Lewiston, NY: Mellen, 1988), 201–2. Davies and Allison, *Matthew 1–7*, 384ff.; Luz, *Matthew 1–7*, 196. Sean Freyne, *Galilee from Alexander the Great to Hadrian, 323 B.C.E. to 135 C.E.: A Study of Second Temple Judaism* (Wilmington: Glazier; Notre Dame: University of Notre Dame Press, 1980), and *Galilee, Jesus, and the Gospels: Literary Approaches and Historical Investigations* (Philadelphia: Fortress, 1988), 167–75, shows that Galilee was predominantly Jewish throughout the Greco-Roman period. In context, Isaiah is referring to the Assyrian conquest of the northern kingdom and to the needs of the Jewish people there for freedom from oppression. The mention of nations is pejorative in Isaiah, but not in Matthew.

43. See Davies and Allison, *Matthew 1–7*, 380, 385, and Harrington, *Matthew*, 71.

44. Matt. 23:4–12, along with 18:15–20, envisions community governance without clear offices and authoritative roles. Matthew probably views all the members of his group as "leaders" and "missionaries" vis-à-vis Israel and the nations.

45. Levine, *Social Dimension*, 224–25. Mark has "you will be hated by all." Matthew adds the word "nations." Contrary to many commentators, nations here need not mean gentiles only.

46. See Levine, *Social Dimension*, 233–39, and the literature cited there for an argument that the universal judgment of all is meant. Douglas R. A. Hare and Daniel J. Harrington, "'Make Disciples of All the Gentiles' (Matthew 28:19)," *Catholic Biblical Quarterly* 37 (1975): 364–65, and Harrington, *Matthew*, 356–60, argue for separate judgments for Jews (19:28) and gentiles (25:31) on the basis of a number of Jewish texts. But John Meier, "Nations or Gentiles in Matthew 28:19," *Catholic Biblical Quarterly* 39 (1977): 100, points out that a universal judgment is presumed by 8:11–12, 11:20–24, 12:41–42, 13:36–43, and also by most apocalyptic literature.

47. The identity of "these my least brothers" *(toutōn tōn adelphōn mou tōn elachistōn)* is disputed. See also 10:40–42; 11:11; 18:6, 10, 14. Some hold that all humans in need are meant. See for example, David Catchpole, "The Poor on Earth and the Son of Man in Heaven: A Reappraisal of Matthew xxv.31–46," *Bulletin of the John Rylands Library* 61 (1979): 355–97. However, Matthew is probably referring more specifically to people's response to his group or its missionaries. See Lamar Cope, "Matthew xxv, 31–46: 'The Sheep and the Goats' Reinterpreted," *Novum Testamentum* 11 (1969): 32–44. Even if he is referring to the response to the Matthean group's teaching, the emphasis is on the deeds of the nations. No mention is made of faith in Jesus or membership in Matthew's group. Levine, *Social Dimension*, 226–27, says that this final parable of judgment concerns the new world and so eliminates any distinction between Israel and the rest of humanity and stresses action, not membership. See also Harrington, *Matthew*, 360.

48. The key phrases are "throughout the whole world" *(en holē tē oikoumenē)* and "to all the nations" *(pasin tois ethnesin).*

49. Levine, *Social Dimension,* 225–27 and 165–92, argues that *ethnē* in 24:14 and 28:19 should be translated "gentiles," with the understanding that Jews are not excluded and that the attempt to win over the Jewish community continues. Davies and Allison, *Matthew 8–17,* 557, say that all the nations in 28:19 almost certainly include the Jews.

50. Matthew uses the singular, *ethnos,* of his own group once in the parable of the vineyard and tenants (21:43). See chap. 3 above.

51. Apoc. of Abr. 29–31; Pss. of Sol. 7, 8; 2 Bar. 26–29, 82; Sib. Or. 2:154–73.

52. Gary Porton, *Goyim: Gentiles and Israelites in Mishnah-Tosefta,* BJS 155 (Atlanta: Scholars, 1988), 287.

53. Though there is controversy over the exact status of the "God-fearers," it is certain from Greek and Roman literature that gentiles were constantly attracted to Judaism. See A. Thomas Kraabel, "The Disappearance of the God-fearers," *Numen* 28 (1981): 113–26, who doubts the existence of a class of gentiles called God-fearers who were associated somehow with the synagogue. For references to subsequent debate and a refining of the categories used, see J. Andrew Overman, "The God-Fearers: Some Neglected Features," *Journal for the Study of the New Testament* 32 (1988): 17–26. For the different intensities of Jewish-gentile relations, see Cohen, "Crossing the Boundary," 13–33.

Chapter Five

1. This treatment of Matthew accepts the majority view that the Gospel of Matthew was composed in the late first century (80–95), after the destruction of Jerusalem in 70. It also assumes that the author made use of Mark in writing his narrative, but it concentrates on Matthew's finished product rather than on the differences from Mark.

2. For example, G. Barth, "Matthew's Understanding of the Law," in G. Bornkamm et al., eds., *Tradition and Interpretation in Matthew* (Philadelphia: Westminster, 1963), 111; R. Hummel, *Die Auseinandersetzung zwischen Kirche und Judentum im Matthäusevangelium* (Munich: Kaiser, 1963), 154; Douglas R. A. Hare, *The Theme of Jewish Persecution of Christians in the Gospel according to St. Matthew,* SNTSMS 6 (Cambridge: Cambridge University Press, 1967), 81ff; Eduard Schweizer, *Matthäus und seine Gemeinde,* Stuttgarter Bibelstudien 71 (Stuttgart KBW, 1974), passim; B. Rod Doyle, "Matthew's Intention as Discerned by His Structure," *Review Biblique* 95 (1988): 34–54. For an analogous attempt to understand the social situation of rabbinic midrash, see Steven D. Fraade, *From Tradition to Commentary: Torah and Its Interpretation in the Midrash Sifre to Deuteronomy* (Albany: SUNY Press, 1991), 13–18. Some literary critics who emphasize the internal world of the text and its effect on readers deny that the social world of the text can be known or is relevant.

3. Ulrich Luz, "The Disciples in the Gospel according to Matthew," in

Graham N. Stanton, ed., *The Interpretation of Matthew* (Philadelphia: Fortress, London: SPCK, 1983), 98–128, esp. 109–11, has an excellent and influential redactional study of the disciples in Matthew as reflective of the Matthean community. See also Barth, "Matthew's Law," 101–25. Jack Dean Kingsbury, *Matthew as Story,* 2d ed. (Philadelphia: Fortress, 1988), chap. 8, uses a more wholistic literary method. For other treatments, see Schuyler Brown, "The Mission to Israel in Matthew's Central Section (Mt 9:35–11:1)," *Zeitschrift für die neuetestamentliche Wissenschaft* 69 (1978): 73–90, esp. 74–77; Hummel, *Auseinandersetzung,* 154; Michael Wilkins, *The Concept of Disciple in Matthew's Gospel,* Suppl. NovT 59 (Leiden: Brill, 1988), 222 and passim; Richard A. Edwards, "Uncertain Faith: Matthew's Portrait of the Disciples," in F. Segovia, ed., *Discipleship in the New Testament* (Philadelphia: Fortress, 1985), 47–61; J. Andrew Overman, *Matthew's Gospel and Formative Judaism: The Social World of the Matthean Community* (Minneapolis: Fortress, 1990), 124–36. Georg Strecker, *Der Weg der Gerechtigkeit: Untersuchung zur Theologie des Matthäus,* 3d ed. (Göttingen: Vandenhoeck, 1971; orig. ed. 1962), argues that Matthew historicizes the disciples for theological reasons. This thesis, which supports his reading of Matthew as a later gentile product, is ably refuted by Luz.

4. Edwards, "Uncertain Faith," shows how the disciples as literary characters in the narrative carry Matthew's comments to his community and so implicitly mirror his group.

5. George Homans, "Groups," in David L. Sills, ed., *International Encyclopedia of the Social Sciences* (New York: Macmillan, 1968), 6: 259–65; G. Duncan Mitchell, "Group; social group," *A New Dictionary of the Social Sciences* (New York: Aldine, 1979), 91.

6. Muzafer Sherif, *Group Conflict and Cooperation: Their Social Psychology* (London: Routledge, 1966), 12.

7. Mitchell, "Community; community centre," *New Dictionary,* 31; Thomas Ford Hoult, "Community," *Dictionary of Modern Sociology* (Totowa, N.J.: Littlefield, 1969), 73.

8. Sherif, *Group Conflict,* 28.

9. Structural functional theory, which sees group activities in the light of a hoped-for social equilibrium and thus views groups as either serving some social function or as a threat, would approximate the views of the leaders of Israel.

10. Realistic conflict theory is also referred to as interdependence or social cohesion or instrumentality theory. In all cases, this approach stresses the meeting of real needs or the solving of concrete problems by aggregates of people who are interdependent, protecting one another in conflict, or seeking to accomplish certain goals through social cohesion.

11. See Donald M. Taylor and Fathali M. Moghaddam, *Theories of Intergroup Relations: International Social Science Psychological Perspectives* (New York: Praeger, 1987), 12ff.; John C. Turner, "Towards a Cognitive Redefinition of the Social Group," in Henri Tajfel, ed., *Social Identity and Intergroup Relations* (Cambridge: Cambridge University Press, Paris: Maison des Sciences de l'Homme, 1982), 15–16: Sherif, *Group Conflict,* is a leading exponent of this approach.

Henri Tajfel, "Instrumentality and Social Comparisons," in Tajfel, *Social Identity,* 500, calls it an instrumentality theory and relates it to rational choice and exchange theory. It often uses economic or utilitarian metaphors.

12. Rodney Stark and William S. Bainbridge, *A Theory of Religion* (New York: Lang, 1987), 56.

13. Murray Horowitz and Jacob M. Rabbie, "Individuality and Membership," in Tajfel, *Social Identity,* 251.

14. Taylor and Moghaddam, *Theories,* 55–57; Turner, "Cognitive Redefinition," 16.

15. Stark and Bainbridge, *Theory,* 36–37. When humans cannot gain desired material rewards, they accept intangible substitutes for the desired reward. These substitutes, called compensators by Stark and Bainbridge, are promises that the reward will be achieved at some future date.

16. The modern emphasis, not to say fascination, with personal identity should not be retrojected into the ancient world, where dyadic relationships predominated. On the other hand, the processes of group formation analyzed by social psychology can be seen in the rhetoric of many documents.

17. The realistic conflict approach, in contrast, explains the bewildering variety of subgroups in society.

18. The simplest definition of a social group is too generic for use in this context: "A social group can be defined as two or more individuals who share a common social identification of themselves, or, which is nearly the same thing, perceive themselves to be members of the same social category" (Turner, "Cognitive Redefinition," 15). The way people see themselves and others and the resultant way they relate to each other within and between groups can be analyzed into abstract social categories. See Henri Tajfel and John C. Turner, "An Integrative Theory of Intergroup Conflict," in William G. Austin and Stephen Worchel, eds., *The Social Psychology of Intergroup Relations* (Monterey, Cal.: Brooks/Cole of Wadsworth, 1979), 40; and Turner, "Cognitive Redefinition," 16.

19. Jean Claude Deschamps, "Relations of Power between Groups," in Tajfel, *Social Identity,* 87. For example, racial biases value or devalue various shades of skin color. In the U.S. African Americans are often referred to as "blacks." Since most African Americans have brown skin, the designation "black" is descriptively inaccurate. It is used to mean nonwhite because American racial bias devalues all who do not have white skin. Recently the term "African American" has replaced "black"; implied is a valuing of African roots and a rejection of white racial categories. Such terms and distinctions of skin color would be meaningless without the presence of racial prejudice.

20. Abraham J. Malherbe, *Paul and the Thessalonians* (Philadelphia: Fortress, 1987), 7–17, places much of Paul's teaching within the household rather than the marketplace.

21. Ibid., 21–33.

22. See the use of brother (in LXX) in a passage concerned with group order and justice, especially the poor (Lev. 19:9–18). The brother and neighbor, whom one is to love as oneself (Lev. 19:18), are the members of the group of

Israel. Matthew uses the same language of his group. See William Thompson, *Matthew's Advice to a Divided Community (Matt 17:22–18:35)*, AnBib 44 (Rome: Biblical Institute, 1970), 179.

23. Many of the parables use the metaphor of servant for the subordinates of the master or king (13:27; 24:45; 25:14).

24. Turner, "Cognitive Redefinition," 16.

25. Yet a group member should not confine his attention to brothers, but salute others (5:47).

26. Overman, *Matthew's Gospel*, 95, notes that the use of "brother" for community life, especially in the Sermon on the Mount, is characteristic of Matthew. On the early use of the term, see Malherbe, *Paul and the Thessalonians*, 49; and Wayne Meeks, *The First Urban Christians* (New Haven: Yale University Press, 1983), 87, and notes on 225.

27. The disciples are sons of the father in nineteen places, most of them unique to Matthew, especially in chapters 5–6, 10, and 18, where instructions concerning communal behavior are given. See Jack Dean Kingsbury, *Matthew: Structure, Christology, Kingdom* (Philadelphia: Fortress, 1975), 55.

28. See Wilkins, *Disciple*, 128–29, for these and other statistics. Wilkins counts thirty three or thirty four instances where the term "disciples" is found in Matthew's narrative but not in the other synoptics.

29. For comprehensive reviews of the disciples as literary characters in the narrative, see Kingsbury, *Matthew as Story*, chap. 8, and Wilkins, *Disciple*, chap. 4. The importance and complexity of their roles is also brought out in the literary studies of Mark Allan Powell, "Direct and Indirect Phraseology in the Gospel of Matthew," in Eugene H. Lovering, ed., *SBL Seminar Papers 1991* (Atlanta: Scholars, 1991), 405–17, and Michael J. Wilkins, "Named and Unnamed Disciples in Matthew: A Literary-Theological Study," in ibid., 417–39.

30. Matthew affirms Jesus' continuing presence in the community at the beginning and the end (1:23; 28:20) and stresses the group's continuing fidelity to their master. But this kind of relationship, which transcends the death of the leader, is not what is meant by factional loyalty. A faction is a temporary alliance of distinct parties recruited personally on behalf of another person. See Jeremy Boissevain, *Friends of Friends: Networks, Manipulators, and Coalitions* (Oxford: Blackwell, 1974), 171–73, 192, 195. The members of the faction are united only by their diverse relationships to the factional leader. If Jesus' disciples had been a faction, they would have scattered permanently after his death, rather than regrouping and persevering. Matthew's group adhered to God through Jesus and thus could believe that God raised Jesus and that God ruled (kingdom of God) even after Jesus' death.

31. Matthew presents a more positive view of the disciples than Mark (Wilkin, *Disciple*, 134–37, 143). For example, in Matthew, the disciples understand Jesus' warning to beware of the leaven of the Pharisees (16:12, vs. Mark 8:21); and the mother of the sons of Zebedee, rather than the sons themselves as in Mark, asks that they sit at either side of Jesus (20:20, vs. Mark 10:35). Mark stresses their lack of understanding; Matthew preserves this theme, but downplays it. See also Edwards, "Uncertain Faith"; Kingsbury, *Matthew as*

Story, chap. 8; and Wilkins, *Disciple,* 222. The disciples are called "men of little faith" in 8:26, 14:31, and 16:8. See also 16:21—23 and 17:19—20. Overman, *Matthew's Gospel,* 126—30, shows that the more positive view of the disciples in Matthew establishes their teaching authority.

32. Wilkins, *Disciple,* chaps. 2—3, argues that schools and relationships of master to disciple were operative in Jewish society. However, the evidence for the level of literacy and the roles of schools in Jewish society is sparse, and its interpretation is controversial. Even if Wilkins is correct, whether there were educational institutions or not is secondary to the crucial fact that these institutions and relationships are not important in the literature. This lack of reference to schools and disciples is in marked contrast to Jews who write in Greek during the first century, for example, Matthew and Philo in Alexandria (cf. Wilkins, *Disciple,* 100—104), and to the rabbis in the second century and beyond, who put great emphasis on master-disciple relationships, the study of Torah, and formal schools.

33. See Anthony J. Saldarini, *Scholastic Rabbinism: A Literary Study of the Fathers according to Rabbi Nathan,* BJS 14 (Chico: Scholars, 1982).

34. See Wilkins, *Disciple,* chap. 1, for a survey of Greek usage.

35. John the Baptist's followers are also referred to as disciples in Matt. 11:2. Later traditions suggest that they maintained a long commitment as well.

36. For a comprehensive treatment of all the roles of the sage in the Near East, see John G. Gammie and Leo G. Perdue, *The Sage in Israel and the Ancient Near East* (Winona Lake: Eisenbrauns, 1990). This Semitic tradition and the Greek tradition of philosopher, sophist, and teacher met in the eastern Roman Empire and undoubtedly influenced one another in ways not yet brought out in most studies.

37. For instance, many people address Jesus as Lord, but Jesus is called Lord by the disciples only in the two sea miracles (8:25; 14:28, 30). At the end of the second sea miracle, they recognize him with Matthew's favorite title, "Son of God" (14:33). The readers come to know Jesus as the Son of God, Son of Man, and Messiah, and perhaps it is implied that the disciples do also. See Kingsbury, *Matthew,* 92—93.

38. Krister Stendahl, The *School of St. Matthew,* 2d ed. (Philadelphia: Fortress, 1968; orig ed., 1954), 30—35, stressed the similarities between the type of interpretation in the Qumran Habakkuk Commentary (1QpHab) and Matthew. He suggested that the subtle biblical interpretation in Matthew implied a formal, trained school of interpreters. His thesis was greeted with skepticism, and in the preface to the second edition (vi—viii, x—xi), Stendahl qualified his original argument substantially. The stability and form of the biblical texts available to Matthew is uncertain, and the formula quotations are thought by many to be pre-Matthean. Thus the activity of a school cannot be proved. See Bertil Gärtner, "The Habakkuk Commentary (DSH) and the Gospel of Matthew," *Studia Theologica* 8 (1954): 1—24, and also the reviews by H. D. F. Sparks in *Journal of Theological Studies* 7 (1956): 103—05; P. Vielhauer in *Theologische Literatur Zeitschrift* 81 (1956): 39—42; and X. Leon-Dufour in *Recherches de science religieuse* 46 (1958): 250—53. For recent reviews of the for-

mula quotation problem, see W. D. Davies and Dale C. Allison, *The Gospel according to St. Matthew* vol. 1: *Chapters 1–7,* ICC (Edinburgh: Clark, 1988), 211–12, and Ulrich Luz, *Matthew 1–7* (Minneapolis: Augsburg, 1989), 156–64.

39. M. Jack Suggs, *Wisdom, Christology, and Law in Matthew's Gospel* (Cambridge: Harvard University Press, 1970), defends this thesis most strongly. See especially Matt. 11:19, 25–30; 12:41–42; 23:34.

40. Marshall D. Johnson, "Reflections on a Wisdom Approach to Matthew's Christology," *Catholic Biblical Quarterly* 36 (1974): 44–64, and Kingsbury, *Matthew,* 64. Johnson argues strongly that Suggs inflates the evidence and that the wisdom aspect of Matthew's Christology is secondary. However, the pattern of wisdom's rejection is stressed by Matthew, according to Russell Pregeant, "The Wisdom Passages in Matthew's Story," in David Lull, ed., *SBL Seminar Papers 1990* (Atlanta, Scholars, 1990), 469–93, esp. 489–93. See the discussion in chap. 7 of this volume.

41. See Abraham Malherbe, *Moral Exhortation: A Greco-Roman Sourcebook* (Philadelphia: Westminster, 1986), 23.

42. In the cities a number of lower-class children received primary education because schools were more available and supported by the municipal government. Henri Marrou, *A History of Education in Antiquity* (New York: Mentor, 1964), 199–203, 358–63.

43. Stanley K. Stowers, "Social Status, Public Speaking, and Private Teaching: The Circumstances of Paul's Preaching Activity," *Novum Testamentum* 26 (1984): 59–82, esp. 65–68, gathers the evidence and applies it to Paul's ministry. On the similarities between popular philosophy and Paul's teaching, see also Malherbe, *Paul,* chap. 1, and Meeks, *Urban Christians,* 81–84. Malherbe estimates that Christian authors generally had at least an upper-secondary level of education (*Social Aspects,* 45). See Robert L. Wilken, "Collegia, Philosophical Schools, and Theology," in Stephen Benko and J. J. O'Rourke, eds., *The Catacombs and the Colliseum* (Valley Forge: Judson, 1971), 268–91, for a slightly later period.

44. Shaye J. D. Cohen, "Patriarchs and Scholarchs," *Proceedings of the American Academy of Jewish Research* 48 (1981): 57–85, points out how the talmudic authorities conceived of themselves as a school. For a critical assessment of Josephus' presentation of the Pharisees as a "school of thought," see Anthony J. Saldarini, *Pharisees, Scribes, and Sadducees in Palestinian Society* (Wilmington: Glazier, 1988; Edinburgh: Clark, 1989), 123–27. Judah Goldin, "A Philosophical Session in a Tannaite Academy," *Traditio 21* (1965): 1–21, shows the influence of philosophic forms on a rabbinic account, though his acceptance of the account as historical is unlikely. For a concise account of Jewish education in talmudic times, see Goldin's "Several Sidelights of a Torah Education in Tannaite and Early Amorical Times," in *Ex Orbe Religionum: Studia Geo Widengren* (Leiden: Brill, 1972), 1:pp. 176–91.

45. Overman, *Matthew's Gospel,* 126–28, notes Matthew's stress on teaching rather than healing or itinerancy. This view is contrary to the thesis of Schweizer, *Gemeinde,* that Matthew's community supports itinerant prophets. The disciples are also given power by Jesus to exorcise, heal, raise the dead and

bear witness (chap. 10), as Jesus himself has done. However, later in the gospel, most notably in the final commission (28:19–20), teaching, not healing, is emphasized.

46. For the types of Cynic teachers found in the literature, see Abraham Malherbe, *Paul and the Popular Philosophers* (Minneapolis: Fortress, 1989), chap. 3. A number of scholars have recently suggested that Jesus operates, not as a teacher of an apocalyptic kingdom of God, but as a wise Cynic, challenging his fellow countrymen. See Burton L. Mack, *A Myth of Innocence: Mark and Christian Origins* (Philadelphia: Fortress, 1988), 67–77. Though Mack and others argue for understanding the historical Jesus this way, it is more likely that any comparisons between Jesus and Cynic teachers would have arisen among Greek-speaking followers, who were familiar with popular teachers.

47. See the analysis of Jesus' confrontations with Herod Antipas in Luke-Acts by John Darr, *On Character Building: The Reader and the Rhetoric of Characterization in Luke-Acts* (Louisville: Westminster, 1992), chap. 6, for parallels with the philosopher unafraid to speak openly. For an extended analysis of Jesus' death in comparison with that of philosophers and martyrs, see David Seeley, *The Noble Death: Graeco-Roman Martyrology and Paul's Concept of Salvation* JSNT Suppl. 18 (Sheffield: JSOT Press, 1990).

48. David Seeley, "Was Jesus a Philosopher? The Evidence of Martyrological and Wisdom Motifs in Q, Pre-Pauline Traditions, and Mark," in David J. Lull, ed., *SBL Seminar Papers 1989* (Atlanta: Scholars, 1989), 542–43, points out that Greco-Roman philosophical students were expected to follow their teacher in suffering and death, a pattern replicated in the early Jesus traditions.

49. Henri Tajfel, *Human Groups and Social Categories: Studies in Social Psychology* (Cambridge: Cambridge University Press, 1981), 255.

50. Turner, "Cognitive Redefinition," 19–20.

51. See Wilkins, *Disciple,* 148–50, 154, and the treatment of the crowds in chap. 2 above.

52. Tajfel and Turner, "Integrative Theory," 40.

53. Jack Dean Kingsbury, "The Verb *Akolouthein* ('to follow') as an Index of Matthew's View of his Community," *Journal of Biblical Literature* 97 (1978): 56–73, and the same article in a modified form in *Matthew as Story,* chap. 9. Kingsbury is concerned to modify the thesis of Eduard Schweizer that Matthew's was a charismatic missionary or prophetic group.

54. In conjunction with the further comments here, see the discussion of synagogue at the end of chap. 3 above. The use of houses as Jewish, Greek, and Christian places of worship has been documented in detail by L. Michael White in *Building God's House in the Roman World: Architectural Adaptation among Pagans, Jews, and Christians,* American Schools of Oriental Research (Baltimore: Johns Hopkins, 1990).

55. Martin Hengel, "Proseuche and Synagoge," in Gert Jeremias et al., eds., *Tradition und Glaube: Das frühe Christentum in seiner Umwelt* (Gottingen: Vandenhoeck, 1971), 157–83; J. Gwyn Griffiths, "Egypt and the Rise of the Synagogue," *Journal of Theological Studies* 38 (1987): 4–5.

56. The discovery of scrolls and ostraca associated with the hall at Masada is

the strongest evidence for religious use of the room. The room in the Herodium is like the one at Masada and so it is labeled a synagogue by analogy. The building in Gamla, dated from the first century B.C.E. to the first century C.E., is consistent with what is expected in a synagogue, but since there are no earlier examples with which to compare it and since it has no religious iconography, S. Gutman's skepticism is appropriate. See "The Synagogue at Gamla," in Lee I. Levine, ed., *Ancient Synagogues Revealed* (Jerusalem: Israel Exploration Society, 1981), 34. Gutman is supported by Levine, *The Synagogue in Late Antiquity* (Philadelphia: American Schools of Oriental Research, 1987), 11. For a more confident argument that it is a synagogue, see Z. Ma'oz, "The Synagogue of Gamla and the Typology of Second-Temple Synagogues," in Levine, *Ancient Synagogues*, 35–41.

57. Synagogues in the diaspora had a similar slow growth from rooms in houses, to houses adapted for synagogue use, and finally to dedicated buildings. See White, *Building*, chap. 2.

58. Luke's version of a synagogue service in 4:16–30 is derived from the diaspora in the postdestruction period.

59. Evidence gathered from diaspora inscriptions indicates that the leaders were not rabbis, but had various titles, such as leader *(archōn)*, head of the synagogue *(archisynagōgus)*, elder *(presbyteros)*, and so on, and that women were sometimes synagogue officials. See Bernadette J. Brooten, *Women Leaders in the Ancient Synagogue: Inscriptional Evidence and Background Issues*, BJS 36 (Chico: Scholars, 1982).

60. Abraham J. Malherbe, *Social Aspects of Early Christianity* (Baton Rouge: Louisiana State University Press, 1977; 2d ed., Philadelphia: Fortress, 1983), 60–70; Meeks, *Urban Christians*, 29–30, 75–77.

61. See Hans-Josef Klauck, "Die Hausgemeinde als Lebensform im Urchristentum," *Münchener Theologische Zeitschrift* 32 (1981): 1–15, for a survey; and White, *Building*, 102–10, for the architectural and inscriptional evidence and for the types of houses which might have been used.

62. See John H. Elliott, *A Home for the Homeless: A Sociological Exegesis of 1 Peter, Its Situation, and Strategy* (Philadelphia: Fortress, 1981), chap. 4, for the household in 1 Peter; and David L. Balch, *Let Wives Be Submissive: The Domestic Code in 1 Peter*, SBLMS 26, (Chico: Scholars 1981), for the household code.

63. In Mark 3:21, Jesus' activity is pictured as causing a rift with his family. Matthew suppresses this tradition. Both Mark and Matthew show Jesus as subordinating his family to his new "family," those who listen to him and do the Father's will (Matt. 12:46–50; Mark 3:31–35). For Paul's solution to the conflict caused by the conversion of one spouse to Christianity, see 1 Cor. 7:12–16.

64. Michael H. Crosby, *House of Disciples: Church, Economics, and Justice in Matthew* (Maryknoll: Orbis, 1988), chap. 2 and Appendix, 325–28, lists an enormous amount of data. The effect of the evidence is to make it probable that the author has households in mind, but since they were constitutive of society, this fact is unilluminating. What is needed is a rigorous analysis of Matthew's underlying world view, usage of words, presentation of narrative relation-

ships, and guiding metaphors so that his precise understanding of fictive kinship relationships and of other kinds of relationships as well can be ascertained.

65. Sin is presumably defined according to the teachings of Jesus and the Bible.

66. Wilson, *Patterns,* 10–20.

67. The focus of chapter 18 is on bringing the straying member back into unity and resolving dissent within the group. See Trilling, *Wahre Israel,* 113; Thompson, *Matthew's Advice,* 264–66; Overman, *Matthew's Gospel,* 103–4. M. C. De Boer, "Ten Thousand Talents? Matthew's Interpretation and Redaction of the Parable of the Unforgiving Servant," *Catholic Biblical Quarterly* 50 (1988): 231–32, stesses the contrast between the normal legal relationships in society and the mercy which should characterize Matthew's group.

68. The Community of Qumran Rule (1QS 5:25–6:1) has similar procedures and makes clear the motive. The offended party is to rebuke his companion the very same day so that he himself does not incur guilt by hating him. Rather, "they shall rebuke one another in truth, humility, and charity." The Community Rule, which is much more institutionalized and elaborate than Matthew 18 lists a number of offenses against the community and its members with appropriate punishments (1QS 6:24–7:25). The Covenant of Damascus (CD 9:2–8) has similar strictures against pent-up anger and for an orderly rebuking of an offender.

69. For a study of explusion, see G. Forkman, *The Limits of Religious Community: Expulsion from Religious Community within the Qumran Sect, within Rabbinic Judaism, and within Primitive Christianity* (Lund: Gleerup, 1972); he notes that expulsion is only the last resort (123).

70. Trilling, *Wahre Israel,* 123, notes that forgiveness, not disciplinary procedure, is the main focus of the chapter. Paul urges similar procedures in 1 Cor. 6:1–11.

71. Hummel, *Auseinandersetzung,* 17.

72. Matt. 9:11; 12:24; 17:14; 21:23; 22:35, 41; 26:3, 47; 27:1. See Overman, *Matthew's Gospel,* 115.

73. Overman, *Matthew's Gospel,* 115–17 and 119–22, notes that teaching was the primary activity of Matthean missionaries.

74. See Gammie and Perdue, *Sage.*

75. Richard A. Horsley and John S. Hanson, *Bandits, Prophets, and Messiahs: Popular Movements at the Time of Jesus* (Minneapolis: Winston-Seabury, 1985); David E. Aune, *Prophecy in Early Christianity and the Ancient Mediterranean* (Grand Rapids: Eerdmans, 1983).

76. Davies and Allison, *Matthew 1–7,* 713–14. Davies and Allison show that subordination of prophecy is a common Christian theme (716).

77. See Aune, *Prophecy,* for a review of the problems and literature.

78. Didache 11:7–12; see also *Shepherd of Hermas, Mandates* 11:7–16. On itinerant charismatics, see Davies and Allison, *Matthew 1–7,* 703–4.

79. Overman, *Matthew's Gospel,* 119–22 and 126–30. Overman is rejecting Eduard Schweizer's thesis that itinerant charismatic prophets and missionaries

were central to the Matthean group. This view has been rejected by most scholars, for example, at length by Kingsbury, "The Verb." Overman (97) offers detailed historical and sociological evidence against a setting of itinerancy.

80. For miracle-working, charismatic prophets as Matthew's opponents, see Barth, "Matthew's Law," 149–54. This thesis is accepted by Kingsbury, "The Verb," 70, among many others. E. Cothenet, "Les prophètes chrétiens dans l'evangile selon saint Matthieu," in M. Didier, ed., L'Évangile selon Matthieu: Rédaction et théologie, Bib. Eph. Theol. Lov. 29 (Gembloux: Duculot, 1972), 281–308, suggests that they are zealot antinomians.

81. See Davies and Allison, Matthew 1–7, 701–19, and W. D. Davies, The Setting of the Sermon on the Mount (Cambridge: Cambridge University Press, 1963), 199–205, for reviews of literature. Davies and Allison (708) suggest that the prophets were a group well known to Matthew and so are not clearly identified in the text.

82. See above, chap. 3, n. 76.

83. David Hill, "False Prophets and Charismatics: Structure and Interpretation in Matthew 7, 15–23," Biblica 57 (1976): 341–48, following and fully defending a suggestion of M. J. Lagrange, L'Évangile selon St. Matthieu, Etud. Bib. (Paris: Gabala, 1923), 152. Note that Hill understands 7:21–23 to be referring to another group (336–38). For a list of possibilities, see Davies and Allison, Matthew 1–7, 701–2.

84. Davies and Allison, Matthew 1–7, 703.

85. For prophecy among the Pharisees, see Josephus, Ant. 14 §172–76; 15 §3, 370; 17 §41–45. For the Essenes, see Ant. 13 §311; 15 §373; 17 §346. On the rabbis, see Hill, "False Prophets," 343–44.

86. Hill, "False Prophets," 336–39; also Davies and Allison, Matthew 1–7, 715–16.

87. See Overman, Matthew's Gospel, 93, 118–19.

88. Hans Dieter Betz, Essays on the Sermon on the Mount (Philadelphia: Fortress, 1985), 154–57, suggests that the opponents were gentile Christians of the Pauline type who did not support the keeping of the whole law.

89. For the activities of some prophets during the first century and an explanation of the Israelite traditions which gave them legitimacy, see Richard A. Horsley, "'Like One of the Prophets of Old: Two Types of Popular Prophets at the Time of Jesus," Catholic Biblical Quarterly 47 (1985): 435–63. For messianic movements, see Horsley, "Popular Messianic Movements Around the Time of Jesus," Catholic Biblical Quarterly 46 (1984): 473–80.

90. On apocalyptic warnings against false teachers, see Strecker, Weg der Gerechtigkeit, 137 n. 4; Hill, "False Prophecy," 339.

91. See Wolfgang Trilling, "Amt und Amtverständnis bei Matthäus," in A. Descamps, ed., Mélanges bibliques, Festschrift B. Rigaux (Gembloux: Duculot, 1969), 31. The titles rabbi and master are rejected, probably because they were common among Matthew's opponents from the emerging rabbinic movement (Overman, Matthew's Gospel, 124).

92. On the missionary's role as teacher, see Overman, Matthew's Gospel, 119–22.

93. Ibid., 121–22.

94. In a review of several theories of deviance, Stephen J. Pfohl, *Images of Deviance and Social Control: A Sociological History* (New York: McGraw-Hill, 1985), entitles his chapter on the traditional idea of deviance "The Demonic Perspective: Otherworldly Interpretations of Deviance."

95. See the seminal study of H. Becker, *Outsiders: Studies in the Sociology of Deviance* (New York: Free Press, 1963); the overview of Edwin H. Pfuhl, *The Deviance Process* (New York: Van Nostrand, 1980); and the studies in Nanette Davis, ed., *Sociological Constructions of Deviance: Perspectives and Issues in the Field* (Dubuque: William C. Brown, 1975).

96. Rodney Stark and William S. Bainbridge, *The Future of Religion: Secularization, Revival, and Cult Formation* (Berkeley: University of California Press, 1985), 49.

97. Benton Johnson, "On Church and Sect," *American Sociological Review* 28 (1963): 542. Emphasis on original.

98. Stark and Bainbridge, *Future of Religion,* 23; *Theory,* 125–26. The two ideal types would be a church that was totally identified with the sociocultural environment and a sect whose members were hunted fugitives. Needless to say, most religious groups fall between these extremes.

99. Stark and Bainbridge, *Future of Religion,* 23.

100. Ibid. Bryan Wilson, *Magic and the Millennium: A Sociological Study of Religious Movements of Protest among Tribal and Third-World Peoples* (London: Heinemann, 1973), 21, relates sects to deviance in this way: "Concern with transcendence over evil and the search for salvation and consequent rejection of prevailing cultural values, goals, and norms, and whatever facilities are culturally provided for man's salvation, defines religious deviance."

101. Nachman Ben-Yehuda, *Deviance and Moral Boundaries: Witchcraft, the Occult, Deviant Sciences and Scientists* (Chicago: University of Chicago Press, 1985), 19–20.

102. Kai T. Ericson, *Wayward Puritans: A Study in the Sociology of Deviance* (New York: Wiley, 1966), 22–23. What we fear is what is likely to emerge as deviance, probably because our fears are centered around what we value. Someone who thinks and acts differently will be labeled deviant by the majority only if they perceive the person attacking matters which are important for all in the society.

103. Stark and Bainbridge, *Future of Religion,* 66–67.

104. For an approach to group definition which depends heavily on social boundaries, see Yehudi A. Cohen, "Social Boundary Systems," *Current Anthropology* 10 (1969): 103–17.

105. Paul Rock, *Deviant Behavior* (London: Hutchinson, 1973), 73.

106. Ericson, *Wayward Puritans,* 10. Ericson quotes Durkheim to the effect that if a society were to be uniformly good by normal criteria, more and more trivial traits of behavior would be marked as deviant (26).

107. Ben-Yehuda, *Deviance,* 1–20, esp. 3.

108. See chap. 1 above for varieties of Judaism and diversity of expression and action.

109. Even though deviant positions are often spoken of as outside the

pale, sociologically and historically they are part of the whole. For example, Reform Judaism is rejected by some Jews today as deviant and not authentically Jewish. Yet even those rejecting Reform Judaism acknowledge that they are Jews by their attack. In addition, the Reform movement is patently Jewish historically and sociologically. Deviant groups remain part of the whole.

110. Davis, *Deviance*, 239–40.

111. Pfuhl, *Deviance Process*, 130–47.

112. N. Davis, *Deviance*, 216.

113. Two standard expositions of this typology can be found in Pfohl, *Images of Deviance*, 315–17, and Pfuhl, *Deviance Process*, 269–73.

114. The Jesus movement was a subculture, in which the members functioned both as members of their group of believers-in-Jesus and as respectable Jews seeking change in society.

115. See Pfuhl, *Deviant Process*, chaps. 5–6, for deviant identity.

116. The concept "master status" denotes a primary trait of a person to which all others are subordinate. Though we all occupy multiple social positions, statuses and roles, one may predominate. In a racially stratified society such as the US, being African American is a master status. Pfohl, *Images of Deviance*, 291; Pfuhl, *Deviance Process*, 163- 65; Everett C. Hughes, "Dilemmas and Contradictions of Status," *American Journal of Sociology* 50 (1975): 353–59.

117. On recruitment, see Pfuhl, *Deviance Process*, 131.

118. Wilson, *Magic*, chaps. 1–2.

119. Ibid., 49, 38, 35.

120. Ibid., 16–26. Wilson's earlier typology had only four types and was based on different principles. See Bryan Wilson, ed., *Patterns of Sectarianism* (London: Heilmann, 1967), esp. the introduction, 1–21, and chap. 1, "An Analysis of Sect Development," 22–45. The latter work contains a list of characteristics of sects, which is often used as a shopping list of things to look for in groups. The presence of a number of characteristics does not make a group a sect unless these characteristics can be related to one another in some systematic way in a theoretical context.

121. Wilson, *Magic*, 16–17, 19. Wilson is generally sympathetic in his analysis of sects, but like most modern Western social scientists, he assumes a "higher absolute value for Western political organization and rationality" (Hillel Schwartz, "The End of the Beginning: Millenarian Studies, 1969–1975," *Religious Studies Review* 2, no. 3 [1976]: 7).

122. For the connection of over six thousand African Christian sects with independency movements, nativizing movements, and myriad other cultural factors, see David B. Barrett, *Schism and Renewal in Africa: An Analysis of Six Thousand Contemporary Religious Movements* (Nairobi: Oxford University Press, 1968). Barrett's typology is concretely related to the African system, while Wilson's is more abstract and universal.

123. Though most modern Christian groups do not stress miracles, the comforting aspect of thaumaturgy is preserved in various aspects of pastoral

practice and care and in the affirmation of personal worth in the face of modern, impersonal, technological society. See Wilson, *Magic,* 502–3.

124. The term "revolutionist" can be misleading. It does not claim that the movement is revolutionary in the modern sense or that it seeks to initiate political upheaval and change. The hypothesis that Jesus was a political revolutionary is weak and has been effectively refuted.

125. Though sects can function as political interest groups seeking to change society, they demand such commitment from members that they usually operate as self-selected and intermittently operative communities (Wilson, *Magic,* 32). This is because "sects are usually value-oriented movements, seeking total change at cosmic, social or individual level" (ibid., 491).

126. When this happens "they obtain a new dimension of social consciousness and create new forms of social organization" (ibid., 494).

127. Overman, *Matthew's Gospel,* 109–13.

128. Ibid., 16–19; 72; 155.

129. In general, the New Testament writings do not envision the reform of the empire at large. The apocalyptic strains of early Christianity, especially the Book of Revelation, envision the destruction of the evil empire, not its reform. This attitude was transferred to Judaism by later generations of Christians who took over the empire.

130. Matt. 16:18 uses *ekklesia* with great solemnity and has Jesus identify it as "my" assembly. Matt. 18:17 assumes both the assembly's existence and its disciplinary powers over its members.

131. Wolfgang Trilling, *Das Wahre Israel: Studien zur Theologie des Matthäus-Evangelium,* SANT 10, 3d ed. (Munich: Kosel, 1964), 154–63, identifies the church with the true people of God; and Hubert Frankemölle, *Jahwe-Bund und Kirche Christi: Studien zur Form- und Traditionsgeschichte des "Evangeliums" nach Matthäus,* NTAbh 10, 2d ed., (Münster: Aschendorff, 1984), 220–47, is most anxious to differentiate Matthew's concept of the church from the Jewish idea of synagogue and the biblical idea of the congregation of Israel see esp. 223–25, 230–32, 245–46). It is true that Matthew's emerging understanding of group is closely tied to his appreciation of Jesus as Messiah, of Jesus' kingdom, and so on, as Frankemölle holds. But this does not mean that Matthew saw his understanding as incompatible or theologically divergent from Judaism. Frankemölle's treatment manifests later Christian theological anxiety about establishing an identity clearly separate from Judaism and Reformation polemics against anything that might smack of law.

132. The presence of God through Jesus and Jesus in the group is thematically central for Matthew. See 1:23 and 28:19.

133. Franz Poland, *Geschichte der Griechischen Vereinswesens* (Leipzig: Teubner, 1909), 332.

134. White, *Building,* chap. 2.

135. K. L. Schmidt, "Ekklesia," *Theological Dictionary of the New Testament* (Grand Rapids: Eerdmans, 1965), 3: 513. n. 25. Note that other terms for cultic associations and private groups, such as *thiasos,* are not found in the New Testament.

136. Davies and Allison, *Matthew 8–17*, 629, gather evidence to show that Matthew is associating his *ekklesia* with the assembly at Sinai.

137. For a full discussion of usages, see Wolfgang Schrage, "'Ekklesia' und 'Synagoge.' Zum Ursprung des urchristlichen Kirkenbegriffs," *Zeitschrift für Theologie and Kirke* 60 (1963): 178–202.

138. See, for a recent example, Ernest Best, "Church," in Paul Achtemeier, ed., *Harpers Bible Dictionary* (San Francisco: Harpers, 1985), 168, under the section "Identity." The Christian church is presented as a full-blown, differentiated, self-conscious institution.

139. *Ekklesia* is also used in James 5:14 and 3 John 6, 9, 10. It is used of the heavenly assembly of the saved in Heb. 12:23.

140. 1 Cor. 1:2, 4:17, 6:4 and frequently, including the salutations of Galatians, 2 Corinthians, 1 Thessalonians, and Philemon (but not Romans and Philippians). This usage is continued in the deutero-Pauline letters, for example, 2 Thess. 1:1; 1 Tim. 3:5; Col. 1:18; Eph. 1:22. That Paul thought of his churches as part of Israel is clear from the metaphor of the olive tree in Rom. 11:17–24.

141. For the former view, see Jack T. Sanders, *The Jews in Luke-Acts* (Philadelphia: Fortress, 1987); also many of the essays in Joseph B. Tyson, ed., *Luke-Acts and the Jewish People* (Minneapolis: Augsburg, 1988). For a more positive interpretation of Paul's view of Judaism, see Jacob Jervell, *Luke and the People of God: A New Look at Luke-Acts* (Minneapolis: Augsburg, 1972).

142. For example, is the final scene in Acts a rejection of Judaism or a continuation of the permanent pattern, first an appeal to Jews and then to gentiles?

143. See Adela Yarbro Collins, *Crisis and Catharsis: The Power of the Apocalypse* (Philadelphia: Westminster, 1984), 85–86. For the social situation of Judaism in Asia Minor, see Leonard Thompson, *The Book of Revelation: Apocalypse and Empire* (New York: Oxford University Press, 1990), chap.8.

144. Schmidt, *"Ekklesia,"* 518. However, the polemics between Matthew's group and the larger Jewish group have prompted him to call his group *ekklesia* in distinction to the assembly from which he had been expelled but still sought to lead. *Ekklesia* and *synagōgē* are used interchangeably in the Epistle of James (2:2 and 5:14). Christian gatherings are named a synagogue in Ignatius of Antioch, *Polycarp,* 4:2, and the *Shepherd of Hermas, Mandates* 11:9. A later witness says that Jewish-Christians in Transjordan called themselves a synagogue. See Schmidt, *"Ekklesia,"* 518 n. 47, citing Epiphanius, *Panarion,* 30, 18, 2.

145. Some scholars have tried to distinguish the local group from the universal or eschatological church, that is, actual assemblies from an ideal theological concept of church. Such distinctions are foreign to Matthew. Schmidt, *"Ekklesia,"* 524–26, wrestles with the local and universal meanings of Hebrew *qahal* and Aramaic *kenishta,* but this problematic stems from later theological categories concerning the universality of the church and the legitimacy of sectarian claims.

146. Others in the narrative have understood Jesus more narrowly, as a

prophet like John the Baptist or Elijah (16:14), but according to Matthew they are incorrect.

147. Kenzo Tagawa, "People and Community in the Gospel of Matthew," *New Testament Studies* 16 (1969–70): 159.

148. Marcus N. Tod, *Sidelights on Greek History* (Oxford: Blackwell, 1932), 76–77; Ramsey MacMullen, *Roman Social Relations 50 B.C. to A.D. 284* (New Haven: Yale University Press, 1974), 18–20, 73–80; Moses Finley, *The Ancient Economy* (Berkeley: University of California Press, 1973), 138; Poland, *Geschichte*, esp. 152–68, and Wilken, "Collegia," 279, for terminology. Robert L. Wilken, *The Christians as the Romans Saw Them* (New Haven: Yale University Press, 1984), chap. 2, gathers evidence for outsiders' views that Christianity was a private association. For an application of these associations to the Pauline evidence, see Meeks, *Urban Christians*, 77–80, and Malherbe, *Social Aspects*, 86–91. For the Pharisees, see Saldarini, *Pharisees*, 67–70.

149. Poland, *Geschichte*, 282–83.

150. For binding and loosing, see Overman, *Matthew's Gospel*, 104–6. For Matthew's claim to authority over the Jewish community, see ibid., 106–13, chap. 3 above.

151. Note that the authority conferred on a small number of believers justifies Matthew's small deviant group in the face of the majority Jewish community, which has traditional authority on its side.

152. Deschamps, "Relations," 87–88.

153. See the emphasis on law in 2 Baruch.

Chapter Six

1. For the various laws discussed in the Jesus tradition, see E. P. Sanders, *Jewish Law from Jesus to the Mishnah* (London: SCM; Philadelphia: Trinity, 1990), chap. 1.

2. J. Andrew Overman, *Matthew's Gospel and Formative Judaism: The Social World of the Matthean Community* (Minneapolis: Fortress, 1990), 16–19.

3. Arland J. Hultgren, *Jesus and His Adversaries* (Minneapolis: Augsburg, 1979), 189–90, notes that Matthew, in contrast to Mark, uses controversy stories to develop a communal self-consciousness distinct from that of the Pharisees and rabbis. See also Overman, *Matthew's Gospel*, 85; R. Hummel, *Die Auseinandersetzung zwischen Kirche und Judentum im Matthäusevangelium* (Munich: Kaiser, 1963), 55.

4. Sanders, *Jewish Law*, 6 and passim, attempts to distinguish disagreements that caused sectarian exclusivism and schism (excommunication) from lesser points of disagreement, which characterized Jesus' controversies with his opponents. Sanders is correct in his ultimate conclusion that Jesus remained within the limits of Jewish debate and that he did nothing deserving of death or total rejection. But the contrast between "trivial and substantial" points of debate is false for two reasons. First, the importance of controversies is very contextual, with what seem to be minor points taking on great significance for certain groups in a given situation and thus exciting

extreme and even violent opposition. Second, from an analytical point of view, those who take extreme views remain within Judaism even if they are sectarians or schismatics.

5. Jerome H. Neyrey, "The Thematic Use of Isaiah 42, 1–4 in Matthew 12," *Biblica* 63 (1982): 460–61.

6. For the same conclusion argued from a different direction, see Sanders, *Jewish Law,* 6–23, esp. 23.

7. See a review of the sources by Robert Goldenberg, "The Jewish Sabbath in the Roman World up to the Time of Constantine the Great," in H. Temporini and W. Hasse, eds., *Aufstieg und Niedergang der Römischen Welt* 2.19.1 (Berlin: deGruyter, 1979), 414–47. There is also a convenient gathering of sources in Molly Whittaker, *Jews and Christians: Graeco-Roman Views* (Cambridge: Cambridge University Press, 1984).

8. See Joachim Gnilka, *Das Matthäusevangelium,* HTKNT, 2 vols. (Freiburg: Herder, 1986, 1988), 2:323; Ulrich Luz, *Das Evangelium nach Matthäus (Mt 8–17),* EKK (Zurich: Benzinger; Neukirchen-Vluyn: Neukirchener, 1990), 233; G. D. Kilpatrick, *The Origins of the Gospel according to St. Matthew* (Oxford: Clarendon, 1946), 116 Eduard Schweizer, "Matthew's Church," in Graham Stanton, ed., *The Interpretation of Matthew* (Philadelphia: Fortress, 1983), 129, says Matthew observes the Sabbath, or at least it was kept for a long time in his community; G. Barth, "Matthew's Understanding of the Law," in G. Bornkamm, G. Barth, H. J. Held, *Tradition and Interpretation in Matthew* (Philadelphia: Westminster, 1963), 91–92, and Robert H. Gundry, *Matthew: A Commentary on His Literary and Theological Art* (Grand Rapids: Eerdmans, 1982), 483, following Hirsch and Schlatter, suggest that Matthew allows flight from the crisis, but fears that other Jews will not recognize the crisis and that this will cause hindrances. This strained explanation is motivated by the unwarranted assumption that Matthew does not observe the Sabbath.

9. See 1 Macc. 2:31–41 for an early stage of the debate about war on the Sabbath. Much later, Num. Rab. 23:1 allows flight from dangers on the Sabbath. The temporal spread of these discussions, from the Maccabees to the midrash, encompassing the Qumran community and extensive talmudic debates, indicates that the precise requirements of Sabbath observance prompted an ongoing dialogue in which Matthew had a small part.

10. This rule is invoked in John 5:10, where it is argued that the cured invalid has broken the law by carrying his mat on the Sabbath. The Mishnah understands carrying as carrying things from the public to private or private to public domains (m. Shab. 7:2, the last of the thirty nine kinds of work). For prohibition of carrying beds, see m. Shab. 10:5.

11. Jub. 2:31; cf. also 50:9–10 on the importance of eating and drinking on the Sabbath. The preparing of food for the Sabbath on the day previous is more difficult.

12. CD 12:1–2 forbids intercourse in the City of the Sanctuary, that is, Jerusalem, because that would defile the holy city. This law comes right after the Sabbath laws but seems unconnected with them. This rule may pertain to

pilgrims visiting Jerusalem. See Chaim Rabin, *The Zadokite Documents* (Oxford: Clarendon, 1954), 59. CD 10:18–19 forbids Sabbath talk about work to be done the next day and about money and gain.

13. For a complete discussion, see Lawrence Schiffman, The *Halakhah at Qumran* (Leiden: Brill, 1975).

14. We take it for granted that Rabbinic literature, dating from 200 c.e. on, cannot be used as evidence for Pharisaic thought in the time of Jesus or for late first-century rabbinic thought at the time of Matthew. Early layers of the Mishnah and Tosefta may be pertinent to these periods, if they can be convincingly unwound from the final texts. For the most part, the Mishnah and Talmuds are cited to show the development of Jewish law over several centuries, into which development Matthew fits. For a recent uncritical use of rabbinic literature in relation to Matthew, see Phillip Sigal, *The Halakah of Jesus of Nazareth according to the Gospel of Matthew* (Latham, N.Y.: University of America Press, 1986), and my review in *Jewish Quarterly Review* 79 (1988): 88–89.

15. For a representative discussion of the biblical passage on gathering firewood, see Mekilta, Tractate Shabbata, chap. 2 on Exod. 35:1–3 (Jacob Z. Lauterbach, *Mekilta De-Rabbi Ishmael* [Philadelphia: Jewish Publication Society, 1933], 3:205–11) where the general topic of doing preparation for the Sabbath on the day previous is taken up. For a list of contrasts between Sabbath and festivals, see m. Betzah 5:2.

16. *Bulmos* probably refers to extreme hunger from fasting that makes one faint or is a danger to health.

17. See an extensive discussion in b. Yoma 84b–85b. Rabbinic literature also cites Lev. 18:5— "You shall therefore observe my statutes and my ordinances, by doing which a person shall live"—as proof that obedience to the commandments is meant to promote life and that if life is endangered, then the commandments may be suspended.

18. In the Covenant of Damascus (10:20–21) even walking about in a field was forbidden. See Schiffman, *Halakah*, 90–91.

19. According to Deut. 23:26, while walking through another person's field one may pluck some grain by hand, but one may not use a sickle. This rule distinguishes casual consumption of a little food for immediate needs with harvesting another's crop, that is, stealing. Mark (2:23) gives no such reason.

20. David Hill, "On the Use and Meaning of Hosea VI.6 in Matthew's Gospel," *New Testament Studies* 24 (1977–78): 114; Kilpatrick, *Origins*, 116, Barth, "Matthew's Law," 81–82.

21. E. Lohmeyer, *Das Evangelium des Matthäus*, (2d ed., ed. W. Schmauch, KEK (Göttingen: Vandenhoeck, 1958), 184; Hummel, *Auseinandersetzung*, 41; Alan H. McNeile, *The Gospel according to St. Matthew* (London: Macmillan, 1915), 168.

22. Even water should be drawn the day previous according to Jub. 50:8. No claim is made that the disciples were fainting or in any danger, so the principle of "saving a life" could not be invoked. According to the Covenant

of Damascus, one could not eat even something lying in the fields (CD 10:22–23), though this sectarian rule is not at issue here.

23. 1 Sam. 21:1–6 (Heb. 21:2–7). Matthew follows Mark here but omits Mark's misidentification of the priest Ahimelech as Abiathar (Mark 2:26). See Lev. 24:5–9 for the laws concerning the Bread of the Presence or Showbread. Twelve loaves were to be laid out each Sabbath on a table in the sanctuary or Temple. The loaves which were removed were holy and eating them was restricted to the priests. This law is referred to in Ex. 25:30 and 40:23. Its observance is assumed in 2 Macc. 10:3 at the rededication of the Temple.

24. Since the Bread of the Presence is changed on the Sabbath, some later rabbinic traditions assumed that David had taken the loaves that had been removed on the Sabbath. But in 1 Samuel 21 the loaves on the table in the sanctuary seem to be the ones at issue. The priest inquires whether David and his men have abstained from intercourse as a condition for eating the holy bread. (See rules for soldiers engaged in holy war in Deut. 23:10–15.)

25. John 7:22–23 argues in the same way as Matthew, using the practice of circumcising on the Sabbath to justify curing a man on the Sabbath.

26. Jub. 50:10–11 is careful to restrict Sabbath work to this case only. Much later, the Babylonian Talmud explicitly articulates what Scripture assumes, the principle that the Temple service overrides the Sabbath (b. Shab. 132b; b. Yeb. 7a).

27. CD 11:17–18.

28. In m. Hag. 2:2, differences on this issue are attributed to the "Pairs" and used as a criterion for distinguishing different schools. Jacob Neusner, *Judaism: The Evidence of the Mishnah* (Chicago: University of Chicago Press, 1981), 57, dates this dispute to the pre-70 period. See also Sanders, *Jewish Law,* 8, 11–12.

29. Neusner, *Evidence,* 55–59.

30. D. M. Cohn-Sherbok, "An Analysis of Jesus' Arguments concerning the Plucking of Grain on the Sabbath," *Journal for the Study of the New Testament* 2 (1979): 31–41, concludes that Jesus' arguments do not measure up to the sophistication of rabbinic arguments. But he is applying criteria from a later stage of Jewish legal and scholastic development to the first century.

31. A similar argument is used later in the chapter when the Queen of Sheba's positive reaction to Solomon is contrasted with the Pharisees' rejection of Jesus, who is "something greater" (12:41–42).

32. Hos. 6:6 was cited previously in 9:13 in connection with God's mercy toward sinners. Mercy as an important principle of law is supported in 23:23.

33. G. Bornkamm, "End Expectation and Church in Matthew," in Bornkamm et al., *Tradition,* 26; Hill, "Use and Meaning of Hos. VI.6," 117.

34. W. D. Davies and Dale C. Allison, *The Gospel according to St. Matthew,* vol. 2: *Chapters 8–17* (Edinburgh: Clark, 1991), 307. Davies and Allison go beyond Matthew's polemic when they accuse the Pharisees of casuistry (307) and rigidity (310–11).

35. Luz, *Matthäus (Mt 8–17),* 233, says that mercy is the center of the Torah for Matthew and individual laws are subordinate to it.

36. Gnilka, *Matthäusevangelium,* 1:445–46.

37. Rabbinic literature has the principle that the Sabbath was made for Israel, but the principle is used as an argument for Israel's election and as an exhortation to observe the Sabbath strictly. See b. Yoma 85b; Mekilta, Tractate Shabbata 31:14, Jub. 2:31. See also Israel Abrahams, *Studies in Pharisaism and the Gospels*, 1st and 2d ser. (New York: Ktav, 1967; orig. eds. 1917 and 1924), 129–35. Since Luke 6:5 also lacks this saying, it is possible that Matthew and Luke had versions of Mark which lacked the saying altogether.

38. Gnilka, *Matthäusevangelium*, 1:446

39. David Daube, *The New Testament and Rabbinic Judaism* (London: University of London Athalone, 1956), 156, calls this story "a halakic lecture by Jesus." Davies and Allison say that Jesus is relatively unsophisticated and brief in his legal arguments because he appeals to human instincts rather than legal nicities. See *Matthew 8–17*, 319, referring to Stephen Westerholm, *Jesus and Scribal Authority*, CB, NT ser. 10; Lund: Liberläromedel/Gleerup, 1978), 101. But the extended legal debates of the Talmuds were not part of the Jewish legal repertoire in the first century, so the comparison is invalid.

40. The episode refers only to "their" (v. 9) and "they" (v. 10) at the beginning. However, the Pharisees in verse 2 are the nearest antecedents to verses 9–10, and at the end "the Pharisees" plot against Jesus (v. 14). Hummel, *Auseinandersetzung*, 28ff. denies that the Pharisees are the opponents.

41. In Mark (3:1–6), the Pharisees were watching Jesus to see if they could accuse him of violating the Sabbath, and so Jesus confronted them with the question of healing on the Sabbath rather than vice versa. In Matthew, the Pharisees challenge Jesus immediately as they would any rival teacher.

42. Rabbinic discussions of these problems are extensive. For example, t. Shab. 15:16–17 argues over whether Sabbath rest can be violated in a case when the threat to life from sickness is doubtful.

43. Thus Geza Vermes, *The Dead Sea Scrolls in English*, 3d ed. (London: Penguin, 1987). Rabin, *Zadokite Documents*, 57, reads this sentence in conjunction with the previous rule that one cannot assist in the birth of an animal on the Sabbath: "Even if she drops her newborn young into a cistern or a pit, let him not keep it (the young) alive on Sabbath." (Sanders, *Jewish Law*, 8, wrongly attributes this interpretation to Vermes.) In either case, the owner is expected to suffer financial loss rather than work on the Sabbath. The Mishnah affirms the general rule of the Covenant of Damascus but makes a distinction (m. Shab. 18:3) between delivering the fetus (presumably extracting it) and helping out after the newborn emerges (catching the newborn to keep it from falling, blowing in its nostrils, and putting the teat into its mouth, according to Rab Judah in b. Shab. 128b). Interestingly, the Mishnah contrasts the case of an animal with that of a human birth. For a mother in labor, they may deliver the child, do other necessary things, and "profane the Sabbath for her sake" (m. Shab. 18:3). Similarly, in CD 11:15 no work may be done for property or gain on the Sabbath, but in 11:16 a human may be raised from a pit or pulled from water.

44. In addition, the young is to be provided food (t. Yom Tob 3:2); later talmudic discussion defends this practice by the principle of relieving the suffer-

ing of a living animal. Rabbi Joshua is more permissive and allows a legal deception by which one does not slaughter the mother and raises up the young also. The Talmud understands Joshua's view to be based on preventing the animal from suffering. For this motive in relieving an animal's burden, see m. Bab. Met. 2:10, b. Bab. Met. 32b, and b. Bet. 37a, based on Exod. 23:5. Interestingly, the financial loss an owner might suffer does not enter into the discussion in the Covenant of Damascus or later rabbinic sources.

45. Although there may be an implied parallel between the limitations experienced by an animal in a pit and a human with a crippled arm, Matthew does not make such an analogy. Luke (13:13–15) does; the cure of a crippled woman is justified by an analogy between untying an animal to bring it to water on the Sabbath and "untying" the woman from her eighteen-year handicap. But this analogy is weak because the life of the beast requires that it be watered daily and the woman's handicap does not endanger her life that very day.

Matthew derived the principle of doing good on the Sabbath from the question which Mark had Jesus ask the Pharisees, abbreviated it, and made it into Jesus' concluding teaching. Sanders, *Jewish Law,* 21, notes that the principle is "too vague and might mean anything."

46. For the development of this principle in the pre-70 stratum of the Mishnah, see Neusner, *Evidence,* 57–59.

47. For the later Mishnaic developments, see m. Shab. 14:3–4; t. Shab. 12:8–14. Neusner's analysis indicates that these rules are from the late first century. Rabin interprets CD 11:10 to mean that one cannot "carry upon himself medicaments [*smnym*] to go out and come in on the Sabbath." The Hebrew *sam* can mean drug, but also spice or dyes and paints, that is, makeup. Thus Vermes's interpretation is more likely, that no one shall "carry perfumes upon himself whilst going and coming on the Sabbath" (*Dead Sea Scrolls,* 95). In either case, carrying on the Sabbath, not curing, is the issue.

Sanders's contention (*Jewish Law,* 13) that minor cures were forbidden on the Sabbath in the first century is based on the later Mishnaic texts (which he claims, without sufficient reason, we may assume contained earlier laws) and on a misunderstanding of the Covenant of Damascus as pertaining to cures, not carrying.

48. There may be an implicit appeal to the love commandment. See Luz, *Matthäus (Mt 8–17),* 239–40; Daniel J. Harrington, *The Gospel of Matthew,* Sacra Pagina (Collegeville, Minn.: Liturgical Press Glazier, 1991), 173.

49. Neyrey, "Thematic Use of Isa. 42, 1–4." O. Lamar Cope, *Matthew: A Scribe Trained for the Kingdom of Heaven,* CBQMS 5 (Washington, D.C.: CBA, 1976), 32–52, develops the connection of the Isaiah quotation with the latter part of chap. 12 and stresses the integral relationship of Matthew's text with conflicts within the Jewish community.

50. Rudolf Bultmann, *The History of the Synoptic Tradition* (New York: Harper, 1963), 17, 81, understands this as an early wisdom teaching that has been subsequently embedded in commmentary. H. Räisänen, "Jesus and the Food Laws: Reflections on Mark 7.15," *Journal for the Study of the New Testament* 16

(1982): 79–100, argues that the saying is Markan or at least from a gentile Christian milieu. James D. G. Dunn, "Jesus and Ritual Purity: A Study of the Tradition History of Mk 7,15," in C. Dupont, ed., *À cause de l'évangile: Etudes sur les Synoptiques et les Actes offertes au P. Jacques Dupont,* LD 123 (Paris: Cerf, 1985), 251–76, suggests that Mark (7:15 and 19c) has modified and radicalized an earlier, more ambiguous, Jesus saying. Dunn further suggests that Matt. 15:11 is closer to the original that Mark.

51. Barth, "Matthew's Law," 86–89, shows how Matthew handles the interpretation of law and tradition; see also W. D. Davies, *The Setting of the Sermon on the Mount* (Cambridge: Cambridge University Press, 1963), 104. Davies and Allison, *Matthew 8–17,* 517, 537, show clearly that the purity laws are affirmed and are still valid in Matthew. Luz, *Matthäus (Mt 8–17),* 425, says that Matthew affirms purity but subordinates it to the love command.

The Markan version of the conflict over purity has been a subject of much controversy. See Roger P. Booth, *Jesus and the Laws of Purity: Tradition and Legal History in Mark 7,* JSNTSS 13 (Sheffield: JSOT Press, 1986); Jan Lambrecht, "Jesus and the Law: An Investigation of Mk. 7, 1–23," *Ephemerides theologicae lovanienses* 53 (1977): 24–82; *Forum* 4, no.3 (1988). For an interpretation of these types of controversies in a Cynic context, see Burton Mack, *A Myth of Innocence: Mark and Christian Origins* (Philadelphia: Fortress, 1988), 189–207.

52. Gnilka, *Matthäusevangelium,* 2:27, notes that Matthew's group possibly kept the purity rules.

53. For Pharisaic traditions as behavioral norms not found in Scripture, see A. I. Baumgarten, "The Pharisaic *Paradosis,*" *Harvard Theological Review* 80 (1987): 63–77.

54. Even in a highly secularized society, such practices persist. In Western culture, people do not eat insects, though they are a rich source of protein. Given the availability of water and indoor plumbing, people in many social strata are expected to shower or bathe often.

55. A variant in Clement of Alexandria's *Protrepticus* 6:79 has "sanctifying their flesh."

56. The evidence is conveniently gathered in Sanders, *Jewish Law,* 258–71.

57. I have seen numerous purification pools *(miqweh)* in Sepphoris, three miles north of Nazareth. Ehud Netzer says there are about twenty in Jericho. See "Ancient Ritual Baths (Miqvaot) in Jericho," in Lee I. Levine, ed., *The Jerusalem Cathedra 2* (Jerusalem: Yad Izhak Ben-Zvi Press; Detroit: Wayne State University Press, 1982), 106–19.

58. In the same Mishnah, the story of Akabya ben Mahalaleel's refusal to submit to the majority opinion and his instruction to his son to submit also serves as an apologetic for accepting rabbinic rulings even if they are not universally traditional or clearly biblical. See Anthony J. Saldarini, "The Adoption of a Dissident: Akabya ben Mahaleleel in Rabbinic Tradition," *Journal of Jewish Studies* 33 (1982): 547–56. See further elaboration in b. Ber. 19a. Regulations concerning handwashing are closely connected to local custom and etiquette as well. See b. Ber. 51a, where one is instructed not to allow someone to hand you your shirt in the morning, not to let someone with unwashed hands pour

water over your hands, and not to return a cup of asparagus brew to anyone but the one who handed it to you. See also b. Shab. 62b; b. Hul. 105b-107b. Observance of handwashing was probably lax in various communities.

59. B. Sot. 4b.

60. M. Ber. 8:2–4; t. Ber. 5 (6): 25–30 (Lieberman, 29–31). For a full exposition of m. Ber. 8 and all related rabbinic sources, see Jacob Neusner, *Invitation to the Talmud* (San Francisco: Harper, 1973).

61. Jacob Neusner, *The Rabbinic Traditions about the Pharisees before 70*, 3 vols. (Leiden: Brill, 1971), 2:45, 48; *Evidence*, 53–54. Booth, *Jesus*, 168–69, argues for a first-century c.e. handwashing rule on the basis of three talmudic rules (b. Shab. 14b). This reconstruction does not succeed in proving that a first-century rule has been uncovered. Booth must assume that the eighteen takkanot (rulings by post-70 rabbis) in m. Shab. 1–4 and parts of their elaboration in b. Shab. 13b-17b are historical and that a reference to "hands" (b. Shab. 14b) means unwashed hands, which transmit uncleanness. The complexity of the talmudic discussion shows that the Amoraim had difficulty understanding and fully explaining the handwashing rules. Attempts to discern from their discussions which understandings were operative several centuries earlier are vary hazardous.

62. This dispute is relevant to the discussion below about the inside and outside and also to Matt. 23:25–26. Handwashing and food purity are part of the same system. See the discussion in the Palestinian Talmud (p. Ber. 8:2 [12a]; Neusner, *Talmud*, 185–90).

63. On the traditions of the elders as practices not found in the Bible, see Baumgarten, "Pharisaic *Paradosis.*" On Matthew's engagement with this issue, see Luz, *Matthäus (Mt 8–17)*, 418–22, 427.

64. Barth, "Matthew's Law," 89–90; Gnilka, *Matthäusevangelium*, 2:24, notes Matthew's narrowing of the saying so that it focuses on real purity from the heart. For an analysis of the various uses of this saying, see Charles E. Carlston, "The Things that Defile (Mark vii.14 [read 15]) and the Law in Matthew and Mark," *New Testament Studies* 15 (1968–69): 75–96. Carlston's understanding of Matthew as mediator in a mixed community of Jews and gentiles differs from the interpretation of Matthew espoused here. For the view that Matthew as well as Mark is revoking the food laws, see John P. Meier, *The Vision of Matthew: Christ, Church, and Morality in the First Gospel* (Ramsey: Paulist, 1979), 100–104, and Ingo Broer, *Freiheit vom Gesetz und Radikalisierung des Gesetzes*, SBS 98 (Stuttgart: Katholisches Bibelwerk, 1980), 114–22.

65. Note that the exhortation to listen and understand also occurs in 13:13. In neither case do the crowds understand, and in both the disciples need further instruction. Jesus' saying is called a parable in 15:15; the parable *(mashal)* here is an unclear saying, a riddle, which challenges the audience. It needed and received interpretation in the gospels and perhaps in Paul (Rom. 14:14). See Davies and Allison, *Matthew 8–17*, 528–29; E. P. Sanders, "Jesus and the Constraints of Law," *Journal for the Study of the New Testament* 17 (1983): 20.

66. Luz, *Matthäus (Mt 8–17)*, 427, notes that handwashing and purity are key disagreements between Matthew and his opponents.

67. 1QS 8:5; 11:8; CD 1:7; Jub. 1:16; 7:13; 21:24; Enoch 10:16; 62:8; 84:6; 93:2, 5,10; Wisd. of Sol. 4:3–5: Pss. of Sol. 14:3. This imagery continues in rabbinic literature, where a dissident apostate, Elisha ben Abuya (called Aher, "Other"), is said to have mutilated the shoots, that is, corrupted the youth (b. Hag. 14b-15a), according to Henry Fischel, *Rabbinic Literature and Greco-Roman Philosophy: A Study of Epicurea and Rhetorica in Early Midrashic Writings,* SPB 21 (Leiden: Brill, 1973), 19–20.

68. These restrictions are concentrated in Leviticus 11 and Deuteronomy 14. For example, eating swarming things is an abomination and brings uncleanness on the person (Lev. 11:43–45).

69. Hans Hübner, *Das Gesetz in der synoptischen Tradition* (Witten: Luther Verlag, 1973), 176–82, notes that Matthew mitigates Mark's teaching on purity by putting it in a new context.

70. Diaspora Judaism often connected purity rules and morality. See Luz, *Matthäus (Mt 8–17),* 425. Davies and Allison, *Matthew 8–17,* 535–36, cautiously suggest some Hellenistic influence.

71. See Margaret Hannan, "The God that Matthew Preaches," (M.A. thesis, Boston College, 1991), 48–56

72. See the treatment of the seven curses in Chap. 3 above.

73. The next curse (v. 27) continues the contrast of inside and outside and brings the charges of greed and self-indulgence to completion. The scribes and Pharisees are compared to whitewashed graves, which look good but have bones and uncleanness inside. This is an allusion to the state of uncleanness caused by corpses. Similarly, according to Matthew, the scribes and Pharisees are filled with hypocrisy and lawlessness *(anomia).* This is the climax of Matthew's attack on the community leaders' integrity and interpretation of the law.

74. The connection of this Q saying with Pharisaic teaching has been worked out by Jacob Neusner, " 'First Cleanse the Inside': The 'Halakhic' Background of a Controversy-Saying," *New Testament Studies* 22 (1976): 486–95. Luke 11:38 has the same saying in a different context and used to make a different point. The fundamental distinctions made in the Mishnah can be dated to the first century using Neusner's method of attestation.

75. Mishnah Berakot and Mishnah Kelim are related to one another concerning this question in p. Ber. 8:2 (11a).

76. Neusner, " 'First Cleanse,' " 493–94. The Shammaite view may have been the dominant view before 70 c.e.

77. For the narrative structure of these stories, see Janice Capel Anderson, "Double and Triple Stories, the Implied Reader, and Redundancy in Matthew," *Semeia* 31 (1985): 71–89.

78. See the treatment of this passage in chap. 4 above.

79. For a review of the evidence for tithing and taxes, see Sanders, *Jewish Law,* 43–51.

80. For a discussion of the Pharisees' legal agenda, see Neusner, *Pharisees,* 3:180–238, and *Evidence,* 45–75. See also Anthony J. Saldarini, *Pharisees, Scribes, and Sadducees in Palestinian Society* (Wilmington: Glazier, 1988), 212–20.

81. Dill and cummin were also used for medicinal purposes. Tithing of dill is mentioned specifically in m. Maas. 4:5. Cummin is transliterated into Greek from Hebrew (Isa. 28:25). See Correns, "Verzehntung."

82. For a review of the evidence for the post-70 priesthood with emphasis on its diversity and complexity, see Seth Schwartz, *Josephus and Judean Politics* (Leiden: Brill, 1990), 96–109, esp. 104–7.

83. Anthony J. Saldarini, "The Gospel of Matthew and Jewish-Christian Conflict in Galilee," in Lee I. Levine, ed., *Studies on Galilee in Late Antiquity* (New York: Jewish Theological Seminary, 1992), 23–38; Overman, *Matthew's Gospel,* 158–61.

84. Dissident groups typically accuse the majority community of misinterpreting the tradition, of missing the main point, and of lack of personal integrity in doing so. Pirke Abot 4:2 has Ben Azzai advise his listeners to fulfill light commandments as they would the weightiest, since one thing leads to another.

85. See the studies of Neusner noted above. Sanders, *Jewish Law,* 134–35, 236–38, and chap. 3 passim, has attacked Neusner's reconstruction of the pre-70 Pharisaic agenda as oriented toward tithing (and eating) their own food in purity in imitation of the priests. Be that as it may, by the late first century, the study of tithing by the early rabbinic group was in progress.

86. R. J. Cassidy, "Matthew 17.24–7—A Word on Civil Taxes," *Catholic Biblical Quarterly* 41 (1979): 571–80, argues that the tax in question was a civil tax levied by the Romans. However, the story implies that the tax is paid to God (through the Temple). For a discussion of the arguments for this possibility, see Davies and Allison, *Matthew 8–17,* 739–41. Both Davies and Allison and Luz, *Matthäus (Mt 8–17),* 529, affirm the religious nature of the tax.

87. See Exod. 38:25–26 for a one bekah (= half-shekel) contribution for the making of silver sanctuary items.

88. Emil Schürer, Geza Vermes, et al., *The History of the Jewish People in the Age of Jesus Christ,* 4 vols. (Edinburgh: Clark, 1973–87), 2:271–74.

89. William Horbury, "The Temple Tax," in Ernst Bammel and C. F. D. Moule, eds., *Jesus and the Politics of His Day* (Cambridge: Cambridge University Press, 1984), 277–79; J. Liver, "The Ransom of Half Shekel," in M. Haran, ed., *Yehezkel Kaufmann Jubilee Volume* [in Hebrew] (Jerusalem: Magnes, 1960), Hebrew section, 54–67. Menahem Stern, *Greek and Latin Authors on Jews and Judaism,* 3 vols. (Jerusalem: Israel Academy of Sciences and Humanities, 1974–84), 1:198–99; J. Liver, "The Half-Shekel Offering in Biblical and Post-Biblical Literature," *Harvard Theological Review* 56 (1963): 173–98, and "The Half-Shekel in the Scrolls of the Judaean Desert Sect" [in Hebrew], *Tarbiz* 31 (1961–62): 18–22. Cassidy, "Matthew 17. 24–7," 573–74, argues that the tax was voluntary, but his textual interpretations are forced.

90. The text is in John M. Allegro, ed., *Qumran Cave 4,* DJD 5 (Oxford: Clarendon, 1968), 7. The translation is the author's own. Strugnell's corrections to DJD 5 contain nothing pertinent to this section. See Liver, "The Half-Shekel in the Scrolls of the Judaean Desert Sect," 18–22, and Horbury, "Temple Tax." Even if the text was not written by the Qumran community (see

F. D. Weinert, "A Note on 4Q159 and a New Theory of Essene Origins," *Review de Qumran* 9 [1977]: 22–30), it witnesses to a dispute over this tax in the Second Temple period.

91. Cicero (*Pro Flacco* 28.66–67) uses popular prejudice against the wealth sent to Jerusalem (*auri illa invidia Iudaici*, "the odium attached to Jewish gold") to defend the notorious Flaccus. Tacitus (*Historia* 5.5.1) complains that Jews keep sending tribute and contributing to Jerusalem.

92. Josephus, *War* 7.6.6 §218; Dio Cassius, *Roman History* 66. 7. 2; Suetonius, *Domitian* 12.2. For the notorious *fiscus Judaicus*, see Schürer, Vermes, et al., *History,* 272–73, and Mary E. Smallwood, *The Jews under Roman Rule* (Leiden: Brill, 1976), 371–78, 385. Nerva reformed abuses connected with the collection of the tax, but the tax was never repealed (contrary to the claim of Kilpatrick, *Origins,* 42).

93. The Mishnah (m. Shek. 8:8) ruled that the half-shekel tax for the Temple need not be paid if the Temple was not standing. Horbury, "Temple Tax," 279–82, reviews Mishnaic evidence with restraint and is not able to draw significant conclusions for the first century. Various authors commented on the half-shekel tax. See sources as diverse as Philo, *De Specialibus Legibus* 1.77, and b. Bab. Bathra 9a.

94. The original tax had been collected from men aged twenty to fifty. The Roman tax was collected from men and women and the age range was wider. Suetonius, *Domitian* 12. 2, reports that as a boy he saw a ninety-year-old man brought to court for nonpayment of the tax.

95. The stater equals the value of a shekel, that is, payment for two.

96. Note that immediately before the story of the tax Jesus predicts that he will be "delivered into the hands of men" who will kill him. The very general designation "men," which Matthew got from Mark (9:31), suggests the governing authorities as a whole, including the imperial authorities who eventually receive the tax collected by the local Jewish tax collectors. See Davies, *Setting,* 391.

97. Davies and Allison, *Matthew 8–17,* 742; see also Horbury, "Temple Tax," 282.

98. R. Bauckham, "The Coin in the Fish's Mouth," in D. Wenham and C. Blomberg, *The Miracles of Jesus,* Gospel Perspectives 6 (Sheffield: JSOT Press, 1986), 230.

99. David Daube, "Temple Tax," in E. P. Sanders, ed., *Jesus, the Gospels, and the Church: Essays in Honor of William R. Farmer* (Macon, Ga.: Mercer, 1987), 121–34, and in *Appeasement or Resistance and Other Essays on New Testament Judaism* (Berkeley: University of California Press, 1987), 39–58.

100. Hugh Montefiore, "Jesus and the Temple Tax," *New Testament Studies* 11 (1964–65): 60–71; Horbury, "Temple Tax," 282–84.

101. Richard Horsley, *Jesus and the Spiral of Violence: Popular Jewish Resistance in Roman Palestine* (San Francisco: Harper, 1987), 279–84.

102. Gnilka, *Matthäusevangelium,* 2:118; Luz, *Matthäus (Mt 8–17),* 536.

103. William Thompson, *Matthew's Advice to a Divided Community (Matt 17:22–18:35),* AnBib 44 (Rome: Biblical Institute, 1970), 56.

104. Gnilka, *Matthäusevangelium,* 2:116.

105. Thompson, *Divided Community,* 56—58 and 61.

106. Gnilka (*Matthäusevangelium,* 2:116—18) interprets the story as a declaration of freedom from Judaism and the Temple by Matthew's group, even as it complies outwardly. Gnilka's interest in "freedom" in this context is a modern concern, not entirely proper to Matthew in his first-century setting.

107. In this interpretation, Jesus and his disciples are identified with the king's family, that is, Israel, who don't have to pay the tax. See Davies and Allison, *Matthew 8–17,* 744—45; Horbury, "Temple Tax," 282—84; and Bauckham, "Coin," 223.

108. See Harrington, *Matthew,* 262; Rolf Walker, *Die Heilsgeschichte im ersten Evangelium,* FRLANT 91 (Göttingen: Vandenhoeck, 1967), 102–3; and Montefiore, "Temple Tax," on the Matthean context of the teaching.

109. Tribute was usually a set sum paid by a community as a whole. Community leaders often had the responsibility for collecting the tax and sending it to Rome, though sometimes individuals had to register and pay yearly or periodically. See Schürer, Vermes, et al. *History,* 401—5. The tax is usually understood as a head tax *(tributum capitis);* see Gnilka, *Matthäusevangelium,* 2:247. For a review of Roman taxation in Israel, see F. F. Bruce, "Render to Caesar," in Bammel and Moule, *Jesus and the Politics of His Day,* 252—54.

110. At the narrative level, Herodians are most likely supporters of Herod Antipas.

111. For a review of coins and an argument that a large-size, second series Tiberian denarius may be the coin in question, see H. St. J. Hart, "The Coin of 'Render unto Caesar . . .' (A Note on Some Aspects of Mark 12:13—17; Matt. 22:15—22; Luke 20:20—26)," in Ernst Bammel and C. F. D. Moule, eds., *Jesus and the Politics of His Day* (Cambridge: Cambridge University Press, 1984).

112. Those who were in favor of another revolt against Rome would have resisted the tax, but they were probably not numerous in the late first century. The pressures which led to the Bar Kosiba War (132—35) took another forty years or so to build up.

There is general agreement that the core saying, "Render to Caesar the things that are Caesar's and to God the things that are God's," goes back to Jesus. Bultmann (*History of Synoptic Tradition,* 26) says that the story is a unified, pre-Markan apothegm. Those who place the saying in the life of Jesus create a number of different scenarios and problems to which it is the response. See examples in Bruce, "Render to Caesar," 259—62. J. Duncan M. Derrett, *Law in the New Testament* (London: Darton, Longman, 1970), 313ff., has an extensive review of the literature.

113. See Neusner, *From Politics to Piety: The Emergence of Pharisaic Judaism* (Englewood Cliffs: Prentice-Hall, 1973), and *Evidence;* Saldarini, *Pharisees;* also Overman, *Matthew's Gospel.*

114. In the wording of Jesus' teaching, Matthew and Luke assume the traditional Jewish custom, that a man divorces his wife. Mark and Paul treat the case of the wife divorcing her husband because this practice was known to their gentile audiences. In 1 Cor. 7:10—15, Paul uses two different verbs, "sep-

arate" and "divorce." However, he uses them once each of the woman and of the man; thus he probably does not make a distinction, and thus does not preserve Jewish custom. See O. Larry Yarbrough, *Not Like the Gentiles: Marriage Rules in the Letters of Paul,* SBLDS 80 (Atlanta: Scholars, 1985), 110–11, and the literature there, as well as Hans Conzelmann, *1 Corinthians: A Commentary on the First Epistle to the Corinthians* (Philadelphia: Fortress, 1975), 120.

115. W. D. Davies and Dale C. Allison, *The Gospel according to St. Matthew,* vol. 1: *Chapters 1–7,* ICC (Edinburgh: Clark, 1988), 273, say that the Pharisees see divorce as a positive command.

116. For example, on the basis of Matthew's text, Davies and Allison (ibid., 529–30), are unable to decide whether only separation or both separation and remarriage are allowed by Matthew in cases of unchastity *(porneia).*

117. Matthew is following Q, which is found in a variant form in Luke 16:18.

118. Mark raises the divorce questions and immediately has Jesus elicit a summary of the biblical practice assumed in Deuteronomy, that a man can write a bill of divorce and send his wife away. This question and answer instructs his gentile community in traditional Jewish practice, which is then modified by Jesus. Matthew assumes that his Jewish community knows the rules and asks a precise question about grounds for divorce, one of which (unchastity) he allows.

119. Rabbinic exegesis holds that there is no "before and after" in Scripture, though some texts still argue on that basis. Paul uses the priority argument concerning Abraham's faith and circumcision (Genesis 12 and 15 prior to Genesis 17 in the argument of Romans 4).

120. Mark (12:5) has *Moses* write a *commandment* allowing divorce. But commandments come from God, so Matthew has Moses allow the practice without sanctioning it as a commandment.

121. Mark (10:10–12) has Jesus teach his disciples in private that remarriage is adultery. However, in Matthew Jesus is a public and authoritative Jewish teacher defending his interpretations among other Jewish teachers. Mark ends with the interpretation of Genesis as the final teaching for his community. Matthew ends his controversy with his oppenents by drawing from his interpretation of the Bible a new rule to govern marriage relationships. Matthew then has Jesus instruct his disciples privately about another pertinent and practical question, whether it is possible to live without remarriage.

122. Paul allows divorce and remarriage when the non-Christian spouse of a newly converted Christian leaves a preexisting marriage (1 Cor. 7:12–16).

123. Matt. 5:32 has *parektos logou porneias,* perhaps modeled on the phrase in Deut. 24:1, ʿ*erwat dabar.* Both phrases mean the same thing.

124. For a review of the extensive literature on the divorce texts, see Bruce Vawter, "Divorce and the New Testament," *Catholic Biblical Quarterly* 39 (1977): 528–42. Ulrich Luz, *Matthew 1–7* (Minneapolis: Augsburg, 1989; orig. German 1985), 301, comments on the flood of literature.

125. Marcus Bockmuehl, "Matthew 5.32; 19.9 in the Light of Pre-Rabbinic Halakhah," *New Testament Studies* 35 (1989): 291–95.

126. The biblical punishment for a "virgin" bride who was discovered to be not a virgin was stoning (Deut. 22:21–22).

127. CD 5:7–10. See Joseph A. Fitzmyer, "The Matthean Divorce Texts and Some New Palestinian Evidence," originally in *Theological Studies* 37 (1976): 197–226; revised version in Fitzmyer's *To Advance the Gospel: New Testament Studies* (New York: Crossroad, 1981), 79–111. Fitzmyer shows certainly that *porneia* could refer to consanguinous unions (97). However, this solution is beset with problems. Nothing in Matthew's narrative indicates an interest in this issue and the dispute in CD 5:7–10 does not seem to have been widely discussed. The Temple Scroll is also relevant (11QTemple 57:17–19). It says that the king shall not remarry unless his wife dies. This is probably a rejection of polygamy, and it may be applicable only to the king. These texts do show that marriage and divorce were a controversial topic in the Second Temple period. See also Davies and Allison, *Matthew 1–7*, 529–30; they opt finally for adultery, but say a firm decision between adultery or incest as the meaning of *porneia* is not possible.

128. See further discussion in b. Git. 90a.

129. Sifre Deut. 269 (Louis Finkelstein, ed., *Siphre ad Deuteronomium* [1939; reprinted New York: Jewish Theological Seminary, 1969], 288).

130. This procedure for dating rabbinic views is found in Neusner, *Pharisees*, 3: 180–238; see esp. 205.

131. Fitzmyer, "Divorce Texts," 96. Fitzmyer's interpretation is plausible but not certain since the texts are less than lucid in their teaching. See the contrary positions cited by Fitzmyer. The point here is that these issues are a matter of intense and sophisticated exegesis and discussion.

132. Davies and Allison, *Matthew 1–7*, 91–92.

133. The interpretation of the saying about eunuchs for the kingdom of heaven (19:10–12) has been controversial for centuries. It may refer to celibacy, to remarriage after divorce, or to the death of a spouse.

134. For example, Ben Sira 23:9–11; Epictetus, *Enchiridion* 33.5; "Avoid an oath, altogether if you can, and if not, then as much as possible under the circumstances." Later, the Babylonian Talmud counsels similarly: "Accustom not yourself to vows for sooner or later you will swear false oaths" (b. Ned. 20a).

135. 11QTemple 53:9–54:7.

136. Josephus, *Ant.* 2.7.6 §135. Josephus notes, consistent with the Covenant of Damascus, that they swore tremendous oaths on admission to the group (2.7.7 §139). Because of their prohibition of public oaths, Herod excused the Essenes from taking an oath of loyalty (*Ant.* 15.10.5 §371).

137. Philo, *Quod Omnis Probus Liber Sit* 84.

138. Philo, *De Decalogo* 84 ff; *De Spec. Leg.* 2.2ff., suggests swearing by one's parents, parts of the cosmos, and so on, rather than by the Creator. In this, he gives the opposite advice to Matthew (23:16–22).

139. CD 6:27–7:2, 15:1–5. See the analysis by Lawrence Schiffman, *Sectarian Law in the Dead Sea Scrolls: Courts, Testimony and the Penal Code*, BJS 33 (Chico: Scholars, 1983), 133–54.

140. Mishnah Shebuot is mostly taken up with judicial oaths and their lia-bilities. Nonjudicial oaths are treated in 3:6 on an oath to nullify a command-ment and 3:7ff. on rash vain oaths. An oath *(shevûʿāh)* is a commitment of the person to do or avoid something, especially to tell the truth in a judicial pro-ceeding. Mishnah Nedarim discusses the forms, validity, and exact scope of a wide variety of vows. A vow *(neder)* is a dedication of something to God and thus a commitment not to benefit from it.

141. See the comparison of rabbinic with Greco-Roman concerns in Saul Lieberman, *Greek in Jewish Palestine: Studies in the Life and Manners of Jewish Palestine in the II–IV Centuries* (New York: Jewish Theological Seminary, 1942), 115–43. For an overview of vows and oaths, see Sanders, *Law,* 51–57.

142. Philo, *De Spec. Leg.* 2.5; m. Sheb. 4:13. Such oaths are encouraged by Philo.

143. "The life of one's head" is an oath formula argued about in m. Sanh 3:2. In m. Ned. 1:3 and t. Ned 1:3, a number of words and phrases connected to the Temple, including "Jerusalem," can be used to dedicate (vow) some-thing to the Temple, or "as if" to the Temple and thus remove it from one's own use. See the discussion of *qorban* below.

144. Similarly, Matt. 23:23 mocks the scribes and Pharisees for tithing herbs because it leads them to neglect more important parts of the Torah. How-ever, in the end, tithing is not abolished.

145. Davies and Allison, *Matthew 1–7,* 535–36, argue that the prohibition of oaths (5:33) is not absolute.

146. Luz, *Matthew 1–7,* 318; see 2 Cor. 1:17–18, where Paul defends him-self against vacillating and denies he is an untrustworthy, insincere person who says both "yes, yes" and "no, no." That one's word should be reliable is stan-dard ethical and wisdom teaching. See for example b. Hul. 94a. The dangers of the tongue and untruthfulness are a standard *topos* of Hellenistic rhetoric and moral literature. See James 3:1–12.

147. James 5:12 does the same. "Yes, yes" and No, no" can also be oath formulas. The short text of 2 Enoch 49:1 has Enoch swearing an oath. The long text tries to rationalize this away, probably under Christian influence. (2 Enoch is known from late manuscripts and has had a long history of transmission. It may contain early material, but separating it is difficult.) In the long text, Enoch denies he swears an oath by heaven, earth, or any creature (= Matt. 5:33?) and then suggests that an oath using "yes, yes" and "no, no" be used. It is doubtful that Matthew understood "yes, yes" and "no, no" as an oath for-mula. Much later the Babylonian Talmud discusses whether a simple yes or no is an oath or whether the word must be repeated twice. Raba's argument that the words must be repeated seems to be definitive (b. Sheb. 36a).

148. See Sophie M. Laws, *The Epistle of James,* Harper's NT Commentaries (San Francisco: Harper, 1980), 218–24; Martin Dibelius and Heinrich Greeven, *James: A Commentary on the Epistle of James,* Hermeneia (Phila-delphia: Fortress, 1976), 248–51, for full treatments of this passage and all its problems and parallels.

149. Luz, *Matthew 1–7,* 313–16, says that all oaths are forbidden; Davies

and Allison, *Matthew 1–7;* 535–36, seem to imply that oaths are not totally forbidden, but on p. 538 they say that they are.

150. Imprecision in the use of oath and vow formulas was common. A. I. Baumgarten, "Qorban and the Pharisaic *Paradosis,*" *Journal of the Ancient Near Eastern Society* 16–17 (1984–85): 6, is correct to distinguish three usages of *qorban:* the strict meaning of something actually dedicated to the Temple, the loose usage for something forbidden to oneself or another by a vow, and an imprecise usage for an oath, rather than a vow.

151. Josephus, *Contra Apionem* 1.166–67. See Stern, *Greek and Latin Authors,* 1:12–23.

152. See B. Mazar, "The Excavations South and West of the Temple Mount Jerusalem: The Herodian Period," *Biblical Archaeologist* 33 (1970): 55. On ceramic and metal containers with *qorban* inscribed on them, see m. Ma'as. Shen. 4:10–11. On the ossuary inscription, see Joseph A. Fitzmyer, "The Aramaic Qorban Inscription from Jebel Hallet et-Turi and Mk 7:11/Mt 15:5," *Journal of Biblical Literature* 78 (1959): 60–65; revised and reprinted in *Essays on the Semitic Background of the New Testament* (London: Chapman, 1971), 93–100. The inscription reads, "Everything which a man will find to his profit in this ossuary is an offering to God [קרבן אלה] from the one within it."

153. M. Naz. 2:1–3; m. Ned. 1:2–4; 2:2, 5; 3:2, 5; 9:7; 11:5. The Mishnah contains a wide variety of popular expressions used for vows and oaths. Lieberman, *Greek in Palestine,* 120.

154. We have no writings from the Pharisees and cannot assume that later rabbinic literature as a whole faithfully reflects their teachings. It is clear, nevertheless, that they had specific traditions about how Jewish life was to be lived, which differed from those of other Jewish groups (Saldarini, *Pharisees,* chaps. 10, 12, and on Josephus' views, chap 6). See also Baumgarten, "Pharisaic *Paradosis.*"

155. In Mark, Jesus immediately quotes Scripture against his opponents (7:6–7) and then follows up with the legal dilemma. He finishes his attack with a broad generalization: "And many such things you do" (7:13). Matthew follows the order of a legal dispute. First, the attack on the opponent's interpretation and then, on the basis of that inadequate interpretation, an attack on the opponent himself, using a prophetic rebuke.

156. The verb in the second clause also has a technical meaning in legal argument, and so the clause simultaneously means "and do not have any support [from Scripture]."

157. Baumgarten, "Qorban," 10–12. See also Jacob Neusner, *A History of the Mishnaic Law of Women,* 5 vols. (Leiden: Brill, 1979–80), 5:107–24.

158. The tone of the attack suggests, but does not clearly entail, that the reason for the man's vow was revenge against his parents. A person is imagined as telling his father or mother, "What you would have gained from me is given to God" (15:5). If this implication is correct, the Pharisees are also charged with aiding a miscarriage of justice. It is unlikely that the Pharisees supported this position in the first century. See Sanders, *Jewish Law,* 56–57.

159. Mark's version of the charge is more rhetorical and less precise. After

the citation of Isaiah, Jesus continues, "'You leave the commandment of God and hold fast to human tradition.' And he said to them, 'You have a fine way of rejecting the commandment of God in order to keep your tradition" (Mark 7:8–9). Matthew focuses more sharply on the behavioral dilemma, transgressing a commandment to observe a tradition.

160. Note that the Sermon on the Mount (5:21–48) contrasts what was said to the ancients and what Jesus says, with the implication that Jesus' teaching is a more adequate interpretation of God's will and teaching given in Scripture. Here the tradition itself is attacked as unscriptural.

161. Matthew does not cite the Hebrew term transliterated into Greek as *korban*, in contrast to Mark, who cites and then translates it (Mark 7:11). Presumably Matthew's audience knows these technical terms in both Hebrew and Greek.

162. Baumgarten, "Qorban," 12–16.

163. See the discussion in Davies and Allison, *Matthew 8–17*, 537–38. They conclude mildly that gentile observance of the law and circumcision is unlikely and that gentile believers kept a minimum number of commandments, sufficient to allow fellowship with Jews.

164. Jacob Jervell, *Luke and the People of God: A New Look at Luke-Acts* (Minneapolis: Augsburg, 1972), 135, points out that Paul's teaching on law and circumcision was not fully accepted by Luke-Acts or Matthew in the late first century.

165. See Roger Mohrlang, *Matthew and Paul: A Comparison of Ethical Perspectives* (Cambridge: Cambridge University Press, 1984), 44–45, for the view that gentiles in Matthew's group were circumcised.

166. John J. Collins, *Between Athens: Jewish Identity in the Hellenistic Diaspora* (New York: Crossroad, 1983), chap. 4, esp. 163–68.

167. Ibid., 211–18; Sanders, *Jewish Law*, 259, 275, notes that Joseph and Aseneth is nonexclusivist.

168. John J. Collins, "A Symbol of Otherness: Circumcision and Salvation in the First Century," in Jacob Neusner and Ernest S. Frerichs, eds., *"To See Ourselves as Others See Us": Christians, Jews, "Others" in Late Antiquity* (Chico: Scholars, 1985), 176. For the possibility that circumcision may not have been universally required, see also Scot McKnight, *A Light among the Gentiles: Jewish Missionary Activity in the Second Temple Period* (Minneapolis: Fortress, 1991), 79–82; Burton L. Visotzky, "Prolegomenon to the Study of Jewish-Christianities in Rabbinic Literature," *Association of Jewish Studies Review* 14 (1989): 56. For a contrary view, see Lawrence Schiffman, *Who Was a Jew? Rabbinic and Halakhic Perspectives on the Jewish-Christian Schism* (Hoboken: Ktav, 1985), 25.

169. Collins, "Symbol," 174–77.

170. For an older view, see K. Kohler, "Circumcision," *Jewish Encyclopedia* (1901–6), 4:94; and more recently, Neil McEleney, "Conversion, Circumcision, and the Law," *New Testament Studies* 20 (1974): 328–33. Schiffman, *Who Was a Jew*, 23–25, defends the standard position on the necessity of circumcision. J. Nolland, "Uncircumcised Proselytes?" *Journal for the Study of Judaism* 12 (1981): 173–79, argues against McEleney.

171. Collins, "Symbol," 172–73; Jonathan Z. Smith, *Imagining Religion: From Babylon to Jonestown* (Chicago: University of Chicago Press, 1982), 12–14.

172. Collins, "Symbol," 171–74.

173. Jacob Neusner, *Judaism and Its Social Metaphors* (Cambridge: Cambridge University Press, 1989), 217.

174. B. Yeb. 46a-48b (on m. Yeb. 4:12). There is no evidence for immersion as a requirement for conversion before the first century, and even in the first century it is controversial. See Schiffman, *Who Was a Jew,* 25–30; Bernard J. Bamberger, *Proselytism in the Talmudic Period* (reprint, New York: Ktav, 1968; orig. ed., 1939), 43–44.

175. For a brief discussion of these and other passages, see McEleney, "Conversion," who argues that they indicate the acceptance of uncircumcised Jews by some, and Nolland, "Uncircumcised," who argues against that interpretation.

176. McEleney, "Conversion," 328, suggests that the lenient and strict advice given Izates shows that circumcision could be omitted in the views of some. Nolland, "Uncircumcised," 192–94, and Schiffman, *Who Was a Jew,* 25, stress the presumption underlying the story, that circumcision is normal and required for a Jew.

177. The ambiguities of the story are well assessed by Collins, "Symbol," 177–79.

178. Ibid., 170–71; for a review of the evidence and basic bibliography, 179–85. The phenomenon of gentiles closely related to the synagogue is crucial here. The controversy over whether they were called "God-fearers" and whether this group formed a recognized category in Jewish social thought and practice is secondary. See also the brief discussion in chap. 4 above.

179. Alan F. Segal, *Paul the Convert: The Apostolate and Apostasy of Saul the Pharisee* (New Haven: Yale University Press, 1990), 204–5, argues that Paul modeled his teaching, that circumcision is not required of gentiles who believe in Jesus, on the acceptance of God-fearers in the synagogues as righteous believers.

180. J. Andrew Overman, "Heroes and Villains in Palestinian Lore: Matthew's Use of Traditional Jewish Polemic in the Passion Narrative," *SBL Seminar Papers 1990* (Atlanta: Scholars, 1990), 593.

181. Ibid., 593–97; Overman, *Matthew's Gospel,* 124–40.

182. Ernst Käsemann, *New Testament Questions of Today* (Philadelphia: Fortress, 1969), 85, sees that Matt. 5:17–20 unambiguously demands obedience to the whole Torah. But since he has detached Matthew from Judaism, he is forced to argue that Matthew is reinterpreting these Jewish-Christian sayings. If Matthew is understood as a Jewish believer-in-Jesus who supports adherence to the law, then in 5:17–20, Matthew is defending his position against Christians who think the law is abolished or greatly changed and against Jews who charge him with failing to teach and keep the law.

For a review of recent interpretations of law in Matthew and the various positions taken, see Klyne Snodgrass, "Matthew and the Law," *SBL Seminar*

Papers 1988 (Atlanta, Scholars, 1988), 536–54. He concentrates appropriately on Matthew's hermeneutic principles and his relating of one law to another (541, 554). Snodgrass's bibliography on law in Matthew, on 5:17–20 and the antitheses in 5:21–48, and on the Sermon on the Mount is extensive. The interpretation of these key passages here is made in relationship with the analysis of Matthew's legal teachings above, which does not pursue, all the arguments and views found in the literature.

183. Chauvanistic Christian comparisons of Judaism and Christianity often arrogate to themselves the love commandment and gratuitously attribute to Judaism a legalistic or spiritually dead adherence to the law. Suffice it to say that in Judaism, as in Matthew, the love commandments and regulations for Sabbath, oaths, and so on, come from the same law, the Torah, which reveals the will of God. The Dead Sea Scrolls, for example, speak of loving God and ones' fellow community members, of covenant renewal, justification by God, repentance from sins, and community life, in terms similar to Matthew's.

184. The nature of the enemies and of nonretaliation has long been controversial. Horsley, *Jesus*, 261–75, suggests that village relationships are at issue and that Jesus promotes solidarity in the face of difficult economic and political circumstances. Davies and Allison, *Matthew 1–7*, 550–51, identify the enemies with Roman and Jewish persecutors and make the contrast between villagers and outsiders.

185. Davies and Allison, *Matthew 1–7*, 508–9, connect the perfect of 5:48 with the greater righteousness in 5:20.

186. On the myriad positions concerning the antitheses, see ibid., 505–9, and Snodgrass, "Matthew and Law," 539 n. 21. Snodgrass correctly emphasizes the integral union of law and interpretation in Matthew's teaching.

187. Overman, *Gospel of Matthew*, 87–89, understands the antitheses as an attack against Matthew's early rabbinic opponents. John Kampen, "A Reexamination of the Relationship between Matthew 5:21–48 and the Dead Sea Scrolls," *SBL Seminar Papers 1990* (Atlanta: Scholars, 1990), 34–59, contrasts Matthean with Essene teaching. H. J. Schoeps, "Jésus et la loi juive," *Revue histoire et de philosphie religieuses* 33 (1953): 1–20, argues that Jesus reinterpreted Jewish law contrary to the Pharisees so that the poor could live it more easily. Benedict T. Viviano, *Study as Worship: Aboth and the New Testament*, SJLA 26 (Leiden: Brill, 1978), 158–95, agrees with Schoeps. Such generalizations are difficult to prove concerning either Jesus' teaching or the Pharisees'. Matthew's late first-century interpretation of Jesus shows no such interest.

188. Tikva Frymer-Kensky, "Jesus and the Law," in R. Joseph Hoffmann and Gerald A. Larue, eds., *Jesus in History and Myth* (Buffalo: Prometheus, 1986), 131.

189. The (ironically) polemical thrust of the love commandment is expounded by Overman, *Gospel of Matthew*, 84–85, and by Terence L. Donaldson, "The Law that 'Hangs' (Mt. 22:40): Rabbinic Formulation and Matthean Social World," *SBL Seminar Papers 1990* (Atlanta: Scholars, 1990), 14–33.

Chapter Seven

1. The neglect of God in New Testament theologies and Christologies has been noted by Nils Dahl in a number of articles reprinted in *Jesus the Christ: The Historical Origins of Christological Doctrine* (Minneapolis: Fortress, 1991). See esp. "The Neglected Factor in New Testament Theology" and "Sources of Christological Language."

2. Ibid., 124, 131, 134.

3. In approaching Christology from the Jewish context of Matthew, I am not foreclosing subsequent Christian reflection, which led to the elaborate Christology of the early church councils. Rather, I am attempting to read Matthew as a first-century narrative, in context, without reference to its history of interpretation.

4. The phrase is from Brian Nolan, *The Royal Son of God: The Christology of Matthew 1–2 in the Setting of the Gospel,* (OBO 23 (Göttingen: Vandenhoeck, 1979), 243.

5. Traditional New Testament theology has analyzed the meanings of the titles attributed to Jesus in the gospels and letters and separated them into Jewish and Hellenistic titles. See two classic studies, by Reginald H. Fuller, *The Foundations of New Testament Christology* (New York: Scribner, 1965), and Ferdinand Hahn, *The Titles of Jesus in Christology: Their History in Early Christianity* (Cleveland: World, 1969; orig. German, 1963). More recent studies have focused on narrative Christologies and, more important, have overcome the artificial distinction between Jewish and Hellenistic titles.

6. I am speaking of Jesus as he appears as a narrative character. Nolan, *Royal Son,* 244, speaks of Matthew's Christology as a "situation Christology," prompted by forces external to Matthew's group and by questions arising within it. Martin Hengel, *The Son of God* (Philadelphia: Fortress, 1976), 58, suggests further that New Testament Christology bears the stamp of Jesus' activities and relationships with his original followers.

7. Both within Matthew's narrative and in New Testament Christology in general, emphasis should be put on the variety of understandings of Jesus and the interplay among them, not on conceptually distinct titles. See Hengel, *Son of God,* 57; Marinus de Jonge, *Christology in Context: The Earliest Christian Response to Jesus* (Philadelphia: Westminster, 1988); W. D. Davies and Dale C. Allison, *The Gospel according to St. Matthew,* vol. 2: *Chapters 8–17* (Edinburgh: Clark, 1991), 5. The main lines for study of Matthew's Christology were laid down by Jack Dean Kingsbury in *Matthew: Structure, Christology, Kingdom* (Philadelphia: Fortress, 1975), and in a number of articles. Kingsbury stresses the subordination of all titles to "Son of God" and the high Christology implied by that title. While drawing on Kingsbury's analyses, we will stress the mutuality of the titles and their roots in Judaism. Though Christology quickly became a problem for Jewish believers-in-Jesus, when Matthew wrote, there was no articulated and theologically sophisticated set of claims for Jesus that could be called a Christology, with all the Trinitarian overtones that term implies.

8. Dahl, *Jesus the Christ,* 133–34, stresses the varied uses to which language about Jesus is put.

9. For the infancy narrative (Matt. 1–2) and its Christology, see Fred L. Horton, "Parenthetical Pregnancy: The Conception and Birth of Jesus in Matthew 1:18–25," *SBL Seminar Papers 1987* (Atlanta: Scholars, 1987), 175–89; Nolan, *Royal Son;* Raymond E. Brown, *The Birth of the Messiah: A Commentary on the Infancy Narratives in Matthew and Luke* (New York: Doubleday, 1977) and "Gospel Infancy Research from 1976 to 1986: Part I (Matthew)," *Catholic Biblical Quarterly* 48 (1986): 468–83.

10. Scholars argue whether the title "the book of the genesis of Jesus" refers to the genealogy, to chapters 1 and 2, or to the whole gospel.

11. Jack Dean Kingsbury, *Matthew as Story* (Philadelphia: Fortress, 1986; 2d ed. 1988), 43–44. Characters refer to Jesus by his name only five times (21:11; 26:69, 71; 27:17, 22). The characters never address him directly as Jesus. He is referred to by his name "Jesus" in the inscription on the cross (27:37).

12. For a careful assessment of the complex development of belief in Jesus as Messiah, see George W. MacRae, "Messiah and Gospel," in Jacob Neusner et al., eds., *Judaisms and Their Messiahs at the Turn of the Christian Era* (Cambridge: Cambridge University Press, 1987), 169–85.

13. For a review of Second Temple literature, see George W. E. Nickelsburg, "Salvation without and with a Messiah: Developing Beliefs in Writings Ascribed to Enoch," in Neusner et al. *Judaisms.* This volume contains an excellent series of articles on the concrete messianic ideas found in various Jewish and Christian documents of the period.

14. See 1QS 9:11 for the prophet (like Moses), and 11QMelch for Melchisedek.

15. See D. Verseput, "The Role and Meaning of the 'Son of God' Title in Matthew's Gospel," *New Testament Studies* 33 (1987): 532–56, who notes that the claim to be Davidic Messiah arouses opposition.

16. Matthew claims that the genealogy is broken into groups of fourteen, though only forty-one names are listed. Fourteen may be simply a multiple of seven or be based on the numerical value of David in Hebrew *(dwd)*.

17. Jesus is legally and socially a member of the house of David through Joseph, who is a "son of David" (1:20). For a full exposition of first-century views of the son of David and their articulation in Matthew's narrative, see Nolan, *Royal Son,* esp. 159–70 and 170–200. Nolan stresses the overlap of Messiah, son of David, and Son of God (the king) in Matthew's presentation of Jesus.

18. Dennis Duling, "The Therapeutic Son of David: An Element in Matthew's Christological Apologetic," *New Testament Studies* 24 (1977–78): 392–410.

19. The irregularity of Jesus' birth is prepared by the naming of four women in the genealogy, all of them irregular in one way or another: Tamar (Gen. 38), Rahab (Josh. 2), Ruth (Ruth), and Solomon's mother, Bathsheba, the wife of Uriah (2 Kings 11–12).

20. Verseput, "Son of God."

21. In Mark (12:35), Jesus asks the question about the Messiah being David's son and identifies it as a scribal teaching. Here, as usual, Matthew turns

the discussion into a scholastic dispute between Jesus and the Pharisees. The dispute about a seeming contradiction in Scripture, in which Matthew has Jesus silence his opponents, prepares for the climactic attack on the scribes and Pharisees in the next chapter (chap. 23). On contradictions in Scripture, see Nils Dahl, "Contradictions in Scripture," *Studies in Paul* (Minneapolis: Augsburg, 1977), 159–77.

22. Mark 12:36; Luke 20:42–43; Acts 2:34–35; 1 Cor. 15:25; Heb. 1:3, 13; plus many allusions. On the use made of this passage, see D. M. Hay, *Glory on the Right Hand: Psalm 110 in Early Christianity*, SBLMS 18 (Nashville: Abingdon, 1973).

23. For the development of the tradition that the Messiah is David's son, see Joseph A. Fitzmyer, "Son of David and Mt 22:41–46," in *Essays on the Semitic Background of the New Testament* (London: Chapman, 1971), 113–26, and Brown, *Birth of the Messiah*, 503–12, and the extensive literature cited there.

24. When needy people petition Jesus to heal for them, they call him both son of David and Lord (9:27; 15:23; 20:30–31).

25. Luke 3:23–38 traces Jesus' ancestry back to Adam and God to emphasize his solidarity with all humanity.

26. The manipulation of membership among the sons of Abraham is matched by the genealogical manipulation of membership among the sons of David.

27. Kingsbury, *Matthew*, 42, notes that Matthew uses "Son of God" twenty-three times, eleven of them redactionally. In addition he argues (40–83) that "Son of God" is central to Matthew's understanding of Jesus. His point is valid, but his goal of subordinating or even collapsing other titles into "Son of God" destroys the rich, connotative texture of Matthew's understanding of Jesus. Nolan, *Royal Son*, is much more true to Matthew in stressing the interplay and interdependence of Messiah, son of David, and Son of God for an understanding of Jesus.

28. Margaret Ann Hannan, "The God that Matthew Preaches" (M.A. thesis, Boston College, 1991), 76, counts forty-four instances of "Father" referring to God in Matthew. Following the hints of Dahl, "Neglected Factor," in *Jesus the Christ*, she stresses the importance of theology proper, that is, an understanding of Matthew's view of God, for the development of an accurate Christology.

29. For fictive kinship as central to Matthew's group, see chap. 5 above. God is referred to as the disciples' Father in 19 places, most of them unique to Matthew, especially in chaps. 5–6, 10, and 18, where instructions concerning communal behavior are given (Kingsbury, *Matthew*, 55).

30. The high priest's rejection is prepared for by the parable of the vineyard, in which the tenants kill the son (21:33–46). There the chief priests and Pharisees perceive that Jesus is speaking about them.

31. For a convenient review of the Second Temple literature, see Gerhard Delling, "Die Bezeichnung 'Söhne Gottes' in der jüdischen Literatur der hellenistisch-römischen Zeit," in J. Jervell and W. A. Meeks, eds., *God's Christ and His People: Studies in Honor of Nils Alstrup Dahl* (Oslo: Universitetsforl., 1977), 18–28; and Hengel, *Son of God*.

32. 4Q174, also called 4QFlor or 4QEschMidr, that is, Florilegium or Eschatological Midrash. See George J. Brooke, *Exegesis at Qumran. 4QFlorilegium in its Jewish Context*, JSOTSS 29 (Sheffield: University of Sheffield, 1985), for a full interpretation.

33. 4QpsDan arᵃ or 4Q246. This text was presented by J. T. Milik in a public lecture at Harvard in 1972 and published by Joseph A. Fitzmyer, "The Contribution of Qumran Aramaic to the Study of the New Testament," *New Testament Studies* 20 (1973–74): 382–407; slightly revised in *A Wandering Aramean: Collected Aramaic Essays* (Missoula: Scholars, 1979), 85–113. Page references are to the revised version.

34. The Greek more cautiously translates, "You will then be *like* a son of the Most High."

35. Dale C. Allison, "The Son of God as Israel: A Note on Matthean Christology," *Irish Biblical Studies* 9 (1987): 74–81, shows that the parallels between Jesus and Israel in the first four chapters are crucial to Matthew's understanding of sonship and Jesus' relationship to the Father.

36. Philo, *De Spec. Leg.* 1.58 § 315–18.

37. For date, nature of the text, and translation, see C. Burchard, "Joseph and Aseneth: A New Translation and Introduction," in James Charlesworth, ed., *Old Testament Pseudepigrapha* (Garden City, N.Y.: Doubleday, 1985), 2:177–247.

38. The reading "firstborn son" is uncertain. See ibid., 233.

39. Ibid., 229.

40. P. Kidd. 1:8 (81c middle).

41. The evidence is gathered by Geza Vermes, *Jesus the Jew: A Historian's Reading of the Gospels* (London: Collins, 1973), 206–13. Vermes's attempt to reconstruct a first-century, Galilean, charismatic type of Judaism from rabbinic sources is weak methodologically. However, the general thrust of his argument is correct. Many of the ways of understanding God's activity through and relations with religious leaders endured for centuries.

42. For the teacher as an example for his students, see chap. 5 above.

43. See Benno Przybylski, *Righteousness in Matthew and His World of Thought*, SNTSMS 41 (Cambridge: Cambridge University Press, 1980), 93–94, on righteousness; and John Meier, *Law and History in Matthew's Gospel*, AnBib 71 (Rome: Biblical Institute, 1976), 76–80, on fulfillment. "All righteousness" refers to all of God's plan according to both Meier and Ulrich Luz, *Matthew 1–7* (Minneapolis: Augsburg, 1989), 178.

44. Jesus defends his disciples for not fasting like the Pharisees and disciples of John the Baptist (9:14–17) by affirming that they will fast in the future. The principle that fasting is normal and required remains secure.

45. The Greek word, *kraspedon*, can mean hem or edge as well as tassel. The crowds in Gennesaret touch the tassels or hem in both Mark (6:56) and Matthew (14:36). The wording of the sentence makes it clear in this instance that the emphasis is on cures caused by touching just the edge of his garment. But in the Septuagint, *kraspedon* refers to the tassels (Hebrew *ṣîṣît*) mandated by Num. 15:38–39 and Deut. 22:12, and that meaning is very likely here. The

woman says to herself that she need only touch the garment, but Matthew has her touch the tassel, contrary to Mark, who has the woman touch Jesus' garment (5:27). For the early date of phylacteries (Deut. 6:8), which have been found at Qumran, see Jeff Tigay, "Tefillin," in *Encylopedia Mikrait* (in Hebrew), 8:883–95. See also the Letter of Aristeas 159, and Josephus, *Ant.* 4.8.13 §213.

46. See E. P. Sanders, *Jewish Law from Jesus to the Mishnah* (London: SCM; Philadelphia: Trinity, 1990), chap. 1, esp. 90–96, for an exhaustive review of the issues in the context of the historical Jesus.

47. The cleansing of the Temple (21:12–13), in which Jesus drives out the merchants and overturns the tables of the moneychangers, is the most striking of these stories. E. P. Sanders, *Jesus and Judaism* (Philadelphia: Fortress, 1985), chap. 1, assesses this incident as historical and understands it as part of Jesus' attack on the Temple. Matthew does not understand Jesus this way.

48. Attempts to identify Jesus as a rabbi have died out as scholars have accepted the development of rabbis and rabbinic Judaism as a postdestruction phenomenon. Some still attempt to associate Jesus with one or another of the Jewish groups named by Josephus, especially the Pharisees. However, Jewish society was complex and contained many social-religious groups and leaders, not just the few mentioned by Josephus. Jesus was one of these leaders with a popular, relatively unorganized following. Though he had characteristics in common with various people and groups, he should not be categorized with one of the few groups we know about.

49. Davies and Allison, *Matthew 8–17*, 296.

50. G. Bornkamm, "End Expectation and Church in Matthew," in G. Bornkamm, G. Barth, and H. J. Held, eds., *Tradition and Interpretation in Matthew* (Philadelphia: Westminster, 1963), 41; Kingsbury, *Matthew*, 92–93.

51. Kingsbury, *Matthew*, 92–93, makes the point that Matthew is claiming for Jesus a higher authority than that of culturally sanctioned teacher. John Meier, *The Vision of Matthew: Christ, Church, and Morality in the First Gospel* (Ramsey: Paulist, 1979), 45–51, sees the basis for Jesus' authority in his roles as Son of God, Son of Man, and Lord.

52. Later interpretation of Matthew has tended to separate the high status and great authority assigned to Jesus from his careful interpretation of Jewish law. Christology has been emphasized and legal interpretation subjected to a quasi-Pauline critique. This separation of Christology from law, symbolic of the later separation of Christianity from Judaism, is not Matthew's position.

53. For comprehensive studies of the miracles in the gospels, see Gerd Theissen, *The Miracle Stories of the Early Christian Tradition* (Edinburgh: Clark, 1983). Howard C. Kee, in *Medicine, Miracle, and Magic in New Testament Times* (Cambridge: Cambridge University Press, 1986) and *Miracle in the Early Christian World* (New Haven: Yale, 1983), places miracles in their broader cultural context in the Greco-Roman world.

54. For the broad sense in which Matthew uses healing, see Duling, "Therapeutic Son," 393–99.

55. For the function of healings in provoking opposition from the leaders

and offering salvation to the crowds, see Joseph A. Comber, "The Verb 'Therapeuo' in Matthew's Gospel," *Journal of Biblical Literature* 97 (1978): 431–34.

56. See Dennis Duling, "Solomon, Exorcism, and the Son of David," *Harvard Theological Review* 68 (1975): 235–52.

57. Hans-Joachim Held, "Matthew as Interpreter of the Miracle Stories," in Bornkamm et al., *Tradition,* 165–249. Held has been followed generally by many commentators, for example, C. Burger, "Jesu Taten nach Matthäus 8 und 9," *Zeitschrft für Theologie und Kirke* 70 (1973): 272–87; K. Gatzweiler, "Les récits de miracles dans l'evangile selon saint Matthieu," in M. Didier, ed., *L'Évangile selon Matthieu: Rédaction et théologie,* Bib. Eph. Theol. Lov. 29 (Gembloux: Duculot, 1972), 209–20; and Jack Dean Kingsbury, "Observations on the 'Miracle Chapters' of Matthew 8–9," *Catholic Biblical Quarterly* 40 (1978): 559–73.

58. Held, "Miracle Stories," 175–77; 244–46.

59. J. P. Heil, "Significant Aspects of the Healing Miracles in Matthew," *Catholic Biblical Quarterly* 41 (1979): 275–79.

60. Kee, *Medicine, Miracle, Magic,* 188–89.

61. Held, followed by Kingsbury, Heil, and others, attempted to associate groups of miracles in chapters 8–9 with particular theological themes such as Christology and faith. Davies and Allison, *Matthew 8–17,* 3–5, show that Matthew's grouping of the miracles is literary and not thematic. The miracles serve a number of thematic purposes at once, so attempts to group them by themes are forced.

62. For the shift of emphasis in Matthew from healing and exorcism to teaching, see J. Andrew Overman, *Matthew's Gospel and Formative Judaism: The Social World of the Matthean Community* (Minneapolis: Fortress, 1990), 127–28.

63. See Carl Holladay, *Theios Aner in Hellenistic Judaism: A Critique of the Use of This Category in New Testament Christology,* SBLDS 40 (Missoula: Scholars, 1977), 237.

64. Vermes, *Jesus the Jew,* 20–26, 58–82.

65. See William S. Green, "Palestinian Holy Men: Charismatic Leadership and Rabbinic Tradition," in H. Temporini and W. Hasse, eds., *Aufstieg und Niedergang der Römischen Welt* 2.19.2 (Berlin: deGruyter, 1979), 619–47, on Honi; Baruch Bokser, "Hanina Ben Dosa and the Lizard: The Treatment of Charismatic Figures in Rabbinic Tradition," *Proceedings of the Eighth World Congress of Jewish Studies,* Div. C, Talmud and Midrash . . . (Jerusalem: Magnes, 1982), 1–6, on Hanina ben Dosa.

66. See Bokser, "Hanina," 4–5; Jacob Neusner, *Talmudic Judaism in Sasanian Babylonia,* SJLS 14 (Leiden: Brill, 1976), chaps. 4, 6.

67. See David Tiede, *The Charismatic Figure as Miracle Worker,* SBLDS 1 (Missoula: SBL, 1972); and Kee, *Medicine, Miracle, Magic,* 84–85. Holladay, *Theios Aner,* esp. 235–39, shows that Hellenistic Jewish literature of the first century did not associate the *theios aner* with miracle working. In addition, this literature kept creator and creature sharply differentiated.

68. Holladay, *Theios Aner*, 238–39.

69. Some authors have subordinated the comparison with Moses in order to affirm Jesus' superiority. See, for example, Kingsbury, *Matthew*, 89–91, and the very influential analysis of W. D. Davies, *The Setting of the Sermon on the Mount* (Cambridge: Cambridge University Press, 1963), 93–108. But Davies has changed his mind in *The Gospel according to St. Matthew*, vol. 1: *Chapters 1–7*, ICC (Edinburgh: Clark, 1988), 190–95, 423–24. For a systematic presentation of the Mosaic theme in Matthew, see Dale C. Allison, "Gnilka on Matthew," *Biblica* 70 (1989): 527–31.

70. Allison, "Gnilka on Matthew," 532, 530.

71. For the connection of Matt. 11:25–30 with Moses typology and Exod. 33:12–14, see Dale C. Allison, "Two Notes on a Key Text: Matthew 11:25–30," *Journal of Theological Studies* 39 (1988): 277–85.

72. Felix Christ, *Jesus Sophia: Die Sophia-Christologie bei den Synoptikern*, ATANT 57 (Zurich: Swingli, 1970); and M. Jack Suggs, *Wisdom, Christology and Law in Matthew's Gospel* (Cambridge; Harvard University Press, 1970).

73. Marshall D. Johnson, "Reflections on a Wisdom Approach to Matthew's Christology," *Catholic Biblical Quarterly* 36 (1974): 44–64; Russell Pregeant, "The Wisdom Passages in Matthew's Story," *SBL Seminar Papers 1990* (Atlanta: Scholars, 1990), 469–93; Davies and Allison, *Matthew 8–17*, 295. Pregeant has a judicious survey of the literature. Davies and Allison emphasize the Moses typology at work in 11:25–30 rather than the associations with wisdom. See the previous section.

74. When Jesus is rejected by his townspeople, they ask sarcastically where Jesus got "this wisdom and these mighty works [*dynameis*]" (13:54). Jesus' works and wisdom are central to Matthew's understanding of him.

75. The theme of Jesus' coming as wisdom or as wisdom's messenger and of being rejected in Jewish, New Testament, and related literature is brought out well by James M. Robinson, "Jesus as Sophos and Sophia: Wisdom Tradition and the Gospels," in Robert Wilken, *Aspects of Wisdom in Judaism and Early Christianity* (Notre Dame: University of Notre Dame Press, 1975), 1–17. For example, see Matt. 12:42, where Jesus is greater than Solomon.

76. Pregeant, "Wisdom Passages," sees the rejection of wisdom as Matthew's main interest in the theme.

77. Davies and Allison, *Matthew 8–17*, 272–73, note that "infants" is used in the Septuagint for the righteous (Pss. 18:7; 114:6; 118:30).

78. Ibid. See also Allison, "Two Notes."

79. See 4Q175 and 1QS 9:11.

80. See Richard A. Horsley, "'Like One of the Prophets of Old': Two Types of Popular Prophets at the Time of Jesus," *Catholic Biblical Quarterly* 47 (1985): 435–63, for a study of the evidence. The rabbinic judgment that prophecy ended with Haggai, Zechariah, and Malachi (t. Sot. 13:2) should not be taken as historical fact. The rabbis saw themselves as authoritative teachers and interpreters who had succeeded the prophets, so they had their own motives for declaring it dead. It is true that prophecy had less of an institutional niche in Second Temple society, but for all that, prophets were common. See R.

Leivestad, "Das Dogma von der Prophetenlosen Zeit," *New Testament Studies* 19 (1972–73): 288–99.

81. Josephus, *War* 1 §78–80; 2 §112–13; *Ant.* 13 §311–13; 15 §371–78; 17 §345–48. See also *War* 2 §159.

82. Josephus, *Ant.* 17 §41–45; 15 §4; 14 §172–76.

83. On Josephus' prediction, see *War* 6 §622–29; also 3 §350–54. Josephus does not explicitly claim to be a prophet. For a similar story, told of Johanan ben Zakkai, see ARNA, Version A, chap. 4 and Version B, chap. 6. On John the Baptist, see *Ant.* 18 § 116–19.

84. Josephus, *War* 6 §288–315.

85. Josephus, *War* 2 §258–599; *Ant.* 20 §168. Josephus condemns anyone who fosters civic disorder. The fact that some prophets were rejected or revealed as frauds does not negate the legitimacy of the phenomenon. In the Israelite period, discerning true from false prophecy was difficult. See David Hill, "False Prophets and Charismatics: Structure and Interpretation in Matthew 7, 15–23," *Biblica* 57 (1976): 327–48; and P. W. Barnett, "The Jewish Sign Prophets, A.D. 40–70," *New Testament Studies* 27 (1981): 679–97.

86. Josephus, *Ant.* 20 §97; Acts 5:36.

87. Josephus, *War* 2 §261–62; *Ant.* 20 §169–70. This happened under the governor Festus (52–60 c.e.). See Acts 21:38.

88. Josephus, *Ant.* 20 §188.

89. 1QS 9:11; 4QTest cites Deuteronomy 18 along with other passages with eschatological implications. Horsley, "Prophets," 441–43, notes that evidence for this sense of prophet is slim. Traditionally great emphasis has been put on the prophet like Moses in the development of Christology. See Hahn, *Titles,* 352–406, and the most thorough study, Howard M. Teeple, *The Mosaic Eschatological Prophet,* JBLMS 10 (Philadelphia: SBL, 1957).

90. Fuller, *Foundations,* 125–29, notes that prophet is an important and original native category in New Testament assessments of Jesus.

91. M. J. J. Menken, "The References to Jeremiah in the Gospel according to Matthew (Mt 2.17; 16.14; 27.9)," *Ephemerides theologicae lovanienses* 60 (1984): 5–24.

92. J. Andrew Overman, "Heroes and Villains in Palestinian Lore: Matthew's Use of Traditional Jewish Polemic in the Passion Narrative," *SBL Seminar Papers 1990* (Atlanta: Scholars, 1990), 597–601; O. H. Steck, *Israel und das gewaltsame Geshick der Propheten: Untersuchungen zur Überlieferung des deuteronomistischen Geschichtsbildes im Alten Testament, Spätjudentum, und Urchristentum,* WMANT 23 (Neukirchen: Neukirchener Verlag, 1967).

93. Kingsbury, *Matthew,* 112, notes correctly that Matthew does not regard "Lord" as an independent christological title. He ably refutes Bornkamm, "End-Expectation," 41–44, and others who see "Lord" as replete with meaning for Matthew. For the ambiguity of the title and the need for contextual interpretation, see also M. Pamment, "The Son of Man in the First Gospel," *New Testament Studies* 29 (1983): 118.

94. For a review of first-century Jewish evidence for the use of *kyrios* for God, see Joseph A. Fitzmyer, "The Semitic Background of the New Testament

Kyrios-Title," in *A Wandering Aramean,* 120–23. Jewish copies of the Septuagint usually designated the Tetragrammaton by some sign rather than the word *kyrios.* Later Christian copyists introduced the widespread use of *kyrios* for God's name in Septuagint manuscripts.

95. W. Bousset advanced this influential thesis in *Kyrios Christos* (Nashville: Abingdon, 1970; orig. German, 1913). It was accepted by Rudolf Bultmann, *Theology of the New Testament,* (New York: Scribners, 1951), 1:52–53, 121ff. Fuller, *Foundations,* 67–68, 119, 156–58, 184–86, 230–31, disputed this claim as did other scholars, and stressed the Jewish uses of "Lord." The sharp distinction between Palestinian and Hellenistic Judaism has been rejected as the overall Hellenization of the Near East, including Israel, has come to be appreciated.

96. 11QtgJob 24:6–7; *mrh* for God is found in the Genesis Apocryphon 20:13, 15. See Fitzmyer, "Kyrios," 124–25.

97. 4QEn[b] 1iv5.

98. For example, Matt. 4:7, 10; 5:33; 9:38; 11:25; 21:9; 27:10; 28:2.

99. The disciples often use no form of address, but when they do, it is "Lord."

100. Note that in the water miracle in chapter 8, Jesus is called Lord (8:25) when the disciples ask for help, but he is not recognized as Son of God afterward. Rather, the disciples wonder what kind of person he is (8:27).

101. Fitzmyer, "Kyrios," 129–31.

102. See the exhaustive review in Joseph A. Fitzmyer, "The New Testament Title 'Son of Man' Philologically Considered," in *A Wandering Aramean,* 143–60. Fitzmyer effectively argues that Vermes's use of later Aramaic evidence from the targums and Talmud cannot determine first-century usage. For a list of the whole Fitzmyer-Vermes debate and an analysis, see John R. Donohue, "Recent Studies on the Origin of 'Son of Man' in the Gospels," *Catholic Biblical Quarterly* 48 (1986): 486–90.

103. See Geza Vermes, Appendix E in Matthew Black's *An Aramaic Approach to the Gospels and Acts,* 3d ed. (Oxford: Clarendon ,1967); *Jesus the Jew,* 163–68, 188–91. Vermes replies to Fitzmyer's objections to his position in *Jesus and the World of Judaism* (Philadelphia: Fortress, 1983), 77--80, 89–99.

104. Davies and Allison, *Matthew 8–17,* 47. The usage is so vague that Davies and Allison suggest, along with many other commentators, that its strange popularity in the gospels rests on Jesus' use of the term.

105. For a recent review of the problem of the origin of "Son of Man," see Donohue, "Recent Studies." Several other reviews are cited in his note 3.

106. Donohue (ibid., 498) suggests that Son of Man gains its primary meaning in the New Testament through Mark's trenchant use of this title in his theology of Jesus. This is consistent with the lack of usage of this figure as a distinct apocalyptic force in Jewish literature. See also Pamment, "Son of Man."

107. Norman Perrin, *A Modern Pilgrimage in New Testament Christology* (Philadelphia: Fortress, 1984).

108. Douglas R. A. Hare, *The Son of Man Tradition* (Minneapolis: Fortress, 1991), 274–75; Davies-Allison, *Matthew 8–17*, 50–51.

109. Hare, *Son of Man*, 280; Davies and Allison, *Matthew 8–17*, 51.

110. Hare, *Son of Man*, 114; Kingsbury, *Matthew*, 114; Luz, *Matthew 1–7*, 74; Davies and Allison, *Matthew 8–17*, 50–51.

111. Davies and Allison, *Matthew 8–17*, 50–51. This tripartitite division comes originally from Bultmann. It was worked out in relation to Markan theology by Perrin. Kingsbury, *Matthew*, 113–22, reviews all the uses of Son of Man.

112. Hare, *Son of Man*, 134, 181. Hare tries to have it both ways: "Son of Man" has no narrative effect, nor is it revelatory. It does not connote anything about Jesus' nature, work, or significance, but it is not trivial. It points to Jesus' destiny. In the end, Hare has said what Davies and Allison say, that "Son of Man" is a title in places.

113. Hare, *Son of Man*, 114–15; Davies and Allison, *Matthew 8–17*, 51.

114. Hare, *Son of Man*, 181; Kingsbury, "The Figure of Jesus in Matthew's Story: A Literary-Critical Probe," *Journal for the Study of the New Testament* 21 (1984): 25.

115. Pamment, "Son of Man."

116. Only a selection of the uses of "Son of Man" will be reviewed here. For a complete interpretation of each saying in order, see Hare, *Son of Man*, 136–80.

117. In the first passion prediction (16:21), Jesus does not refer to himself as Son of Man because he has just done so previously (16:13) and been identified as Messiah and Son of God.

118. Kingsbury, *Matthew*, 114–15, 119–20.

119. In 4 Ezra the expression "something like the figure of a man" occurs only once (13:3) and is missing in the Latin. It must be reconstructed from the versions. Elsewhere in Matthew 13, this figure is referred to as "man" or "the man." See Michael Stone, *Fourth Ezra*, Hermeneia (Minneapolis: Fortress, 1990), 381–84; particularly his discussion of the redeemer figure and "Son of Man" (211–12).

120. For the sophisticated structure and themes of the passion, see Frank J. Matera, *Passion Narratives and Gospel Theologies* (New York: Paulist, 1986), and J. P. Heil, *The Death and Resurrection of Jesus: A Narrative-Critical Reading of Matthew 26–28* (Minneapolis: Fortress, 1991).

121. The addition of "for the forgiveness of sins" to the liturgical formula in Mark (14:24) specifically fulfills the promise of Jesus' name in Matt. 1:21, "that he will save his people from their sins."

122. See Davies and Allison, *Matthew 8–17*, 642, for a cautious appraisal.

123. This treatment of Jesus in Matthew is far from complete. Many other biblical types and narrative roles of Jesus could be expounded. For example, Jesus is presented as the merciful servant of God who suffers in 3:17, 5:3–12, 8:17, 11:2–6, 12:18–21, a role which is folded into that of the suffering messiah in the last half of the gospel.

Chapter Eight

1. Quotation is from Hans Dieter Betz, "The Sermon on the Mount in Matthew's Interpretation," in Birger Pierson et al., eds., *The Future of Christianity: Essays in Honor of Helmut Koester* (Minneapolis: Fortress, 1991), 275.

2. For example, W. D. Davies and Dale C. Allison, *The Gospel according to St. Matthew,* vol. 2: *Chapters 8–17,* ICC (Edinburgh: Clark, 1991), 603, say that in chapters 11–16 Matthew depicts the rejection of Jesus by corporate Israel. But Davies and Allison have imposed the concept of "corporate Israel" on Matthew. Matthew, as was shown in chap. 2 above, continues to differentiate the leaders from the people and to hope for the conversion of the people to his way of thinking right to the very end.

3. Strecker and Betz are good examples of the imposition of historicizing schemes onto the Matthean narrative.

4. David Flusser, *Judaism and the Origins of Christianity* (Jerusalem: Magnes, 1988), in "Two Anti-Jewish Montages in Matthew," 552–60, alleges that Matthew has changed the wording of an earlier version of 8:11–12 to make it virulently anti-Jewish. (Flusser does the same with other passages as well.) But his case rests on interpreting 8:11–12 as a complete and blanket condemnation, something the saying does not claim explicitly, and on applying the saying to the relationships of Jews and gentiles seen as mutually exclusive groups, again something the saying does not explicitly do. In "Matthew's 'Verus Israel,'" 561–74, Flusser alleges that Matthew's real views can be found in 5 Esdras and Justin Martyr. But in each case, Matthew does *not* say what Flusser claims. Matthew differs essentially from the second-century Christian writers, who condemn Judaism and claim to be a new Israel or to replace Israel, precisely because he does not say what they say, but holds onto membership in Israel.

5. Contrast the revised Schürer (Emil Schürer, Geza Vermes, et al., *The History of the Jewish People in the Age of Jesus Christ,* 4 vols. [Edinburgh: Clark, 1973–87]) with the late nineteenth-century original (Emil Schürer, *A History of the Jewish People in the Time of Jesus Christ,* 5 vols. [Edinburgh: Clark, 1885–91]). For the effect of modernity and anti-Semitism on historians' treatments of Judaism, see Christhard Hoffmann, *Juden und Judentum im Werk Deutscher Althistoriker des 19. und 20. Jahrhunderts,* Stud. Jud. Mod. 9 (Leiden: Brill, 1988). For bias against Judaism in Christian theology, see Charlotte Klein, *Anti-Judaism in Christian Theology* (Philadelphia: Fortress, 1978). For anti-Judaism in New Testament study, see Anthony J. Saldarini, "Judaism and the New Testament," in E. J. Epp and G. W. MacRae, eds., *The New Testament and Its Modern Interpreters* (Atlanta: Scholars, 1989), 27–54, esp. 28–29.

6. The importance of Second Temple Judaism has been highlighted by the appearance of numerous books on this period in the last few years. See Alan F. Segal, *Rebecca's Children: Judaism and Christianity in the Roman World* (Cambridge: Harvard University Press, 1986); Shaye J. D. Cohen, *From the Maccabees to the Mishnah* (Philadelphia: Westminster, 1987); Frederick J. Murphy, *The Religious World of Jesus* (Nashville: Abingdon, 1991); Lawrence H. Schiffman,

From Text to Tradition: A History of Second Temple and Rabbinic Judaism (Hoboken: Ktav, 1991); Gabrielle Boccaccini, *Middle Judaism: Jewish Thought, 300 B.C.E.–200 C.E.* (Minneapolis: Fortress, 1991); Lester Grabbe, *Judaism from Cyrus to Hadrian,* vol. 1: *The Persian and Greek Periods* (Minneapolis: Fortress, 1991), vol. 2: *The Roman Period* (Minneapolis: Fortress, 1992); James J. G. Dunn, *The Parting of the Ways* (Philadelphia: Trinity, 1991); Shemaryahu Talmon, ed., *Jewish Civilization in the Hellenistic-Roman Period* (Philadelphia: Trinity, 1991); E. P. Sanders, *Judaism: Practice and Belief 63 BCE–66 CE* (Philadelphia: Trinity, 1992).

7. Elizabeth Schüssler Fiorenza, "The Ethics of Biblical Interpretation: Decentering Biblical Scholarship," *Journal of Biblical Literature* 107 (1988): 3–17, develops a rationale and method for including minority concerns and views in biblical interpretation so that it may criticize and enlarge the dominant traditions.

8. See Arthur A. Cohen, *The Myth of the Judeo-Christian Tradition* (New York: Harper, 1969); and recently, Jacob Neusner, *Jews and Christians: The Myth of a Common Tradition* (London: SCM; Philadelphia: Trinity, 1991).

9. The historical facts of the overlapping of Christianity and Judaism, extending into the fourth and even seventh century in the East, undercut the recent theological thesis of Jacob Neusner that the essential core of Christianity and of (formative, rabbinic) Judaism were present and effective in the first century. See Neusner, *Jews and Christians,* chap. 2. Neusner is on much more solid ground in subsequent chapters, where he defines the separate systems of talmudic Judaism and classical Christianity in the fourth century and beyond. Still, the analysis of thought systems must not be allowed to obscure the lived reality of religious communities in all its diversity and "messiness."

10. For the literary influence of Matthew in the second century, see E. Massaux, *Influence de l'évangile de Matthieu sur la littérature chrétienne avant saint Irénée* (Louvain: Publications Universitaires, 1950); reprinted in 1986 with a review of subsequent scholarship by Leuven University/Peeters and translated as *The Influence of the Gospel of Saint Matthew on Christian Literature before St. Irenaeus,* ed. Arthur J. Bellinzoni, 3 vols (Leuven: Peeters; Macon, Ga.: Mercer, 1990–93). See also the German translation by Wolf-Dietrich Köhler, *Die Rezeption des Matthäusevangeliums in der Zeit vor Irenäus,* WUNT 2, no. 24 (Tübingen: Mohr, 1987). Köhler takes into account the effect of oral tradition more adequately than Massaux's older study.

11. See Burton L. Mack, *Rhetoric and the New Testament* (Minneapolis: Fortress, 1990), 93–102.

Index

The Gospel of Matthew

Verse numbers are in italics.

Ancient Sources

Books are listed alphabetically. Under Hebrew Bible, New Testament, and Deuterocanonical Books, the books are listed in their traditional order in the original language. Under Mishnah, Midrash, Talmud, and Tosefta, tractates are listed alphabetically. References to the Gospel of Matthew are in a separate index.

Modern Authors

Subjects